HE LEADS, I FOLLOW

The Life of Mother

Maria Theresia Bonzel

He Leads, I Follow
The Life of Mother Maria Theresia Bonzel

Foundress of the Sisters of St. Francis of Perpetual Adoration

P. Lothar Hardick, O.F.M.

Translated from the German by Sister M. Honora Hau, O.S.F. and Sister M. Clarahilda Fischer, O.S.F.

Our Sunday Visitor
www.osv.com
Our Sunday Visitor Publishing Division
Our Sunday Visitor, Inc.
Huntington, Indiana 46750

Nihil Obstat
John A. Schulien
Censor Librorum

Imprimatur
✠ William E. Cousins
Archbishop of Milwaukee
March, 25, 1971

The *Nihil Obstat* and *Imprimatur* are official declarations that a book is free from doctrinal or moral error. It is not implied that those who have granted the *Nihil Obstat* and *Imprimatur* agree with the contents, opinions, or statements expressed.

23 22 21 20 19 18 2 3 4 5 6 7 8 9

Our Sunday Visitor Publishing Division
Our Sunday Visitor, Inc.
200 Noll Plaza
Huntington, IN 46750
1-800-348-2440

ISBN: 978-1-68192-272-0 (Inventory No. T1960
eISBN: 978-1-68192-273-7
LCCN: 2018930279

Cover design: Lindsey Riesen
Photos: courtesy Sisters of St. Francis of Perpetual Adoration

PRINTED IN THE UNITED STATES OF AMERICA

CONTENTS

FOREWORD

His Excellency Archbishop of Paderborn, Dr. Lorenz Jaeger, in the preface of his festive talk celebrating the centenary of the Congregation of the Sisters of St. Francis of Perpetual Adoration in Olpe, wrote: "We hope confidently this jubilee year 1963 will give us a new and comprehensive biography of the life and works of Mother Maria Theresia." Unfortunately, this wish, expressed also by many others, could not possibly be accomplished during the jubilee year of the Community. A biography of this nature above all demands a progressive development through research to discover the greatness and value unsurmised at first. Whoever wishes to write such a biography must first allow himself to be led by the person whose life he wishes to portray. He must learn to really love that person to be able to place himself into his life and thinking. Only then can he attempt to delineate this life for others and awaken in them a like love and respect. Therefore this book should not be written hurriedly but with ever renewed, though time-consuming, examination of the sources.

An attempt was made not to write so much of the various periods and problems of Mother Maria Theresia's life, but to let her own words speak as far as possible. One could select words ever so honorable and pleasing regarding her heroic endurance, her quiet patience, her maternal goodness, but these, however, would be the words of another. Consequently, they are not so valuable as her own. In her modest and unassuming manner, her own words disclose all. In using this method there is hope that her life will draw the reader close to Mother Maria Theresia.

Her own writings constitute the most valuable source material of her life. From her hand we have the following:

a. *Records* relative to the beginning of the Community. These are characterized by extreme poverty and are displayed in a small notebook of 116 pages of which only pages 3-35 have writings on them. The paging of the notebook is not hers. Between pages 12 and 13 some sheets are missing which certainly had writings on them as the interruption of the text on page 12 shows. The entries are sometimes made in ink, sometimes in pencil. Numerous corrections are made in the entries, which points to the fact that these records were not made at the same time. They range from September 1859 to early May 1864.

b. *Instructions* given her Sisters in preparation for profession. These comprise 192 pages, collectively there are 31 discourses. Discourses 1-9 were first given on April 8-10, 1872; discourses 10-16, July 14-16, 1872; discourses 17-26, December 5-7, 1872; discourses 27-31, February 21-22, 1875. In all probability, Mother Maria Theresia later relied more or less on these written notes as references.

c. *The Oldest Statutes of the Congregation* which Mother Theresia drafted and compiled up to March 25, 1865. With full authority and justice one can call these statutes the foundation of the spiritual life the foundress pursued in her community.

d. *Letters* she wrote to the sisters, to the superiors, to the ecclesiastical and civil authorities. The originals are filed in the archives of the archepiscopal general vicariates in Paderborn, in the archives of the town of Olpe, and in the archives of the motherhouse in Olpe. In addition there are a few letters and writings in various places, and some also in private hands. Many official letters are also in the archives in the motherhouse. Attested copies of all these letters have been made. For the sake of clarity these have been divided into seven groups, numbered consecutively.

To prevent bulky documentation of sources in this book, an abbreviated method was chosen that numbered the specific copies of the letters and also the groups under which they fall. the groups are as follows: I) letters to Sister Deogratias; II) letters to the sisters in the United States; III) to the sisters in Germany; IV) feastday letters; V) to superiors; VI) to ecclesiastical authorities; VII) to civil authorities.

Unfortunately, a large group of letters is missing in this collection, namely, those written to Sister Hildegardis Schelle and preserved by her until her death. These would have cast precious light on Mother Maria Theresia's art of directing souls. The reason given by the local superior for destroying the letters after the death of Sister Hildegardis is that they dealt too intimately with the personal affairs of her soul. Fortunately, some fragments of these letters exist in Sister Hildegardis' notebook. Rev. Salesius Elsner, OFM, in his work of 1925 had some of these original letters, which no longer can be found.

Besides the various official documents in question, written records of Sisters, collected previously at an earlier time, were examined. These were without evidence and without names. How to question the eye witnesses still living at that time was not properly understood. The collected testimonies of the Sisters since 1961 and later have better content.

Of special value are the records of Sister Hildegardis Schelle, bound into two volumes in 1917. Besides her own remembrances, she was able to record those of Sister Deogratias Schaefer, Sister Martha Vormberg, Sister Paula Thomas, Sister Verena Schulte, Sister Bonaventura Claes, and many others. The knowledge of family connections was also at her disposal: town commissioner, Justus Bonzel (Olpe); merchant, H. Hellinghaus-Börsch (Drolshagen); member of the Board of Health, Dr. Joseph Kaufmann (Berlin); mayor, Liese (Olpe); local council member, Ruegenberg (Olpe); and district judge Schelle (Olpe).

As mentioned previously Sister Hildegardis made available personal letters she received from Mother Theresia. All we know of Mother Theresia prior to 1859 goes back to the records of Sister Hildegardis. It is unfortunate that she did not have the same inclination to gather the important happenings of Mother Maria Theresia's childhood and youth as of her later years. Since Mother Maria Theresia died in her seventy-fifth year, there were certainly a few sisters living at that time who knew her in her youth. But family tradition has provided much since 1917. At that time Sister Hildegardis was too absorbed in extraordinary happenings to pay much attention to the quiet normal day-by-day events of human living. Nevertheless she wrote the records in this area with great exactness. After the first draft, she would rework it for the finishing touches. Thus her records carry great evidence.

Sister Andrea Bussien gives the best information of the last years of Mother Theresia's life in the Chronicles of the congregation which were written with great exactness. They extend to 1910. From February 19, 1903, it becomes clearly evident that she wrote as an eye witness and often made her entries of the happenings she wished to record on the same day they occurred. It was her desire to write more about past happenings, but Mother Theresia was of the opinion that not too much should be written concerning her, for it was not she who accomplished the work, but God who used her as his instrument.

The citations of all those records were kept in the original as far as possible. However, at times it seemed proper to change the antiquated forms of letters and records to present day forms lest the difference in style cause a deviation in meaning. Special care was taken to preserve the original as a whole. The title of the book, *He Leads, I Follow* is Mother Maria Theresia's own expression. It seems that this title best reproduces the meaning of her life.

The literature available and used in this work are: Salesius Elsner, OFM, *Mother Maria Theresia and Her Foundation,* Werl i. Westfalen, 1926; Bonaventure Hammer, OFM, *The Congregation of the Poor Franciscan Sisters of Perpetual Adoration,* Lafayette, Indiana, 1910; Rosanna Peters, OSF, *The History of the Poor Sisters of St. Francis Seraph of the Perpetual Adoration* 1875–1940 (History of the Community), 1944; Brunhilde Siegel, *Lebensbild Der Mutter Maria Clara Pfänder, Stifterin Der Franziskanerinnen von Salzkotten*, Lippstadt, 1957; August Hirschmann, *Geschichte Der Pfarrei Olpe im Rahmen und Landes-Geschichte Olpe in Westfalen,* 1930.

Since the Church in the inauguration of the informative process has placed the life of the servant of God under its own jurisdiction, the contents of this book, in accordance with the Decree of Pope Urban VIII, are completely and unreservedly submitted to the judgment of the church.

Rev. Lothar Hardick, O.F.M.
The Foundation Day of the Franciscans of Olpe
July 20, 1964
Münster, Westfalen

CHAPTER I

THE YEARS OF CHILDHOOD

Whoever sees the life and works of an individual disseminated before him naturally endeavors to discover the guidelines that gave direction to that life and its accomplishments. He searches for events, words, and deeds that stand out as signs revealing the deeper and inner motives of action. Such signs can knowingly be determined by the respective person himself as clear expressions of his will. But it can also be that subsequent reverential reflections reveal the coming together of events, not by chance, but as an indication of God's management and providence.

Mother Maria Theresia Bonzel's day of birth can be considered such a sign. She herself never considered it mere chance that she was born in 1830 on September 17, the day on which the church celebrates the Stigmata of St. Francis. Although she often mentioned in jest that she had crawled "from the wounds of St. Francis," this jest nevertheless expressed her joy that her first day of life bore the sign of St. Francis. Many an occurrence, many a severe struggle, and many a bitter sorrow in her life can be understood, in fact, only if one knows of her desire to attain the Franciscan ideal in its fullness. It is as one of her spiritual daughters said of the Mother foundress: "Her deep love of St. Francis motivated her to follow in the footsteps of the great Franciscan founder." Thus the very first day of her existence illumined her whole life and work.

She was born in Olpe, a small town in southern Sauerland, Germany. In baptism she received the name of Regina Christine Wilhelmine. Her first or Christian name was Wilhelmine, abbreviated to "Aline." Up to the time of her religious investiture she signed her name as "Aline." This she also did in all her official correspondence. The fact that her name sometimes appeared as "Adelina" shows that her Christian name Wilhelmine was scarcely or never used.

Aline's father was Frederick Edmund Bonzel, a merchant, and one of the wealthiest citizens of Olpe. Her mother was Maria Anna, surnamed Liese. The families of both the father and the mother were of long-resident stock. Documentary evidence shows the Bonzel family was established in Olpe in 1625. Even at that time a family possessed great wealth. The Liese family settled in Olpe in mid-sixteenth century according to authentic records. After Aline a second daughter, Emilie, was born to the family. She later married Dr. Lorenz Kaufmann of Olpe.

Not only because of their wealth were the Bonzels highly respected in Olpe. Their excellent reputation was due in large measure to Aline's paternal grandfather, Franz Joseph Bonzel. That he was commander of the militia and also town councilor shows the great confidence the citizens placed in him. Only a man of great integrity, with ample evidence that his power would be used for the welfare of the people, could have been chosen for such offices. Born in 1783, during his later years he experienced turbulent times caused by the French domination and the Wars of Liberation. He had many good opportunities for using his great influence for the good of his fatherland and the benefit of the citizens. Possessing an energetic spirit of enterprise, he founded a new rolling mill at the beginning of the industrialization of the Sauerland. From this industry came the great wealth of the Bonzel family. From the first marriage of the grandfather to Maria Wilhelmine Gummerbach three sons were born, Arnold, Xavier (who died in childhood), and Edmund, Aline's father, who was born in 1808. In his second marriage to Maria Josepha Liese, he was further blessed with four sons and five daughters.

To characterize adequately the family into which Aline was born, one must give consideration to Arnold, her paternal uncle. It is important that a family leave economic status and security to the oncoming generation, but of greater importance is its spiritual legacy. A righteous family pride centered in Arnold because of his great spirituality, for the Bonzel family considered it a matter of honor to remain true to the ideals of its forefathers. Although Arnold did not enter a religious order, he worked in his surroundings as a religious in secular garb. Nearly all of his chief traits of character are found again in essence in his niece Aline.

Uncle Arnold was in very good financial circumstances, but he was not concerned in keeping a close watch over his possessions. The word of God, "Give to the poor" (Mt 19:21), he fulfilled with great liberality. Since he remained unmarried, he was under no obligation to lay money aside. He did not exercise his generosity as many another man of wealth, who holds himself at a distance and supports charitable projects of others with money. Arnold assisted personally in cases of emergency. It happened at one time as he was making a pilgrimage, he met two unhappy and weeping children abandoned by their parents. He took them with him, provided for their keeping, and cared for their future. Whether or not this happened on the pilgrimage to Werl is not known. Uncle Arnold made the pilgrimage to Werl fifty times; still he did not disregard the smaller shrines in his vicinity.

An outstanding trait of his piety was his extraordinary love and veneration for the Holy Eucharist. To accompany the Blessed Sacrament in solemn procession only on the feast of Corpus Christi was not enough for him. Every Thursday evening for the entire year he prayerfully retraced the Corpus Christi procession route. It was his method of keeping the Thursday Holy Hour. A simple, homelike, and devout piety has its own norm which is not easily influenced by a general although legitimate norm, and above all, not by a rigid one. The Eucharistic piety of Arnold had special consideration for the house of God. Whatever was needed for decoration or otherwise he supplied from his own means. It is no wonder that the sacristan maintained a good friendship with such a generous helper. The Poor Souls held a special place in his heart. Even in the last days of his life, he collected money in their behalf for Mass stipends. Up to his last day, bowed with age, he took his customary walks, in his right hand a supporting cane, in his left hand a rosary. He was no longer interested in events occurring about him. He no longer cared. He prayed.

To withhold nothing from the poor and the ornamentation of the church, he saved on his own clothing. Often and justly so, his relatives severely reproached him and tried to persuade him to buy new clothes for himself. Serene as he otherwise was, he became quite angry with them for their prodigality in the use of money. That it was not stinginess of age, but his personal unpretentiousness is proved by his otherwise exceptionally great meekness. Although not formulated in the following manner, he lived according to the principle: One should give with warm hands what otherwise would fall from cold hands. When he died in 1879, his entire wealth had been expended for the poor. In his death he was serene and resigned. His last words were: "Praised be Jesus Christ forever and ever. Amen." His eyes then closed in death.

Since Aline's father died in 1837 before he was thirty years of age, her eyes turned toward her Uncle Arnold in a special way. In the fullest sense, he was the only surviving brother of her father; the others were only half-brothers. Perhaps the daughter sought in this uncle the image of her deceased father. It is singular that the chief characteristics of the uncle found expression in her life also; love of the poor and orphans, deep veneration for the Holy Eucharist, a personal unpretentious modesty, and a firmness to follow with implicit fidelity a way of life considered as right without permitting any interference from others.

Since she lost her father at the age of seven, her memories of him were not especially clear. The mother who pursued the development of her eldest daughter, wielded the greater influence in her life. Mother Maria Theresia writing the following letter to one of her sisters seems to have been reminded of the death of her own father:

> I have received your letters telling us of the death of your good father. You have the Sisters' and my deepest sympathy. We shall pray with you, dear Sister Viridiana, that our dear Lord may grant eternal rest to his beloved soul soon. Offer the next six weeks for your dear father. Since you can no longer meet him in life, may his blessings rest upon you from above. The loss of parents is always a great sacrifice and tears flow justly. Still through our total surrender to God we have detached our hearts and thus — as brides of Christ — we can through prayer be of greater assistance to our loved ones. (III 22)

In these lines definite reference is made to detachment of heart and total surrender to God. The meaning here is entirely different from that of a cold turning away from our relatives. In certain religious communities there are directives of piety which understand surrender to God as a radical thrusting aside of parents, brothers, and sisters. The foundress of the Olpe Franciscans was never in harmony with this idea. Her Sisters should attend their own parents in serious illness and endeavor to be with them at the hour of death. She considered that God himself implanted the love of parents in the hearts of children. The grief of a child over the loss of a father was sacred to her. But she also realized that a religious in this grief, when everything reminded her of the love and warmth of her own parental home, must remain true to her total surrender to God. For her, grief at the death of parents may not become an occasion for a flight back into the past. In a situation of this nature, the dedicated bride of Christ can, through faithful perseverance on the way of love, obtain ever greater graces for her dear ones.

Such beautiful adjustment God grants to a Sister who shows such love for her parents. Certainly there exists — exteriorly — a separation, as also the married daughter must go her own way in the new unity of marriage. But the religious should not only preserve the love of parents but should know that God wishes to bless her parents in a special way through her religious vocation. Mother Maria Theresia in making it possible for her Sisters to show their love and gratitude to their parents by actually assisting them in their last illness and in death, gave clear evidence of how truly human her guidance of the Sisters was and what she herself felt toward her own parents.

In touching warmth this rings out from the letter she wrote to Sister Eustella in 1902:

> The news of the bitter sufferings of your dear mother has saddened me deeply. Let me trust in God, dear Sister Eustella, and beg him fervently to alleviate her pain and grant her great patience to persevere in resignation. The consolation of having you, dear child, at her bed of suffering to care for her, I gladly permit the dear sick one and you also, that you may lighten her suffering as much as possible and support her in her last hour. We shall pray with you, dear

> Sister Eustella, and also for you. I am certain that your comforting and assisting love will be a source of many blessings for your loved ones. Sister Casilda will gladly take care of your little ones. Fulfill your filial duties loyally and lovingly to your good sick mother. Please assure her and also your good father of our prayers and many greetings. We are with you in sympathy and in prayer. If you are able, keep us informed. I greet you in the love of Jesus and Mary. (III 52)

Does not the sympathy with the sorrows of the sisters resound as an echo of the wholehearted love and fidelity that she as a child offered her own parents? Unfortunately, we have but few instances of Aline's childhood in her parental home. The way she saw the sisters' relations to their parents reveals much of the atmosphere in the Bonzel home.

The family home was in the immediate vicinity of the parish church. Aline grew up under the influence and in the shadow of the House of God. Did the nearness to the church leave its impress on the lives of the children? The mother took the children to church with her at an early age. At one time during the so-called "Perpetual Prayer," she took Aline with her into the festively flowing church. Most likely at home and again at the church door came the motherly warning that in church one must be good and quiet. But as the little one saw the numerous brilliantly lighted candles on the altar, silence was flung to the winds. Joyously her spirited child voice rang out clear and loud with the silent church, "Oh, how many lights!" Immediately her jubilant outcry was smothered by the mother: "Here you may not talk; you must be very quiet; God is there upon the altar." One wonders what went on in the mind of the child that often prayed with its mother to God and now was told distinctly: "There before us on the altar is God."

Aline said of herself later that she joyfully joined all childish pranks. Was it the Bigge River flowing past the motherhouse, constructed in after years, that kept her memory alive as to her youthful frolic in skating? Many girls are able to recall a period of life in which they loved to imitate boys, yet, better even excel them.

This was also true in regard to Aline; in retrospect she considered herself a vivacious girl. Olpe offers children many possibilities for play and adventures. There are the hills of the Sauerland with their extensive woods to allure youth; the Bigge and the smaller streams to offer them the whole romance of running waters. Winter with its ice and snow gives children the liberty to romp about joyously in the invigorating air. All this one can project into the childhood and youth of Aline. Unfortunately but few incidents of this period of her life are available. The smaller and the greater joys, the smaller disappointments and the real sorrows of the child have not been recorded as research into the life of Mother Theresia revealed. Today, unfortunately, the possibilities of obtaining particulars of Aline's childhood are irretrievably lost.

The exact year of Aline's First Holy Communion cannot be ascertained. Most likely it followed the universal custom of the time, namely, at the completion of the elementary school. She was then fourteen years of age. It was only through the endeavors of Pius X that children were permitted to approach the Table of the Lord at an earlier age. It was not impossible that, in exceptional instances, children were permitted to receive Holy Communion earlier. If such an exception had been Aline's, she would certainly have registered her joy, since she preserved an animated and exact account of the day of her First Holy Communion.

To judge correctly what she later told a Sister, one must take Aline's age into consideration:

> On the day of my first Holy Communion I was unspeakably happy. Before that I was a vivacious child, ready to take part in every prank. But after I received the Lord into my heart and returned to my place in the church an indescribable feeling came over me. In the joy I experienced, but one thought filled my whole being. As Jesus had given himself entirely to me, I must give myself entirely to him. Without really knowing what I was saying I repeated over and over again, 'O Lord, I am your victim, accept me as your victim; do not reject me.' This prayer silenced every other thought and raised me to a state of indescribable blessedness.

Nearly all whom God calls in a special way know very precisely at what time God's will was first consciously experienced by them. Was this the hour in Aline's life that opened to her the path of her life? That she later remembered so exactly her prayer at that time makes one surmise it was. She spoke of the experience of that hour: "One thought filled my whole being, as Jesus had given himself entirely to me, I must give myself entirely to him." This in a noticeable way reminds us of the words of St. Francis of Assisi: "Keep nothing of yourself for yourself that he may accept you completely who gave himself to you completely." Whoever comprehends God's great gift of himself, must in answer give him a mutual love of surrender. Thus the youthful heart answers in readiness: "O Lord, I am your victim; accept me completely as your victim; do not reject me."

Eucharistic piety at that time was characterized chiefly by adoration of our Lord in the Blessed Sacrament. Only on special occasions were the faithful granted the great grace of union with our Lord in Holy Communion. In the piety of all, Communion was considered as the "coming of the soul's sweet Guest to dwell in the human heart." Undoubtedly, one believed the Holy Sacrifice of the Mass was the sacrifice of Christ and also our sacrifice. Faith also recognized Holy Communion as the banquet of the soul. But to the individual these thoughts remained ineffective. Thus it is rather surprising that Aline, also a product of the times, in reference to the grace of the Eucharist should understand and speak out so clearly of the idea of sacrifice. Is this not evident: He who gives himself completely to God, to him God grants the fullness of his mysteries?

CHAPTER II

MATURING OF VOCATION

Aline's mother was a good example to her daughters both in vigor and in piety. Undoubtedly the relatives, after the premature death of the father, rendered the widowed mother and her children all necessary assistance. But the education and the development of the children devolved upon the mother who possessed the necessary capacity to take that responsibility in hand. Between her and her daughters there naturally existed a very close bond of union. Even in later years the mother was always concerned about her daughters. This was manifested especially in regard to Aline, who during the early years of her religious life, was ever able to rely on the ready help of her mother.

As a child Aline gave evidence of rich intellectual endowment and outstanding strength of character. Because of her natural ability and qualifications, her future way of life could well be developed. The mother placed high hopes on her elder daughter. These hopes were not entirely unselfish. However, one may not blame her for this. The widow clung tenaciously to her children and because of the early death of her husband she looked to them for her future security. It seems that she harbored the thought of having in Aline a support for her declining years. Therefore she believed that somehow Aline must remain with her. As Aline later spoke to her about her call to the religious life, the mother was not enthusiastic about the prospect, and did not give an immediate "yes" to the idea. She put her off by saying that she needed more time to consider it.

In the more affluent families of Olpe, to which the Bonzels belonged, it was customary to send their daughters, after the completion of the elementary school, to a *pensionat*, that is a girls' boarding school, for some time. The purpose was not only the acquisition of more knowledge, but above all the formation of character and proficiency in the social graces. Tradition has it that the girls were sent to the Ursulines in Cologne. Thus Aline, with good grades and excellent recommendations from the elementary school, went to Cologne to the Ursulines. Apparently she was there more than a year.

Unfortunately, the reports of the Ursuline-Pensionat were lost during the Prussian *Kulturkampf*. Thus the time Aline spent in the boarding school cannot be established definitely. The Ursuline convent in Cologne was later able to give only the following: "Without doubt she (Aline) was in our boarding school for the name of Bonzel is still known here and has a good reputation." If the name Bonzel was still in clear remembrance in 1925 in the Ursuline boarding school, it could also be associated with the fact that at the close of the *Kulturkampf* a great niece of Mother Theresia, called Adele Maria Theresia Bonzel, was accepted in Cologne in the boarding school.

Inquiries as to Aline's classmates at that time were not made early enough to obtain particulars of the actions and experiences of the girls in the school. Although there are no extant facts, one can nevertheless state that this period must have had great significance in the development of the young girls. It was the first time Aline was away from the parental home and her native town for a long period of time. She had to adjust to unknown people in new surroundings and prove herself in a firmly organized environment. The tried tradition of the Ursulines laid great stress on cultural and character formation and true cultivation of piety. The constant association with religious women must have had great influence on the girls. It is true in all *pensionats* that the girls are deeply interested in the life of the religious; as much as possible they try to discover many of the so-called "conventual mysteries."

Such interest often enough may have been only a romantic curiosity. But in the overall atmosphere of the *pensionat* many a vocation has been awakened. This seems also to have been the case with Aline. Although we know scarcely anything of her stay in Cologne, it is certain however that before she left the *pensionat*, she spoke to the superior of the Ursulines of her desire to become a religious. At that time her desire may not have been firm; it needed to mature. At all events the farewell words of the superior influenced and encouraged her to consider earnestly taking such a step. The consent of the mother however, was wanting. Aline also conferred with her confessor on this point. He reacted positively but counseled her not to act hastily, to wait some time in order to test the genuineness of her decision. Concerning this talk with her confessor we know from her friend, Emma Deimel, to whom she had entrusted it. Emma Deimel harbored like thoughts; she later entered the Carmelite Convent in Echt, Holland, and was invested as Sister Maria Walburga. The little information we have today of Aline's youth came largely from her.

After Aline's return to the parental home, the mother valued it most highly that her daughter become deeply involved in the social life of Olpe. What mother would not have had a like ambition? Before the critical eyes of relatives and acquaintances, her daughter should give evidence of her grace and charm in the refined manners she acquired at the *pensionat*. As Aline now had to participate in all the yearly festivals and amusements of Olpe and its surroundings, more than she herself liked, her mother must have had another design in this. She hoped that her daughter's idea of the convent would pass over and prove to have been but a romantic enthusiasm resulting from the conventional atmosphere of the *pensionat*. If through experience in social activities, the daughter's thoughts would be deflected from the convent and in consequence acquire a new interest, this indeed would be a highly prized method.

All this of course was not according to the thinking of Aline. She would have liked to enter a convent immediately. However, her inner nobility of character did not allow her to frown upon those festivities nor to enter them with a dejected countenance. Her cheerful and open disposition made it easy for her to participate with genuine joy. What the mother had hoped in her inmost heart, and here and there contrived, was happening to some degree: Aline had several offers of marriage, in itself an honor for a young girl. In jest, although clear and determined, she withdrew from the young men who persisted in their offers.

At her First Holy Communion, she had prayed: "O Lord, I am your victim; accept me entirely as your victim; do not reject me." Soon after her return from the *pensionat* she experienced how our Lord accepted the oblation of herself as a victim. She was afflicted with a heart condition that lasted during her entire life. If a young person not yet twenty years of age be afflicted with a disease and experienced the infirmities of man in suffering and in pain, if he saw boundaries set to his energies, how do you think he would react? Many would complain, bearing the disease with an exhibition of suffering to evoke sympathy. Or, they would rest upon their misfortune unable to develop their capabilities and go through life in bitterness of heart. Again, others despairing would thrust themselves into all possible gratifications to glean something from life. Aline realized that God had accepted her offer. She saw in this, the affirmation that God had accepted her as his victim. It was not enough for her to bear this illness patiently, she also was prepared to follow Christ in an all-embracing surrender. Her cardiac condition was not the end of her endeavors, but in reality only its beginning. According to human estimation, she was scarcely equal to the tasks life set for her. As she bore her infirmity in the right spirit, she was able to accomplish much. Her strength was not an explosive energy, a reckless creative muse, with disquiet scheming. With a heart condition like hers, she would soon have come to the end of her capacity. But she lived and worked over fifty years with this ailment because she possessed the gift of expending her energy with serenity, wisdom, and tenacious regularity.

Throughout her entire life one can observe a display of these characteristics. They are clearly seen in the way she strove amidst all difficulties to enter the religious life. It was true of Aline, and in fact of all girls who attended the *pensionat*, that the social life experienced there was later preserved in close friendships. Several Olpe daughters had been with Aline in Cologne. They soon formed a unique circle whose objective was certainly not the revitalizing of an exhausted friendship. They united to venerate the Blessed Virgin Mary, a devotion endeared to them by the Ursulines. They formed a Marian Alliance of which Aline became the leader. The tasks undertaken by this alliance were the yearly decorating of the May altar, the assembling for prayer in honor of Mary, and the engaging in works of Christian charity and beneficence. This Marian Alliance was the initial realization of their later religious life, not only for Aline, but also for two of her friends. One was Emma Deimel referred to previously. The other was Regina Loeser. She was invested with Aline on December 20, 1860, but died prematurely on May 27, 1861.

Aline realized her call to the religious life very definitely at the age of nineteen and one-half. From March 28 to April 8, 1850, she took part in a parish mission in the neighboring town of Drolshagen, conducted by two extraordinary priests. Their names were known far and wide: Missionary Hillebrand and the Franciscan Father Kaspar Heimer. Aline made a general confession of her entire life to the leader, Missionary Hillebrand. She was so moved that her handkerchief was wet with the tears shed in the confessional. With her the missionaries accomplished their purpose completely. The method of the mission was set especially on stirring the feelings powerfully. The sermons resulted in a strong awakening of the emotions. Missionary Hillebrand must have been deeply impressed by Aline's confession in which he was given a more penetrating glimpse into her soul than others were. The experienced director of souls perceived the genuine in Aline; he saw clearly that hers was a soul God had taken into his care in a special way. He offered her his wish to become the director of her soul and that she should contact him whenever he should be in the vicinity. That a missionary so much in demand should make this offer to her shows his concern for this chosen soul to walk in the way of God. He wished to be the instrument for fulfilling the will of God completely in her. Aline confided this offer to one of her friends. She followed the counsel of the confessor.

At the mission renewal, which usually took place the following year, she again confessed to Father Hillebrand and most likely also during the Olpe mission in 1851. The missionary realized that this penitent needed to be confirmed in her ideal to be able to withstand the great opposition her mother voiced to her entrance into religious life. It may be that he harbored the thought that the mother would relent if she were confronted with completed data in a positive way. Therefore after confession, Aline pronounced a vow of perpetual chastity. She went a step farther and soon after the mission entered the Franciscan Tertiaries of the world. Her name as a tertiary of St. Francis was her future name as a religious: Maria Theresia.

Thus interiorly she had bound herself completely. Now there was but one conclusion she could draw: as she had proceeded on this way and gave up all claims to marriage for the sake of heaven, she must endeavor to enter the religious state as soon as possible. But for this she needed the consent of her mother. She realized this permission would provoke much discussion. Most probably Missionary Hillebrand had counseled her after taking the vow of chastity to have a decisive talk with her mother and explain fully to her that she had destroyed all bridges behind her.

The exact day on which Aline had her discussion with her mother is not known, but it seems to have occurred toward the end of May or the beginning of June, 1851. She talked openly with her mother telling her that marriage could no longer be a thought of hers for she had bound herself in another way. Her decision to leave the world and to enter the convent was irrevocable. She begged for her mother's consent, but her request was ill received. The mother refused resolutely. No matter how urgently Aline pleaded, or how warmly she begged, her mother remained adamant in her refusal. Did the mother really believe she could change the mind of her daughter? She must have known Aline better than that. It was against Aline's nature to become hard and inconsiderate under opposition. She did not push her opinions by hurting others. But she was not to be turned from the course on which she felt herself called.

After the fruitless discussion she went to the One who had called her. She knelt before the tabernacle in a nearby church. That the Lord really called her, she was positive. Still her heart was so very heavy. In her mind rang the question: "Why?" From the vantage point of the completed work of Mother Theresia in retrospect to this day, one realizes: It was necessary that she pass through all this suffering to grow in maturity for the future work God had determined for her. But at that time she was to carry the full weight of the question. The words of Christ might have entered her mind: "Who loves father and mother more than me is not worthy of me" (Mt 10:37). Was her vocation sufficiently clear at that time to enable her to bring about a hard, conclusive break with her mother? The command of love of parents also entered her mind. She still trusted that sometime and someday she would get the consent of her mother. There was so much to consider. What was right?

As Aline went to her room that evening, she could find no respite in sleep. Her thoughts were too agitated. Out in the open a nightingale began to sing, at first soft, in dull and plaintive tones, then assured, ever more joyous and clear, until the song became a jubilant outburst of exultation. The nightingale sang peace into the heart of Aline. She felt that somehow she was not alone in the dark. God wished to have her and he would also determine the time in which she would go. He alone knew his designs for her. Therefore he placed these obstacles in her way. It was not easy for Aline to realize that she must wait still longer.

In her discussion with her mother, Aline's heart condition may have militated against her call to the religious life. It appeared as a clear sign. Normally one would consider seriously before admitting a young girl with heart trouble into the convent. It is strange Aline never considered that a reason for doubting her religious call. At this period she suffered rather severe heart attacks; she was quite ill, bedridden, and required nursing care. When recovered somewhat in health she often assisted her sister Emilie in her household tasks. Emilie had married in the meantime and also suffered from a prolonged illness.

Concerning the inner attitude of Aline during these times, her friend and confidant, Emma Deimel, remarked: "The inner urgency of my friend was always to lead souls to God, and how wonderfully our Lord brought it about that her wish was fulfilled. She was sickly and often seriously ill; but that did not satisfy her zeal. She made novenas to beg for suffering and our dear Lord also fulfilled this wish." Considering these remarks, one could get the impression that Aline herself at times scarcely believed she would ever be a religious. According to human judgment it was unwise for a sick person to pray for more suffering, if she really wished to enter the convent. To enter a convent, at least a reasonable condition of health is required. However it may have been, it required special courage for a sick person to pray for the grace of suffering in this way. One can explain it only in the light that at this time she recognized her vocation as that of suffering and she was prepared to answer the call.

Still, she must have realized that her vocation in life was not to exhaust itself in suffering only. An incident that played an important role in the life of the sick one is related by Emma Deimel: "Once when Aline was bedfast, I visited her. She mentioned that she saw a nun in a brown habit standing at the foot of her bed. She was firm and maintained that it was St. Clare." No further details are known regarding this incident to permit a fuller explanation. However, with Aline it had the effect that she felt herself more definitely called to the religious life.

Her idea gained stability with Rev. Rector Hesse, who understood the nature of his penitent thoroughly. Was he fearful of using his influence outside the confessional in Aline's behalf? He felt that it could be readily construed that he divulged the secrecy of confession if in a talk with the mother he should give the reasons for Aline's vocation. He counseled Aline to contact Rev. Hengstebeck. She did so and with great confidence and made a complete manifestation of conscience to him. She felt a sense of security in his real support and was especially grateful that he offered to talk with her mother concerning her vocation. Through his authority, the pastor succeeded in finally winning the consent of Aline's mother. Aline now thought she had reached her goal. She consequently took the necessary steps and applied to the Salesians in Hoexter for admission. She was most likely drawn to the Salesians through the influence of Missionary Hillebrand who knew the convent in Hoexter well. He had also previously counseled the Salesians to make a foundation in Mülheim, which they did in 1859.

Her day of admission was determined. The required dowry was procured. Aline bade farewell to her friends, acquaintances, and relatives. Then something very unusual happened. As Aline went to a neighboring woman, Jaeger by name, who was an intimate friend of hers, to bid her goodby, she said to her: "Unpack your trunk, dear Aline, you are called to found an order of perpetual adoration here in your home town." From where did this woman have the certainty for such a statement? Did it rest merely on the supposition that Mrs. Jaeger knew Aline well? Aline did not have much time to reflect on the occurrence nor to ponder whether God really wanted to make something known to her through this statement, or whether it was merely the spontaneous outburst of a soul well known to her. However, Aline was unable to travel the next morning for erysipelas had suddenly attacked her. Again she was confronted with the reality of being unable to carry out the cherished ideal of her heart as she had planned. God wanted otherwise. In consequence, she decided not to apply again to the Salesians for admission.

In later years, she told one of her Sisters that about this time she had had a strange dream. She saw St. Francis of Assisi and St. Teresa of Avila having a debate. It was concerning Aline. The saints could not come to a decision to whom Aline should belong. At length St. Francis won and took Aline as his daughter. But St. Teresa did not relinquish her claims so readily. With hands stretched out over Aline, she gave her a blessing. Surely this was but a dream and an experience not too readily supernaturalized. But somehow the dream was a mirrored picture of what went on in the mind of Aline. After the collapse of her plan to enter the convent with the Salesians, the question as to where she should now apply was but natural. She had received the name of Maria Theresia as a Franciscan Tertiary; her friend Emma Deimel had entered the Carmelites, daughters of St. Teresa. Aline and Emma most certainly talked with each other about their inclinations to enter the convent. From their confidential talks, St. Teresa could have entered her dream. On the other hand, Aline as a Tertian, was bound to St. Francis, her birthday on the Stigmata of St. Francis gave her further connections with the saint. Therefore, was she not destined to become a Franciscan? Men doing research work, sometimes take very insignificant data as reasons for their conclusions. Who would question that God also uses insignificant things, such as a dream, to draw them into his plan in order to reveal his designs for them?

CHAPTER III

NEW BEGINNINGS

Aline had now reached the age of twenty-nine. During the past nine years she had repeatedly sought to enter a religious community, but her plans were always thwarted. The year 1859 brought for her a turn in events although not in decisions. Seemingly it had never occurred to her to found a religious order of her own, although in those days the idea was not a strange one. The Catholic Church in Germany at that time enjoyed a spring-like blossoming of foundations in religious orders. Every year new ones came into being. Frequently the founders were quite ordinary people. They all knew themselves called to serve the needs of the church and of mankind. Often enough the only basis for a foundation was a generous heart ready for all sacrifices. Aline certainly knew of many of these foundations. But her endeavors of entering religious life were always directed toward an established congregation. In 1859 she was faced with a fact of becoming a co-foundress of a new community of women.

In the Olpe circle of Aline's friends was Regina Loeser, who also harbored the thought of entering religious life. The idea of joining the religious state was circulated among the group of friends and was instrumental in bringing together Aline and a Sister of the Congregation of Christian Charity, Sister Clara Pfaender. Sister Clara was born on December 6, 1827, in Hallenberg, Sauerland, and was baptized as Anna Theresia. Later her family settled in Liesen in the vicinity of Hallenberg. Soon after her completion of elementary school, she felt an ardent desire to become a teacher. In this she was strongly supported by the young and energetic pastor, Rev. Loeser. She even lived for a period of time in the parish residence. Here she became acquainted with the pastor's younger sister, Regina Loeser, and formed a close friendship with her. In 1848, the Rev. Loeser was summoned to Paderborn as Seminary Procurator. Because of his influential position, he was able to do much for Anna Theresia Pfaender. She pursued her vocation and on November 4, 1850, was invested in the Congregation of the Sisters of Christian Charity in Paderborn under the religious name of Sister Clara Pfaender.

She had been troubled for some time with thoughts as to whether the Congregation of Christian Charity was the right one for her. Entering a stricter order also occupied her thinking for she was attracted to adoration of the Blessed Sacrament. Shortly after, she felt a strong urge to found a congregation of her own with the objective of combining the adoration of the Blessed Sacrament with deeds of charity.

In the summer of 1859 the two friends in Olpe, Aline Bonzel and Regina Loeser, decided definitely to enter the religious life. The community each had in mind, or whether both had planned to enter the same community, is not known. It is probable that Regina Loeser wrote to her friend Sister Clara Pfaender regarding their plans. Sister Clara somehow had the information and considered it as providential, a sign from heaven. Here she had two willing souls with whom she could perhaps start a new community. She invited her friend, Regina Loeser, to Witten for a discussion and begged her to postpone for several weeks her decision to enter the convent. Most likely she had also invited Aline Bonzel. At all events, Aline Bonzel and Regina Loeser drove to Witten. How extensively Sister Clara divulged her plans to the two at that time is not known. Regina Loeser was prepared immediately to join in the plan. Aline Bonzel was more conservative. The whole idea was still too new, too uncertain. She promised only that she would support the project financially as far as it lay in her power.

Upon the return of the two friends to Olpe, their plans were naturally discussed with relatives and acquaintances. Aline's uncle advised her that a foundation in Olpe would be unsuccessful, for the Vincentians, a charitable congregation, were active there. As a foregone conclusion, Regina Loeser conferred with her brother, the Rev. Loeser. He not only knew Sister Clara Pfaender well but had always encouraged her. His reaction to the plan was positive. Thereupon Aline's doubts seemed to have vanished. A second discussion took place in Witten, in which their plans took on concrete form. On September 9, 1859, Sister Clara received an answer to her request from the major superior, Mother Pauline of Mallinckrodt. Approbation for withdrawal was granted her. She was to leave Witten for Paderborn on September 20, and from there travel to Olpe on September 23.

In the meantime, the two in Olpe who had joined with her drew the spiritual Rector Hesse into their confidence. In their behalf he wrote to the Bishop of Paderborn, Dr. Konrad Martin, on September 11, 1859, as follows:

> *Your Excellency (Grace) Most Reverend Bishop:*
>
> Two young ladies have for a long time been determined to enter the convent. After several years of investigation and preparation, they were at the point of fulfilling their desire, when an urgent request was received from a certain nun, Sister Clara Pfaender, that they should postpone their entrance for a few weeks. The two women came to me for advice. As the respective Sister had given no further information, I thought they should not consider the non-motivated request as weighty, but ask her for an explanation. A second, still more urgent request, was the answer with the following information. She was planning a project and these two women seemed to be just God's instruments for its accomplishment. The two traveled to Witten and brought back the following communication from Sister Clara, namely that she intends to found a new congregation and has presented her plan to the Most Reverend Bishop who gave his approval most graciously. Thus far Sister Clara's project has a secure basis and a hope for success.

The answer of the bishop to this letter came only later with a copy of the decision (decree) sent to Sister Clara upon her request for September 22, 1859. Also her statements upon her withdrawal from the Congregation of the Sisters of Christian Charity, made to the bishop, are as follows:

Your Excellency, I am taking the liberty of presenting the following to you with great reverence and in deep submission and obedience:

After I have worked peacefully in God for nine years in the Congregation of the Sisters of Christian Charity and devoted my energies, both spiritual and physical, to the service of the blind, especially in their instruction and education, I have experienced for several years a calling to a stricter and more perfect way of life for the greater glory of God and the salvation of souls. After earnest prayer and mature deliberation, I have often sought permission from my superiors for withdrawal from this congregation although very dear to me. The superiors after several years of investigation have granted the permission. It is now my desire to follow this long-recognized will of God, and together with several other young women of similar mind to live under the Rule [name not given], based upon a Constitution approved by the bishop, to lead a life of perfection in the religious state, to pray fervently for the needs of Holy Church, and to care for poor, neglected, and orphaned children. We wish to offer our weak prayers according to the will of God for the propagation of the Faith, for the Holy Father, for bishops and priests, for all the clergy, for the conversion of sinners, for unbelievers and those wavering in faith, for the poor souls, and especially for our bishop and his cherished diocese. In this our age, we also with to venerate the Sacred Hearts of Jesus and Mary with deep devotion and to further these devotions as much as possible. Likewise we wish to serve our dear Lord in his poor, neglected and orphaned children and devote our energies for their instruction and education. In deep acknowledgement of our nothingness we shall place our complete trust in Almighty God who is the strength of the weak and who with his supporting grace will be our help. To maintain an intimate union with the Church, we beg Your Excellency to take us under your protection. With deepest humility we ask in the Hearts of Jesus and

> Mary that Your Excellency will give us your most gracious approval to our plans and your episcopal blessing.

The answer of the bishop came the same day:

> Concerning your request of September 22, 1859, I reply that regarding your plan of forming a congregation with other pious women by leading a secluded life, and devoting your energies to orphaned children, I see no objection, provided that at all times you let yourselves be guided by the norms of genuine piety and Christian wisdom. Ecclesiastical approbation of your way of life will depend upon the favorable progress made in accordance with the requirements of the church.

This decision of the bishop was also sent to Rector Hesse of the secondary school in answer to his letter of September 11, 1859. Thus all preliminaries in the first steps of making a new foundation of a religious community in Olpe had been completed.

If at this point an inventory were taken of the objectives given for the new foundation, one would come to the following conclusions. The outlines for its future were not very clearly drawn. Regarding the apostolate as spelled out, one could readily ask if the new foundation was really necessary. The care of orphans, as Sister Clara mentioned in her letter of September 22 to the bishop, was likewise possible in the Congregation of the Sisters of Christian Charity. The same holds true for all prayer intentions given as purposes of the congregation. Every religious community offers its prayers for the intentions of Holy Mother Church. However, a justification could exist if these were carried out in a special way, such as, perpetual adoration. But perpetual adoration was not mentioned. In the new foundation, however, it became a reality. Why did Sister Clara not mention it in her letter to the bishop? The character of her whole letter will probably give the answer. The letter was most likely written during the last moments she spent in her previous congregation. Under existing conditions, the necessary calm for drawing up an orderly and consistently organized program for the new foundation was lacking. There are quite clear indications that is was Sister Clara's will that the new community be characterized by a special austerity of life. A statement as to the spiritual life of the foundation is missing. However, its importance was not so great in those days. During the same era similar foundations flourished which at first simply set up the activities and objectives of the apostolate and later wrote the rule and constitutions. Often enough at the very beginning it was purely accidental rather than a conscious effort that one or the other rule took hold. That the situation was quite different with Mother Maria Theresia Bonzel, who from the beginning thought only of Franciscan spirituality and consequently of the Franciscan Rule, the following events will show.

Of the three persons involved in this new undertaking, Sister Clara Pfaender was assumed to be superior from the very beginning. She had brought much with her of incalculable value to a new foundation. She had experience in religious life, had held the office of superior in Solingen and in Witten, had practice in teaching and ability to impart knowledge to others. She had exercised the initiative. Although unable to contribute financially, she was recognized as great spiritual capital. That her experience in religious life could be a disadvantage was not conceived at that time. One must bear in mind that in the Congregation of the Sisters of Christian Charity, under the leadership of the great Mother Pauline of Mallinckrodt, Sister Clara had received a very distinctive education emanating from the Augustine Rule. Such impressions cannot be shaken easily. It is therefore difficult to change over to a spirituality of another characteristic religious community. That was expected in this situation.

The town of Olpe was chosen for the foundation. It was given preference because both Aline Bonzel and Regina Loeser were natives. Their families were wealthy and could provide the necessary financial security. Religious are poor in their own private lives. To care for others, however, they must have a sound economic basis. On the other hand, Olpe presented some difficulties as a foundation site. The Vincentians had operated St. Martin Hospital since 1856. Could the small town of Olpe cope with two active religious orders of women? Would not one community prove a detriment to the other? Many of these questions which in themselves foreshadowed the future development were probably seen at that time. But as a whole there was much rejoicing among all who shared the longed-for beginning. Such joy is adapted to dull the sensibilities of foreboding difficulties encountered in such an undertaking.

On September 23, 1859, Sister Clara withdrew from the motherhouse of the Sisters of Christian Charity at Paderborn. Before departing for Olpe, she visited the Franciscans at Paderborn and had herself enrolled as a tertiary in the Franciscan Tertiaries for the laity. From this it can be judged that she was willing, if possible, to switch over to a Franciscan way of life. She arrived in Olpe on September 24, 1859.

One can readily imagine that the following days were well filled. Aline and Regina certainly did not await the event with hands in lap. With the arrival of Sister Clara, the little community was complete in numbers. All that had been discussed and weighted previously could now take definite form. It was under stood that as a new community, they should approach the pastor and mayor of the town.

To give their new foundation the correct impetus, it was necessary for the candidates to prepare themselves spiritually. For this a retreat was the proper means. The character of the retreat should be adjusted to the religious life and likewise to the locality and the surrounding areas. This was scarcely possible in Olpe. Hence the three journeyed to Aix-la-Chapelle, now called Aachen. Why Aix-la-Chapelle? This city had two communities of women founded just recently and living under different rules: Sisters of the Poor Child Jesus founded by Mother Clara Fey, and the Poor Sisters of St. Francis founded by Mother Francis Schervier. It would seem advantageous to seek counsel from both orders. But the probable reason for going to Aix-la-Chapelle was that Aline had an acquaintance, Sister Laurentia (Pauline Deimel), in the community of the Poor Child Jesus. She could question her more readily than the other.

Mother Theresia reported on the trip to Aix-la-Chapelle:

> In 1859 on the feast of St. Michael, three young women from Olpe journeyed to Aix-La-Chapelle to make a retreat in preparation for the foundation of a new congregation

> in Olpe, diocese of Paderborn. They celebrated the feast of the holy seraphic Father Francis in Aix-la-Chapelle, and by a sermon on the happiness and tremendous value of holy poverty were deeply inspired to follow the poverty of Christ. After a previous discussion with Bishop Laurent, Mother Frances, superior of the Poor Sisters, and a Jesuit priest, Sister Clara, Regina Loeser, and Aline Bonzel, commenced their retreat in the convent of the Poor Child Jesus. Sister Alphonsa directed the retreat.

Bishop Laurent of Luxemburg had counseled them to adopt the Rule of the Third Order of St. Francis for their foundation. During a visit with Mother Francis Schervier, the three received their first equipment as religious. As a gift, she presented each with a book of the Little Office of the Blessed Virgin Mary. Mother Maria Theresia Bonzel cherished this book to the end of her life; the book is still preserved in the motherhouse of the Olpe Franciscans.

Mother Maria Theresia commented further that the Sisters of the Poor Child Jesus endeavored to win Regina and her for their community. Sister Laurentia especially tried hard to influence them, for she herself, Pauline Deimel, was also from Olpe and sincerely interested in securing more girls from her native town. Undoubtedly one does not know all that was discussed among them at that time in an endeavor to persuade the two Olpe girls to enter the community of the Poor Child Jesus. Mother Maria Theresia has made clear the readily understandable situation. Sister Laurentia at that time reacted to Sister Clara Pfaender, the future superior, very critically and spoke accordingly to Regina and Aline. Could pride in her home town have aroused unknowingly an unconscious antipathy toward Clara Pfaender? That could have been possible, for with persons deeply conscious of home, it is not easy to see a stranger come in to found a new community with the home girls. To them it seemed an enigma that Clara Pfaender had entered a community and then withdrew to found another one.

The first obstacles, even before the actual start of the foundation, were the hardest to bear. Later on it became apparent that difficulties had their good points, because every detail was examined more carefully, haste was prevented, and blind idealism eliminated. To the above difficulties others were added, as Mother Maria Theresia mentioned in her later record that "even the father confessor pointed out how dangerous it is to found something new, for all is already provided for in the church; he advised us to enter an established community of which there are many with excellent reputations. He referred to Aix-la-Chapelle as an example."

The hearts of Regina and Aline were heavy. They were tortured with many doubts. One of them determined to drive to Witten on the next morning to enter the congregation of the Liguorians where she could find rest and tranquility in the cloister. Apparently, the "Witten" referred to is in Holland and not in the Ruhr. It is not mentioned directly which one had decided to enter a contemplative order to evade all difficulties in the way of their new foundation. But one can say with certainty that it was not Aline. In her honesty she would have mentioned her discouragement as she did in the beginning of this brief chronicle. Here her name was not omitted where disagreeable things were concerned. Also, it was not consonant with Aline's character to give up readily, for she had the firm support of her family for the Olpe foundation.

At all events, Mother Theresia wrote about their leaving Aix-La-Chapelle and the overcoming of their difficulties:

> Almighty God willed otherwise. He gave strength and courage to their souls to overcome all kinds of hardships in the fulfillment of his Holy Will. After a stay of three to four weeks in Aix-la-Chapelle, which time was devoted chiefly to spiritual exercises, they returned by way of Cologne to Olpe. In Cologne they celebrated the feast of St. Ursula and were encouraged by a Jesuit priest to continue in their plan of a new foundation. They arrived in Olpe by post chaise about five o'clock in the morning and took up residence in a rented portion of the private home of widow Schuerholz.

During their absence the people of Olpe were not idle. The Bonzels and other benefactors rented the required space for living quarters, where the small group began their new life. Special concern was exercised to find quarters for a convent near the parish church of St. Martin:

> Within a few days all was arranged for conventual living as much as was possible in a private residence and Sister Clara appointed superior. As no constitution existed, they lived according to the Rule of St. Francis, the determined order of the day and the directives of Sister Clara. No mortification was too severe and the practice of penance was sweet and agreeable. During the month of November a brief devotion was held for the Poor Souls which was attended by the people of Olpe. By means of alms from the Loeser and Bonzel families, several weeks passed in relative peace and quiet during which the three Sisters prepared for investiture through prayer and good works.

These sketches by Mother Maria Theresia of the first days in the newly founded religious community are certainly not abundant. One ardently desires far more particulars. Still something previous lies in this treasured background of their first days in Olpe. The beginning was established. Now they had to prove themselves; with wholehearted zeal they undertook to prepare themselves worthily. They were able to begin their apostolate for the care of orphans immediately. At first their charges numbered four children. The Sisters provided for their care and educational development. Later as the children attended the city schools, they had charge of them outside school hours. The number did not remain at four but increased rapidly.

It must have been a great consolation for the three to see their apostolate flourish so well in the very beginning of the foundation. Success in their sphere of work proved the necessity for a new community in the active life. On this point we have an evaluation by Dean Goerdes of Drolshagen in a request he wrote to the bishop of Paderborn on October 25, 1860. Among other items was the following:

> Views in regard to the new foundations vary. Many are in favor; many others are in opposition. Their objectives certainly are good and praiseworthy, provided they are carried out in a suitable and prudent manner. To my knowledge not a single institution exists in the whole of Sauerland for the care of orphans. Here a great need could be served. Such children are often obliged to earn much money for their upkeep under poor conditions. Their education is almost entirely neglected. They are employed to herd cattle or like jobs. Their school and church attendance is poorly provided for. There is no question that the orphans of this locality could be placed in their institutes, as I have learned from the Land and Administrative Councilor Meeting in Freusberg several days ago.

Here a great need is pointed out in a few brief sentences. Without doubt the parishes were responsible for the poor conditions that existed for the care of orphans. It is true that some families carried out their responsibilities toward these children very conscientiously. Others, however, just used these children. Child abuses were lessened considerably after the passage of the child labor laws. It would be an advantage basically for child placement in the home, if the respective families fulfilled their duties toward the child. But it happened too often that orphans were adopted for ruthless use in labor; their educational development and religious instruction were sorely neglected. The oft reiterated complaint of the sorry plight of orphans could not be denied. Thus it meant much for Olpe to have a group of idealistic minded women form a new community and dedicate their services to the care of orphan children.

Prospects for the new foundation in Olpe were favorable not only with respect to the apostolate but also to the increase in numbers. Following is a quotation from Mother Maria Theresia's Chronicles:

> Soon the daughter of Widow Schuerholz entered the small community as lay-sister and as postulant was called Miss Louise. Then Miss Lisette, a small foster-sister of Sister Clara was admitted. As seamstress she helped in the

> sewing room to make clothes for investiture. She herself was determined to remain a postulant. A young girl from Paderborn, who had previously been granted admission from Sister Clara, now entered. The entrance of Fredericka Boehmer, who had sought admittance, was postponed because of lack of space. In the following year, a house that had served as quarters for the soldiers, but was now vacated was remodeled as a convent for the Sisters. They moved into these quarters several weeks after Easter. Since this location had only a small space for a garden, the sisters utilized the garden of Widow Schuerholz near their present location. Fredericka Boehmer from Paderborn, Theresa Eisenbach from Olpe, and Anna Clemens from Rueblinghausen soon entered.

The new house into which the Sisters had moved was called the Zimmermann house, located on the street known today as the Railroad Station Street. The residence was acquired by Aline's mother and placed at the disposal of the Sisters. Secured in early March, the house was remodeled and ready for occupancy by the Sisters several weeks after Easter. Since it was more spacious, it could accommodate the admission of additional candidates. One wonders whether by admission of the candidates, the new foundation wished to show its importance and give evidence of its purpose and vitality? Perhaps relative to Clara Pfaender, the bishop's approval to occupy the new convent was a foregone conclusion. Otherwise, if there were not some certitude regarding the future, the simple acceptance of girls into the new foundation would be beyond comprehension.

It was evident to the energetic superior, Sister Clara, that the time of probation should not be filled just with prayer and work. While awaiting the final results, she endeavored in the interim to engage in some undertaking. Therefore, in 1860, before Pentecost, she went to Paderborn to report to the bishop on the progress of the new foundation and at the same time beg for investiture for herself and the other Sisters. Bishop Dr. Konrad Martin explained that first they must choose a Rule and then write a constitution. After that investiture would be in order.

Of the deliberations that must have gone on in the community, nothing is known. Discussions were held regarding the Rule to be adopted as a basis for community living. Aline Bonzel wanted the Franciscan Rule by all means. But seemingly she was not well acquainted with the basic Rules of religious orders, for with the exception of Aix-la-Chappelle, she had not come in contact with the Third Order Regular of St. Francis. Besides her stay with the Schervier-Sisters was more in the character of a visitor than otherwise. Clara Pfaender knew the Augustinian Rule from her convent days with the Sisters of Christian Charity. She felt she could write a constitution based on that Rule. Since she was the superior and responsible for admitting candidates into the community, it seemed advisable, in this very beginning, that she have the liberty to employ her full experience in religious life. Only on this basis, can one explain how a community which uniformly desired to live according to the Franciscan Rule, began with the Augustinian Rule, but with the intention of later converting to the Franciscan rule. In this procedure the character of the times can readily be detected. Many most likely saw basically little difference whether one lived according to the Augustinian or the Franciscan Rule. The development of a specialized spirituality came later and in many instances very much later. As mentioned before there might have been good reasons for the action at that time, but these are lost on the present generation. Still that decision was the source of very many difficulties in the future. Therein lay the cause why in a few years two communities developed from the one.

In the summer of 1860, in the joys of a successful and flourishing beginning one never thought of the sorrows to set in later. The constitutions were drafted and sent to the bishop for approval. That happened in August. The days passed quickly and foundation day was drawing nearer. But the approval of the constitutions and the permission for investiture still awaited a reply. With great impatience, Clara Pfaender wrote to the bishop on September 29, 1860:

> ... although for several weeks I have twice daily sent to the post office for the mail, I have thus far not received your

gracious reply relative to the approval of the constitutions and the happy day of our investiture.

In all, three letters dated September 29, 1860, were sent to the bishop with the same request and with the probable idea that the request would carry more weight if the three first candidates — Clara Pfaender, Aline Bonzel, and Regina Loeser — would write the bishop simultaneously, individually, and in the same tenor. The letter bearing Aline Bonzel's signature is of special interest to us. It is as follows:

> *His Excellency the Bishop!*
> *Most Reverend Bishop!*
>
> Your Excellency will graciously permit me to venture to write to you also to make known my most urgent requests and humbly to explain them.
>
> One year has now elapsed since we engaged in our well-known work for the honor of God, under the leadership of our dear Sister Clara, who came here for the happiness and welfare of many. As our venerable Mother we obey her in childlike and sincere love. We have overcome many difficulties by the grace of God, for He often answered the tears and burning petition of his beloved daughter and spouse (Sister Clara). Through her pious and saintly life she has won the hearts of the well-disposed for this good cause. Through steadfast confidence in God and in your pastoral support, she founded and furthered a community here in Olpe, without all human support and assistance under all sorts of difficulties and far from that fatherly care bestowed so lovingly upon the community established close to you.
>
> Long have we felt sincerely grateful to God and to Your Excellency for the treasure shared with us and our native town through and in our beloved Sister Clara. She is the instrument of God, the grain of mustard seed. She willingly permitted herself to be trodden on and here under the loving protection of Your Excellency, now blossoms, grows, and renders the fruit of Catholic love and

joy for the glory of God and the good of the Church. At the least sign of Your Excellency, we are prepared to leave our native town with our dear Sister Clara and to reside wherever you in your goodness will determine.

With an ever increasing longing, we have waited for Your Excellency's ecclesiastical approbation of our constitutions and the appointment of the blessed day on which we shall have the happiness of receiving the holy habit from your hands. Not only we, the small group of your least servants, but also our families, after some minor obstacles from their side have been eliminated with the help of God, are now in most favorable frame of mind and ready to support us as much as lies within their power. All Olpe is of the same opinion with the exception of a few to whom the pious life of our dear Sister Clara and our seclusion and contempt of the world are a constant reproach.

Without our suggesting it, there is among all the expressed desire that Your Excellency, after the completion of your confirmation schedule in October, honor our native town with your august presence and officiate at our investiture.

We also have a firm confidence in God that the many prayers, fasts, and mortifications offered daily by us and others will ascend to our good Father in heaven and be received graciously. With your kind cooperation may our work soon be crowned. All preparations have been made. The chapel is furnished, the vestments are on hand, the religious habits are in readiness. The only thing missing is a set day for the investiture and our joy will be complete.

The ending of our trial period is especially important to our dear Sister Clara for the repeated delays are proving detrimental to her health; and we fear lest a longer and painful postponement will undermine it completely.

Also, Your Excellency, the confidence now engendered in this work for the greater glory of God the Father and also its support could be weakened very much and result in impaired development. It could also create a new hardship for my family in regard to succession of property.

Up to this time we have limited our activity to the care of six orphan children and are unwilling to increase this number before our investiture. Strengthened through ecclesiastical consecration and vested with the blessed habit of the order, we shall with the help of God fulfill our obligations with great courage, deep humility, and intense love, and thus bring honor to the diocese and joy to your fatherly heart.

May we humbly ask Your Excellency to honor the feast of St. Theresia or a beautiful feast of the Blessed Virgin in October by granting us the happiness of receiving the long-desired religious garb. We shall be grateful to you throughout our lives and pray for you daily as we have done for a long time.

Please forgive my liberty, Most Reverend Bishop, brought on by the great desire of investiture, and pardon it kindly. Again I plead for it most earnestly with a worthy desire for the development of our work.

With deep respect and confiding reverence

Your Excellency
Your least
Aline Bonzel
Olpe, September 29, 1860

This letter is informative in more respects than one. Whoever must wait is easily subjected to fears for he endeavors to seek reasons why no reply has come. Was it wise to make the new foundation in Olpe? Olpe is relatively a great distance from Paderborn. Whoever lives in Paderborn can readily clarify a situation through personal contact. Could the bishop even harbor the thought that the new foundation should be made elsewhere? Olpe is not the only place where the foundation could be made.

Noticeably, Aline Bonzel's letter revolves strongly around the person of Clara Pfaender. Is it the expression of implicit obedience that Aline also at this time offered her superior? That well may be assumed. For somehow all beginnings center in reverence around the personality of the leader. Still the letter gives a very individualistic impression. Written according to the established usage of the times, it naturally went farther in its submissiveness than is customary today. But upon closer scrutiny, many turns of expression appear that stand out as rules. Relative to what has been known of Mother Maria Theresia heretofore, the letter as a whole is rather strange. It is not in her style of writing. She wrote in a more straightforward manner, more naturally. One cannot but surmise that the letter was not written by her alone. Deliberations as to content were most likely considered in common. United action was probably taken regarding the best approach for such an affair. For, since three letter writers sent letters to the bishop of Paderborn on September 29, 1860, it can be readily determined that they were not of a spontaneous character. Only in that light can one understand this letter of Mother Maria Theresia, so different in style and feeling from all her other known letters.

Before the bishop answered the requests, he took the last steps to clear the way for the new foundation. He did not wish to rely solely on the good will of the petitioners. Thus on October 8, 1860, he asked Dean Goerdes in Drolshagen to make a confidential investigation concerning the successful prospects for the community in Olpe. On October 25, 1860, he reported to the bishop. In this report he stressed the necessity of an orphanage. In regard to the prospect of the institute, he continued:

> To the question as to whether Olpe can maintain the institute, I can only answer, yes. Two Franciscan communities (Attendorn and Friesenhagen), in this vicinity have had sufficient sustenance, why not this one? If in the beginning, the care of orphans will gain prominence, consideration will need to be given to the financial resources of candidates admitted (other things being equal) at least for the time being. Then the industrial demands will be unable to harm them.

A calm and thinking religious also considers the domestic economy of the whole without which a new foundation cannot be made.

Whoever neglects this phase runs the danger of wrecking the whole idealism of such an undertaking, for not only the livelihood of the Sisters must be maintained but also that of the orphan children. After Dean Goerdes had given the above information, he posed the question of superiorship for the new foundation:

> Sister Clara has been described to me as an energetic, talented person, one fully capable of directing a community. Also very capable are Regina Loeser and Aline Bonzel, who besides have significant wealth. Therefore, I cannot oppose the wish of the petitioners for investiture.

The bishop replied on October 30, 1860, as follows:

> Upon reading your revered report of October 25, 1860, I am not unwilling to approve that Clara Pfaender and the young women associated with her bind themselves into an ecclesiastical congregation. I also grant further that they may live under the title of Sisters of St. Francis, Daughters of the Sacred Hearts of Jesus and Mary, according to the Constitutions submitted to me and which I have reviewed carefully.
>
> I intend to appoint Your Reverence superior of this newly founded congregation and my representative. Therefore I desire that you contact the proposed Clara soon, acquaint yourself with the Constitutions, and examine the young women who wish to join the congregation and be invested with Clara Pfaender, in regard to their vocation, using the questions outlined in the requirements. Report the results to me immediately that I may grant you faculties deemed appropriate and worthy as my representative to officiate at the investiture in the parish church of Olpe.

By the end of November, Dean Goerdes had completed the canonical examination of the candidates required by the bishop. Regina Wurm had joined the group in November; her name had been added to the list mentioned previously. Then on

December 10, 1860, Bishop Konrad Martin granted faculties to Dean Goerdes to invest the first nine Sisters of the new congregation. The date of investiture was left to the decision of the Sisters. They set it for December 20, 1860, and chose St. Martin Parish church as the place for the reception of their religious habits. Clara Pfaender drew up a rite for the reception ceremonies and submitted it to the bishop. He rewrote it and according to this rite the investiture ceremonies took place on December 20, 1860.

After the celebration of Holy Mass in which the postulants received Holy Communion, the celebrant Dean Goerdes gave a brief talk. Thereafter, he asked, "Dear daughters, what is your desire?" The nine postulants answered, "We desire to be admitted to the novitiate of the Sisters of St. Francis." The celebrant asked further, "What is your purpose in desiring this admission?" The answer: "We cherish the wish to perfect ourselves more and more in this way of life to be able to serve God and the Congregation of the Sisters of St. Francis more intimately and to become more serviceable to our neighbor through prayer and good works." Thereupon the celebrant continued: "Let us, dear daughters, plead in prayer that God ratify your purpose and bless it." The singing of the Litany of All Saints followed during which the postulants lay prone. After the invocation *Veni Creator*, the postulants approached the altar singly while the choir sang *Jesu Corona Virginum*. After this, each in turn had her hair cut, and she received the blessed religious habit. All clothed in the habit returned to the chapel and again approached the altar. The celebrant read the list:

> In order to remind you that from now on your whole way of life must be new since you have died to the world and live only for Christ, you shall receive a new name today. Thus:
>
> Miss Clara Pfaender shall be known as: Sister Maria Clara of the Sacred Hearts of Jesus and Mary.
>
> Miss Aline Bonzel shall be known as: Sister Maria Theresia of the Blessed Sacrament,
>
> Miss Regina Loeser shall be known as: Sister Maria Antonia of the Immaculate Conception,

> Miss Fredericka Boehmer shall be known as: Sister Maria Franziska of the Five Holy Wounds,
>
> Miss Theresia Eisenbach shall be known as: Sister Maria Magdalena of the Precious Blood,
>
> Miss Lisette Pfaender shall be known as: Sister Maria Agnes of the Sweet Name of Jesus,
>
> Miss Luise Drexelius shall be known as: Sister Maria Josepha,
>
> Miss Anna Marie Clemens shall be known as: Sister Maria Margaretha,
>
> Miss Regina Wurm shall be known as: Sister Maria Gertrudis.

(The three last named were invested as lay sisters; the first six, as choir sisters. Mother Maria Theresia abolished the institute of lay Sisters immediately after the separation of the congregation.)

After each Sister was crowned with a wreath of flowers, benediction with the Most Blessed Sacrament was given. The Sisters were then conducted to their convent. There Dean Goerdes announced that Sister Clara had been appointed as superior by the bishop for a period of two years. Thus a new congregation had in reality been brought into being. The Sisters approached their superior and kissed her hand as a sign of willing obedience. The remainder of the day they passed in quiet and recollection. No visitors were permitted lest the tranquility be disturbed. The work had begun. Perhaps in the stillness throughout the convent the motto that Dean Goerdes gave them at the opening talk that morning burned itself into their souls: "Leave all to God! If this work is of God, it will endure; if it is not of God, it will of itself fall into ruin."

In the December 10, 1860, letter giving permission for investiture, the bishop also wrote:

> In virtue of the faculty granted me by the Holy See, I will allow the congregation to have a private oratory (provisional for one year) and permit the Blessed Sacrament to be preserved in this oratory with the stipulation that a perpetual light be kept burning, the key of the tabernacle

> be in the custody of a priest, and that Holy Mass be celebrated in the oratory at least three times a week.

It is significant for a religious community, at its very beginning, to be permitted to have the Blessed Sacrament preserved in its midst and Holy Mass celebrated in the convent oratory. Thereby a community is given a real heart center. That is probably the reason why the Sisters wished to spend the remainder of investiture day in quiet and recollection. They wished to prepare themselves for the following day, December 21, when Holy Mass would be celebrated for the first time within their convent home.

Mother Maria Theresia gives a graphic account of the significance of this day in a later chronicle:

> The next morning, the feast of St. Thomas Apostle, Holy Mass was celebrated for the first time in the beautifully decorated chapel and the Blessed Sacrament was placed in the tabernacle for adoration. Touching and festive was the singing of the Sisters. Their desire and yearning rose ever higher and higher manifesting itself in sobbing as at the Sanctus the hymn, *When Will You Come, My Redeemer* was intoned — no heart remained untouched — no eye dry, when at the consecration the tremulous voices of the Sisters began: *Welcome, Consolation of the Devout, You Sweet Jesus.* After the Communion of the priest, the Sisters received Holy Communion. Filled with joy and gratitude to God, their Savior in their hearts, the Sisters began the Perpetual Adoration of the Most Blessed Sacrament in hourly rotation, day and night, after Holy Mass. Adoration is the chief objective of the congregation.

And this last paragraph added later to the chronicle — "Adoration is the chief objective of the congregation" — has a very special significance. One of the main objectives was attained in the Perpetual Adoration to which the congregation had pledged itself. It had now begun. After the investiture this was their most important accomplishment. The care of the orphans had started earlier. Now as it were, the crowning of the whole was acknowledged. Everyday life according to their high ideals had now begun.

CHAPTER IV

THE WAY OF THE CROSS BEGINS

It is seemingly a law in religious life that everyone who is called by God to follow him in a special way must first walk the way of the cross. To mature life to its fullest, he must pass the test of perseverance by enduring sorrows and hardships of various descriptions. What can be said of the individual can also be said of the congregation as a unit. In the latter instance this manifests itself strongly and forcefully. Upon perusing the list of founders and foundresses one sees this verified always and ever again. Each congregation must first walk the way of the cross before it can see its way clearly into the future. According to human judgment many founders and foundresses became frustrated in their work. Many who began a congregation were later removed from the leadership of that congregation and were forced into public disgrace that through humiliation they might contribute more effectively to the growth of the congregation. But also in other situations, where such was not the case, the cross in the first years stood in grim seriousness and willed to be borne.

The new foundation in Olpe proved no exception to the rule. Here also the cross made its appearance and that at an early hour. Even before the first Sisters were invested with the religious habit, thoughts as to whether Olpe was really a favorable place for the foundation of an active charitable congregation began to rise to the surface. Bishop Konrad Martin had written to Dean Goerdes on November 20, 1860, as follows:

> I have learned from a reliable source that the town of Olpe is not an appropriate place for the foundation of a Franciscan congregation nor for an orphanage, and that Elspe would be far more suitable for both institutions. Will Your Reverence please examine and weigh the situation with Rev. Hengstebeck, the parish priest in Elspe, and then report to me?

The Dean accordingly made the contacts and found the house in Olpe roomy and uninhabited at the time. But plans to move into this house did not materialize.

On the other hand it was evident because of its rapid growth that the congregation needed territory that could offer it a longer future. Negotiations were started regarding the Chapel of the Cross and its surrounding grounds, but these came to naught, probably because the cemetery was connected with them. Soon another possible land purchase came up for consideration, which was located on the western boundary of Olpe. Dean Goerdes informed the bishop on March 23, 1861, in the following:

> The house the Sisters are planning to purchase is very roomy, well situated, and besides has garden area surrounding it. If a house for a convent is to be purchased in Olpe, this one would be the most favorable. I have no misgivings regarding this purchase other than the world political conditions and I have talked with the superior, Sister Clara, concerning these, with the remark that I consider it advisable to delay purchase for several months. The universal need for money might cause the lowering of the set price. It will definitely be in the interest of the congregation to purchase the property later, for the Bonzel and Loeser families who are expected to finance the purchase will only with difficulty be persuaded to do so if a house was to be purchased in another locality. At least during the lifetime of the parents of Aline Bonzel and Regina Loeser, this should not take place. Since the railroad now passes near Elspe, all prices have been advanced – making costs significantly higher than formerly. From what other sources could the money be obtained if not from the aforementioned persons?

Under pressure of conditions the house was purchased sooner than had been planned. On June 10, 1861, the legal procedures had been transacted with the businessman William Weber, the merchant Christian Loeser, and the widow Bonzel. The mother practically purchased the property for her daughter, Sister Maria Theresia. A singular situation! One could have transacted the business by having the superior purchase the property and the relatives of the co-founders finance the undertaking as a gift to the Sisters. Was the principle of Franciscan poverty accomplished by their way? Or did the relatives wish to gain greater security for their daughters through the method that was employed? After the completion of the business deal, renovation of the house took place immediately. Foremost, arrangements had to be made for a chapel. By July 31, 1861, the convent was ready for occupancy. The Blessed Sacrament was borne to the new chapel in solemn procession. The young Community now had a definite convent home.

The bishop was very hesitant in giving his approval. As late as August 29, 1861, he wrote to superior Dean Goerdes as follows:

> Rather for the sake of peace, I wish that the Franciscans would investigate other areas to see if they could not locate more suitably in some other place. It would be very agreeable to me if Your Reverence, by your advice, would support some other suitable place.

What were the reasons for recommending the foundation to be made in some other place outside of Olpe? In itself Olpe seemed the most suitable. Three Olpe girls were among the first nine Sisters. The affluent families of Bonzel and Loeser backed the foundation and made possible the first steps in its economic support. Were the citizens of Olpe not justly proud that such an undertaking took place in their town? All told, the difficulty was linked with the fact that the Vincentians, an active charitable order and operating St. Martin Hospital in Olpe, were already established there. The Vincentian Sisters really had the first right. Through their charitable activities they had deserved the gratitude and the attachment of the citizens of Olpe. Must not the Vincentians, and above all their responsible superior, the suffragan bishop of Paderborn, be concerned that their activities in Olpe be maintained?

As long as the Sisters of the newly founded congregation under Mother Clara Pfaender were few in number, there was not thought of defining the operations of each community in detail.

Why should it have been done? Their fields of work were well outlined. The Vincentians operated the hospital and nursed the sick; the Franciscans had opened a small orphanage and otherwise devoted themselves to Perpetual Adoration. Each congregation had its own spheres of activity without the one interfering in the work of the other; so it seemed.

There was no reason why the young congregation should have made known its first Constitution to the world. If it had done so, one would have become aware earlier that difficulties were bound to arise. For the Constitution drafted by Mother Clara and approved by the bishop gave as objectives not only the "care, education, and instruction of youth, but also the nursing of the sick in hospitals and in homes ..." In the beginning, this second point did not come to the fore in the activities of the Sisters as can be learned from the fact that the people called them the "orphan sisters." Also, the task of nursing was not sought by the Sisters themselves. It happened incidentally. It was really unavoidable.

When the Sisters on their begging tours entered the homes of their benefactors and saw a sick person who needed nursing care, it was but an act of charity to do more than just say a kind and encouraging word. When the families begged the Sisters to come again to see their sick, what else could the Sisters do? The sick are particularly attached to those persons in whom they have once confided. Could the Sisters refuse when people approached them to come and see their sick relatives? The instances increased. That aroused the feelings of the Sisters at the hospital and also those who saw in the Vincentians "their" sisters. Was not the newly established congregation forcing its way into the sphere of activity belonging to the long established charitable Sisters?

These feelings might have been augmented by the surprisingly rapid growth of the newly founded congregation. At that time Olpe was but a small town with a population of 2,200. Now if a really large motherhouse of the congregation should be established, could the Vincentians, who justly had priority, maintain themselves in Olpe? One must bear in mind that in October, 1859, the Sisters resided in the house of Widow Schuerholz; after

Easter 1860, they moved into the Zimmermann house. On July 31, 1861, they moved into an established convent. Between these transactions there were negotiations for Elspe and the territory bordering on the Chapel of the Cross. Such restless activity could readily give opportunity for malicious talk.

Representing the interests of the Vincentians, Auxiliary Bishop Freusberg appealed to the bishop. The bishop presented his considerations to the superior of the Franciscans in Olpe. He announced by letter dated March 23, 1861:

> As the activities of the Sisters of Charity are confined chiefly to the one special building, I do not believe that they suffer anything out of the ordinary if the Franciscans visit some of the sick to whom they are called. Likewise it is questionable whether the money bestowed upon the Franciscans would be given to the Sisters of Charity if the former were not there.

These words of the superior show quiet reflection. Unfortunately such careful thought was not the case of all concerned. For as the letter of the superior discloses, a strong apprehension had arisen that the Vincentians could possibly lose their successful operation and economic status if another congregation with great strength should develop in Olpe.

The situation did not quiet down. That occasioned the bishop to write to Mother Clara on April 18, 1861:

> I have very carefully scrutinized the complaints leveled against your congregation in Olpe. The complaint is that the nursing of the sick in the homes is being usurped. I do not recognize this to be an established fact. On the other hand I see unfortunately that although your congregation should give no cause for dissention, the conflict will continue and grow into an uncontrollable scandal.... I assure you that I embrace your congregation with sincere pastoral benevolence and shall acknowledge it at all times; but because I heartily wish you well and would not like to see you, even though innocent, give occasion to scandalous conflicts.... I beg you through the love of Christ to offer

> this sacrifice to God: either change the location of your motherhouse from Olpe or refrain from nursing the sick in Olpe. I realize how very difficult either decision will be. My pastoral heart is greatly grieved to have to come to such a decision. But the greater the sacrifice the richer the reward that will rest upon your congregation.

The bishop's letter was clear. Why were his urgent wishes not followed immediately and another site sought? In the first place the superior Dean Goerdes was of a different opinion. He was acquainted with the immediate and prevailing circumstances and knew that the Sisters in transferring the congregation out of Olpe would be hanging in midair. In Olpe they were established economically through the energetic assistance of widow Bonzel. Besides at this time negotiations were in progress for purchasing property that would provide a convent for the Sisters. Since widow Bonzel was prepared to finance the purchase of the property, stability for the new congregation could be realized. Should one disregard this possibility and begin in another place under great uncertainty? The repeated shifting of locale would prove a detriment to the young congregation.

But the opposition did not relent. Consequently, the bishop was induced to write a personally handwritten letter to Dean Goerdes in which he said:

> More complaints have come from Olpe recently regarding the usurpation of the nursing activities by the Franciscan Sisters. These had the signature of the parish priest. As always I was unable to find guilt on the part of the Franciscan Sisters, but the Sisters of Charity are greatly irritated. The auxiliary bishop begged me most urgently to have the Franciscan Sisters move from Olpe, or at least forbid them to engage in nursing activities in Olpe. This is becoming very difficult. But on the other hand peace especially among religious communities is so great a good that I cannot but assume the responsibility to prevent scandalous conflicts, which under existing circumstances appear unavoidable if the Franciscans continue their activities in Olpe.

He added:

> For the sake of peace, above all I wish the Franciscans would look around to see if they can find another suitable place in the surrounding areas outside of Olpe to make their foundation. I would be very pleased if Your Reverence would support them by counsel and advice in the choice of another special site. At my next visit I shall take the opportunity to confer with you and with the Sisters in person so that we can resolve this conflict favorably.

Shortly before writing this letter, the bishop had been in Olpe. He visited the convent of the Franciscans and held canonical visitation. On this occasion, August 26, 1861, he himself officiated at the investiture of nine candidates. The Sisters who had been invested on December 20, 1860, pronounced their vows. Among them was Sister Maria Theresia Bonzel. The bishop voiced his joy and praise that the young congregation developed so obviously under the blessing of God. Did he not endeavor at this time to guide the situation in such a way as to voice his expressed wish that the Sisters should not limit their activities to Olpe alone, but work prosperously within the confines of the entire diocese? Before he returned to Paderborn, he revisited the Franciscan convent. Certainly his words of appreciation, gratitude, and encouragement were not mere generalities. He undoubtedly informed himself of the existing situation and the controversial activity of the Franciscans. At all events this personal visit bore results. The bishop saw the situation in a different light although more time was still required to solve the controversy.

On March 21, 1862, the congregation received a new spiritual superior, Rev. Schmidt from Wenden. At the very beginning of his activities, he had to cope with disagreeable quarrels, as seen in a letter he received from Bishop Konrad Martin:

> Acquainting myself first hand with the true conditions relative to the controversy in Olpe, I was favorably impressed. Even before I received your report I had to calm an apprehension. The district magistrate of Olpe had written a letter to the auxiliary bishop which he read to me

> in person. It was a scathing letter. In reply I wrote to the Board of Trustees of St. Martin Hospital informing them that I had no intention whatever of removing the Sisters of Charity from the hospital. This point had to be settled first. That the Franciscan Sisters do some home nursing should be no obstacle. They however are not to intrude themselves, but if their services are requested they may go in the name of God. It is hoped that in this way they may gain a firmer foothold in Olpe until something else can be worked out. Difficulties and obstacles will not harm the young congregation. These constitute a trial and bring out the good in the undertaking. You, dear Father, accept them with a kind and fatherly heart and consider the beautiful reward you will receive from God. Furthermore, I shall look into the situation of the Sisters in Olpe more closely and study the controversy with a view of further clarification.

This letter seemed to end the controversy; however, it was not solved until much later. Difficulties from this source repeatedly came to the surface. These continued almost to the end of Mother Maria Theresia's life and terminated in the year 1900 when the Franciscan Sisters assumed the operation of St. Martin Hospital. One must be acquainted with these difficulties to understand why Sister Clara Pfaender searched for another place to relocate the motherhouse and found one in Salzkotten.

"Difficulties and obstacles will not harm the young congregation. They constitute a trial and bring out the good in the undertaking," thus the bishop wrote. Difficulties were not wanting. Added to the external problems were those arising within their own ranks. In May 1861, Mother Clara became seriously ill. Sister Antonia Loeser who had nursed her, contracted the same illness, typhus. In the early days of their foundation in Olpe, she had established a close relationship between Mother Clara Pfaender and Mother Maria Theresia Bonzel. At that time, she little thought that the length of her convent days would be a meager five months. Her fellow sisters held her in high esteem for she lived her religious life of prayer and penance very seriously. As a native of Olpe, Sister Antonia rejoiced greatly to see the congregation firmly established in Olpe in 1861. Her happiness was great as they moved into their newly acquired house. She toured it but once and then had to return to bed immediately. The seriously ill Sister kept repeating, "Observe the rules! Observe the rules!"

When on Trinity Sunday the procession with the Blessed Sacrament was passing her window, she raised herself upright in bed with all her remaining strength, and in a weak voice joined in the processional singing, a hymn of praise in preparation for her death. In the afternoon of the same day she sank into a semi-conscious state. Sister Maria Theresia and Sister Francesca remained with her during the following night. In a moment of consciousness, Sister Maria Theresia asked the dying sister to beg our Lord that she also may soon join her in heaven. Sister Antonia in a certain and determined voice answered: "No, you will not die yet. You still have a long way before you." On the following day she again and again called out: "The virginal crown! The virginal crown!" She must have recalled the exhortation her own sister once gave her. Her sister had entered the convent with the Clemens Sisters in Muenster, and on a visit had counseled her: "Regina, ever preserve the virginal crown." The words seemed to have made a permanent impression on her for she lived her life accordingly. At the moment of death it must have been a great comfort for her, adorned with the virginal crown received at investiture represented by a circlet of flowers, to meet her eternal Bridegroom. She breathed her last quietly in the arms of the friend of her youth, Sister Maria Theresia Bonzel.

The cross marking the grave of Sister Antonia was not alone for long. On May 3, 1862, Sister Maria Theresia wrote in the chronicles:

> Today the new superior, Rev. Schmidt, officiated at the investiture of the following sisters: Sisters Alphonsa, Mechtildis, Thecla, Ottilia, Liboria, Antonia, and several others. Sister Clara accompanied by Sister Maria Theresia and Sister Alphonsa, the latter ailing, traveled to Rosellen. For the interim period Sister Francesca was designated as

temporary superior; but shortly before they left, the appointment was changed and Sister Agnes, the half-sister of Sister Clara Pfaender was to act as superior. Sister Clara and Sister Maria Theresia spent the first night of their trip in Cologne and Sister Alphonsa traveled on to Rosellen. His Excellency Bishop Dr. Konrad Martin was in Cologne at the time and from there, accompanied by Auxiliary Bishop Baudri, he would make his episcopal visit to Rome. Sister Clara and Sister Maria Theresia visited His Excellency from Paderborn in the archbishop's residence to discuss various matters. Their stay in Cologne was prolonged to several days, and during that time they visited various convents in the city and purchased needed supplies. On Sunday they arrived in Rosellen where Sister Alphonsa awaited them in her parental home.

The superior Sister Clara contracted a cold and had to spend several weeks in bed. A priest, Vicar Adams, who understood the principles of homeopathy, took Sister Clara and Sister Alphonsa under his charge. Sister Maria Theresia became nurse. Sister Alphonsa's condition worsened daily despite the excellent care she had from all sides. Because of repeated night watches and otherwise overtaxing of strength, Sister Maria Theresia's strength began to fail. She was not strong physically. The physician-acting priest, Vicar Adams, asked Mother Clara to have another Sister come from the motherhouse to release Sister Maria Theresia to give her some rest.

In the meantime the presence of either the superior or her assistant, Sister Maria Theresia, was mandatory at the motherhouse because of the unbearable behavior of Sister Liboria. Sister Francesca came to relieve Sister Maria Theresia, who left for Olpe on the Friday before Pentecost Sunday. She went by way of Wenden to confer with Rev. Schmidt relative to the conduct of Sister Liboria and arrived at the convent in Olpe at eleven o'clock at night. The next morning at four o'clock she dispossessed Sister Liboria of her religious habit and dismissed her as a trouble maker from the convent.

As the report clearly shows, Vicar Adam, must have sensed tensions in the congregation. He counseled Sister Maria Theresia and also Sister Francesca to seek admission into some other congregation if they were not happy. The chronicles of Mother Maria Theresia continued as follows:

> Sister Clara remained in Rosellen with Sister Francesca several weeks longer. After completing the milk diet, she returned to Olpe improved in health. Sister Alphonsa remained in her parental home until fall and then returned to the convent. After several weeks, she received the last anointing, pronounced her religious vows in the arms of her superior, made her Last Will and Testament leaving one thousand dollars to the superior, Clara Pfaender. She died on November 26, 1862, among her Sisters to whom she had been an inspiring example in sickness and in health. Soon thereafter Sister Bernhardine Schamoni died of tuberculosis; the superior had made a recovery trip with her to Paderborn, but to no avail. Our dear Lord called the saintly Sister to himself to give her the crown of faithful perseverance. Also some orphan children died.

Thus the young congregation in its early years stood beneath the cross. It was indeed bitter to see the Sisters die, who with all readiness had dedicated themselves to God to work for the welfare of the needy, to see them snatched from life before they had even begun their active apostolate.

Nevertheless the number of Sisters continued to increase. This enabled the superior to open the first affiliation, in October 1862, in Much in the archdiocese of Cologne. Sister Francesca Boehmer was appointed its first superior. She was assisted by two Sisters and a lay instructor. The daring venture of establishing the first foundation was richly rewarded. Mother Maria Theresia's chronicle reports: "Soon many postulants entered from Much and the surrounding areas. These were accepted into the congregation."

Since the existing obstacles to their active apostolate in Olpe did not lessen, Mother Clara determined to centralize the motherhouse in another locality, as the bishop had counseled at various times. Reverend Heissing in Verne, indicated to her that Salzkotten might be a good possibility. Thus accompanied by her assistant, Sister Maria Theresia, Mother Clara traveled to Salzkotten on November 15, 1862. Here she was able to purchase a larger house with barn and garden area in the eastern section of the town. To make it practical to move the motherhouse as early as possible, renovations were begun immediately. In the spring of 1863, all was in readiness. Sister Maria Theresia wrote:

> On Easter Monday some of the Sisters left, several days later another group followed, and finally on April 25, Mother Clara and other sisters who were unable to make the trek on foot went by post. The convent in Olpe became an affiliation with Sister Maria Theresia as superior. Stationed with her were Sister Juliana, Sister Ignatia, Sister Ursula, Sister Johanna, Sister Margaretha, Sister Gertrudis, and one postulant, Miss Josepha. Fourteen sisters and fifteen postulants went to Salzkotten.

The situation in Olpe had become fundamentally different through this change of status. "Because of the decrease in [the] number of Sisters, it was impossible to continue the Perpetual Adoration in Olpe." Sister Maria Theresia gave this as the first consequence. After that statement she placed in brackets how very sorry she was and closed it with an exclamation point. One can perceive how she valued adoration. She mentioned that primarily, for her Perpetual Adoration was the chief objective of the congregation. Only thereafter she enumerated further effects of the removal of the motherhouse from Olpe. It is understandable that the new motherhouse should be equipped with all requisites. Consequently, only the bare necessities were left in Olpe. Without any bitterness the new superior in Olpe wrote:

> The Sisters full of joy over the great treasure of holy poverty, entrusted themselves completely to the loving providence of God. All endeavored to strive for perfection and through diligence and work to draw down the blessings of God upon themselves.

That Sister Maria Theresia Bonzel should remain in Olpe as superior, as she herself wrote, was in consideration of her relatives and friends in the town. It was not a matter of exclusive trust. Soon thereafter it became evident that an estrangement and a wariness had set in between the two who together with the deceased Sister Antonia Loeser had begun the new foundation. Mother Clara had secretly appointed a certain Sister in Olpe to spy on all that Sister Maria Theresia did and to report her conduct and the condition of affairs to Salzkotten. On her side Sister Maria Theresia was also informed of all that happened in Salzkotten. She herself declared that it happened "through blameworthy underhandedness," and acknowledged openly: "I committed a great injustice in that I engaged in secret correspondence with a certain Sister in Salzkotten." In this way Sister Maria Theresia learned all those things which the Sister thought might be of interest. This confession of her own guilt was most probably recorded later. At a time when others looked upon her with esteem and as an example, she acknowledged her injustice in humility. If she had covered her guilt with a cloak of silence, it could not have been established easily at another time.

What could have caused such an estrangement between the two co-founders? Mother Maria Theresia herself has referred to some of the issues. But it is worthwhile to consider other things also. In the first place the characters of the two Sisters were very different.

Consequently, they probably viewed the prospects of the congregation in different ways. Mother Clara came from an established congregation already engaged in extensive activity in various affiliations. With Mother Theresia all was new. One must also consider that between October 22, 1859 and April 25, 1863, the motherhouse was moved three times, involving much labor and restlessness; one affiliation was opened; and the superior was often ill and away from the motherhouse for weeks at a time. Where was the time for guidance so necessary for a young congregation? Guidance is so important in the very beginning that the congregation may mature in tranquility. But owing to circumstances this tranquility was never present.

Mother Maria Theresia's decision as written in the chronicles in her own words is as follows:

> From the very beginning it was determined to follow the Rule of St. Francis, but the Rule of St. Augustine was adopted as a basis with the promise and wish to convert to the Franciscan Rule later. The Augustinian Rule as basis was also very painful to Sister Francesca. Both sisters had developed a great love for holy poverty and felt that only as Franciscans could this great happiness be theirs. The Rule of St. Augustine was precious and dear to both Sisters for most congregations follow its precepts. Many have attained happiness and salvation through its observance. But here there was placed in the hearts of the two Sisters by God himself a desire to be poor, really poor and unassuming and this desire could not be fulfilled in the established congregation.

Sister Maria Theresia confided all her difficulties to Sister Francesca as the latter stopped in Olpe on her way from Much to Salzkotten. At that time Sister Maria Theresia was very weak physically and ill, so much so, that one feared for her life. The many worries of the immediate past had aggravated her heart condition. She considered leaving the congregation as the simplest solution. Sister persuaded her to postpone the decision at least for the present. In this matter of conscience, Sister Maria Theresia consulted not only the Superior Revered Schmidt, but also, outside the confessional, the Reverend Rector Hesse. Accordingly her spiritual director reported it to the bishop who summoned Mother Clara for a discussion in which Sister Francisca also participated. At this time it was also learned how Sister Maria Theresia had obtained such detailed information of all that happened in Salzkotten. Mother Clara determined to call Sister Maria Theresia to Salzkotten for a retreat after Pentecost, and in all probability, transfer her from Olpe altogether. But events took a different turn: Owing to physical weakness, Sister Maria Theresia was unable to travel, and because of lack of money, others could not do so either; besides, the Reverend superior forbade it, Mother Theresia reported later.

At that time it had not been known to Mother Maria Theresia that the bishop had written to the Superior of the congregation on June 5, 1863, in the following term:

> I am convinced that under the prevailing conditions it is an imperative necessity to leave Sister Maria Theresia in Olpe for the time being. I therefore commission you to refrain summoning her to Salzkotten until further instruction. I approve Sister Francesca functioning as superior in Olpe in the meantime.

Thus Sister Francesca came to Olpe as superior. She was lovingly devoted to Sister Maria Theresia. Concerning her report of conditions in Olpe – as Mother Maria Theresia later wrote – from Salzkotten, "there were no loving considerations for Olpe consequently the dispositions of all Sisters became embittered." Before long Sister Maria Theresia and Sister Francesca petitioned the bishop for a dispensation from the present congregation in order to enter a Franciscan congregation.

The bishop in the meantime had determined otherwise. Two letters followed in rapid succession. The first was in answer to a petition submitted by the leading townsmen in Olpe for the re-establishment of the Perpetual Adoration. The bishop granted the petition in a letter dated July 17, 1863. The second letter, dated July 20, 1863, was addressed to Superior Revered Schmidt in Wenden and directed that he should, "to prevent further agitation and dissensions between the institution in Olpe and the motherhouse in Salzkotten, withdraw the first completely from the jurisdiction of the latter and from the temporary official direction of Mother Clara."

The bishop continued:

> As you informed me the institution in Olpe needs several Sisters more. After a consultation with Sisters Maria Theresia and Francesca, inform me as soon as possible how many and what Sisters should be sent from Salzkotten to Olpe. At the same time consider authoritatively whether Sister Maria Theresia or Sister Francesca should function as local superior in Olpe; if the first, whether Sister

> Francesca should be appointed as assistant or whether she should return to Much as local superior.

The superior answered by letter on July 30, 1863:

> Unfortunately, I was unable until yesterday to discuss the alleged highly honorable disposition of the questionable situation in Olpe with Sister Maria Theresia and Sister Francesca and to make the provisional arrangements. After due deliberation and after the Sisters had made a novena to the Holy Spirit for enlightenment, at my suggestion, permit me to submit the following to Your Excellency for your pastoral approval and decision:
>
> 1. With reverence to the new superior in Olpe, I observed relatively little difference in spirituality between Sister Maria Theresia and Sister Francesca; both are well qualified for the office of superior. But in behalf of the material interests of the institution, I decide in favor of Sister Maria Theresia. Since she is no longer superior, the alms of the town have lessened considerably, as well as the food supplies, according to the Sister cook. The world, especially that of the aristocrats, voice their opinions in such fashion, certainly very imperfect in motive, and one cannot but take it into account. Sister Maria Theresia's family is not only the wealthiest in Olpe, but also under all circumstances, the most influential. Sister Maria Theresia will use her influence to improve the orphanage and consolidate the institution, if she wields the superiorship among her spiritually inclined and respected relatives. How fearful Sister Maria Theresia is of this dignity! Yesterday she pleaded very earnestly amid tears and on her knees that she be spared that responsibility giving as reasons her poor health and confessing her spiritual disqualification; she pleaded urgently that Sister Francesca continue in office. The latter also begged to be relieved of the superiorship. Nevertheless for reasons mentioned above, I beg most fervently that Sister Maria Theresia be installed as the superior. She suffers from spasms at times (at present she appears in perfect health).

> Sister Francesca works with her in exceptional harmony and love and shows outstanding ability in teaching. She could be spared from Much at least until winter and ought to remain in Olpe as assistant. In addition she could be novice mistress and instructor. Because of her ascetical formation and her loving prudence, she is especially qualified to teach. Almost daily instruction in catechism is very necessary not only for the novices but also for the professed Sisters for in the previous years these instructions were almost entirely neglected.
>
> 2. The letter Your Excellency wrote, dated July 17, granting the re-establishment of Perpetual Adoration in the convent chapel was a source of great joy to the Sisters and to the people of Olpe. It created the necessity of a greater number of Sisters. Even without it, more Sisters would have been required. In consulting with Sister Maria Theresia and Sister Francesca, I concluded that ten Sisters would be sufficient for the time being. Since two of the seven sisters assigned originally to Olpe did not make the necessary adjustment they would need to be transferred. Consequently five new Sisters were required in Olpe.

Further recommendations of the superior as to transfers of Sisters could certainly not be considered from every point of view by the bishop. The results of the many deliberations were announced by the bishop in his letter of August 3, 1863, wherein is written as follows:

> In conformity with your proposal of July 30, 1863, I shall hereby appoint Sister Maria Theresia as local superior of the Franciscan congregation in Olpe, and designate Sister Francesca as her assistant, with the expectation that both will administer their offices for the glory of God and the good of the congregation.

The letter closed with the following:

> The following Sisters are assigned to the convent in Olpe: Theresia (as superior), Francesca, Juliana, Johanna, Margaretha, Ignatia, Gertrudis, Dominica, Ursula, and Stan-

> isla. On the other hand to the convent at Much, which naturally must remain under the jurisdiction of the motherhouse, are assigned the three Sisters: Thecla (as superior), Armella, and Laurentia.

Hereby the separation was finalized. Sister Maria Theresia was compelled to accept the superiorship of the independent congregation in Olpe and to chart its future course. She herself did not want the office. Together with Sister Francesca she had pleaded with the bishop to enter another well established Franciscan congregation. The petition was refused. When the two Sisters realized that an independent congregation was to be formed in Olpe, they begged the bishop that an older and experienced religious be given them as superior to lead them in the correct way instead of experimenting at what they would need to do. This request was also refused.

The feast of St. Bonaventure, July 14, 1863, impressed itself indelibly on the mind of Mother Maria Theresia as the day on which the Sisters learned that Olpe was left to its own resources. She wrote: "The Sisters were really abashed that they had to rely on their own resources," for all of them had but very little experience in the religious life. In comparison with today's program for young Sisters, they would just have completed the novitiate. Their congregation had been in existence only that length of time and even that period was a very disturbed one. Therefore they hesitated to undertake the responsibility. Above all Mother Maria Theresia, whose spirit impressed itself so lastingly on the congregation, had to be vaulted by God into her position. But even at that time, as demonstrated later so often in her life, when she recognized the Will of God, she gave herself quietly and with a firm purpose to the task. It is a testimony to her character as she writes of the young congregation: "With trust in God and under the Rule of St. Francis, the Sisters were confident that they could expect the blessing of God."

CHAPTER V

COMPELLED INTO HER CHARACTERISTIC WAY OF LIFE

The separation occurred. Neither of the two religious founders had wished nor perpetrated it. God had manifestly employed the talents of both co-founders in order to accomplish more for the church and the whole of mankind. If there had been but one congregation, its activity could not have spread so extensively as with the two of them. One must recognize that the determining factors leading to the separation were not planned by Salzkotten nor by Olpe. Much less were they managed nor brought to completion by them. Those spiritually responsible for the Sisters, especially their spiritual director and the bishop, were the only ones involved during the period of decision. The final decision was contrary to the wishes of Mother Clara Pfaender as superior and Sister Maria Theresia Bonzel as subject. Both had their ideas as to how the crisis could be solved. However, both submitted to the decision of the bishop. Both became enriched by the experience.

The bitterness that these days concealed for both congregations, led them on the way of the cross, a blessing for both. In the great Franciscan Family, both institutes today rank as strong congregations, for both are animated with a fine spirit and render great services. From this point we will not develop further the history of the Salzkotten Franciscans, but to say only this: Mother Clara Pfaender energized the congregation with great ability toward fruitful activity and development in Europe and in North America. What she contributed to the Sisters was manifest in 1880, when it was demanded of all the Sisters to separate themselves from the Mother. At that time Mother Clara went her sorrowful way alone, a tragedy recognized only later. Her spiritual daughters on that occasion demonstrated an admirable, truly heroic obedience in faith to ecclesiastical authority, which later resulted in great blessings for them.

When a congregation arises from an existing one, it is not enough to separate them in leadership and administration. The church demands specifically that the congregations be adequately distinguished from each other: individual name, individual garb, and individual statutes. Just as in transference from one congregation to another, there must be a period of renewed probation followed by profession, this also obtained in Olpe. The church ordains in such instances that life in the threefold profession of vows is no longer valid without renewed ties. Complete religious life is not undertaken by investiture, but a life in compass with the new congregation according to its special obligations. Thus if a new period of probation is required by a congregation and closes with profession, the procedure certainly does not indicate that the former congregation is to be regarded with distrust. The church thereby signifies a new congregation has been formed which follows its own rule and constitution.

Thus Sister Maria Theresia and Sister Francesca began the framing of a new constitution. They also fashioned a new religious garb, which consisted of an unhemmed coarse woolen undergarment and a like habit with a white cincture. As footwear only sandals were considered. The head covering consisted of a white cap protruding somewhat in the front; a strip of stiff white paper was set in the seam to give it a definite and firm shape. A black veil was draped over this with a large overflap in front which could be lowered over the face when going out of doors. The mantle worn by the Sisters was of the same style as commonly worn by Franciscans. After the test of daily wear some changes were made in the religious garb. Shoes were permitted. The sisters lived in the Sauerland which is noted for its cold and snowy winters. The practice of lowering the veil over the face when leaving the convent was also discontinued. It savored too much of contemplative orders and was impractical for active orders. A scapular with a black cross sewed on it was added. The garb of the Olpe Sisters remained essentially unchanged for almost one hundred years, until the present era when a modernized form was adopted to meet the present situation. The pictures of the original religious garb of the Olpe Franciscans reminds us forcefully of the way the Poor Sisters of St. Francis in Aix-la-Chapelle (now called

Aachen) wore their veils. The foundress of the Aix-la-Chapelle Sisters, Mother Francis Schervier gave much to the Olpe sisters and shared ideas with them. Probably the new name of the congregation, "Poor Sisters of St. Francis of Perpetual Adoration," was a suggestion from the "Poor Sisters of St. Francis."

In Reverend Schmidt from Wenden, the congregation had a director who did all to give it a genuine foundation. He energetically set guidelines to overcome the difficulties of beginning. This exemplary, zealous, and devout priest was himself a member of the Franciscan Tertiaries. In all probability that increased his interest to support Sister Maria Theresia's idea of guiding the formation of the Sisters of the congregation according to the spirit of St. Francis. He wished a Franciscan priest to come as soon as possible to fire the Sisters with the genuine spirit of St. Francis by giving them an animated retreat, so he wrote to the guardian of the Franciscan monastery in Düsseldorf for a suitable retreat master. In that letter he made an amusing error in expressing his desire that the Rule of the First Order of St. Francis be introduced to the Olpe Sisters to be adopted by them. He most likely reasoned that the Second Order of St. Francis was that of the Poor Clares and the Third Order that of the people of the world, and the First Rule for all the others. The guardian in Düsseldorf, Reverend Aegidius Jonas, set him right in his answer of September 13, 1863. He referred to the Third Order Regular of St. Francis which in conformity with its statutes could form a good foundation. Regarding a retreat master, he referred him to Provincial Othman Maasmann.

On October 23, 1863, Reverend Schmidt wrote the following, among other things, to the provincial:

> The Olpe Sisters now numbering ten have in addition to the Perpetual Adoration added another objective – caring for poor, orphaned, and neglected children. They now have forty children in the house. The Sisters desire to live as genuine Franciscans according to the Rule of St. Francis. Their way of life meets the warm approval of the bishop. The undersigned priest, spiritual director of the Poor Franciscans in Olpe, begs Your reverence in the name

> of His Excellency the bishop to send a suitable priest of your order in the near future to give the sisters a retreat to introduce them into the Franciscan way of life and ordain what is prescribed by the precepts of the church that this congregation may enter into a genuine union and the graces of the Seraphic Order. If any definite preparations are to be made, please advise me.

The provincial answered immediately and on October 26, 1863, wrote: "In compliance with the wish of the Most Reverend Bishop Konrad Martin, I shall send a suitable priest to Olpe as soon as possible for the specified purpose." Thus in November of the same year the Reverend Bonaventure Wessendorf came to Olpe to give a spiritual retreat to the Sisters. The Franciscan Province of the Holy Cross, Saxony, could scarcely have sent a more suitable priest for this task. Holy in his way of life and blessed with an all-embracing spirituality, he was well qualified because of his rich experience. He was the spiritual director of Mother Francis Schervier, foundress of the Poor Sisters of St. Francis of Aix-la-Chapelle. This very fact alone should prove very significant for the Olpe Sisters.

Sister Maria Theresia in her intensive discussions with Father Bonaventure Wessendorf concerning the formation of the congregation had most likely reiterated her desire of having an experienced religious come to Olpe who with advice and deed might help in the difficulties of beginning. Father Bonaventure encouraged the Sisters and promised to commend them to the bishop of Paderborn. His report to the bishop concerning the Sisters and their congregation had good effects. The bishop agreed favorably with all the suggestions submitted by Father Bonaventure for the development of the congregation.

In Olpe Father Bonaventure had promised the Sisters that he would see that Mother Francis Schervier would assist them with valuable counsel through her fruitful experience and give them the correct introduction into religious life. God provided that he soon had the opportunity to contact Mother Francis for shortly thereafter she came to Paderborn. When Father Bonaventure presented his request, she was prepared to do her utmost, and promised that she herself would go to Olpe. The Sisters were not complete strangers to her for the three founders had visited at the convent of Aix-la-Chapelle in the beginning of October 1859. At that time she had given each a copy of the Little Office of the Blessed Virgin Mary as the first equipment for the religious life. Father Bonaventure must have realized her wholehearted selflessness when, in addition to the great task as Mother of her own congregation, he asked her to be concerned in the same way with another congregation. When Sister Maria Theresia wrote in the Chronicles that "this servant of God was prepared to shy from no sacrifice that concerned the honor of God," her every word carried its weight.

Most assuredly Mother Francis had intended to go to Olpe as soon as possible. But the pressing work as major superior of a rapidly growing congregation held her bound to Aix-la-Chapelle. Sister Maria Theresia saw the danger of further uncertainty clearly. She consequently engaged in a written correspondence with Aix-la-Chapelle, and in February 1864, went there to discuss urgent matters with Mother Francis, for some questions pressed for decision. When she and Sister Francesca, her assistant, arrived in Aix-la-Chapelle preparations for investiture ceremonies were in progress. Sister Maria Theresia later wrote in the Chronicles that at that time in Aix-la-Chapelle "many candidates" were invested and among them was the Countess Merfeld. The uncle of the countess, the Most Revered Bishop von Ketteler of Mainz, was officiating officer at the investiture ceremonies. How small and insignificant the two Sisters from Olpe must have felt as they experienced the rhythm of a strong and growing congregation in Aix-la-Chapelle! The Olpe congregation numbered only ten Sisters! They rejoiced on February 12, when Regina Schaefer of Olpe became their first postulant. Their Community could not be compared with what they saw in Aix-la-Chapelle. Would it not be natural to lose courage under such a situation?

Owing to the numerous guests who came to Aix-la-Chapelle for investiture, the two Sisters were housed in Burtscheid, an affiliation of the congregation. As soon as the celebration was over Mother Francis with sincere love extended motherhouse hospitality to them. Now they could communicate all their problems and worries to this great servant of God. They confided all to her as to a mother, as seen in the following instance. Sister Francesca Boehmer was in great spiritual need for she feared she might not have been baptized validly. Her Protestant mother had her baptized by a Protestant minister who had the reputation of not performing his obligations conscientiously. Mother Francis solved this need by having Sister Francesca baptized conditionally by a Franciscan priest, Reverend Romuald Terhaag; she herself was sponsor. Thus this point was solved satisfactorily.

What seemed the most pressing problem at that moment was the discussion of a well-intentioned plan by the director, Reverend Schmidt, to establish a governing body as help and security for the Sisters in Olpe. The members were to manage the external business of the congregation. Mother Francis recognized such a governing body as one limiting the policy-making decision of the young congregation and circumscribing it greatly. Lay personnel would assume the right of making decisions. She objected resolutely to the plan. Urged by experience she counseled the congregation to keep itself free and independent. Upon her return to Olpe, Sister Maria Theresia informed Superior Schmidt of Mother Francis' decision. He gave up the plan immediately, although he had developed the program rather extensively and had outlined it on paper.

Before the two sisters left Aix-la-Chapelle, Mother Francis told them that she would visit them in Olpe at her earliest convenience to help regulate all necessary matters there. It was June before she could keep her promise. At this time she learned to know the Sisters' way of life and to give them wholesome counsel. She was convinced that zeal was not lacking and that their overzealous spirit must be tempered with wisdom. At this time Sister Maria Theresia again attempted to evade the responsibility of founding a congregation. Together with Sister Francesca she pleaded that their congregation be accepted into the Aix-la-Chapelle congregation. Mother Francis felt the great sincerity in this request made with such humility. She on her part also demonstrated humility, for she did not consider the aggrandizement of her congregation through an easy annexation of another house in a new area. Through such a maneuver she would have rewarded herself for her service in Olpe. She, however, acted in accordance with the will of God and placed her experience and knowledge at the disposal of others as instruments of the Lord. She also recognized that the Olpe Sisters were called by God to follow their own way of life; at least, they must try it. She told the Sisters that they should proceed on their own specific way with great confidence in God. Should it become apparent that they could not possibly succeed, then and only then would she be prepared to integrate the Olpe congregation into her own.

Superior Schmidt also took this opportunity to discuss all problems with Mother Francis. Seemingly, he took no offense that she objected to his plan of a governing body. To him, also, she spoke of her willingness to be of assistance in every possible way.

Because of this proffered assistance, Sister Maria Theresia was able to go to Aix-la-Chapelle for a spiritual retreat and remained at the motherhouse there for an additional six weeks. She was permitted to take part in all conventual exercises. Her objective was to learn the right way of religious living through first-hand experience in a well-regulated congregation. She realized that entering exactly into the spirit was the best way of learning that life. At this time also she was briefed by Mother Francis Schervier concerning all particulars and important matters regarding the formation and guidance of a congregation. In the six weeks she had ample opportunity to ask questions.

Mother Francis in the interim had the opportunity to mull over the impressions of her visit in Olpe and was now able to present her ideas in a more instructive way. She had no need of exhorting the Sisters to zeal, mortification, and penance. On the contrary, it was even a question of too much zeal in adopting extraordinary austerities as penance. These penances required the reins of wisdom. She counseled moderation and later advised urgently against such daily penances as the discipline, the penitential belt, fasting and the like, and counseled to abandon them. There was danger lest the young enthusiastic religious would soon undermine their energy and health. She also advised that the coarse clothing be changed, for associations with children and the sick make frequent laundering a necessity. She advocated linen wear.

During these hours of reflection Sister Maria Theresia realized ever more clearly the plan she was to follow in guiding her congregation according to the will of God. In Aix-la-Chapelle she was a great learner. Many ideas began to mature, thanks to the kind instructions she received. She did not conduct herself as one realizing her own mission, nor as one who waives advice from others relative to things which concern her alone and should be managed by herself. Because she sought and accepted counsel from the wise, she spared herself and her Sisters many an experiment and many a bitter experience. In regard to Mother Francis Schervier it must be said, she did what is exceptionally rare in religious congregations.

As foundress of a flourishing congregation, she in a selfless way placed her experiences at the disposal of a newly founded sisterhood. She advised that this new congregation maintain its own character, for in serving the will of God, she did not present her own congregation as a standard for all things. Whoever regulates his life entirely according to the will of God is capable of seeing the will of God in others and will not impose upon them his own way of life.

How grateful the foundress in Olpe always felt toward the foundress in Aix-la-Chapelle is seen from the letter she wrote shortly after the death of Mother Francis, on December 17, 1876, to Aix-la-Chapelle. Therein she called her a "dear spiritual mother and counselor in all things." When she learned that a biography of Mother Francis was to be written, she expressed in detail her many reasons for gratitude to this great woman. In her letter of May 22, 1887, to Mother Vincentia in Aachen she mentions these with other statements:

> Our congregation has experienced the self-sacrificing love and benevolence of this good and venerable mother in manifold ways. I would be glad if the following statement could be inserted (in a biography) as a manifestation of our gratitude. In April of the year 1864, accompanied by another Sister, I made a trip to Aix-la-Chappelle to seek counsel from Mother Francis and to beg her assistance. We found her prepared for every sacrifice for the

glory of God; she promised to come to Olpe and arrived at our convent in July of the same year. The good mother remained with us for several days; she helped us in difficult situations, instructed, and directed the Sisters of the young congregation in their conventual exercises. She gave wholesome counsel and won the love and confidence of the Sisters and also the respect of all who had the good fortune to come in contact with her. She showed a special love for the children in the orphanage and loved to spend some time with them. Before she returned, she promised that if possible she could continue her care of our congregation — and this she did.

In the fall of the same year she caused great joy by offering me the opportunity to make a spiritual retreat in the motherhouse at Aix-la-Chapelle and thereafter remain for six weeks to study the organization of their convent and learn what might be beneficial to our own. When in Olpe, the venerable mother had noticed that our chapel lacked some necessities for the worthy celebration of the Sacred Mysteries. She supplied a chasuble, rochet, and stole. We experienced her generosity again in a supply of office books and others for spiritual reading. For all we are most grateful.

When after several years I informed the dear mother that our assistant, Sister Francesca, was suffering from tuberculosis and that a change of air was recommended for her, she lovingly provided that the sick one come to Aix-la-Chapelle and was devotedly cared for there by the Sisters. Up to that time our Sisters had very little experience in the care of the sick. The venerable mother arranged that two of our Sisters be educated in nursing care in Euskirchen. For the same reason, she provided that two other sisters be admitted to the nursing school of the large Hospital of Our Lady of Perpetual Help in Aix-la-Chapelle. I went to her often in difficult situations for counsel. A friendly correspondence was constantly carried on between us. At that time as well as at present, there was good rapport between the congregations. We were sincerely

> grieved by the illness and quick death of our dear and unforgettable Mother Francis who had done so very much for us. She who in life manifested such great love for us in so many ways will also intercede for us above that, after we have served our purpose well here, we shall be united again in heaven.

In the beginning of her account, Mother Maria Theresia expressed the wish to have her sketch included in a biography of Mother Francis. In fact, Reverend Ignatius Jeiler used this valuable contribution scrupulously in his biography of the Aix-la-Chapelle foundress. One senses Mother Maria Theresia's great gratitude in every sentence. Even later after her own congregation had grown strong and she felt secure, she ever maintained the role of learner.

After the death of Mother Francis, she requested a photograph of her and a small personal remembrance. When in 1867, her Sisters adopted a definite religious habit, the style chosen closely resembled that worn by the Sisters of Mother Francis. The Sisters wore this garb practically unaltered until 1960. It cannot be established definitely whether the similarity of religious habit was chosen intentionally or not. But certainly it points to the close spiritual relationship between the two congregations.

After her period of apprenticeship, as one may readily call the time she spent in Aix-la-Chapelle, the returning superior was confronted by three weighty questions in addition to her daily cares; the redrafting of the Constitution, a legal foundation for the orphanage, and an economic basis for the congregation in respect to the inheritance of Mother Theresia herself. Of course, these problems did not arise at the moment, but for some time had been awaiting cooperative decisions. Since all three questions were of greatest importance for the efficient development of the small congregation, the Sisters were greatly interested in all of them. It is to be noted that in the question of their own inheritance, which touched the Sisters so closely, they manifested the greatest reservation.

ECONOMIC SECURITY OF THE CONGREGATION THROUGH THE INHERITANCE OF MOTHER MARIA THERESIA

What was the situation relative to the inheritance of the Widow Bonzel to her eldest daughter? In an order without any exterior apostolate, such as the contemplative order of the Poor Clares, the question of an economic basis is not so important although here also it plays a role. But in an active order serving in an educative or in a nursing capacity, a secure economic basis is wise and all-important. Only under such conditions can the congregation follow its apostolate of charity. Under other situations love soon becomes exhausted by the many demands for consolation and encouragement placed upon it. Consequently, there can be no valid objection to the influence the Bonzel family exercised in the decision of 1859, to make the original establishment in Olpe, and again in 1863 to have at least a foundation in Olpe. Considerations for establishing the motherhouse in Elspe were discussed earlier. These were abandoned lest the foundation would not have the economic backing of the Bonzel family and consequently lack a sound economic basis.

The first transfer of abode for the young congregation was from the so-called Schuerholz House. For this, the Sisters were grateful to Mrs. Bonzel. After Easter in 1860, Mrs. Bonzel purchased the Zimmermann House as a dowry, to be divided equally between her two daughters Aline and Emilie. An uncle of Sister Maria Theresia bequeathed an inheritance of real estate and between four and five thousand *Reich* dollars to his niece. Mrs. Bonzel also purchased the so-called Weber House for a motherhouse in Olpe. To have the diocese of Paderborn purchase the property was under deliberation for a long time. The experience in Italy, however, was fresh in their memories, in which the political unification of Italy with one stroke confiscated all convent and church property. Dean Goerdes in his letter to the bishop dated April 16, 1861, had counseled the bishop not to make it too easy for "rapacious hands" to obtain possession of convent property, if in Germany as now in Italy, the hour of visitation should strike. Did he have a premonition of the *Kulturkampf*? At all events his counsel was followed by Mrs. Bonzel, for the purchase of real estate and a house was transacted in her name.

The question concerning the inheritance of Sister Maria Theresia Bonzel, especially a suitable gift to the Episcopal See in Paderborn, busily engaged Reverend Schmidt. A long and extended correspondence resulted between him and the General Vicariate. Mrs. Bonzel rightly exercised justice to her second daughter Emilie also.

The fact that Reverend Schmidt assumed the difficulties of negotiating these personal matters manifests his great zeal as spiritual director of the Olpe congregation. He spared no hardship to bring this affair to a successful conclusion. Seemingly, Sister Maria Theresia personally did not enter into any of the deliberations. In the negotiations, there is no trace of her attitude toward the question. That she understood the problem is certain. In all these negotiations no one questioned her in regard to the facts because she remained silent throughout. At that time she was a subject; the reins of authority were in other hands. She took the expression "Poor Franciscan" very seriously. For this reason, Director Schmidt had a poor assistant in her. After the prospective donation to the Episcopal See had been considered and justly approved, difficulties arose between the sisters of Salzkotten and those of Olpe.

Thus Reverend Schmidt was obliged on June 20, 1862, to report the following to the General Vicariate:

> Because of a higher mandate, I contacted Mrs. Bonzel in Olpe yesterday concerning the settlement of the donation to the episcopal See. She mentioned that a settlement would be impossible until the confused situation of the Franciscan congregation becomes stabilized and the convent becomes secure. She declared her willingness to place the entire inheritance at the disposition of the bishopric. But since the property is the dowry of her daughter, Sister Maria Theresia, she cannot contract that until there is certainty that the future of her daughter is secure. She begged that the settlement be postponed for the present until the investigation relative to the Franciscan superior be con-

cluded — since her reasons are fundamental, I am not in a position to oppose her views and her explanation.

Only on November 16, 1863, was Revered Schmidt able to inform the bishop that he had again contacted Mrs. Bonzel concerning the donation. On October 4, 1864, the negotiations were finally and definitely closed. By signature Mrs. Bonzel ratified the transaction through which the property of the Olpe orphanage, secured through the dowry of her daughter Aline, now Sister Maria Theresia, was transferred to the Episcopal See in Paderborn. The pastor of St. Martin Church in Olpe, Reverend Hengstebeck, accepted the property in the name of the Episcopal See in recognition of the terms stated in the contract. In substance these terms were: the Episcopal See accepted the gift donation for the foundation of an institution in Olpe for the care of neglected and poor orphaned children. This institution was assigned to the management of the Poor Franciscans. If said congregation should cease to exist, the orphanage was to be reassigned to another Catholic congregation. This gift contract was also licensed by civil authority on March 1, 1865.

One may ask why such a complex negotiation was pursued. The reason is found in the first statute of the congregation in Chapter II, Article 3, which states: "Poverty without property. As daughters of St. Francis the congregation possesses no property and utilizes a house with garden and real estate loaned by the bishop." These statutes were not approved by the bishop until July 6, 1865. But the provisions for a life of poverty without property had to be set up beforehand. Sister Maria Theresia understood St. Francis of Assisi's concept of poverty very well. She endeavored to introduce this same idea of poverty into her own congregation, the essence of which is based on the abrogation of all possessions and claims to possession. In Franciscan orders, the Pope possesses the right of all property servicing the order. In the young congregation in Olpe, the Episcopal See in Paderborn possesses the right and exercises proprietorship when the congregation has to testify. Ten years after the so-called *Kulturkampf*, this very contract was the cause of much sorrow and grief and even occasioned a lawsuit. More on this point later.

The avowal of Franciscan poverty was the only reason in the foregoing of the gift contract. Although Sister Maria Theresia apparently did not enter into the difficult and laborious negotiations, these, however, were necessary because she wished poverty without property. However, this was not the only way that the title "Poor Franciscan" was justified. The first stages after the separation brought day-by-day evidence of actual poverty in Olpe. The Chronicles of the Congregation report concerning these days: "Poor as the life of St. Francis also should be the life of his daughters; and as the 'poor' Christ, their life of privation should also resemble that of the poor." Poor were the accommodations of the convent, poor their hard straw beds, poor their simple table. How often the Sisters lacked even the bare necessities and had to beg bread for the orphans from generous benefactors. Frequently the Sisters had no money whatever on hand. When a Sister was obliged to take a trip they resorted to the poor box. If nothing was found therein, they had to borrow money. Then the Schmidt Brothers, or the Loeser, Bonzel, and Kaufmann families came to the rescue. One or the other of these always gladly helped in every situation. Although the Sisters themselves lived the life of poverty, they were ever solicitous that the orphans were well supplied in all their needs. At this time the bed sheets and other linens were used for the orphans, and only later after nine postulants entered did the congregation obtain sufficient money from their dowries to supply the convent with the needed linens.

REGULATIONS FOR THE ORPHANAGE

In October of the year 1863, the "orphan sisters," as the people of Olpe called them, cared for forty orphans. These children were their chief concern. From the very beginning they were active in this apostolate for in this sphere of activity they feared no opposition from the other religious congregation. Consequently, it was of special concern to the superior, Sister Maria Theresia, that the orphanage be established on an adequate legal basis. That also, in retrospect, had necessitated the gift contract of Mrs. Bonzel to the Episcopal See. The pivotal point of this gift was that she succeeded in this for the benefit of the orphanage in Olpe.

Therefore a suitable statute for the orphanage was an urgent task, and obviously it was framed after the visit of Mother Francis Schervier to Olpe. The document is dated August 1, 1864. Its plan followed that of Reverend Superior Schmidt's statute for the proposed but relinquished sanatorium. It ensured corporation rights to the Sisters.

STATUTE FOR THE ORPHANAGE OF THE POOR FRANCISCANS IN OLPE

1. Under the title of "Poor Franciscans" a congregation of women has been formed in Olpe, the chief town of the district, whose main objective is to care for and instruct neglected and orphaned children in Olpe, and if desired in other areas also; however, other works of Christian charity are not to be excluded.

2. In admitting children, first priority is given to those of the Catholic parish and the district of Olpe. When the authorities of this district wish to admit such children, their requests should be granted as far as possible. Children from outlying areas whose instruction and education are in greatest danger are to be given the preference.

3. According to rule, children are admitted after the completion of the second year. However, urgent conditions may dispense with the age rule.

4. Admissions are granted through the decision of the superior and her council. In exceptional cases, the decision depends upon the spiritual director.

5. The children begin their elementary education at the age of six years. They attend classes in the orphanage and are taught by a qualified Sister or instructor. Girls are instructed in all the feminine arts and housekeeping: knitting, patching, sewing, washing, etc. In their free time the children are urged to engage in domestic work and lighter tasks of the garden and the fields.

6. Instruction and practical training of the children for later life come to pass in a stabilized and well-regulated house under the constant observance of ecclesiastical and also civic regulations. The congregation must keep abreast of developments to revise its instruction and education as well as the diet and rearing of children accordingly.

7. Ordinarily, children are not dismissed from the orphanage until they have completed their elementary education. However, those who remain incorrigible in spite of all counsel and endeavors to turn them to better ways and who consequently give bad example to the other children, are dismissed by the superior with the consent of the spiritual director. These children are returned to the care and watchfulness of those who had previously arranged for their admission to the orphanage.

8. The Sisters will consider it their duty to arrange for the moral well-being and favorable placement of those children leaving the institution. They will continue to regard these children as theirs and take the place of father and mother with reference to them. They will preserve contact with the children by inviting them on Sundays from time to time to visit the orphanage together with their teachers or employers to influence their further educational development. For those children who left in good standing the orphanage remains a home where they can spend their days of vacation or the intervening days in a change of employment.

9. All that pertains to the economical or the spiritual life of the Sisters is under the jurisdiction of the diocesan bishop, who is represented by a director.

10. For nourishment, clothing, instruction, and education of the children, the congregation utilizes the means at its disposal (cf. 12), also donations, the work of the Sisters and the children, and prospective collections. In addition, the rule prescribes an annual charge to be paid for each child accepted in the orphanage. In exceptional situations,

this sum may be reduced or remitted altogether depending upon the circumstances of the congregation. If public funds are given to the congregation for specific purposes of education or charity, the institution is to render an account of expenditures to the administrative authority.

11. Together each evening the Sisters and orphans pray for their benefactors in the chapel of the institution. During the octave of All Souls they hold a solemn anniversary for all deceased benefactors of the orphanage, either in the chapel of the institution or, pending the consent of the pastor, in the Olpe parish church.

12. The Congregation of the Poor Franciscans of Olpe, organized for the care and education of orphaned and neglected children, transferred property by a legal donation to the Episcopal See in Paderborn. This property at present consists of a large house with real estate and garden valued at ten thousand dollars.

13. The superior of the orphanage functions in all legitimate civic relations and performances. All important economic negotiations of the congregation that exceed the value of one hundred dollars, such as acquiring additional property, sale of immobile property, building, borrowing, or lending capital, require the approbation of the diocesan bishop. In all such matters the congregation is also subject to civic regulations.

14. If the congregation of the Poor Franciscans of Olpe should unite with another congregation, then that congregation should likewise agree to operate the orphanage. Should this congregation, however, dissolve, or in any way be dissolved, then the diocesan bishop is empowered to transfer the operation of the orphanage to another congregation.

This statute was signed by Director Reverend Schmidt on October 5, 1864, who then sent it to the bishop for his approval, which was received on January 7, 1865.

In many respects the Statute of the orphanage mirrors exactly the existing situation in Olpe at that time. For instance, Paragraph 14 states the possibility of the Congregation of Olpe Sisters uniting with another congregation. This was not mere theory. It had a factual background. For at that time there was uncertainty that the congregation could survive on its own. Sister Maria Theresia had endeavored to unite the Olpe congregation with the Franciscans at Aix-la-Chapelle. Mother Francis Schervier had declined. She thought that an attempt should be made in Olpe, and if the going was simply impossible, then the question of union could be considered further.

Although several points refer directly to the Olpe orphanage, they have much wider significance. There is, as example, mention made of working in other places. Thought is given to expanding the apostolate. In Paragraph 1, relative to the objectives of the congregation, mention is made for the instruction and education of "neglected and orphaned children in Olpe and also in other areas, if requested." That Perpetual Adoration is not mentioned here as the chief objective can readily be understood. The statute for the orphanage is an instrument of public and civic character. It states that "other works of charity are not excluded." A very wise and prudent formulation! The statute of the first beginning in Olpe spoke much more directly of the special objectives of the congregation as not only "care, education, and instruction of youth, but also the nursing of the sick in hospitals, homes … and in general, the practice of all needed works of charity." In the meantime added knowledge was acquired. The bitter conflicts over the care of the sick were heated. Thus, no one spoke openly of the fact that the Sisters considered working at other charitable activities, including the care of the sick. They not only desired the right to care for the sick in special situations only, but to include it among the works of the active apostolate.

In Paragraph 5, there is a statement to the effect that elementary schooling will be provided in the orphanage itself by a qualified Sister or a lay instructor. This was a goal-setting regulation. Prior to this time, the congregation had made no provision for the preparation of teachers. It was necessary to provide for teacher certification. In the beginning the orphans were instructed by a lay teacher. Miss Tillmann was the first to undertake this task. In the meantime, two postulants entered on October 18, 1864, Regina Schaefer and Sybilla Heiliger. Both began study immediately to prepare for teaching. The assistant headmaster Lohre instructed them in the various subjects. For this purpose he donated his free time, which was not very plentiful, for besides this, he managed a large industrial school. Consequently, he came early in the morning, even before Mass, to teach the two postulants. This was a great sacrifice on his part, and also a great hardship on the postulants. Later, the two candidates went to Karthaus near Trier to continue their studies under the Franciscans. After they had successfully passed the certification tests, one of the sisters was able to take the place of a lay instructor in Olpe.

It was very important in the beginning to choose the right spheres of work. To bake hosts, a task begun in early 1865, could well be combined with Perpetual Adoration. To acquire this skill the assistant, Sister Francesca, spent some time in Koblenz with Sisters from Aix-la-Chapelle Franciscans. Certainly in the apostolate of a large congregation, this task is not in the foreground. But one must also consider the small congregation, which in this way can contribute toward the celebration of Holy Mass in many parishes. Did not St. Francis also supply his brothers with host-baking irons that they might contribute toward the worthy celebration of the Holy Eucharist?

The education of the Sisters in the care of the sick began in 1868. After a request for their training had been made to Superior Kaiser of the city hospital in Cologne without results, Sister Maria Theresia turned to Mother Francis Schervier. This worthy helper in need for the Olpe Sisters made it possible for two Sisters to be sent to Euskirchen in November 1868, to become proficient in the nursing of the sick from the very rudiments. Two other Sisters went to Essen where in a hospital conducted by the Elizabethan Sisters they learned the nursing of the sick. The fifth and sixth Sisters went to Aix-la-Chapelle to study nursing care in St. Mary Help Hospital. For all this assistance the Sisters were grateful to Mother Francis Schervier.

Thus in large measure, the apostolate of nursing the sick was made possible. It was evident to the superior of the Olpe Sisters that the effectiveness of the sisters in active charitable works does not depend upon good will alone. Sister Maria Theresia herself had not the experience of a special education in any specific field. But she did all within her power that her Sisters become highly qualified through the best education to render possible a rich and fulfilling apostolate.

THE FIRST CONSTITUTION OF THE CONGREGATION

The chief endeavors of Sister Maria Theresia were concerned with the inner development of her Congregation of Sisters. Essential to this formation was their very own constitution. The drafting was not to be done hastily. Too much depended upon it. Not that the congregation have a constitution of some sort, it must be good and conform to the best — that was of greatest importance. It was understood from the very beginning that the Olpe Sisters must have conventual regulations. The general character of the new constitution was foreshadowed in the letter Reverend Director Schmidt wrote to Bishop Konrad Martin on August 10, 1863. His statements are almost prophetical:

> Should a religious congregation endure and not carry the germs of dissolution within itself from the very beginning, it must above all endeavor to be what its name signifies.... If the sisters are to be genuine Franciscans, the congregation will receive graces from above and will coalesce with the Catholic people, as the Franciscan Fathers, and will thus have a glorious future. Therefore they must imbibe all that is Franciscan in so far as is compatible with religious women. First there is the Rule of St. Francis ... closely allied therewith is the clothing ... all must bear the imprint of poverty, and this makes the greatest impression on the people; one also witnesses by his so highly treasured worn habit, grown old together with him.... If the Sisters, I re-

> peat again, become true Franciscans, interiorly and exteriorly, then their future is assured.

Bishop Konrad Martin himself had counseled in August 1863 that the Olpe Sisters should frame a constitution based on the Third Order Regular of St. Francis. Utilizing this as a basis they should add their own worthwhile experiences.

All who were in any way concerned, with one accord, manifested a favorable spirit. From the very first, the will of the Olpe Sisters was in agreement with that of Director Schmidt and also with the expressed wish of the bishop. It now depended essentially upon Sister Maria Theresia to activate the wishes and the task. She had no desire to frame the new Constitution solely upon her own decisions. She wished to integrate her congregation completely into the great family of the saint of Assisi, and therefore sought counsel in following the Franciscan way of life exactly. She and all her Sisters made a retreat conducted by Reverend Bonaventure Wessendorf to induct them into the Franciscan way. For the same reason she took counsel from the great Franciscan Mother Francis Schervier, to profit from her rich experience. Although she alone had sought counsel from this great religious woman in Aix-la-Chapelle, she provided that all her Sisters gained deeper knowledge of Franciscanism from Mother Francis during her visit in Olpe. The superior in Olpe did not wish to have this knowledge for herself alone and thus be the only one to give it to others. All Sisters from the very beginning should be informed in the Franciscan way of life. When her assistant, Sister Francesca, was in Koblenz to acquire the skill of host-baking, she had many opportunities of speaking with Mother Francis, who also at that time was there. Upon Sister Francesca's return, she and Sister Maria Theresia drafted the Constitution. They completed the work on March 25, 1865.

Since the Constitution breathes the genuine spirit of the first beginning, it is an especially primary document, and we shall enter somewhat deeper into it. The manifestation of its spirit is a permanent testament for the Poor Sisters of St. Francis of Perpetual Adoration. We shall explore the characteristic features and observe especially the situation existing at that time. The Rule of Pope Leo X written for the Third Order Regular of St. Francis in 1521, and used as a basis, appears first. Then follows the Constitution. The objectives of the congregation are given first as follows: "After the example of our holy Father Francis, the Sisters will endeavor to unite the contemplative with the active life: in the Perpetual Adoration and in the practice of works of charity."

"After the example of our holy Father Francis" — when one considers the foregoing — a person senses how much there is in the first words and how great the reaction. Francis serves as a guideline along which the congregation is to formulate its way of life. This guideline of the saint of Assisi, is not determined by insignificant, individual, and external ways, but from the basic goal here established: "the contemplative life combined with the active life." Here in this synthesis of the contemplative and the active is expressed the fundamental characteristic trait of St. Francis. When one considers his prayer life, one gets the impression that he must have been a contemplative through and through. If one follows his active life, then he appears an outstanding example of the active orders. Nevertheless he united both in a unique way within himself. His contemplative life made him clearly recognize the will of God who called him to the service of others. In the midst of active life he was never in danger, even in the most absorbing activity, of losing himself in the activity. He was active but not enamored of the activity; he loved the will of God. He saw the contemplative and the active life not as two separate entities, but as one life — the contemplative seeking and discovering the will of God and the active fulfilling it in order to know God more intimately.

This synthesis of the contemplative and the active life finds its expression for the Olpe Sisters in the "Perpetual Adoration and in the active apostolate of charity." Combined, both are clearly defined literally: "Through the Perpetual Adoration of our divine Lord in the Blessed Sacrament, the Sisters seek to make atonement and to pray for the general intentions of Holy Mother church. In the active apostolate the congregation pursues principally the instruction, education, and development of youth, especially poor, neglected and orphaned children."

The Franciscan way of life is also expressed thusly: "The Sisters live according to the Rule of holy Father Francis as approved by Pope Leo X for the Third Order Regular with the exception of those changes appearing in the Constitution." Historically, it is not quite correct to call the "Leo-Rule" the Rule of St. Francis. Does not this very point in its formulation betray the great joy of really belonging to the family of St. Francis? That the statutes deviated from the "Leo-Rule" was caused by necessity owing to the character of that Rule. Some of its regulations were no longer observed in the nineteenth century, for example, those regarding the divine office and the reception of the sacraments. The rule of fasting needed to be modified although the Olpe statutes had endeavored to adhere strictly to the "Leo-Rule." Through personal experience the Sisters realized that a change had to be made and the severe rule mitigated. The "Leo-Rule" was not formulated for an active apostolate of charity, but for the contemplative orders. The effect of all this was that in 1927, the church gave a new rule to the Third Order Regular of St. Francis, more in keeping with the character of an active apostolate.

Also, the mention of the three vows is entirely in keeping with the character of St. Francis: Poverty without property, chastity, and obedience. The addition "without property" to poverty indicates the wish of the poor man of Assisi.

The work is organized into chapters regulating the special areas of religious life. At the very beginning before the Constitution proper, appears the daily horarium of the Sisters. Up to the present day, this order of the day has undergone many changes. A congregation is fully authorized to adjust to the changing conditions of the time. The future development of a religious congregation should not be hindered nor choked by the rules of its first beginning. It is well, however, to know the original order of the day, which shows the external framework within which the Olpe Sisters operated. The horarium was as follows: The Sisters arose at 4:30 a.m. and engaged in pious thoughts and ejaculatory prayers while dressing. After fifteen minutes they repaired to the chapel. The Angelus, a short morning prayer, the usual adoration, self-dedication, and prayers to the Blessed Sacrament were said. The Hours of the Little Office of the Blessed Virgin Mary were then recited. After reading a selection, the Sisters meditated until the offertory of the Mass. The Sisters had breakfast accompanied by spiritual reading after Holy Mass. They then engaged in their specific tasks until 10:45 a.m., when they assembled in the chapel for examination of conscience, spiritual communion, and a few vocal prayers. At 11:00 a.m., the noon meal, preceded by a short prayer, was served. This was accompanied by spiritual reading and terminated at 11:45 a.m. with a prayer of thanksgiving and the Angelus. The Sisters then engaged in recreation until 12:30 followed by the recitation of the rosary in the garden when possible. Working at their assigned tasks followed until 2:00 p.m., when Vespers and Compline were said in the chapel. At 3:00 p.m. prayers for the dying were said honoring the agony of Christ; thereafter the works of the apostolate were continued until 5:00 p.m. Either instructions, or confession, or chapter followed and at 6:00 p.m., the Sisters had their evening meal also accompanied by spiritual reading until 6:30 p.m. They had recreation until 8:00 p.m., when evening prayers, examination of conscience, and reading of the meditation were then followed by Matins and Lauds. The Sisters retired at 9:00 p.m. while their mind was engaged in private prayers. Day and night in hourly rotation the Sisters held the adoration of the Most Blessed Sacrament. All exercises were announced by the ringing of the bell.

The first chapter of the Constitution treats of the admission of candidates into the congregation and regulates the six-month postulancy and the one-year novitiate. The Second Chapter deals with profession and the vows. Here the Franciscan way of life is signified for it stresses that the Franciscan Ritual is to be used. The "small profession" (for temporary profession) at that time was pronounced for a period of five years. During this time the Sisters remained under the direction of the novice mistress. After five years the Sisters made their final profession. There was great idealism in the treatment of the vow of poverty. The idea of poverty without property was securely anchored in the Constitution: "As children of St. Francis, the congregation possesses no property and uses a building with garden and real estate loaned to them by the bishop.... Since the congregation has no burdensome revenue, is poor, and wishes to remain so, it relies entirely upon divine Providence and cooperates in the spirit of St. Francis, in the name of the poor Christ, and is willing and glad to beg." The spirit of Franciscan poverty could not have been stated in a more radical way. Here the title "Poor Franciscans" was raised to an all-embracing program. It was not a blind, romantic, and fanatic poverty. Sister Maria Theresa and her Sisters had felt this poverty in all its severity; their avowal of such poverty was made with all knowledgeable earnestness.

The third chapter deals with fasting and other penitential practices. Here the Constitution followed the "Leo-Rule" exactly which states: "The Brothers and Sisters shall abstain from meat on Mondays, Wednesdays, Fridays, and Saturdays.... From the Feast of All Saints until Easter they shall fast on all Wednesdays and Fridays, as also on all Fridays of the year. From the Feast of St. Martin until Christmas, they are to fast daily. The Lenten fast they shall begin on Quinquagesima." Other prescribed practices of penance were that discipline is to be taken daily and the penitential belt (Zilizium) be worn two hours daily. Work was treated in this chapter also. The entire chapter breathes of penitential severity. Here the zeal of the young congregation went too far. More moderate objectives were set up later owing to the counsels of Mother Francis Schervier to lessen the severity of the works of penance. This capability to learn from the wisdom of others and to lessen severity in her objectives manifests Sister Maria Theresia's genuine way of thinking. For whoever falls in love with his own zeal in such areas is unteachable. It must also be remembered that all these severities were not invented in Olpe. They rather portrayed an up-to-the-present picture of the religious communities conceived purely for contemplative living. Every biography of the saints dwelt with special delight in the description of these severities. It was, therefore, not easy to disassociate oneself from these and to program a new course more suitable to active religious life.

The fourth chapter deals with prayer, silence, the Sacraments of Penance and the Holy Eucharist. A statement relative to the annual retreat mentions that the Mother wishes these retreats to be conducted by Franciscan masters. This sounds like a personal reference to the superior of that time. It shows also that even in the first years the Sisters called the superior "Mother." The specific days for the reception of Holy Communion were designated in accordance with the practice of piety in that era. It stated, emphatically, "Seldom, and only to souls of advanced virtue, was daily Holy Communion allowed with permission of the confessor and the mother superior." But considering the customary practices of the day, there were, all in all, still many days for the reception of Holy Communion. The professed Sisters received on Sundays, Tuesdays, Thursdays, Fridays, and Saturdays of each week, on all feast days of our Lord and the Blessed Virgin Mary, all indulgenced feasts of the order, the feast of St. Joseph, All Saints, and All Souls. In addition, there were the memorial days of the individual Sisters, such as, the day of their profession and their nameday. The last point precipitates others. In all fixed norms of the congregation, the individual Sister was not to be overlooked. Concessions were to be made for her personal intentions. What is further said relative to Perpetual Adoration in this chapter is in summary a good ascetic instruction for discharging the atoning adoration correctly.

Two points in the fourth chapter of the Constitution are geared to the future. Things are mentioned which could not possibly have been realized at that time and therefore operate now as a legacy of the superior. The first has reference to the strictly contemplative life for a group of the Sisters. There is added:

> Although the contemplative life, in the mind of the Church, ranks higher, the great objective of Adoration on earth never achieves complete perfection. The congregation endeavors with the grace of God that some of its members, schooled in virtue and who experience a call and a desire for this way of life, be given the opportunity. This embraces enclosure and life according to the Rule of St. Clare as reformed by St. Colette. As soon as possible a link would be established for the above mentioned adoration. It is readily evident that through this adoration, the other Sisters as shown above, would not be excluded.

The idea of a group of strictly contemplative Sisters is treated in Article 10 of Chapter Five, which deals with the election of a superior. It reads as follows: "Should a superior have a call to the contemplative life and express a desire for enclosure, she should be given the opportunity if another Sister can replace her in the same office. If, however, this cannot be done, she must remain in office." Here one questions, why this one exception since the enclosure quarters had not been established previously and no regulations had existed at that time? Does this betray something individual? Mother Maria Theresia and Sister Francesca had drafted these Statutes. Both must have thought along the lines of being reckoned among the contemplatives one day. There are various reasons why the idea of having "a group of Poor Clares" within the convent could not be realized during the time of Mother Maria Theresia. There was the uncertainty of the survival of the religious orders brought on by the *Kulturkampf* and continuing to the present day. Also, the conditions existing in the old motherhouse would have made its realization impossible.

The idea of a strict contemplative unit within the congregation seems to have originated with Mother Francis Schervier of the Franciscan Sisters of Aix-la-Chapelle. Many congregations founded at this time had embodied such a unit with great success. According to the plan contained in the oldest Constitution, Perpetual Adoration is a duty of all the Sisters and is not to be taken over exclusively by the contemplative group. Adoration so definitely emphasized in the title of the congregation is to give a religious consciousness to all the Sisters. Mere activity can lose itself in the forces of involvement. Should not the contemplative group be a constant exhortation to all Sisters in their activity not to forget the interior union with God?

A second reference in the Constitution relative to long-range objectives appears in Article 9 of Chapter Four. Here the possibility of the congregation establishing itself in different localities is considered. Whoever has knowledge of the one-hundred-year history of the Olpe Franciscans finds these various foundations self-evident. However, in 1865 it was but a look into the future amidst great uncertainty.

The long-range foreign mission activities of Mother Maria Theresia were furthered during her life span. According to His Excellency the Bishop, and accompanied by his blessing, "the congregation will rejoice later by sending some qualified Sisters of the congregation to China and to other lands as missionaries." Although Mother Maria Theresia was unable to establish foreign missions during her life, her daughters were not oblivious to those plans. In 1962, the first foreign mission was established in the Philippines and in August 1963 the jubilee centenary of the congregation, the first five Sisters were sent to found a mission in the northern part of Brazil, South America.

The fifth chapter treats of offices and elections. Here we have a unique document of Mother Maria Theresia herself. The very first paragraph gives a full account of the office of superior and embodies a "mirror of perfection" for the administration of that office. One can scarcely find another document that spells out so well the duties of superior as given by Mother Maria Theresia. She held that office at this time. What she considered important she committed to paper. Whoever reads these statements of the foundress of the Olpe Sisters, discovers them verified in her way of life. The title of superior is designated as "mother" in the Rule; in this capacity she is to consider herself as the servant of all. She accepts the imposed heavy duty as a sweet burden, undertaken in obedience and borne for love of the congregation; but the honor, she considers an oppressing burden which in self-righteous charity she gladly places on other shoulders. The mother superior guides the congregation and exhorts the Sisters to live according to their vows and to observe the Rule and Constitution. She is zealous for the purposes of the congregation especially for the one nearest her heart — the sanctification of the Sisters. She endeavors to be a real mother to them, one whom they can easily approach in confidence to manifest their conscience and their bodily infirmities; she easily dispenses from corporal austerities as good reason dictates. Her maternal love, however, should not be too natural as to prevent her from admonishing, correcting, and punishing whenever necessary. To encourage and inspire the Sisters, the mother, unless hindered by illness or extraordinary duties, is to be first in all conventual exercises. She will not permit demonstrations of too natural affections of the Sisters toward herself nor among themselves; she is an enemy of fondling, even more of flattery; she tends toward straightforwardness and simplicity, which are the marks of the children of St. Francis. In wisdom she turns the dutiful respect and affection of the Sisters to God instead of to herself in order that their hearts dedicated to him in service remain his. She tries more through virtue than through office to be their superior before God. Also, to local superiors she exhorts the Sisters to obedience. The superior is to be a docile instrument in the hands of God and to deal with all in wisdom and to keep her eye on the will of God.

This is the ideal Mother Maria Theresia set for her own life. Because she lived it completely, she left her Sisters a precious legacy of the art of living. The office of councilor to the Mother was especially stressed by the foundress of the Olpe Sisters in this same chapter: "The councilor has the obligation to advise the Mother in charity by calling her attention to her failings under all circumstances, to remind her of her duties, and to dispense her from one or other conventual exercises." Under such conditions, the superior, in whose hands lay the obedience of all the Sisters, would also have a share in the blessings of obedience.

The sixth chapter of the Constitution treated *Interior and Exterior Conduct.* It considers love among the Sisters and their relations with the laity. The seventh chapter treats of special love of all Sisters. The eighth chapter speaks of visitations conducted by ecclesiastical superiors, such as, the canonical visitation conducted by the bishop or other delegated by him. The ninth chapter deals with obligations toward deceased Sisters. The tenth chapter treats of obligations to the Constitution.

Under the caption, *Reasons for the Constitution*, is the following conclusion:

> In obedience to the request of the Most Reverend Bishop, dated August 1863 and with confidence in God, we endeavored to compile this Constitution. This work is based on the Rule of St. Francis for Tertiaries living in community. It lends itself to the observance of the vows and our heretofore established objectives. Our way of life organized according to this Rule and on our experiences thus far, we submit to your pastoral and fatherly care for approval. We beg Your Excellency to recognize our small

> community as an ecclesial organization and to grant us your episcopal blessing and approval of our Constitution.
>
> *Olpe, March 25, 1865*
> *Sister Maria Theresia*
> *Sister Maria Francesca*

The entire document was written personally in manuscript form by Mother Maria Theresia herself. It was first given to their director, Pastor Schmidt, who signed it on June 16, 1865, and sent it to the bishop with a petition for approval. Bishop Konrad Martin returned it on July 6, 1865, with his approval in the following statement:

> The Constitution submitted by the Poor Sisters of St. Francis of Perpetual Adoration is approved provisionally by ecclesiastical authority to permit later necessary or useful changes to be made. The desired episcopal blessing is granted the Sisters.

CHAPTER VI

WITH THE BLESSING OF GOD

The episcopal approval of the Constitution of the Poor Sisters of St. Francis of Perpetual Adoration gave their community security as an organization of the church. It now devolved upon the members to achieve the goal set by the Constitution. With the approval, the bishop in further correspondence opened the door to future growth, by granting permission for investiture of two postulants and for temporary profession of four novices. The ceremony took place on August 2, 1865. Rector Schmidt officiated. The other Sisters had previously made their profession according to the Franciscan Rule. The first postulant after approval, Regina Schafer of Olpe, received the name of Sister Maria Deogratias of St. Francis. She had entered the congregation on February 2, 1864. In her entrance, Mother Maria Theresia saw the goodness of God in a very special way. She had dedicated the Sisters completely to a Franciscan way of life and the first Sister to join was to receive the name of Sister Maria Deogratias of St. Francis. This Sister satisfied her deepest desires. The letters Mother Maria Theresia later wrote her are among the most important documents in the life of the servant of God. Sibylla Heiliger, the second invested, received the name of Sister Maria Bonaventure of the Immaculate Conception.

Before the foundation was canonically established in Olpe, the bishop had appointed Mother Maria Theresia as superior. Now that the Constitution was approved, the Sisters prepared to elect their own superior. The Constitution allowed for various possibilities and difficulties that might occur in the elections. The election is to be conducted by secret ballot. A two-thirds majority vote is required. If in the first balloting a two-thirds is not achieved, a second balloting takes place. In the second balloting an absolute majority is sufficient. If an absolute majority is not achieved then, the diocesan bishop appoints the superior. Who could have surmised that at the very first election the last alternative had to take place! In the election of August 12, 1865, on the feast of St. Clare of Assisi, the first balloting resulted in a tie vote for Mother Maria Theresia and Sister Maria Francesca. The second balloting showed the same results. The bishop decided in favor of Mother Maria Theresia for three years, while Sister Maria Francesca remained as her assistant and as novice mistress. The fact that the election results did not in any way alter the existing friendship of the two Sisters speaks much for the character of both.

In the year 1866, three Sisters were invested. On February 10, Sister Josepha Hundt of the Sacred Heart of Jesus became a member of the congregation. Reverend Ludgerus Barkhofen, O.F.M., officiated at the ceremony. Mother Maria Theresia and Sister Francesca, her assistant, pronounced their final vows according to the Third Order Rule of St. Francis at the same ceremony. On August 25, the postulants Margaret and Katherine Thomas were invested and received the names of Sister Paula Thomas of the Holy Spirit and Sister Clara Thomas of the Queen of Heaven, respectively. Sister Paula pursued studies to become an instructor. Assistant headmaster Lohre prepared her for the professional examinations. The congregation is greatly indebted to Father Lohre for his unselfish assistance. His ever-ready help ameliorated the difficult beginnings. His selfless attitude is shown in the following: "I will be all I can be to the poor Sisters who have so little support."

The year 1867 showed no increase in membership for the congregation, but the following year two candidates were admitted on June 4, and four on October 3. In all, eleven had entered the congregation since the approval of the Constitution. The number of Sisters more than doubled within three years. The increase manifested the blessings of God upon the Poor Sisters of St. Francis of Perpetual Adoration and his intentions of leading the congregation to great objectives.

Still the years were not all joy. The Sisters were eager to test the Constitution in everyday living. Mother Maria Theresia doubted that all the articles of the Constitution would be practical in every detail. In this she was and remained human, capable of mature judgment. It soon became evident that modifications needed to be made in the matter of wearing apparel. She applied to the bishop for the necessary changes in the Constitution. He granted the requested permission, August 17, 1876.

Reverend Schmidt, Rector of the Sisters, a true and loyal organizer during the difficult and formative years of the congregation, was transferred to Hüsten as pastor in September 1867. It was a difficult parting. The bishop appointed Reverend Kaiser von Rhode as the new Rector. He also became renowned as a true father and protector of the Sisters. The fall of 1867 proved a severe time for Mother Maria Theresia. She must have felt that God had taken all support away from her and placed her more and more upon her own resources and initiative. Assistant Headmaster Lohre was also removed at the same time. He became Rector at Hamm. Besides his essential duties, Father Lohre had prepared a Sister for professional examination and had been the ordinary confessor for all the Sisters. He was replaced by Vicar Schmidt. Father Schmidt in turn was transferred in November of the same year. The bishop then appointed Vicar Schroeder as ordinary confessor for the Sisters.

A further vital and very painful loss threatened. The ill health of the assistant and novice mistress cast a gloom over all the Sisters. They feared the worst. Overtaxing her strength in the care of the sick, Sister Francesca had contracted a heavy cold, and soon a severe case of tuberculosis set in. Mother Francis Schervier, informed of Sister's condition begged to have her transferred to Aix-la-Chapelle in July. She hoped that in the milder climate of that city Sister could more readily recover than in the rigorous climate of the Sauerland. Besides the city had better and more efficient doctors who could undertake the case. It happened that this year was the assigned time for a pilgrimage to the holy places in Aix-la-Chapelle. Sister Francesca, along with all the Sisters, set their hope for recovery upon touching the holy relics. During the day the throng of pilgrims seemed too much for her. Consequently she went to the cathedral in the stillness of the evening hours to pray undisturbed to God and beg him for her recovery. According to human judgment, the young congregation was unable to spare Sister at that time. But it soon became evident that all must pray for tranquil resignation to the holy will of God.

In September, 1867, Mother Maria Theresia, just recently recovered from a serious illness, journeyed to Aix-la-Chapelle to see Sister Francesca and to take her home for she was homesick for Olpe. She had recovered her strength somewhat in Aix-la-Chappelle. In the August 12, 1868 elections, Mother Maria Theresia was reelected as superior. She reappointed Sister Francesca as assistant and novice mistress. Did she do this to avoid hurting one doomed to an early death? In November 1868, Sister Francesca began to fail rapidly. She herself did not realize her condition and hoped constantly for recovery. Her head was filled with plans for the future of the congregation. All the other Sisters could readily see that her days were numbered. To see her loyal Sister so deceived as to her true condition saddened the heart of Mother Maria Theresia. Difficult as it was for her, she felt responsible to help her to accept all in perfect resignation to the will of God. When Sister Francesca again spoke of her future plans, Mother Maria Theresia said to her in serene tranquility: "Dear Sister Francesca, it is time that you banish all the earthly more and more from your mind that you may spend the moments in unbroken love of God, for if our love of God is great at the hour of death, it will remain so for all eternity." "Mother, am I to die soon?" asked the sick one surprised. "Yes, I think so," was the answer, "therefore, I must make you aware of it." Both were silent. The sick one wept and after some moments said: "Oh, I would so gladly help longer! There is so much to do for the congregation."

Sister Francesca asked her doctor on the morning of November 17: "What is your opinion, doctor, how much longer have I to live?" "Scarcely twelve hours," he replied. Then he was silent. After he had gone, Sister Francesca said to Mother Maria Theresia: "He can talk! Just listen how well I still can breathe!" Then she took a deep breath to show how much alive she still was. But shortly thereafter she herself felt the nearness of death. She begged to talk to all the Sisters once more. The Sisters assembled in her room and she spoke an encouraging word of farewell to each Sister, individually. Shortly before six o'clock in the evening she breathed her last. She was the first Sister our Lord took to heaven from the young congregation of the Poor Sisters of St. Francis of Perpetual Adoration.

The offices of the deceased were given to two other Sisters. Sister Deogratias assumed the duties of assistant and Sister Bonaventura that of novice mistress. Since now her entire time was devoted to the formation of the novices, Sister Bonaventura had to relinquish her teaching position in the orphanage. Thus the education of the orphans was again given into the hands of Miss Kortmann, a lay teacher.

In the meantime the civic authorities demanded a separate building for the orphan children and the Sisters caring for them. They feared the Sisters doing home nursing among the people of Olpe would endanger the health of the orphans by their contacts with contagious diseases.

In cooperation with the government, the congregation acquired the Koester residence in the spring of 1868. This building was situated opposite the convent of the Sisters. Renovations and adjustments were completed in April of that year, and the orphans and the Sisters moved in immediately. Business negotiations by contract were closed in June of that year.

Three more postulants were invested on April 16, 1869. The director of the Sisters in reporting the investiture ceremony wrote to the bishop: "The new foundation must in truth be a work of God. Innocence and humility, piety and spiritual moderation, severity and joyfulness, appear to blossom here in pairs." A beautiful judgment concerning the spirit of the congregation!

Although the Sisters had been willing to put up with limited living quarters, space was simply entirely insufficient. Above all it was expedient to provide suitable support for the orphans. Mother Maria Theresia consequently decided to begin an addition on the northwest side of the convent and also the construction of a chapel.

Work was begun on both in the fall of 1869. Construction had scarcely begun when Mother Maria Theresia experienced the hardships of foundresses — those dealing not only with interior formation but also with building adequate structures for the housing of a growing congregation. Brother Paschalis Gratze was the architect of the new wing and the chapel. When Bishop Konrad Martin came to Olpe in August 1869, to administer the Sacrament of Confirmation, he also invested six postulants at the convent. On the same day he solemnly laid the cornerstone for the new wing and chapel. Building progress was very slow in the beginning. Mother Maria Theresia was in constant need of funds to finance the project. When the Franco-Prussian War broke out in 1870, construction came to a complete standstill. The erected walls were covered to protect them against weathering. Only after the war had ended could the work be resumed. Toward the close of the year 1871, the building was in readiness for occupation by the orphans. The Sisters moved into the former Koester residence which previously had served as quarters for the orphans. The completion of the chapel required more time.

In her deep concern to secure funds for the building project, Mother Maria Theresia turned to St. Joseph in confidence and made him her paymaster. If in her average daily needs she had to count the pennies, how difficult it must have been for her with the added expense of a building project. She promised her heavenly paymaster if he would see that the necessary funds were at hand on time, she would add "of St. Joseph" to every Sister's name. Up to this time each Sister of the congregation had an individual supplementary title attached to her name. This sign of gratitude still characterizes all the Sisters of Mother Maria Theresia's congregation.

Another matter that caused Mother Maria Theresia great anxiety ran parallel with her building worries, namely, the opening of an advanced education school for girls in Olpe. At this time the young congregation lacked professionally trained qualified teachers for the undertaking. The townsmen of Olpe had approached her with the request. The Sisters' former Rector, who had been transferred to Hamm, possessed the requisite qualification. Always having had the welfare of the congregation at heart, he offered his services as administrator of the school. Accordingly, on May 5, 1869, he submitted his request as spiritual director of the Sisters in Olpe. But the bishop was not ready to release his able Rector of Hamm. Mother Maria Theresia entered into the deliberations with great intensity. Those who knew her heretofore had not expected her to exert herself with such self-possession as superior to battle for the good of the congregation.

Conditions forced her into the open to act as superior of the congregation. She showed she had matured in her office of superior. Again and again she turned to the bishop and to the general vicariate with her petitions. She even suggested a replacement for Rector Lohre in Hamm. Several misunderstandings resulted and had to be resolved under difficulties. How entangled the affair finally became can be seen readily in the letter Mother Maria Theresia wrote to the bishop on June 7, 1870. It portrays the tenacious energy and wisdom of the servant of God in the interests of her congregation. The bishop was in Rome at this time. Because of its urgent character, the letter was sent there.

> *Your Grace, Your Excellency, Father and Bishop:*
>
> Your Grace will forgive me, the poorest child of St. Francis, who is compelled again to bring the urgent need of our congregation for consideration to your fatherly heart and pastoral attention. With permission of Your Grace, Rector Lohre received a license from the Royal Government to establish a school for the higher education of girls and to conduct courses to qualify the Sisters for teaching. Although Rector Lohre could not be freed at Easter, he nevertheless opened the school fearing that he might lose his license. He then returned to Hamm. The Sisters in the meantime conducted the school. The Royal Government issued an announcement, under my name, that we were conducting a school without being licensed. It ordered the school closed on the third of this month. Rector Lohre not understanding the situation clearly and believing his license lost wrote to the general vicariate that he was willing to remain in his present position. After he was later informed correctly concerning the situation, he tried to retract his previous statement, for he wished to abide by his promise to help the Sisters. In Paderborn we learned that in all probability he would not be free although we have a letter under date of May 6 that he would definitely be with us in three months. His license will run out on July 4, and under present conditions, it would be difficult to have it renewed by the Royal Government. Mr. Kroll, the

education authority in Arnsberg, said Mr. Balkenhol, Vice Rector in Hamm, could secure a license for Hamm upon promise that he would take examinations in the summer.

I consider this embarrassing situation in our congregation unnecessary, for our beloved Father and Rector of past years is convinced that it can be remedied by the promised assistance of the Rector Father Lohre. He is willing and is only awaiting your word.

Entire Olpe, the pastor, the city and school authorities have sent a petition to the general Vicar for the transfer of rector Lohre to Olpe, but to date without effect. The citizens of Olpe and the district magistrate are all for the congregation and wish most ardently that the school situation be settled soon. But if the initiated work be postponed longer and disturbed again by the absence of Rector Lohre, our reputation in Olpe will become questionable. We have engaged in home nursing again at the request of Your Grace and now beg you, our dearest Father and bishop, to help us in this dilemma. Grant a favorable answer to our petition, namely, that Father Lohre receive his assignment to Olpe before the expiration of his license on July 4. The consensus of opinion of all is that Hamm can manage without him but not Olpe. As we were told in Paderborn a successor to Rector Lohre was found in Hamm in the person of Rector Parensen of Erfurt, who wishes to be transferred.

It grieves me to burden Your Grace with this problem at a distance, but I can see no other alternative. Poor, forsaken, and distressed, I know of no one else on earth who is so noble and generous to bear our burdens and willing to lift our drooping spirits as you, the best of fathers and pastoral superiors. We are in need of urgent help since our only human support, the Pastor Kaiser in Rhode, our cherished spiritual superior is seriously ill with a nerve fever and beyond hope of recovery.

May the divine Heart that accepts our hymns of praise, thanksgiving, and petition listen to our constant pleas for the welfare of our Bishop. May the Holy Spirit who guides and governs the church strengthen the Episcopal Shepherd of our diocese with special wisdom and fortitude to accomplish his high purpose among the Fathers of the Council for the honor of God and the salvation of Christendom in the spirit and courage of the apostles. With childlike confidence, we again lay our urgent plea for help in our distress and need before you for a speedy answer and beg your blessing upon our congregation. May Your Grace remember our petition while celebrating the Holy Sacrifice on the glorious tomb of the Prince of the Apostles and send us your blessing from afar. We beg this with deep respect, reverence, and thanksgiving.

Your Grace's unworthy servant
Sister Maria Theresia
Superior of the Poor Franciscans

The bishop could scarcely decide against his vicar. He consequently forwarded Mother Maria Theresia's letter to Paderborn under date of June 11, with the remark "to investigate further whether and how the Franciscans are to be helped." Thus the vicar wrote on June 22, 1870:

Venerable Mother Maria Theresia
Superior of the Franciscans of Olpe

Your letter of June 7 to His Grace our Most Reverend Bishop at Rome has been forwarded to me under date of June 11, 1870, for further consideration. Since Rector Lohre has expressed his wish personally to remain at Hamm; since I have informed all the authorities concerned to that effect; since a substitution for rector Lohre during the semester, apart from his expression of will, would be an impossibility; since I have informed the bishop concerning this entire matter, we must consider the affair settled. At present we can only repeat to let the affair rest with our previous arrangement, namely, that rector Lohre remain in Hamm and that he renounce the design of founding and directing a school for girls in Olpe.

Therewith the plan was definitely shattered. Another priest who could have qualified as administrator of the school could not be found. For this reason the district magistrate recommended Rector Lohre simply to open the school and then await his transfer to Olpe. His recommendations were followed and the school opened under the temporary leadership of a secular instructor, who was certified to do advanced teaching. The Sisters undertook instruction on the elementary level. At all events they opened the school and endeavored to keep it open as long as there was hope that Rector Lohre would come eventually. It was evident to all that Father Lohre's license could not be renewed. Regarding this the district magistrate had informed Mother Maria Theresia. The Sisters could congratulate themselves that a license was granted in the first place. A renewal was out of question since the rising standards of certification were becoming more complicated. The effects of the *Kulturkampf* were being felt gradually.

THE FIRST FOUNDATIONS

Mother Maria Theresia spent all her energy in the attainment of a school for the advanced education of girls in Olpe. In opening such an educational institution she sought the manifestation of a recognized activity in line with the care of orphans, one completely in agreement with the Constitution. The main objective of her apostolate was the care of youth more so than an activity for the Sisters. At this time the first possibilities of opening new foundations were apparent.

The first foundation of the young congregation was at Blankenstein on the Ruhr. In the spring of 1869, Father Bonsmann approached Mother Maria Theresia with a request for Sisters to engage in home nursing and to instruct girls in the domestic arts. Mother Maria Theresia felt prepared to undertake the work. The membership of the congregation permitted a new foundation. She thought it would develop the self-reliance and the responsibility of the older members. Also, since their situation in Olpe was still not clearly defined, she thought it well to have a place of activity in another area. On June 1, 1869, the bishop gave his permission for the new foundation. Various circumstances, however, caused delay, but it was established on November 9 of the same year. Mother Maria Theresia accompanied her Sisters to their new place. With Sisters Agnes and Petra she boarded the stage coach in Olpe as far as Finnentrop. From there they took the train to their destination. The railroad between Olpe and Finnentrop was not built until 1872-74. Previously, travel between Olpe and Blankenstein was troublesome. In Blankenstein they leased several rooms, where the Sisters lived and began their apostolate of home nursing. Somewhat later Sister Agatha joined them and commenced her instruction for the girls in domestic arts. The foundation was placed under the protection of St. Elizabeth. In the lapse of years this mission developed into a hospital and a convalescent home.

A few months after establishing her first mission, Mother Maria Theresia was approached for a second one. The request was made by Reverend Father Schmidt in Hüsten, who had been the superior of the Sisters until September 1867. In his parish, the Countess Karoline of Fürstenberg had a hospital constructed which she donated to the Catholic parish with the stipulation that it be administered by the Franciscan sisters for the welfare of the sick. Although Father Schmidt had no hand in the stipulation, it nevertheless must have pleased him greatly. He knew of the difficulties under which the Olpe Sisters labored to carry on their nursing apostolate in the city. If they assumed charge of the hospital in Hüsten, it would enable them to develop their nursing arts more fully and qualify themselves better for other hospitals. These were sufficient reasons to undertake charge of this hospital. Reverend Father Kaiser together with Mother Maria Theresia accompanied the first Sisters to Hüsten on January 7, 1870. Four sisters comprised the nursing staff there. Since the wounded of the Franco-Prussian War were brought to Karoline Hospital, a fifth sister was sent to aid the four.

In the following year, 1871, three new foundations were made: Wissen on the Sieg, Morsbach, and Eckenhagen, making inroads into another diocese, namely, the domain of the Archbishop of Cologne. Olpe is situated in the southern section of the Diocese of Paderborn. In the expansion of the congregation, it seemed but natural that sooner or later the neighboring archdiocese of Cologne should come under consideration. But it was not easy to take that step. A request for a foundation in Morsbach, District Waldbröl, came to Mother Maria Theresia in the previous year. She endeavored to meet the preparations for expansion. Work for the Sisters outside the diocese was close at hand, as the demand came from the Archbishop of Cologne. He wished only those Sisters to work in his archdiocese who had their motherhouses in his territory. That kept the Olpe Franciscans at a distance, for a time.

An additional request for Olpe Sisters came from Wissen which also belonged to the Archdiocese of Cologne. Reverend Steinbusch, pastor in Wissen, was especially fond of them, for he was uncle to Sisters Hugoline and Heinrica, both members of this group. He did all within his power to secure the Olpe Sisters. His endeavors were successful in changing the decision of the archbishop.

Mother Maria Theresia was not awaiting the outcome passively. On January 26, 1871, she wrote to the diocesan bishop of Paderborn to mediate in their behalf:

> The year before, Morsbach located in the Archdiocese of Cologne, requested us to make a foundation there. At that time Your Grace was prepared to give us your episcopal blessing for the undertaking; but just before the Sisters were to leave, they met with an obstacle. The Most Reverend Archbishop Paul of Cologne determined to have only those congregations laboring in his archdiocese who had their motherhouse established in the archdiocese. Just recently two more requests from the archdiocese of Cologne have been received for Sisters, namely, Hilden near Düsseldorf and Wissen. We were on the verge of giving up the idea of making foundations in the archdiocese when Father Peters of Hilden informed us that the archbishop is reconsidering and is gathering more information. As our bishop you know our spirit of simplicity and poverty and have given us the assurance of your help. with hearts full of thanksgiving for all your condescension and goodness, we beg Your Grace to aid us graciously in this situation

and put in a good word for us to the archbishop that he permit the Olpe Franciscans to work in his archdiocese.

The bishop answered her letter immediately: "In reference to your letter of yesterday, I must say that within these days I have urgently recommended your congregation to the Most Reverend Archbishop of Cologne."

After such endeavors, results finally took shape: the Olpe Sisters were admitted into the Archdiocese of Cologne. Thus on March 27, 1871, the foundation at Morsbach was established. Suitable preparations had been made long in advance. On July 1 of the same year, a convent house was opened in Wissen, adequately prepared for three Sisters. In both foundations the Sisters engaged in home nursing.

Hilden near Düsseldorf requested Olpe Sisters as teachers. The pastor of Hilden, Father Peters, had previously obtained permission from the Archbishop for the establishment of the school. The plans were that by Easter, 1871, six Sisters would be stationed there; consequently preparations for the foundation were readied. But in March when the sisters were registered with the existing administrative authorities they were met with a decisive prohibition through public ministerial prescription that there would be no further appointment of religious as educators. Those engaged in places where they had previously taught were to be exceptions. Thus their plan was shattered. As a result the Olpe Sisters did not arrive in Hilden until 1926. In the shattering of her plan, Mother Maria Theresia met her first repercussions with the government brought on by the measures of the *Kulturkampf*.

Still a fifth foundation was realized before the outbreak of the *Kulturkampf*. Reverend Wimmer of Eckenhagen, district Waldbröl, asked for sisters to take charge of the institute for communicants, do home nursing, and conduct instruction in the general arts. The Archbishop of Cologne not only granted his permission but gave, without being solicited, a donation of two hundred dollars for the preparation of the house. The bishop of Paderborn also agreed to the new foundation. Eckenhagen was opened on December 21, 1871, with three Sisters. This establishment ended the new foundations in Germany temporarily. The

Kulturkampf made further expansion an impossibility. Only after twelve years were two new foundations, Heimerzheim and Jülich, opened.

The fact that five foundations were opened in a period of three years proves the interior and exterior growth in strength of the congregation. For the major superior, the growth added greatly to her tasks and labors. Many and difficult negotiations were required before the activities of the apostolate and the support of the Sisters in their new localities could be made secure. Mother Maria Theresia not only accompanied each group of Sisters to their new destination but visited them often thereafter and endeavored constantly to encourage the Sisters and maintain a loving union with and among them through correspondence. Her letters portrayed the painstaking care she took of the Sisters. Her written correspondence is a very special chapter in her dealings with them. She did not limit her letters to the superiors. If any Sister was in need, or if any one of her relatives met with death, a letter of consolation or condolence could be expected from Mother Maria Theresia. Spoken words are readily forgotten after the person to whom they were spoken has passed away. But in Mother Maria Theresia's correspondence the words to her Sisters live. Although much of her writing was not preserved, enough of her numerous letters are extant to reveal the precious knowledge of heart of this great woman and expose her excellent character. Through circular letters on great feastdays she created an atmosphere of unity among the Sisters, no matter where they were stationed. In later days, it became noticeable that on feastdays her letters to the various houses were not drafted similarly. In this way she wished to personalize her messages to the individual convents.

As major superior of the congregation she stressed the importance of superiors of the various convents to report regularly to her all significant events of their houses. She wished to know the conditions of her Sisters at every moment. If a superior was negligent in this matter, she would receive a letter of warning from Mother Maria Theresia. In one of the preserved letters we read: "It is very conspicuous that you write so seldom. With all my manifold duties, it is impossible to answer every letter; still

I think that superiors should write to me every month. Improve yourself in this matter." Thus she tried to develop a spirit of unity throughout the entire Community, to be near to all, to warn and encourage the Sisters along the way they were following together for the greater glory of God.

In opening new foundations there was a willingness by the congregation to aid to the fullest extent wherever the need of mankind called. Normally, a religious works outward from within the convent to maintain a regulated religious life and at the same time be of service to mankind. Mother Maria Theresia, however, was willing, if a definite need existed in a locality, to send her Sisters there even though there was no convent in the place nor did she have an idea of establishing one. In such instances she considered the need — to help was law. One knew that she would do all within her power to give aid. Proof of this is seen in a letter written by Superior Kaiser on June 18, 1870, from Rhode:

> *Venerable Mother*:
>
> I have a letter from Reverend Stollmeyer at Grafschaft near Smallenberg to the effect that typhus has broken out in the village. Lest it spread further, he requests the service of two Sister nurses from our congregation to be sent there. The pastor will pay the traveling expenses and care of the Sisters. He wishes an immediate answer whether the Sisters will be coming or not. He asked that I inform him immediately. Thus I beg you to let me know at once whether you can meet his request, or better still, you inform him directly.

Mother Maria Theresia was willing. But in the meantime, the disease had run its course and further aid was not necessary in Grafschaft. Requests such as nursing contagious diseases are always indicative of great confidence placed in the Sisters. In those days such care demanded greater personal resignation on the part of nurses than would be the case today since medicine has made great strides.

The letter of the Superior had an interesting postscript which is added here: "My hearty thanks for your valuable nameday gift! But for the future I must forbid you, in the interest of holy poverty, to give such expensive gifts to me." The above speaks for the modesty of the Superior and his readiness to guide the Sisterhood entrusted to him. The circumstances of the gift are unknown. Most probably Mother Maria Theresia had desired to give special joy to the spiritual father who had done so very much for the congregation and to grant him strength in his illness. But she took his admonition to heart. Later she wrote to a local superior as follows: "For nameday give the pastor a beautiful bouquet of flowers and do not begin to give gifts." Evidently she did not want any artificial display but an expression of sincere and heartfelt wishes. One would need to have more intimate knowledge of the situation to judge the affair accurately. A situation relative to the Superior of the Sisters was surely different from that of the local pastor in the place where the Sisters worked.

THE FRANCO-PRUSSIAN WAR 1870–71

With a special spirit of sacrifice, the Olpe Sisters devoted themselves to the service of love as the Franco-Prussian War broke out in 1870. Mother Maria Theresia was ready immediately to send all of her Sisters, who could possibly be spared, to care for the wounded and sick soldiers. As her Sisters were assigned to duty in the military hospitals and barracks in Kreuznach, she accompanied the first group of Sisters in August, 1870. Eighteen Sisters, more than half of those in the Olpe motherhouse, were active in Kreuznach in the beginning of 1871. Five Sisters cared for the wounded in Hüsten. In Kreuznach eight hundred wounded soldiers were entrusted to the care of the Sisters. Mother Maria Theresia was unable to remain any longer, for her presence was required in Olpe. Seven postulants were to be invested on August 19, and three Sisters were to pronounce temporary vows. The number of Sisters in Olpe decreased considerably as even seven novices were helping in Kreuznach. The congregation in Olpe spared no sacrifice aiding those in need because of the war. After the war, which ended early in 1871, the Sisters were free to return home.

Their selfless spirit won recognition from the highest government authorities of the country. The Empress presented

Mother Maria Theresia with the distinguished service medal for the services of the congregation in its voluntary care of the sick and wounded. This was an honor designed for the sacrificial generosity displayed by women during the war. Somewhat later Mother Maria Theresia received in addition the Red-Cross Medal of the Third Class and then of the Second Class in acknowledgement of the splendid services of her congregation. Twenty Sisters who nursed the wounded during the war were honored by the Emperor on February 15, 1873, with his Commemorative Medal. Soon after their return in January 1871, Sister Michaele and Sister Martina died of typhus contracted in the hospital at Kreuznach. Three others died later. It was very difficult for Mother Maria Theresia to see those young sisters die who had so trustfully dedicated their young lives to God and placed themselves in his provident care.

DIFFICULTIES IN NURSING THE SICK IN OLPE

While the Sisters' services in nursing the sick were sought in various places and recognized by the highest government authorities, in Olpe they met with great difficulties. One automatically thinks of the Words of Christ: "Nowhere does a prophet carry less honor than in his own country and in his own house." (Mt 13:57), if one may interpret the words in a somewhat different sense. The obstacles arose not so much from the citizens of Olpe as from another source. In November of 1870, the Auxiliary Bishop Freusberg of Paderborn came to Olpe. He visited the Franciscan motherhouse. As spiritual superior of the Vincentian Sisters who conducted St. Martin Hospital there, he took sides completely with his Sisters and attempted above all to give them an unhindered charge of nursing in every way. To have him, in view of his office as opponent, was not easy. In the episcopal see of Paderborn the Sisters of Christian Love as well as the Vincentians had their motherhouses. Here he brought about an agreement with the former to devote themselves exclusively to the education of youth and leave the apostolate of the sick entirely to the latter. He wished to make a similar settlement in Olpe. In conversation with Mother Maria Theresia he announced his intention openly. She informed him with composure that she was a Franciscan and that it had been a tradition in the Franciscan Order from its very inception to engage in service to the sick and the poor. Therefore, she could not deviate from the principles of the Order to accede to his demands. Her Sisters would continue to go to the sick and the poor in Olpe, especially upon a personal request. The auxiliary bishop said that Rome had issued a bulletin to the effect that various congregations in the same town should not engage in the same apostolate. Mother Maria Theresia answered that if such a bulletin had been issued the bishop of the diocese would certainly be aware of it; he had permitted them to engage in the apostolate of the sick. The auxiliary bishop asked, "Has the Reverend Bishop permitted this?" "Yes, Your Grace." "That will lead to rivalries," the auxiliary bishop said. Mother Maria Theresia answered: "Certainly not through us, Most Reverend Bishop, as we work only for the greater honor and glory of God; if that happens, peace cannot be disturbed." Then the auxiliary bishop ended the conversation with a warning: "If you practice the nursing of the sick, I shall be your opponent, and you shall only harm your congregation."

He then went to the chapel where the Sisters were waiting. After a few words he gave the congregation his episcopal blessing remarking that he was giving the blessing "for the Perpetual Adoration and the education of youth." He had intentionally omitted the apostolate of the care of the sick. Nothing remained for Mother Maria Theresia to do but to beg for a complete blessing including the care of the sick in the name of him from whom every blessing on earth comes.

Sometime later she indeed mentioned the incident to the diocesan bishop. On January 26, 1871, she wrote relative to the foundations made and added:

> Our spiritual superior has certainly informed Your Grace that several of our Sisters were occupied for five months in the care of the sick and wounded; they have been home now for a few weeks for their patients have mostly recovered. Here in Olpe we have to date not undertaken the

practice of nursing because we thought you considered it best to delay it somewhat longer. Several weeks ago Bishop Freusberg visited us unexpectedly to give us God's blessing upon our apostolate in the education of youth and expressed himself our friend and protector; but if we should engage in the care of the sick in Olpe, he would do all possible against us and thusly we would but harm the congregation. I answered him that from the beginning the care of the sick was an objective of the Franciscan Order and that in Olpe we would gladly just go to the poor; but in general I would pursue the objectives of our congregation and that I also had the permission of our beloved bishop. I mentioned further that I could not see why he objected so much to the idea that we and the Sisters of Mercy work together in the care of the sick here in Olpe. I could certify that we work only for the honor of God and that under such conditions peace could not be disturbed. To prevent all disturbances, I shall rejoice when we have a foundation established where our Sisters can engage in the care of the sick. I ask again in this matter that you grant us your blessing and protection. Permit me also to beg you to recommend us for Treffurt where we heard, Sisters will soon be requested.

How the bishop reacted to the above could not be determined. In his answer to Mother Maria Theresia's letter he did not mention the affair. Did he probably have a discussion with his auxiliary bishop? At all events he did not forbid engaging in the care of the sick but permitted conditions to stand as heretofore.

Auxiliary Bishop Joseph Freusberg threatened the Olpe Franciscans that if they did not willingly and on principle relinquish nursing the sick, their congregation would experience his power as an adversary. In fact, soon serious difficulties did arise relative to the nursing of the sick, but this time from the government authorities. If the statements of the auxiliary bishop had not taken place, probably it would not have entered the mind of anyone to take the same stand as that of the town. In this regard, the state likewise sought express opportunities to cause hardships for the religious congregation. Often in such cases, the subordinate officers did not use their own initiative but acted on the orders of their superior officers. A peculiar reaction was experienced as among the names of petitioners on the list of the district magistrate against the Sisters engaging in nursing, the name of Adolph Freusberg appeared.

It is not clear who reported the nursing apostolate of the Poor Franciscans. At all events the Royal Government in Arnsberg wrote to the district magistrate Freusberg on May 12, 1871, as follows:

> According to our information the Franciscans there are conducting a licensed orphanage, an educational institution, and an apostolate of home nursing in the city. Investigate the situation and advise us within three days if it be true. If necessary forbid the respective Sisters the nursing of the sick because through these services they expose children to the great danger of contracting contagious diseases.

The district magistrate sent this correspondence of the government to Mother Maria Theresia on May 24, 1871. He added the following:

> In this situation I shall share a copy of directives dated May 12, with you. This was issued by the Royal Government. I am also sending a list of favorable names for your further information. It has been reported to me that the Sisters of the local Franciscan convent did home nursing in the case of a wife of a day laborer. Although I recognize favorably the noble endeavor of the Franciscans to be of service to their suffering fellowmen in caring for the sick; yet, I cannot refrain from bringing to your notice that this cannot be permitted for sanitary reasons. Persons certified for conducting orphanages and institutions for the education of children are endangering the health of these if, at the same time, they engage in nursing the sick. There is great possibility of contracting contagious diseases. You and those in the local Franciscan convent will therefore in the future

> refrain from home nursing in the local town and in the surrounding areas, or else pay the penalty of five dollars and run the possible risk of losing your given license.

It is absolutely not true that Mother Maria Theresia through sympathy recklessly disregarded the directives of the town official in the administration of an orphanage. The point of danger made by the district magistrate was the exact one Mother Maria Theresia had foreseen and considered carefully.

What should she do now if further requests for home nursing should come to them, especially in instances when the Vincentians for some reason or other are unable to give the service? What line of action would be weightier — that of the directive or the command of love? For Mother Maria Theresia the answer was simple. Under such working conditions difficulties were bound to arise. On July 16, 1872, the district magistrate wrote the following to her:

> It has been reported to me that the Franciscans were repeatedly (namely, were from eight to fourteen days) doing home nursing for the wife of the cabinet maker, Joseph Gipperich, although the Royal Government at Arnsberg had forbidden you and your Sisters to perform these services on May 24, of the previous year under threat of penalty of five dollars. It is unpleasant for me to fine you, but you have engaged in the nursing of the sick in spite of the command. Your penalty is two dollars to be paid to the town treasurer, Mr. Willmes, within the next eight days. I call your attention to the fact that repeated transgressions of this nature will call for a large fine by the Royal Government. Total disregard of regulation will be reported.

Mother Maria Theresia needed to vindicate herself. She did so in a brief message to the district magistrate and in a longer explanation to the Royal Government on July 20, 1872. To the district magistrate she wrote:

> Sir: the undersigned takes the liberty relative to the district magistrate's order of the 16th of this month to answer

> obediently that the Franciscan Sisters were not engaged in nursing at Carpenter Gipperich's home, but in housekeeping. Therefore I beg you submissively to revoke said order and to cancel the imposed penalty. (VII 2)

To the Government Mother Maria Theresia wrote a comprehensive letter giving a complete and cohesive report detailing the particulars of the situation:

> Several years ago an epidemic of typhoid fever broke out in the town and also in several villages in the vicinity; among these was Germinghausen, a very poor village under the jurisdiction of Drolshagen about one and one-half hours from here. The local Vincentian Sisters, who cared for them for a short time, could, would, or dared not continue their services there any longer. Because of the great need, Mr. Amtmann Neuhaus in Drolshagen, the inhabitants of the village and also their doctor, Dr. Fuchsius, begged us to undertake the care of these poor and otherwise forsaken sick. We willingly undertook the task to the satisfaction of all concerned. Briefly thereafter a certain woman of the town was delivered by Caesarean section; our Sisters also cared for her because the Vincentian Sisters did not wish to take the case. After this patient recovered and no longer required nursing care, we received a signed warning and threat of punishment from the local district magistrate to the effect that our Sisters are not to nurse the sick, through a law forbidding us to do so because we are connected with an orphanage and an educational institution. If we had known beforehand that such a law existed, we would not have violated it. We had no idea of such a law especially since the Sisters who administer St. Martin Hospital have at the same time a school for girls in the domestic arts along with the hospital. Also there are several hospitals in the neighborhood for the care of sick with contagious diseases which also have no small number of poor or orphan children. I shall point out Neheim, Werl, and Lippstadt. Our orphans are cared for in a building apart from the convent by a wide street. The Sisters in

> charge and caring for the orphans have scarcely any contacts with the other Sisters. We refrained from the service of the sick until now. Several days ago, in a local family of three, father, mother, and son, the mother became ill mentally, and at the request of the father, one Sister went there to keep house.
>
> Mr. Freusberg, the district manager, fined us two dollars as penalty, which however will be canceled when the truth of the situation will be known. We have arranged our housing in such a way that those who are to nurse in private homes in and out of the town will live in another building apart from that of the orphanage, at a distance of sixty-four feet from it. These will have no contacts with the orphans whatever. Will your Royal Government, therefore permit us a license for the Sisters who live apart to engage in nursing the sick in and out of town? Is our present arrangement compatible with the law, for we do not wish to transgress it under any condition? (VII 2)

This correspondence is intelligible and shows clearly that the difficulties did not arise from the fact that Mother Maria Theresia simply wished to intrude herself and her Sisters nor disregarded directives. Her difficulties arose from her great sense of duty in practicing the commandment of love though others interpreted her actions otherwise. She had sent her Sisters into those areas only in which the energies of the Vincentians did not reach. The Vincentians above all had to give their thoughts and care to the hospital in Olpe. It may be that in consideration of the hospital in Olpe, extraneous nursing, such as in the epidemic of typhus, had been rescinded. For if the same Sisters who nursed in the hospital also cared for the typhoid patients, there would have been danger of contagion. On the other hand, patients could be isolated in the hospital much more readily than in the private home.

One point in the correspondence of Mother Maria Theresia that portrays her attitude must be brought to light, namely, her resolute and straightforward way of giving information. This she also taught her Sisters. Today no one makes an issue of religious women taking care of maternity cases. At that time it was not done. Even religious congregations devoted to the care of the sick did not practice that service for reasons scarcely understood today. Mother Maria Theresia's thinking was otherwise. She was simply open to the conditions of human life, calm and certain in facing conditions. Regarding her sisters, she never sought to stifle the God-given ties of love between parents and child. What many congregations are discovering today, she practiced naturally a century ago. When parents were seriously ill, she sent the daughter to the bedside of the father or mother to care for the parent. Some of her letters to Sisters under such conditions are still extant. Why should not the Sisters care for their parents who under great danger gave them life and now are in need of their help? That this was a matter of course with Mother Maria Theresia and mentioned without comment, speaks clearly and forcefully of her charitable way.

Especially her theories relative to nursing of the sick reveal that she understood how to argue clearly and openly when there was a challenge to the congregation. But when the struggle concerned only herself personally, she gave an impression of aversion to explain. God called her to serve a large group of religious. She must have realized that he ordained her as mother and leader of the Sisters and that her way was not a tranquil and unpretentious one. Since she had given a "yes" and an approval to her religious life, she embraced it with all the energy of her heart in the position assigned her and revealed that she possessed the qualities a foundress of a religious congregation should possess. Thus she became a true mother to her Sisters not only in loving care and guidance in their way of life but also in a courageous and tenacious pledge for her Sisters.

In her presentation to the Government she had petitioned the state's approval of her Sisters nursing the sick, where such approval would be demanded. On November 21, 1872, the Government gave the requested approval. It demanded that the Sisters caring for the sick be separated from the orphans and from the Sisters caring for the orphans to avoid all danger of infectious diseases. This stipulation was readily met since two separate houses were at the disposal of the Sisters.

Mother Maria Theresia had struggled with utmost energy and tenaciousness that nursing the sick become a possibility for her Sisters. She shied from no opposition. It seemed as though she had a premonition that the destiny of her congregation would soon depend upon its being reckoned as a congregation devoted to the care of the sick.

CONCERN FOR THE SPIRITUAL LIFE

Relative to the active apostolate of her Sisters, the servant of God had accomplished much between the approval of the Constitution and the *Kulturkampf.* Still, she was not the type to spend all her energies on external activities and then have no time for things more essential to the congregation. Unfortunately, the early years left no reports of the more important task of the congregation: the formation of the Sisters in the spirit of religious life. The title *Poor Franciscans of Perpetual Adoration* had deep significance for the servant of God and the congregation. It was an acknowledgement of earnest religious endeavor through a spirit of prayer, as St. Francis said, "all temporal things must be subservient to it." In reality between the years 1865 and 1872, we have but one sign of how greatly Mother Maria Theresia strove to adjust the life of her Sisters to her conceived idea of Perpetual Adoration. It was not sufficient to achieve an active apostolate. The Sisters could only be steadfast and stand firm in their external activities if in the early years at the motherhouse they had been steeped in the spirit of prayer. At all events, it was necessary to make certain provisions for the motherhouse that did not depend solely upon the Sisters.

Mother Maria Theresia wrote to the bishop on February 4, 1868, in the following vein:

> With benevolent sanction of our Most Reverend Father and Bishop, our chief objective as Poor Franciscans of Perpetual Adoration is to pray before the tabernacle in hourly rotation, day and night, for the universal and special intentions of Holy Mother Church. In every hour certain prayers will be said for our dearly beloved Holy Father and also for our ardently cherished Bishop and Master. In addition at various periods of the day, together with our

> orphan children, additional prayers will ascend to heaven for His Holiness and Your Excellency. Now we should also like to offer our prayers conjointly with the fervent and devout souls of the town parish in honor of the Sacred Heart for the vicissitudes of Holy Mother Church. Therefore I beg Your Excellency most earnestly for the love of God for your gracious permission to conduct an evening devotion to the Sacred Heart every Sunday in our convent chapel. The inhabitants of Olpe love to participate in the devotion of the Poor Franciscans and confidently turn to the Sacred Heart to pray very specially for the Holy Father and for Your Excellency. Devotions in the local parish Church on Sundays close about four o'clock in the afternoon. The devotions in our chapel would not interfere with these. With confidence in Your Excellency, I venture a second request — on Thursday Sexagesima called the Feast of Atonement, on which the Blessed Sacrament is exposed in some congregations of Perpetual Adoration — to offer reparation to our dear Lord for the many dishonors he suffers in the mystery of his love especially on Shrove Tuesday and the closing days of the Carnival. We beg Your Excellency to grant us permission for exposition of the Blessed Sacrament on that day. We shall certainly double our petitions for the Holy Father and for our Bishop.
>
> As a poor child of St. Francis, a beggar, I venture to ask a third request. St. Joseph, who was such a loving protector and foster father of the Savior, is also our foster father. Will Your Excellency permit us exposition of the Blessed Sacrament during Holy Mass in the morning on March 19, the feast of St. Joseph, and again during the devotions in the evening?

On February 9, 1868, the bishop conferred with Superior Kaiser regarding the requests of Mother Maria Theresia to obtain his opinion, and instructed him to consult the priests of the Olpe parish, for it depended upon their willingness to permit this added service. The superior consulted Father Hengstebeck in Olpe. Previously, the priests who had been in Olpe, Father Lower, Vicar

Schroeder, Vicar Droege, and assistant Director Buesse, had declared themselves willing to conduct the devotions Mother Maria Theresia requested. Father Hengstebeck was not opposed to the devotions; however he judged that it might become burdensome to one or other priest because of the duration of the devotions.

On March 4, 1868, the superior wrote to the bishop that he thought the requested solemn adoration for the Great day of Atonement and for the feast of St. Joseph could readily be granted; but the Sunday devotions could be permitted from the beginning of November until the end of March, or for every first Sunday of the month throughout the year. In this connection the superior made some very characteristic remarks about Mother Maria Theresia. He said: "The granting of all the petitions might easily lead to further petitions, for the pious desires of a woman can easily overstep appropriate bounds, if all are granted — moreover it is true Venerable Mother Maria Theresia without doubt will have many requests of this nature in her mind." The superior understood the servant of God very well. He recognized that just in the point of adoration she strove for the utmost; thus he advised not to grant her requests in their entirety, for she would soon follow with others of a similar nature. At all events his characterization of Mother Maria Theresia is noteworthy; as "good Mother," "really worthy Mother." This characterization came from a spiritual person, whose contacts were many, who knew her well, and whose word carried weight.

CHAPTER VII

THE KULTURKAMPF

The year 1872 brought about a transfer in the office of spiritual superior. Father Kaiser, who had been the superior of the congregation, was transferred from Rhode to Bremen near Werl. Mother Maria Theresia was not passive in this change of superiors. Much depended upon the person selected to this office for the congregation, since religious life was threatened more and more in Germany. She realized that the bishop himself would give great consideration to finding a qualified spiritual man for this position, one whom the Sisters could unhesitatingly trust. Thus the servant of God with great sincerity wrote to the bishop on June 26, 1872:

> Through the present transfer of our Reverend Father superior we are temporarily in a very great dilemma. After we Sisters prayed for enlightenment and deliberated among ourselves, we cannot refrain from begging Your Excellency kindly to send Reverend Vicar Schroeder, who in an untiring spirit of sacrifice and love had been confessor for our congregation for a long period of time, as our provisionally appointed spiritual superior. Father Schroeder through long service among us has won the love of the entire congregation and possesses the confidence of all the Sisters and also the love and admiration of the members of the Olpe parish. Father Rector Klueppel and also assistant Rector Tigges serve the hospital. Toward the pastors in Wenden or in Drolshagen we cannot turn with confidence for we are unable to find in them the qualities requisite for the office. To be without spiritual direction in these difficult days would be dangerous especially as we live so far distant from our bishop. Most likely the pastorate in Rhode will soon be filled, and the future pastor of Rhode may be the one our dear Lord has destined for our superior at a later time.

Her prodding had the desired results. On July 2, Vicar Schroeder was appointed superior. With great zeal he conducted this office until his death in 1876. Then Dean Pielsticker of Attendorn assumed the functions of the office without a formal appointment, for it was the period of the *Kulturkampf.*

In all probability there is not a biography written of a founder or a foundress, or a history of a religious congregation in the nineteenth century, that does not contain a chapter on the *Kulturkampf.* Also, in the life and activities of Mother Maria Theresia this period has left its impress. In many respects the state, in fact, was not so brutal as that under the nationalistic Social Regime of Hitler. The measures of the state in its actions against the Church left little to be desired. Basically the *Kulturkampf* was a sharp reaction against the growing strength of the Catholic Church. Similar reactions against the Church took place outside of Germany as well as in many German lands. However, when the *Kulturkampf* is mentioned the Prussian State stands out foremost. Why this? This question needs a more comprehensive explanation for only then will the difficulties that confronted the Poor Franciscans of Olpe and their combat be clarified.

HISTORY OF THE PRECEDING PERIOD

In Prussia during the first half of the nineteenth century, a bitter conflict arose between Church and state, inflamed chiefly by the question of mixed marriages. The fact was that the Catholic Church required that the non-Catholic partner promised to agree to the Catholic rearing of all the children. During the arguments, the Archbishop of Cologne, Klemens August of Droste-Vischering, was arrested on November 20, 1837, as prisoner of the State and brought to the stronghold of Minden. This so-called "Cologne Affair," a deed of violence, happened in the Catholic western section of the Prussian territory, in the Rhineland and Westphalia, keeping the sharpest protests and universal provocations aroused. To quell the anger of the multitude, the government finally gave in.

With the new king, Frederick William IV, Prussia had a monarch who placed great significance on religion and was prepared to give due justice to the Catholic Church. Under his administration the regulation by which an ecclesiastical edict required the permission of the government was abolished. The bishops were again permitted free communication with Rome. Heretofore the Prussian bishops were allowed only such transactions as were regulated by the state. In 1841, the Minister of Public Worship and Education had an office for Catholic Counseling and one for the Evangelical, that is, Protestant and Lutheran. Finally the state relinquished all interference with mixed marriages and left that area to the jurisdiction of the bishops.

The Prussian State, after the confusions of the 1848 revolution organized a new system of government and rose to power in 1850, permitted further liberties to the Church. The government granted the churches, both Evangelical and Catholic, the power to regulate their own affairs and to administer and transact their own business. Thus the Catholic Church was able to develop with energy in Prussia. In consequence, the state through its secularization acquired large tracts of Catholic holdings. As to the Catholic orders the universal right of "freedom of association" worked to their advantage. Thus many newly founded congregations and monasteries resulted in a springtime of religious orders. There was scarcely another German land in which the Catholic Church, in a general or in a particular way, enjoyed such a fruitful era in its religious orders.

The state also was very well satisfied with this blossoming of religious orders. The Prussian King William I even in 1866 often called attention to it. The state experienced how the numerous religious energetically and selflessly undertook the education of youth, the care of the sick and the orphans. These endeavors for the welfare and social progress of the people won appreciative approbation.

Soon, however, discords had crept into the fine relationship between state and Church. Anti-ecclesiastical liberals questioned anxiously whether the Catholic Church had not won too great an influence in the state. It had according to their thinking. The Prussian Chamber of Deputies, formed in 1852, was first called the "Catholic Parliamentary Party" and later in 1858, the "Central Parliamentary Party." A few years later, in 1866, Prussia won the war against Austria and also the Franco-Prussian War in 1870-1871. Austria and France had a predominantly Catholic population, while Prussia in spite of its greater Catholic holdings was predominantly Protestant. Winning both wars was considered a triumph for Protestantism over Catholicism by the National Liberal Party and celebrated as such. On January 18, 1871, the Prussian King was declared head of the German Empire, and attempts were made immediately by the Liberal Party to renew the previous Prussian-Church affair.

Pope Pius IX saw himself forced to speak out against the errors of his time through a special "Syllabus" issued on December 8, 1864, in which among other issues he rejected the trends of modern liberal culture which were in opposition to supernatural revelation. This caused a reaction of disapproval and enmity in the state *"Kultur"* on which naturally the opponents of the Church did not fail to capitalize. When Vatican Council I declared the Dogma of the Infallibility of the Pope on July 18, 1870, the opponents saw evidence that the Church was a danger to the state and above all threatened the Evangelical Empire. The danger of the so-called "Ultramontanism" was played up beyond measure. The powers decided to take liberty away from the church in Prussia again and as well as from all the churches in Germany in order to destroy their organization, to subjugate them completely to the state. Since with the removal of ecclesial political conflict, there emerged simultaneously a conflict of various philosophies of life in opposition to each other, the movement was soon designated as the *Kulturkampf,* or "struggle for civilization."

THE STATUTES OF THE KULTURKAMPF

The real force behind this conflict without doubt was Prince Otto von Bismarck, who at that time was chancellor of the new German Empire (1871-1890). He could count on the National Liberal Party to bolster his leadership. He could risk that the Minister of Public Worship and Education, Adalbert Falk (1872-1879), would carry out the measures of the conflict. The minister proved himself a loyal servant of his master. The *Kulturkampf* began in Prussia with the demonstrative abolishment of the Catholic section in the Department of Public Worship and Education on July 8, 1871. In December of 1871, the so-called "Pulpit-paragraph" of the German Penal Code was issued, and in March 1872, the Prussian school inspection rules were promulgated. The Ministerial Decree followed in June 1872, declaring that members of religious orders may no longer be employed as teachers in the schools; and where valid contracts had been issued, these were to be reported by the inspectors immediately. The law against the Jesuits and related orders was issued on July 4, 1872, by which the Jesuit order was abolished and expelled and its members banished.

The *Kulturkampf* reached its climax between May 11 and 14, 1873, by the issuing of the Prussian May Laws. These laws referred to the formation and employment of religious, the powers of ecclesiastical discipline, the limits of ecclesiastical criminal law, defections from the Church, and the organization of an imperial law court for the settlement of ecclesial affairs. As the Imperial Government had guaranteed independence and autonomy to the church, paragraphs relating to these measures were at first altered and then abolished completely in 1875. Justice by law was no longer a possibility, for injustice was rated as justice.

Bishops and clergy refusing to submit were fined, if not imprisoned. The archbishops of Cologne and Gnesen-Posen, as also the bishops of Paderborn, Breslau, Münster, and Limburg were deposed from their bishoprics by the state. Pope Pius IX in his encyclical of February 5, 1875, declared the laws to be in enmity to the Church and not binding. Thereupon, the state intensified its measures. It sought to render the priests docile by suspending clergymen's livelihood through the *"Sperr-Brotkorbgesetz"* beginning April 1875; in May of the same year it canceled the exemption of the clergy from military service.

The time had come for priests to offer the Holy Sacrifice of the Mass and to dispense the Sacraments secretly, for the state had forbidden the clergy to exercise their priestly functions. No replacement was permitted for a deceased priest. On May 31, 1875, the Cloister Decree was issued, which abolished all religious orders except those caring for the sick, and banished the members of the expelled orders from the country. In a deliberation of the decree a motion was made to the effect that as soon as possible the Catholic orders caring for the sick should also be abolished for they are the strongest propaganda for the Catholic Church. The motion would have carried had it not been for the Secretary of War of Kameke who spoke out clearly in their defense. He declared in the committee that he was not in a position to wage a possible war, if he did not have the Sisters of Mercy to care for health and sanitary conditions. He spoke in very clear terms of his experiences during the last war. But it was demanded that the Sisters adjust to all other social demands: for new investitures they must have permission of the state; they must be under the constant surveillance of the police; and they may be banished if they become irksome to the state.

The results of the *Kulturkampf* proved devastating to the Church in Prussia. In 1878, only four of the twelve bishops still functioned in office; convents and seminaries were closed; and about one thousand parishes were quarantined and no longer conducted regular services. Hundreds of priests and numerous religious were banished from the land. But the Catholics stood firm and won the combat under great hardships. Finally, in 1880 Bismarck began to relent gradually the laws of the *Kulturkampf.* But it was not until 1887 that a great number of the banished orders were able to return.

EFFECTS ON THE FRANCISCANS IN OLPE

During this period the Olpe Sisters experienced many difficulties. The important phases and the various laws of the *Kulturkampf* have been designated briefly. For from that point of view only can the sorrows endured by Mother Maria Theresia at that time be clearly understood. The Diocese of Paderborn and the town of Olpe were especially dealt a heavy blow. In Olpe the Reverend Hengstebeck died early in 1874. Bishop Konrad Martin appointed the former Vicar Schroeder as pastor there; in replacing a clergyman, he acted contrary to the May Laws. Because he had also replaced pastors in other places, on August 4, 1874, he was taken into custody, and sentenced to twelve weeks in prison. There followed adjudication of all episcopal rights and on the part of the state the suppression of all episcopal functions. Finally he was condemned to confinement for nine months in the citadel Wesel. From there he escaped to a foreign country on August 4, 1875. He died on July 16, 1879, in Mont St. Guibert in Belgium.

Since the parish in Olpe opposed the May Laws, all the property of the parish was confiscated, on August 4, 1875 including revenue, improvements, and sources of income. The state appointed the Commissar to keep a watch over the confiscated property. In addition the Reverend Schroeder of Olpe and the Reverend Cordes of Rhode were accused of taking census in a forbidden pastoral letter, but they were freed finally because of lack of sufficient evidence.

Although the plight of the bishop and pastor did not touch Mother Maria Theresia directly, it was all within close range. She suffered keenly with the Catholic Church in its oppression and very especially with the Bishop of Paderborn. She felt that a word of sympathy from her might give him some little joy. Thus she wrote to him on June 18, 1874:

> With deepest reverence and full of sorrow and sadness, I venture to send a few words expressing our inmost, sincere sympathy concerning the disastrous misfortune that has come to you, our most beloved, most reverend father and bishop, in conformity with the unsearchable designs of a provident God. Each one of us Sisters is gladly willing to endure all, if it will alleviate to some degree your grievous affliction. Still we can do little else than pray and sacrifice and this we do willingly day and night. May the Sacred Heart, knowing only goodness and mercy, be merciful to the oppressed Church and grant her peace and rest soon.

As this letter was written, an important step had been taken to obtain future economic security to the congregation. After the town had taken the initiative, a fear arose that the state might sooner or later seize the patrimony of the Church. The confiscation of the Papal territories in Italy reminded Germany of the secularization just seventy years ago. Was another expropriation of Church possessions threatening?

Under community property regulations at that time, all the property of the Sisters belonged to the bishopric of Paderborn. That was brought about through a donation gift negotiation of 1864. The Constitution of the Sisters contained the following clause in Chapter 2, Article 3a: "As children of St. Francis the congregation possesses no property and uses a home loaned by the bishop and a nearby garden with some real estate." This regulation gave further expression to Franciscan poverty without property. However, during the *Kulturkampf* there was real fear regarding the security of the congregation because the buildings belonged to the bishopric of Paderborn.

If this had effected only the Poor Franciscans, they would readily have awaited further developments. The Sisters would have acquiesced. But the superior knowing her responsibility, had to consider other aspects. She had the obligation to provide not only for the Sisters but for the upkeep of the buildings and the grounds, and also for the orphans and other needy persons. A weighty decision had to be made by Mother Maria Theresia whether the principle of "poverty without property" could in justice be preserved under present situations. In this predicament she turned to the bishop as advised by Mother Francis Schervier. The bishop himself had felt concern to provide security, as far as possible, to existing congregations laboring under great difficulties. Through a notarized deed, dated July 1874, he had the donation gift of 1864 revoked; the real estate was made over to Mother Maria Theresia under her maiden name of Aline Bonzel. The attorney of this transaction for Mother Maria Theresia was Dr. Kaufmann, her brother-in-law, who also was the doctor for the Olpe Sisters. It was considered plausible not to enter the real estate under the name of the congregation, for as possession of the order it would have been endangered at that time. Instead, it was designated as the property of a single person of the state.

Other orders acted differently to obtain security for their possessions and convents. At this time there were many fervent Catholics belonging to the royalty. They obtained possession of convents by a fictitious sort of purchase in order to save the congregations. Later after the banishment terminated, the convents were returned. Mother Maria Theresia took a different way, which in her situation was feasible since it dealt with her parental inheritance. But the transfer of property to her name became a sad event. For after the arrest of the bishop of the diocese, the state appointed Himly, assessor for the government, as royal commissioner of the diocese. He complained that the transfer of property on the part of the diocese to the superior of Olpe was underhanded; and consequently the notarized deed of 1874 was not valid in law. This caused a long drawn-out lawsuit which reached the appellate court in Arnsberg. June 1, 1878, the court finally reached a verdict: the plaintiff lost the case and had to pay all the costs of the lawsuit. The destiny of the congregation had depended on the outcome of this trial. As urgently as the Sisters stormed Heaven, so sincerely joyous were they at its outcome. That St. Joseph was their great helper in their hour of need impressed itself very deeply into their memory. On April 16, 1872, the Sisters, five in number, had first added "of St. Joseph" to each Sister's name at investiture. Mother Maria Theresia made this promise during her building program. It appears that placing all her Sisters under the protection of St. Joseph in 1872, had connections with the *Kulturkampf* also. In this sense the name "of St. Joseph" later came to be understood by the Sisters.

Was the revoking of property rights not a deviation from the ideals of the congregation? Did not "poverty without property" become an illusion when the superior herself became the possessor and transacted business with the public? Does this not show clearly here that the principle of the lack of all property as practiced by St. Francis was no longer feasible in the changed world of the nineteenth century? Did one not follow a romantic ideal that was shattered by the reality of life? What then remained after the bishop returned the property rights?

As long as the bishop retained the legal ownership, one could of course allude to and affirm the living in poverty without property. But really was poverty without property assured, although honestly, through this procedure? The question is justified. Fundamentally the Franciscan "will" to be poor cannot be forced through any external measures. It depends much more upon the question of personal will, whether a person wishes to renounce legal ownership rights or not. One who is really striving to become poor in heart cannot rest satisfied that legally he possesses no property, but must constantly scrutinize himself personally relative to poverty and repeatedly forego all claims of possession. In the life of St. Francis one can clearly see his essential detachment from all possessions which the egoism of man loves so much to display before men of the world.

Mother Maria Theresia understood St. Francis very well in this regard. Therefore she could, also after 1874, advance the idea of Franciscan poverty to her Sisters as detachment from all possessions as the central idea of poverty in her congregation. She did not have to give up her ideal of poverty but could retain it in its entirety and explain its profound spirit to her Sisters. This is manifest in the instructions she gave the eight Sisters in preparation for their final vows, February 21-22, 1875. Her last direction, which gives a summation of her explanations of poverty in spirit and the formation of the Sisters in this aspect, is given here in two brief phrases as guiding principles in their formation. These are "renounce and endure" and "desire nothing and refuse nothing." Thus the servant of God endeavored to guide her Sisters in the exterior insecurity of the *Kulturkampf* and in the interior security of comprehensive poverty. As an example for her Sisters she pointed to Christ who renounced all and chose poverty. She closed her discourses with a reference to Christ: "According to his example we shall refuse nothing and desire nothing. All that Divine Providence sends us we shall accept with the tranquility of mind, whether it be in Germany or in America. May God grant us this great grace." As superior she was definitely better informed and aware of the perils of the times than her Sisters. One recognizes readily how earnestly she endeavored to be a true spiritual leader to her Sisters and to prepare them mentally and spiritually for all that might come. She had many cares indeed, but she created no panic among the Sisters and led them to certitude, that characteristic mark of souls who place their full confidence in God.

How involved the police supervision of convents could become for the administration of superiors is clearly shown by the reports to the mayor. On November 2, 1872, an ordinance was issued from the office of the district magistrate that every change of locale and position of the Sisters must be reported. The reports of December 28, 1872, and of May 20, 1875, are examples of conformity with the regulation. To the local Mayor Halbfas: "Hereby I inform you that Sister Maria Agnes Hund has been transferred to St. Joseph Convent, Sister Aloysia Lennenberg to Hüsten, Sister Mechtildis Lennenberg and Sister Aegidia Schwartecoppe to Wissen. Besides Sister Maria Angela Puppe has been transferred from Herschberg and Sister Theresia Sonntag from Elspe to Olpe." Until January 2, 1899, the Office of Mayor had received annual reports concerning the Sisters and their positions together with lists of Sisters living in Olpe and all transfers made during the years. The first detailed report was made on May 17, 1873, stating:

> Our motherhouse is located in Olpe. The objectives of the congregation are: the care of the sick in homes and in hospitals; the care of orphan children and otherwise the practice of the spiritual works of mercy. Our congregation is self-supporting and not dependent on any other order; our superior and delegate of the Most Reverend Diocesan Bishop is Reverend Vicar Schroeder in Olpe. Toward the end of September 1859, the congregation was founded in Olpe. In the beginning there were three members. Now it numbers forty-seven members in the motherhouse and in six other foundations. The congregation is administered by a superior and her assistant. There are thirty-five professed Sisters and ten novices. The congregation has no lay Sisters.

If one marvels at the courage of those who in these troubled times remained loyally true to their religious vocation, then one must surely call it holy gallantry to permit young girls to apply for the religious habit. Thus Mother Maria Theresia experienced great joy when six postulants were admitted on June 2, 1873, and two more on August 12, of the same year; again on June 2, 1874, two were invested and on May 18, 1875, five more. After that there were no more investitures in Germany for some time. The Cloister Decree of May 1875, forbade the Catholic orders to admit any new members unless permission be given by the government. It was evident that the objective of this decree was the extinction of all religious orders. The great uncertainty of this period made it advisable for Sisters in temporary vows to renew annually for one year. That is what the Sisters did in February of 1873. Since the congregation did not depend upon Germany alone for its continuance, the Sisters were permitted to pronounce their final vows somewhat later.

The administrative public authorities kept close surveillance that convents did not transgress the anti-religious order laws. Many an incident is related of how by legitimate strategy tricks were played on the state during these strenuous days of the "Kampf." Mother Maria Theresia tried this once and with good results. Sister Hildegardis Schelle relates the incident:

> One afternoon she received a call from the Mayor N.N. that within one hour his officials would visit the convent. What could they want? Mother Maria Theresia divined their objective. Without delay the wise Mother gave orders that all the sought after should seclude themselves in the convent garden. After this she met the officials calmly and respectfully. To the inquiry: "Are there any newly invested Sisters here in this house?" Without telling a falsehood she could answer, "No!" Whereupon the stern man of the law withdrew.

The incident must have happened shortly after May 22, 1877. At that time more Sisters were preparing to travel to America. Three postulants were in readiness to go. Since they were destined for America, they were invested secretly in the stillness of the night on May 22, 1877. On the following day they laid aside their religious habit and in secular dress remained a month longer in the motherhouse. Most likely someone had knowledge of the nocturnal investiture and reported it. Thereupon, Mayor Halbfas had to follow up with some sort of investigation. The mayor had given a one-hour notice before the appearance of the officials. Evidently, he did this as many other good Catholics did under similar circumstances, namely, he effected failure in spite of fulfilling official duties. He gave opportunity to those concerned to be prepared when the officials arrived to inquire if there were any newly invested members in the house. In fact they were not in the house but hidden in the garden. That the officials also inquired about foreign members, points to the fact that the report was to rest on very exact information. The Sisters, however, were destined for foreign countries. The whole situation appears as a scheme and was evidently so arranged that nothing resulted from it. The mayor could report the incident to the higher authorities as one without incidence.

One must remember that the mayor was the brother of Reverend Father Vincenz Halbfas, who later as Provincial of the Franciscans helped the Olpe Sisters in North America.

Even though one or the other hardship was avoided and passed over, crucial situations were unavoidable. The state also learned much from this struggle and endeavored to close the back doors by means of which people tried to evade the published decrees. Mother Maria Theresia also received an edict, dated April 7, 1877, issued by the Minister of the Interior and the Minister of Spiritual Affairs, which read:

> The understanding of the Superior General that the profession of vows relative to novices need not have the approval of the state, does not hold. As far as the novitiate is concerned, the religious belong temporarily to the congregation. Their final reception depends on the final profession of vows. Article 2 of the Law of May 31, 1875, refers to these as also to the regulations of universal provincial law, (1160 ff II. ii), that the entrance into a convent and the profession of vows requires the knowledge and permission of the state. In the nineteen cases mentioned no formal profession of vows should take place; the respective novices should make their profession into the hands of the superior general and not those of a delegate of the bishop. It is not his business. The forms used in the profession are not subject to state control and therefore profession, whether temporary or final, limited or lasting, with or without the permission of the diocesan leader, will be valid only with the previously obtained permission of the state. Accordingly the superior general is forbidden the temporary profession of novices without permission of

> the state; nor may she inaugurate the return of members who have left the congregation without that permission.

This edict was not occasioned by Mother Maria Theresia, but it affected her and her congregation.

It cannot be detected in this edict with what bitterness the state considered the religious orders. But this is not the only discouraging point. The Sisters were forbidden to accept new members. Also, they were systematically restricted in their apostolate. On December 23, 1875, Falk, the Minister of Public Worship and Education, issued a directive from Berlin pertaining to this. It is noticed that this directive though issued January 3, 1876, by the government in Arnsberg to the district magistrate in Olpe, was not forwarded to Mother Maria Theresia by the mayor until January 31 of the same year. Subordinate officials could dare to delay sending official messages, but not indefinitely. The local magistrate received the following communication:

> Most humbly, I inform Your Honor that the Minister of Public Worship and Education has ordered the following matters by means of the Rescripts of December 23, 1875, No. 2222 B. The local foundation of the Poor Franciscans, who are engaged in the activities of caring for the sick and of conducting an institution for orphans, by permission of Article 2 of the Decree of May 31, is no longer to operate the orphanage. The minister ordered further that the private elementary school conducted by the convent is to be closed by Easter of this current year. The children, from that time, are to attend the local elementary school. By October 1 of this year the children are to be provided for otherwise. I have informed Your Honor and take it for granted that you carry out these ministerial rescripts and make further arrangements for their publication.

The disbandment of the orphanage began. Forty children were returned to parents or guardians. The Sisters were obligated to release their charges into an uncertain future. Otherwise, why had these children been entrusted to them previously if not that the Sisters were considered better prepared to care for them than either parents or guardians? By this action, the title "orphanage Sisters" by which the Sisters were known by the people came to an end. Whether or not the magistrate thought the disbanding of the orphanage progressed at too slow a pace and needed some prodding from him, he appeared personally on the scene and repeated the demand of dissolving the institution. With but little discussion, Mother Maria Theresia laid bare the situation. She assembled all the children still at the orphanage and brought them into the presence of the magistrate, saying: "Now, Lord Magistrate, take all these children with you." He of course could not do that, nor could the decree of the minister be abolished.

After the orphanage was closed, Mother Maria Theresia endeavored at least through a sewing school for children to save a part of the Sisters' apostolate among youth. Through information from the mayor, October 20, 1876, it was learned that this activity was forbidden also to religious according to the decree of May 31, 1875. Did the servant of God have a foreboding when she struggled so bravely to retain the nursing of the sick in Olpe?

As a climax to difficulties, Reverend Superior Schroeder of Olpe died on June 19, 1876. On account of the disfavorable times, a new superior could not be appointed. Father Pielsticker of Attendorn assumed the duties of superior temporarily. He did all within his power. But it was always a short distance to Attendorn when one wished to confer in person. A superior in Olpe could have helped and counseled more.

The situation grew extremely severe. The presence of great difficulties can readily be gleaned from the few words Mother Maria Theresia wrote in a letter of January 12, 1877:

> Our orphan children according to the arrangement of the government should have been placed in homes or suitably cared for otherwise by October 1 of last year; the Sisters are engaged in the care of the sick. If the fortune of many other congregations (in conformity with law) were to become ours, then the selling of our house and acreage would provide the means by which we could emigrate into another country." (VII 6)

Still she did not lose hope. On August 12, 1877, the Sisters confidently elected her again as superior general. Thus it happened every three to six years. The office of the major superior and the person of Mother Maria Theresia had become an identity with the Sisters; they had no other thought on the subject. Although banishment of the Sisters was feared, the servant of God continued the construction work on the new chapel at the motherhouse. To her it was a faithful confidence in God at a time when there was no room for hope. Construction was slow. Materials were wanting. But Vicar Droege was able to offer the Holy Sacrifice of the Mass with the Congregation of Sisters for the first time in the new chapel on the First Sunday of Advent 1877. Are not the prayers of the First Sunday of Advent filled with hope giving new inspiration in these dark times?

> To you I lift up my soul;
> in you, O my God, I trust;
> Let me not be put to shame;
> Let not my enemies exult over me.
> No one who waits for You shall be
> put to shame.

Poor Franciscans of Perpetual Adoration, that was their title. And that title became an acknowledgement. The times led them into the bitterest, almost irremediable poverty. They were accepted by God in the full meaning of the term. But they remained steadfast through adoration and total surrender of their lives to him for whose homage they built a chapel in their poverty.

CHAPTER VIII

NORTH AMERICA

"Accept all with equanimity that Divine Providence sends! Whether in Germany or in America! May God give us this great grace!" With these words Mother Maria Theresia closed her instructions on February 22, 1875, to eight of her Sisters in preparation for their final vows. They were: Sisters Paula, Bonaventura, Clara, Angela, Margaretha, Agnes, Agatha, and Bernardis. Was it definitely known on the eve of their profession day to Sister Clara, Agatha, and Bonaventura that on November 25 of the current year that they, together with three other Sisters, would depart for North America? Scarcely. There are many indications that Mother Maria Theresia harbored quite definite notions concerning the possibilities offered her congregation at that time.

Not only in Olpe were thoughts of America discussed at that time. Many congregations which found the exercise of their apostolates impossible in Germany, especially in Prussia, looked for new openings in other lands for their members. Above all the powerful development in the United States of America attracted attention. Also many emigrants of Germany had already settled there. To provide for the spiritual needs of all in that rapidly developing country placed heavy burdens on the priests and religious. Disastrous as the *Kulturkampf* was for the fatherland, just so filled with blessings was it for the Catholic Church overseas. Banished from Germany by the state, or restricted to the utmost in their apostolates, great multitudes of German religious crossed the ocean in search of new areas of activity in the service of God and mankind. It was mainly the young who took the step. As a result the Catholic Church, especially in the United States, was enriched with a numerous and valuable commitment of forces.

The Franciscans of Saxony, Province of the Holy Cross, had taken the same step. They adjusted readily to the New World. Mother Maria Theresia always considered it well to keep close ties with the Franciscan Fathers, who had often given retreats in the motherhouse at Olpe. Thus the Mother in Olpe certainly was well aware of the adjustment of the Franciscans to American conditions, after their monasteries had been closed by the state during the *Kulturkampf*. That knowledge most likely awakened an idea in Olpe of doing likewise. Because of the uncertain conditions at home, a responsible superior must naturally consider the possibility of having a suitable new area of activity for her Sisters, should there be an eventual banishment from the homeland. Nevertheless great as was her confidence in God, Mother Maria Theresia realized that man under adverse conditions may not remain passive.

Her first contact with ecclesiastical authorities in North America was occasioned by Father Steinbusch in Wissen. To him the Poor Franciscans are indebted for very much. In 1871, he made possible a new foundation for the congregation in Wissen. Toward the end of the *Kulturkampf*, he as a political representative in Berlin pledged much for the Olpe Sisters. Through a Franciscan who at the time of the *Kulturkampf* went to America, he became acquainted with Bishop Joseph Dwenger of Fort Wayne, Indiana. Father Steinbusch pointed out to the bishop that a Congregation of Sisters in Olpe was harboring the thought of sending Sisters to America. As the bishop was very interested, he made a trip to Olpe in person to secure help for his diocese and if possible reach a concrete agreement. He was able to assure Mother Maria Theresia that his diocese offered a large and fruitful area for genuine missionary work. Both were of the opinion that the Sisters could begin by caring for the sick in Lafayette, Indiana. The bishop and the servant of God were both receivers of gifts and donors as well. The Olpe superior gave proficient helpers for the Fort Wayne diocese, and she received assurance that her congregation would have permanent existence and an apostolate in a new land. The date fixed for the departure of the first Sisters was in the fall of 1875.

As we have seen in February 1875, Mother Maria Theresia began to prepare her Sisters mentally and spiritually for adjustment to this new development. For their first foundation in Lafayette, it was planned that Sister Clara serve as superior and

Sisters Bonaventura, Agatha, Rosa, Augustine, and Alphonsa accompany her. They embarked on the *Holland* from Rotterdam on November 25, 1875. Mother Maria Theresia had been accustomed to accompany the Sisters to each new foundation. Unable to do it this time, she and Sister Paula, her assistant, did accompany them to the ship. The parting was not easy. The thought must have occurred to them that probably many more Sisters of the congregation would be making a similar journey. The disastrous conditions in the homeland forced such a bold venture. It was undertaken with confidence in divine Providence.

On the evening of December 12, 1875, Sister Clara could write to Mother Maria Theresia that they had arrived in New York after a "very fortunate journey and that they were well and in good spirits." They remained in New York for two days with the Franciscan Sisters whose motherhouse is in Aachen, and were warmly received. Again the Olpe Sisters experienced the ever ready and helpful assistance of Mother Francis Schervier. On December 14, the Sisters ventured on the last part of their journey and reached their destination, Lafayette, Indiana. They first turned to the bishop. He had, upon his return from Europe, contacted Father Accursius Beine, a Franciscan, born in Luegeneder near Warburg, then pastor of St. Boniface Church in Lafayette. He would care for the Sisters upon their arrival in the city and help to facilitate their beginning. The bishop had evidently taken for granted that the Sisters were supplied with sufficient money to begin the construction of a hospital immediately. He had not reckoned that they were poor not only in name but also in fact. Besides their great readiness for service, they had brought only their necessary personal effects and no sums of money whatever. Their money just paid their traveling expenses, for Olpe undoubtedly did not realize distances in America; hence, no funds remained with which the Sisters could establish themselves. The whole undertaking as seen here shows a complete and implicit trust in divine Providence. Also, their knowledge of the language was meager as they touched land in the New World.

Still the venture was successful. Sometime later, August 13, 1878, Father Accursius wrote Sister Therese, his sister, concerning this beginning. In his letter, he described how the bishop had contacted him and asked him as a Franciscan to care for the Franciscan Sisters when they arrived. His letter to her is as follows:

> The Most Reverend Bishop told me that the Sisters would bring sufficient funds with them from Germany to begin the construction of a hospital immediately. Naturally I was prepared to assist them with counsel and deed. The Sisters went to the bishop first. He telegraphed me immediately. I had to rush about to find a house that I could rent for them. I soon found one. The Sisters, six in number, came to Lafayette during the night in bitter cold weather. I met them at the station and conducted them to a guest house near the station. In the morning I discovered that the Sisters had no money left. "The realization came upon me," Sister Clara said, "I have begun this work and I must also finish it." After they took possession of their new residence, we arranged all provisionally according to their needs. I obligated myself to say Holy Mass for them in their chapel twice a week and with permission of the bishop installed the Blessed Sacrament. That was a great joy for the Sisters. In the spring of the year, I built a nice hospital for the Sisters and had them teach in a school for girls connected with St. Boniface Church. Now they are well established.

From this letter one readily senses the good fortune the Sisters had in encountering this energetic Franciscan. From the information the bishop had given him, he had expected an entirely different situation. But when he recognized that really poor Franciscans had come, he managed without any complaint, seized the situation as it was, and assisted in every way possible. The residence rented for the Sisters was located on Cincinnati Street. There the Sisters began the nursing of the sick without delay. Here they made the necessary contacts with the people. The residents of Lafayette soon recognized what a treasure they had in these Sisters. Early in 1876, Mr. Albert Wagner donated a large tract of land for the building of a hospital and a convent. With genuine American energy the construction began in the spring. Bishop Dwenger officiated at the laying of the cornerstone on the feast of the Holy Trinity, June 11, 1876. Construction progressed rapidly. On the feast of St. Elizabeth, November 19, 1876, Father Accursius dedicated the new structure and thus ended his task of supervision.

Here God had opened a door into the future for the congregation. The Sisters found numerous benefactors. The great difficulties under which the Sisters struggled in Germany were absent here. The singular happened: while in Olpe the education of youth was denied the Sisters, in the United States it was offered them together with the nursing of the sick. Thus in 1877, the Sisters undertook teaching in the German St. Boniface School in Lafayette, Indiana. They definitely incurred difficulties in the beginning, especially in adapting to the American mentality and meeting the standards of the country. But with diligent work they made strides and the confidence of the people grew. Soon six Sisters were engaged in teaching two hundred children – surely sufficient reason for thanking God most heartily. They had been in Lafayette less than two years when they were already able to invest two American postulants, August 25, 1877.

In Germany at this same time Mother Maria Theresia needed to muster all her energy and wisdom to save, at least to some degree, the apostolate of the Sisters. In America, on the other hand, there was a most unexpected development. Tasks and possibilities multiplied so rapidly that the number of Sisters, although increased by two, was not sufficient for the work. More Sisters were needed. Willingly and with a purpose to serve God in the religious state, three candidates were prepared to go to America. They felt that in their homeland there was no opportunity to live as religious. Where youth manifested such clear signs of a divine call as to include the will to leave the fatherland, Mother Maria Theresia thought this wish should joyfully be granted. She invested them secretly during the night. Then they laid their habits aside until they reached America. Judging from the existing laws of the *Kulturkampf*, this was indeed a great risk. But the issue proved successful, as seen. In secular clothes the three novices embarked at Rotterdam on June 23, 1877. Again Mother accompanied her Sisters to the ship.

The number of Sisters in Lafayette had now increased substantially. There surely was a constant flow of communication between Lafayette and Olpe. Mother Maria Theresia urgently fostered this exchange of correspondence with North America. She especially felt the necessity of manifesting herself a true mother to these Sisters, and with words of advice to further their religious spirit. Through the letters she was also well informed of the actual details surrounding their arrival in Lafayette. However, even the best exchange of correspondence cannot take the place of a visit in person. She felt obligated to convince herself that both the locality and the situation were suitable. As a possibility of further foundations existed, the visit was deemed advisable. Many arrangements had to be made first to insure the unity of the congregation in spite of the great distances involved and, second, to give the American group the necessary freedom to carry on normal business negotiations and still remain in unity. The superior, Sister Clara, in Lafayette was ill and a new superior would have to be appointed.

Thus Mother Maria Theresia decided to make the trip to America. On August 12, 1877, she had been reelected as Mother General. Healthwise she considered that she was well able to undertake the journey, and on May 4, 1878, embarked at Bremen. Sister Deogratias accompanied her as the designated new superior in Lafayette. Although enroute the weather was often stormy, the trip as a whole was good. The joy of the Sisters in America over this visit can readily be imagined. While in Lafayette, Mother Maria Theresia had the great pleasure of accepting the final profession of several of her Sisters, and also the investiture of the third American postulant from Lafayette. The servant of God remained here with the Sisters for an entire year. To learn the day-to-day life through personal experience must have proved very valuable to Mother Maria Theresia. She knew that conditions in Germany were well taken care of by her able assistant, Sister M. Paula.

While in America, Mother Maria Theresia in person established a new foundation, namely, in Columbus, Nebraska. The German Franciscan, Rev. Ambrose Jansen had invited her there. In October 1878, the servant of God and Sister Deogratias made the seven-hundred mile trip to Columbus. Because of traveling conditions at that time, the trip was not only difficult but hazardous. At one time the train was stopped on the open prairie in the middle of the night. All the passengers had to alight. Until the train could go farther, they waited in a lonely public house. It just happened to be a Saturday. A Sunday without Holy Mass was unthinkable for Mother Maria Theresia. Upon inquiry about a Catholic Church nearby, she was informed that a missionary lived in the vicinity. Both Sisters left the strange train in search and found him in his residence. In answer to their inquiry he told them that Mass would not be celebrated until 11:00 a.m. and not there but in the next mission place. Undoubtedly, Mother Maria Theresia and Sister Deogratias were in need of some refreshment, but theirs was a great desire to receive Communion. At that time a complete fast from midnight was still required. Consequently, both Sisters waived the offered refreshment, and later accompanied the priest to his next mission and there attended Holy Mass and received Holy Communion.

Mother Maria Theresia had many other adventurous experiences in North America. Unfortunately, it is not known definitely whether the above mentioned incident happened during this trip or a later one. But since the servant of God recognized the special protection of divine Providence in this incident, the details should not be passed over in silence.

Once when Mother Maria Theresia was traveling and the train stopped for the night, she and her Sister companion were obliged to lodge in a lonely and weird guest house. Suddenly in the night they were awakened by distressing cries from a nearby room and among the voices distinctly recognized that of the landlord. The next morning with all possible haste they departed from that den of thieves. Somewhat later they related the episode to a priest who knew that area, and he asked immediately: "Did you say anything?" She answered, "No." He said, "You have a good guardian angel, that you are still alive, for the house in which you were is a bad house. If you had said anything, they perhaps would have killed you, lest you betray them."

At another time Mother Maria Theresia with another Sister arrived in a town in which neither was acquainted. They confidently asked a seemingly respectable man for information. He indicated exactly the direction in which they should go and added that he himself had some business in that area, too. The Sisters followed his directions. But as they went on they became more and more apprehensive. The streets became narrower and the rabble milled about among the lanes and alleys looking boldly and audaciously at the Sisters. At this moment a man stepped out from around the corner and walked directly to the Sisters, and said: "Sisters, I believe you are going the wrong way, you should go in the opposite direction. Hurry, get out of this section of the town." They had been sent into the most disreputable quarter of the town. When the Sisters turned to thank the kindly stranger, he had disappeared.

On a journey through hilly country in North America where the road ran flush along a high precipice, Mother Maria Theresia suddenly saw a stranger at the coach door who commanded her to alight. Since he was a stranger, she gave no heed to his command. But again he ordered her to leave the coach. The Sisters becoming fearful stepped from the vehicle to make the hazardous way on foot. The driver tried to reason with them that there was no danger nor cause for alarm. But after a short distance the horse suddenly shied and with driver and coach plunged into the abyss with a deafening noise. Mother Maria Theresia attributed their deliverance from danger to the powerful help of St. Joseph whose care and protection she always sought in all her travels.

After wearisome travel, the Sisters finally reached Columbus. Upon investigating the situation there, they determined to make a new foundation. To secure money for the construction of a hospital the Sisters undertook the tedious task of canvassing to solicit funds. Columbus shortly received word that Sister Clara had died on October 26, 1878. On February 4, 1879, Sister Agatha, the assistant to the provincial, also died. This double loss was a very hard blow for it affected the two Sisters who wielded the administration of the small congregation, and through their solicitous care became the actual foundresses of the apostolate in America. Sister Deogratias was appointed superior to replace Sister Clara, and became the director of the American foundations. In the spring of 1879, she and her assistant went to Columbus.

Under great difficulties, the construction of St. Mary Hospital had been completed and now was ready for occupancy.

Before returning to Germany, Mother Maria Theresia had made another trip to Columbus, Nebraska, to study the progress and to bid farewell to the Sisters. From Columbus she wrote to Sister Deogratias in Lafayette and among other matters informed her that a postulant, Maria Schneider, would enter: "I have accepted her and may God grant his blessing that all may go well." Two days later she wrote from Hoboken: "This afternoon we shall embark; the Blessed Mother will be our help; Sister Hyacinth and Sister Hildegardis both send their heartiest greetings to you. As I have learned several priests will make the voyage with us. I must close. The ship will leave port at 2:00 p.m. It is now 12:00 noon. God speed!" (I 2).

A brief account of the journey was received on June 13:

> Most likely you have learned that the steamship *Rhein* arrived on the 5th of this month. We had a wonderful voyage, weather and wind were mostly favorable; and we were free from seasickness. A thousand thanks to God for all his love and mercy! We were taken to Bremerhafen by a small steamboat and reached our land destination about 8:00 a.m., and Bremen by 10:00 a.m. We had hoped to arrive in our convent by evening. But since we could drive only to Hagen, we stayed at Hüsten, and arrived safely at our convent on Saturday evening. (I 3)

The letter also gave news from Olpe:

> We now have a new altar in our chapel. On Sunday, the feast of the Blessed Trinity, the Vicar said the first Mass on that altar. Oh, how I rejoiced! God be praised and thanked for his great love and mercy! The new Way of the Cross should also be beautiful and be here soon. Father Tigges ordered the pictures in handsome frames. A new communion rail has been ordered also, and Johann Schmidt is decorating the chapel. All the Sisters are well and concerned. My dear Sister Deogratias, how overwhelmed I am by all this. Let us endeavor to become, to be, and to remain

> true and good children of St. Francis. God's grace will not be wanting to us.

It was typical of Mother Maria Theresia to admonish her Sisters in such a way as to include herself in the admonition. Thus from the same letter:

> May the Most Sweet Heart of Jesus imbue us all with a true religious spirit and grant us zeal and fidelity to live according to our Vows, Rule, and Constitution; then our Lord will keep order in everything. Become one in his love; then you will be strong against seductions from the outside world. (I 3)

The following excerpt from her letter of June 13, 1879, confirms the fact that conditions were not without any possible ripple. This can be sensed from one of her letters:

> How are you and all the Sisters? Write me lest I become restless. I do hope and trust that all is well after the storm. … I am sorry that you have so much to endure, but be brave and do not become faint-hearted. The Lord leads; we shall follow, as he directs!" (I 3)

It is not easy to get a clear idea of the difficulties Mother Maria Theresia refers to in her letter and which worried her. Perhaps the following extracts from some of the letters of that period may shed some light. But what stands out especially in this letter is the admirable reserve of the servant of God in the face of attacks on her person and her whole-hearted willingness of reconciliation. Just this reserve makes it difficult to learn the exact nature of the difficulty because she did not retaliate nor in lengthy explanations try to excuse herself. Evidently, she had given some directives relative to the school in Lafayette that met the disapproval of a Franciscan who taught there with the Sisters. In a letter carrying no date but obviously written in early July of 1879, we find:

> Dear Sister Deogratias!
>
> Your loving letters were received and I thank you most sincerely. How happy I am for the information regarding

conditions there. What you, dear child, must have suffered. The whole incident often flashes upon my mind, but then again I am soon at peace, for I am not conscious of having in bad conscience done or said anything. Place all, all in the Providence of God; he will bring order. But, dear Sister, do not let it distress you so! It is not the first storm that has come over your Mother; nor in all probability will it be the last. I can tell you sincerely that my heart is at rest relative to all I have said or done during my last days there. I am very, very sorry that Father Agnellus has become so unhappy. May he soon find peace through the grace of God and be blessed a thousand fold for all! You, dear Sister Deogratias, observe the Rule, Constitution, and Customs as learned in the motherhouse, and have confidence; pray much and do not readily omit the community exercises. All will turn out for the best. I told Sister Vincentia all about it. She said that she was once involved in a similar situation and would like to share some advice. Above all the Sisters must hold together in unity and loyalty.

You wrote that Father Agnellus said the confessional was misused — yet, no, dear Sister Deogratias, I will not justify myself; no matter what is said against me, against my person, but shall thank the Sacred Heart for all. May Christ our Lord protect our congregation, keep our Sisters true and in the right spirit, and save them from the world — that is my desire. Then if I can be pleasing to him as a sacrifice, I shall gladly stand beneath the cross with his sorrowing Mother. I desire nothing from the world, but trust firmly in God. You, dear sister Deogratias, remain steadfast and true! We are children of St. Francis and must follow our exemplar.... Please write to Father Vincenz and ask him to espouse the cause of our Sisters in America.... Father Agnellus sent me the regulations of the bishop before you did although he knew very well that I was acquainted with them.... Today I shall write to Father Superior. May the Lord enlighten my mind, direct my words, and keep my heart within his own that I write only what he wills. (I 211)

On July 22, 1879, Mother Maria Theresia wrote to Sister Deogratias that she had been advised to write to the North American Provincial Vincenz Halbfas, O.F.M., to explain the difficulties existing in the Lafayette school. She was of the following opinion:

> I would gladly have done so, but considered it better that you together with Sister Alphonsa or any other Sister thoroughly acquainted with the affair, visit the bishop and personally explain the whole situation and ask his assistance. He surely knows Father Agnellus very well and would be in the best position to help. If I should discuss the entire matter from here, it would indeed be a sorry concern if the letter should be lost or fall into other hands. Plead urgently with the Provincial in my name and beg him for the sake of God to assist us by bringing order into the situation there. Ask him to advise and assist you as he deems proper according to God's Will. May it please Almighty God to bring the truth to light and permeate all our Sisters with a truly religious spirit, then all will be well. (I 4)

A letter of July 25, 1879, reveals a lack of complete unity among the Sisters in Lafayette as to the manner of conducting the school. Some held with Father Agnellus and others followed the directives of Mother Maria Theresia (I 5). In all her successive letters the servant of God refers repeatedly to this matter and pleads for unity and fidelity among the Sisters. It is apparent that Father Agnellus did not always see clearly that the unity of the congregation may not be infringed upon under any conditions. For example, in a vivacious manner he was a little too outspoken that the American Sisters must be independent of Olpe. Outside the school question, this thought will come up again and will be treated further in another section. Probably he did not wish to be controversial relative to Mother Maria Theresia, but when in a highly resentful mood he let some words slip that in a more thoughtful time he would never have uttered. This can readily be perceived from a letter, unfortunately not dated, of Mother Maria Theresia to Sister Deogratias:

> It seems strange to me that Father Agnellus takes it hard that I do not write to him. He probably has forgotten what he wrote to me. Otherwise, as I mentioned previously, I should think a letter from one whom he considers a liar would not be agreeable. I reread his letter of July 14, of the previous year and believe that it is better for me to be silent. God knows all and he will be judge of us all. When Father Agnellus at some time meets me in heaven, as I hope, then he will no longer think that Sister Maria Theresia is a liar and a hypocrite. It has been a consolation for me to pray much for that good and pious priest, although often with an aching heart. (I 212)

If in these difficulties Mother Maria Theresia had obstinately demanded amends to be made to her honor, the situation probably would never have become clarified. As a responsible superior she remained consistent throughout the affair. But she never avenged personal offenses, made no judgment over the intention or will of another, and to the very end credited others with acting in good faith. She never defended herself personally, no matter how great the hurt when others spoke ill of her. And when an opportunity presented itself, she was in charity prepared to forget all. The whole situation cleared up later. Father Agnellus returned to his home country and several Sisters were transferred from Lafayette. But even prior to this, Mother Maria Theresia gave expression to her great joy in a letter to Sister Deogratias, dated June 23, 1882, saying "that Father Agnellus is again devoted to you and to the congregation" (I 18). Soon after Father Agnellus left North America, Sister Deogratias received the following reprimand from Mother Maria Theresia:

> As far as your last relationship with Father Agnellus is concerned, it would have been much better and more in keeping with wisdom if you had brought it about that the recent mutual understanding had not been disturbed and that your farewell had been one of mutual peace. I am very sorry, but since he permitted it so, we shall draw a profitable lesson from it for the future.

As early as September 15, 1882, Mother Maria Theresia wrote a rather detailed letter to North America reporting Father Agnellus' visit to Olpe. Not a trace of the difficulties between her and the priest can be discovered in this letter. It reads:

> Now with great joy I must tell you of the good and Reverend Father Agnellus' visit with us in Olpe. He arrived on Friday evening and gave all of us a great surprise and great joy. On Thursday morning I had received a letter from him, postmarked Cincinnati, stating that since he was traveling with a sick brother, he would not come to Olpe. Friday noon a dispatch came from Sister Angela from Blankenstein stating that she would bring Sister Martina, who was ill, that evening. Consequently two Sisters went to the station to meet them. There a priest came to Sister Scholastica asking her to greet me sincerely and tell me that he would be at the convent the next morning to say the 6:00 a.m. Mass. He said that he was the priest from Lafayette, who had worked with our Sisters there. Then Sister Dominica and Sister Scholastica brought us the good and Reverend Father Agnellus. How happy I was and how blessed the hours were that the pious and sorely-tried Father spent here with us. He is really quite ill and often feels miserable, but the few days he spent here with us improved his health considerably. Father Agnellus repeatedly said to me and to the other Sisters: "Since I left Tyrol seven years ago, I have not experienced such happy days as here in Olpe." He left on Wednesday noon. All the Sisters and others with whom he came in contact while here respected him highly. He mentioned that he would continue to bless our congregation and pray for all the Sisters. He asked me to send greetings to the Sisters in North America and mentioned that he would never forget us. Dear Sister Deogratias, Father felt hurt at much that happened there, but he is an upright God-loving soul, one who readily becomes reconciled. He means well. (I 22)

The entire exchange of letters relative to this problem shows how difficult, under such circumstances, it can become for a major superior to get a clear picture. Just this instance clearly displays Mother Maria Theresia's reserve. A person must realize that the communication was not direct between the two parties. The interchange was addressed to a third party — Sister Deogratias — as a confidant. Under such conditions how readily a harsh, trying word enters! But the situation in this case is entirely different: the honor of the one, whom the other perhaps considers an opponent and adversary, is not injured in the least. What Mother Maria Theresia otherwise wrote to her daughters is certainly very valuable. How she conducted herself in this difficult affair shows her admirable greatness of soul. Here St. Francis' attitude toward priests becomes visible in her:

> The Lord gave and gives me such great confidence in priests who live according to the precepts of the Roman Catholic Church because of their consecration, that I, although they persecute me, would still seek refuge in them. And I will show them love and honor them as my masters. I will not take notice of their sin because in them the Son of God and they are my masters.

In this vein the servant of God had written to Sister Deogratias amidst the turmoil: "We are the children of St. Francis and must form ourselves according to his example" (I 211).

Another event in the American situation was perhaps more serious in nature. The bishop apparently was of the opinion that he should have direct control over the Sisters in America, as the bishop of Paderborn had over the Sisters in Germany. He even intended to appoint a superior for the North American group to govern the Sisters in his name. Mother Maria Theresia saw with fear that such a measure would lead to a separation of the congregation. But could she oppose the bishop, especially Bishop Dwenger to whom she felt so greatly indebted? She wrote of her great anxiety to Sister Deogratias:

> As concerns the office of superior, our congregation would become separated if there were a second superior. In Germany our Sisters are also serving in various dioceses, but under one superior; the same should also hold for Ameri-

> ca. The Franciscans of Cincinnati, to my knowledge, have no other superior. Father custodian is confessor, but does not concern himself with other matters. Should the bishop in the meantime have appointed a superior, it would be better not to say anything until a convenient time. The duties of the superior are listed in the Constitution. We recognized that only too well previously, and it was also often said of Father Schroeder of blessed memory that the office of superior and confessor were incompatible. But at that time we could not do otherwise. Should I no longer know how our status is to be understood and how our life is to be regulated, although after much prayer together with Sister Francesca, I composed the Constitution and submitted it to the Most Reverend Bishop Konrad? (I 5)

To avoid a separation, it certainly was most important to stress the idea of a unified congregation among the Sisters sent to America. To note how consistently Mother Maria Theresia followed this principle is very instructive. She reasoned that if this awareness was kept vitally alive among the Sisters across the ocean, there would be no danger of separation because the Sisters themselves would not desire it. Whoever is conversant with the history of congregations realizes that not all of them have accomplished what Mother Maria Theresia did through her maternal goodness and consistent manner of governing. Even in the same country congregations have been separated because bishops permitted only those Sisters to serve in the diocese whose motherhouses were located there. If this has not happened to the Olpe Franciscans, it can gratefully be attributed to the fact that Mother Maria Theresia had always been a true mother to her Sisters. All her spiritual daughters realized this. To the Sisters in America she gave the freedom of decision in their affairs; nevertheless she admonished and advised when this freedom was extended too far in one point or another.

In the early years the major superior chose the religious names given the newly invested Sisters, both in Germany and America. But already at the first investiture, October 19, 1879, she wrote: "The religious names of the newly invested could be:

Maria Gertrudis, Ignatia, and Rufina, all of St. Joseph. If, however, owing to conditions there, you think otherwise, you may make the change" (I 7).

Especially informative as to the manner in which the servant of God was persistent, but not autocratic, upon unity is seen in a letter addressed to Sister Deogratias. Unfortunately, this correspondence is not dated, but apparently was sent to America in 1880:

> I hope the Sisters have arrived safely upon your receiving this letter. Mutually you will have much to tell each other. You were perhaps quite surprised to see Sister Johanna instead of Sister Hyacinth, but by now you surely know the reason for the change. I am glad that Sister Johanna is with you, for as a Sister Councilor she will be able to glean exact information of situations there. I am sure you must be glad, too. Sister Johanna will hold visitation in all the American houses; this is good, for to be independent from the motherhouse could only be a disadvantage. Now you, dear Sister Deogratias, must not think that I distrust you, no, most certainly not. I think this move is in God's wise providence and will be for our good. In your last letter you stated that you have been urged to admit Sister Agnes to profession. Good, dear Sister Deogratias. If you and the older Sisters are in agreement, it will not take long to obtain the consent of all the superiors of the whole congregation. Then you asked whether the postulants are to wear satin clothes, or whether black woolen ones would do just as well? After you have made the decision, you are to write here for consent. I beg you, dear Sister Deogratias, for the sake of God, do not initiate new ideas independently, for it will bring no blessing. Our status is established, and when there is a necessity to introduce a new custom, here is the place it must be done, and not in America. What was told you previously concerning this by Father Agnellus, let it be a thing of the past. Such matters are the concern of the major superior and her council. I will understand your situation there and can only counsel you to depend upon

> your lawful superiors in the various circumstances. Your agreement to the Statutes of the local bishop would mean a separation in our congregation. Since Sister Johanna is there with you now, discuss all with her. But the Statutes are not to be approved. Sister Johanna will tell you what our superior, Father Dechant, who has all the rights of a bishop, said. He expressed the wish that you and all the Sisters should hold with Father Vincenz; and if his opinions and counsels are not adequate in the more important issues, then you and the Sisters should turn to this place. You realize that the priests there love to mingle in everything. I long and yearn for the day when the main house there will be under the direction of a German Franciscan. (I 212)

To preserve unity among the Sisters amidst various pressures, Mother Maria Theresia realized only too well that from Olpe she could not always know or judge all things exactly in the United States. Many decisions of the Sisters had to be made there even when in close contact with the major superior in Germany. Therefore, on May 20, 1881, after she had written rather definite suggestions for transfer, she added: "All this is only my counsel ... from a distance one cannot always judge correctly" (I 12). Somewhat later she wrote: "From here it is not easily recognizable what the situation is and how it should be managed. If after prayer you have decided something with the older Sisters, proceed with it" (I 18). This wise realization of different conditions in North America shows clearly that she felt not all depended upon her opinion and judgment. In such actions are the essential characteristics of good leadership manifested in a major superior, when she entrusts minor details of government to the judgment and responsibility of the local superiors.

Repeatedly, Mother Maria Theresia manifested her love for the Sisters in America. Although she maintained a unity among the Sisters, she did not do this by calculation but from the deep love in her heart. She was personally interested in the Sisters individually and often gave valuable counsel to local superiors on how to accept and guide individual Sisters. All vocation crises of the Sisters, all their illnesses, and their other cares found an echo in the maternal heart. Perhaps no other letter is so expressive, so filled with maternal goodness as the one of November 16, 1881, written in grateful response to greetings on the occasion of her nameday. It reads:

> *My dearly beloved Sisters,*
>
> Greetings in the Sacred Heart! I thank you most sincerely for your felicitations on the occasion of my nameday. We shall trust that it be God's will to give us many graces through the intercession of St. Theresa; above all, great love of God and neighbor, qualifying us to achieve great things for the honor of God and the welfare of our neighbor. Our dear Lord knows how gladly I would have written some words of love and encouragement sooner to each of you individually, my dear good Sisters, but my time is limited and my energy often quite meager. I live under a firm conviction that you know my love and care for you never shrinks from sacrifice and pain for your welfare when the Lord lets me know it is his will. I rejoice greatly that you are so busily engaged in qualifying yourselves in your branches of study. May our dear Lord strengthen our weak energies that through his grace we may contribute toward spreading his Kingdom on earth and leading souls to heaven.
>
> Our first task however, my good Sisters, is self-sanctification. We all know how easy and sweet the hardest difficulties and greatest sacrifices tend to become when we are intimately united with God. What can our divine Bridegroom refuse us when we are faithful to our vows, devoted to his guidance, and honor his interests with complete detachment of self? Our dear Savior willed to give each five full talents, together with holy zeal for souls, conscientious fidelity in his service that gleaning profits here we may reap a glorious reward. How often, dear Sisters, I think of you, mornings and evenings, and many times during the day and in the sleepless nights. To whom else could I bring my yearnings and petitions for your sanc-

tification than to the Sacred Heart of Jesus, in whom we are all united in an intimate, holy, and never-abating love. In this heart you should find your consolation and peace, for dreary hours are never wanting and the cross is in Lafayette as well as in Olpe. It must be borne, it must be suffered and battled; therefore, embrace it heartily, persevere courageously, no matter what may come over us. We wish to surrender completely to Christ; he also sacrificed himself completely; therefore we as his brides may refuse him nothing. If we are but valiant and resolute then most of the battle is won. Let us crucify the ego even if the heart in consequence beats louder and the tears flow causing the cheeks to become reddened. One good action or deed will not win the battle; we must daily begin anew. May the loving Mother of God obtain for all of us the grace of perseverance.

Now, my dear Sisters, I beg earnestly for your prayers and remain with best wishes from all the Sisters here. In the Sacred Wounds of Christ,

Your devoted
Sister Maria Theresia, Poor Franciscan
(I 14)

Through such letters, and there are many, Mother Maria Theresia voices her concern for the spiritual advancement of her Sisters. That these letters are preserved is a clear indication of how much the Sisters treasured them. If the foundations in North America had not been made, much of Mother Maria Theresia's character would not be so perceptible today. Under the existing circumstances she had to write; and she fulfilled this apostolate with greatest zeal. It is precisely these letters, from Olpe to North America, that manifest most of the spiritual thinking of this true Mother relative to her spiritual daughters. What was spoken in the homeland and faded away was preserved in these letters. Even as major superior, she was not of the opinion that everything in the congregation should relate to her alone. This idea is clearly indicated in a special letter she wrote to Sister Deogratias on July 15, 1882:

> Now I must call your attention to something that somewhat disturbed me. The Sisters in Omaha, Columbus, St. Mary's, and Reynolds did not write to Sister Paula for her nameday. Although this is not strictly obligatory, it nevertheless hurt me very much. I have written to Sister Alphonsa. It would please me if you, dear Sister Deogratias, would remind the superiors of the places designated of the custom, not in a conspicuous way, but quietly and by word of mouth. It is not necessary that all the Sisters write for some do not have the time. But I think that the superiors should write a letter on such occasions and also tell the Sisters lest gratitude vanish and the bond of love uniting all the Sisters intimately be lured away. (I 19)

The congregation faced many tasks in North America where the Poor Franciscans were highly esteemed. A really graphic sketch of their activities is drawn by Reverend Bonaventure Hammer, O.F.M., in his book of the Poor Franciscans of Perpetual Adoration, especially their apostolate in the United States. He writes:

> The principles guiding the activities of the Sisters on American soil are the same that reaped such rich results in Europe. Animated by a true Christian love of neighbor, they endeavored to do as much as possible in the care of the sick and the education of youth. In their hospitals where labors of charity are carried on in the true sense of the word, they accept patients without distinction as to race, color, denomination, nationality, social standing, or class. The rich are not preferred to the poor. The rule, first come, first served, is activated here. Those entering the hospital unable to pay, receive the same attention as those paying in full or in part. All receive the same service. The Sisters care for them, prepare their meals, and professionally provide for their needs. They are visible in the kitchen, in the laundry, and in the operating rooms. They are always the kindest and most concerned nurses, always busy, always cheerful with a kind word on their lips. One never notices that long watches and endless toil fatigue them. If

> persons scrutinize these unassuming and reserved Sisters more closely their only ambition seems to be to console the sick and to supply them with all necessities for their well-being.... As religious instruction is not permitted in the public schools of this land, Catholics saw no other way to provide religious education for their children than to establish their own schools. This they did in spite of the hardships resulting from supporting a double school system, the public and the parochial. The Franciscan Sisters upon their arrival in this country were well prepared to teach in the parochial schools on the elementary level and also on higher levels. Under the guidance of their pastors they taught in all the grades taught in the public schools; and besides, which is of the greatest importance, they taught religion. The Sisters taught in St. Boniface School, Lafayette, almost immediately upon their arrival, as soon as they had pupils in sufficient numbers. To this day pupils taking the examinations in all eight grades together with those of the public schools, invariably rank higher in the results.

Today in our critical times, we are not so prone to sing such an absolute hymn of praise for we have the conviction that all that is great and praised is tinged with human weakness which in its humanity will exact its toll. Nevertheless, if someone becomes so enthusiastic for these Franciscan Sisters, he must have seen greatness in their activities and way of life and considered all from that point of view.

At this stage one must at least enumerate briefly the rapid spread of foundations in North America. Mother Maria Theresia's Sisters also became imbued with the pioneer spirit which at this time was so alive in the United States and ever ready for new risks. In 1880, St. Joseph Hospital was founded in Omaha, Nebraska; in 1881, a school in St. Mary, Nebraska. The year 1882, saw the founding of St. Anthony Hospital, Terre Haute, Indiana; St. Mary Hospital, Emporia, Kansas; St. Francis Academy, Columbus, Nebraska; Sacred Heart School, Emporia, Kansas; St. Bernard School, Lindsay, Nebraska. In 1883, St. Francis School was founded in Humphrey, Nebraska; and in 1884, St. Alexis Hospital, Cleveland, Ohio. Upon a close look at the map, it can be recognized readily that Lafayette and Columbus were the two focal points from which the other foundations radiated.

From this enumeration it is readily seen what possibilities America offered for a rich apostolate. Mother Maria Theresia must have followed this glorious development with great joy. In all this she was concerned above all lest religious life be endangered through too much activity. Consequently the letters to North America are filled with repeated exhortations to great fidelity in religious life. The very first letter Mother Maria Theresia wrote to the Sisters upon her return from the North American trip contains the following passage: "Most likely you can undertake Perpetual Adoration now" (I 211). She realized how much depends upon organized adoration, through which the whole life becomes dedicated and firmly anchored.

Verily the foundation in North America has proved to be of greatest significance in the biography of the servant of God. In perfect justice, it must be said that without this foundation we should lack those exact particulars revealing her very nature. Directing the congregation in unity, she had to give guidelines repeatedly. Hence we have the numerous letters to North America addressed chiefly to Sister Deogratias, which constitute a true storehouse for the characterization of the foundress.

At that time the directors of the congregation were cognizant of several serious problems that held the foreground. Activities multiplied rapidly; many areas applied for Sisters; bishops pleaded urgently to have them undertake various spheres of activity. Overactivity could easily endanger the spiritual life of the Sisters especially since the congregation was still young and still engaged in its own development and formation. Was there not a temptation in all this to be generous in the acceptance of candidates for a greater number of Sisters would increase the feasibility of more foundations? Could not a comparison with older congregations, grown strong through increased membership, awaken the ambition to use all means available to grow likewise?

Mother Maria Theresia saw the situation clearly. What did she do? We are intensely interested in the period between the foundation in North America in 1875 and the year 1882. During this time it was impossible to receive new members in Germany; but in America ever more candidates applied for admission. Mother Maria Theresia the servant of God wrote on July 22, 1879:

> As I learned from your letter, you now have several postulants. Thanks be to God! Form them in a truly religious spirit, in simplicity and humility. If you find vacillation and dissatisfaction in any of them, it is better to dismiss them early than burden the congregation with a cross later. (I 4)

Even under the best assumptions, she was unwilling to shorten the time of the postulancy. "Be very careful in accepting candidates" (I 8), is an advice she gave repeatedly. She advised against putting up with obstinate characters in silence, but rather counseled dismissing them: "Be resolute in dealing with recalcitrant characters. We should not always keep silence, for it will not better conditions but only aggravate responsibility" (I 20). Once when she learned that a Sister gave too free vent to her feelings, she answered that lack of self-control is very serious. "This cannot continue. It would be better if she returned to the world; then others would be unharmed through such an example. If you are of the same opinion, then I shall write to her soon." (I 25)

These counsels show that the servant of God stressed greatly the spirit of true obedience, one without obstinacy. On the other hand, she insisted energetically that a congregation does not exist to harbor persons of weak will who cannot control themselves and good-naturedly just drag along. With understanding she bore human peculiarities as well as the unavoidable conditions of life in common, if at some time or other no unified pattern of living could be reached. Thus at one time in a strain of humor, she remarked. "See it is the Lord who has so jumbled us together." (I 25)

It was of great importance to her that the young Sisters received a genuine solid foundation for the apostolate and especially for the religious life. In this connection we have her letter of October 2, 1882:

> From a sense of duty I must admonish and beg you again and again to be careful in the acceptance of postulants. You must first test their suitability and ask yourself what value there is in numbers if the candidates cannot renounce themselves. Also the young Sisters are not to be sent to the missions immediately; that may not be. Those who enter should make their novitiate in Lafayette and should stay there at least one year. They may attend classes in subjects pertaining to religious life. These classes should be held in the convent.... Recently many elderly priests were here and all remarked that we should seriously watch the formation of the Sisters in America; they agree with me." (I 23)

The many petitions for new foundations in America became a very taxing problem for Mother Maria Theresia. She desired ardently to devote the energy of her congregation to the services of God and the welfare of mankind. But she also had the responsibility to take care that the development did not advance prematurely. The congregation was young, and lacked Sisters who through years of experience had proved themselves capable of becoming superiors. In her letters she stressed this point repeatedly. She wished the houses to be not only places of activity but real convents. She realized only too well that all or very much depended on the superior. On August 18, 1882, she wrote as follows:

> With reference to undertaking more missions in Nebraska, you know that I would as gladly as you concede to the wishes of the bishop of Omaha. But, dear Sister Deogratias, we lack superiors. How can such young Sisters, who themselves are not firmly grounded, form and lead others? Oh, the responsibility is great. I think we should wait a year, by then conditions will be better. Do you not think that it is better to delay for a while? Religious life is no child play. If the ABC's of religious life are neglected in the beginning, they can scarcely be made up later. With anxious care I think of the young Sisters who are superiors now; our dear Lord must freely substitute, but we on our part must exercise prudence." (I 20)

On the other hand she knew that priests were pressuring much for another hospital here and another school there. But she also had to keep the religious life of the Sisters in mind; therefore she put on the brakes repeatedly to avoid premature expansion. From another of her letters we glean:

> Relative to another branch establishment if you think the foundation should be made, examine the situation closely. If you have sufficient personnel, I shall be happy. But, dear Sister Deogratias, you know we lack superiors; all depends on that. Young Sisters, still children in the congregation, cannot form other Sisters, and ours is the responsibility. God will demand justice. One cannot request nor depend on diocesan priests for that; they do not know religious life in community, but demand much of a religious whether they be old or young. I would rather that you accept fewer places and staff these with conscientious and faithful Sisters. That would be better than too many foundations that would bring the sorrow and discouragement in which some would seek their own honor instead of the honor of God. (I 21)

This letter reveals how profoundly Mother Maria Theresia understood the office of superior. She shied from expanding the congregation in its activities to promote her own honor. That would happen if the numerous foundations and expanding activities would feed personal pride. Also, those engaged in charitable works or in this apostolate may be tempted to take the credit themselves of the great results of their labors. The servant of God withstood this temptation. She was ever conscious of her responsibility to the Sisters in religious life and saw clearly that in all the activities of religious life the honor of God could be sought and promoted. She at one time admonished clearly:

> We cannot possibly accept all the offers there and besides your chief duty is the sanctification of the Sisters. For this we must one day give a strict account. We shall certainly not be asked how many foundations we have made.... Besides, what shall we accomplish by sending young, inexpe-

> rienced Sisters to the missions who pine away and expose the congregation to ridicule? That is not proper! (I 22)

In the same letter she betrays that she herself follows the same plan in Germany: "Here also we have many requests for new foundations; just lately we have been petitioned for four; to date I have not accepted any, for we wish first to staff those adequately that we already have" (I 22).

This era has been called the period of foundations. There has been hectic urge for ever new undertakings. As to Mother Maria Theresia we see plainly that her congregation could have expanded much more rapidly as far as externals are concerned. But she heeded the interior life and wished to assure her congregation of the possibility of maturely meeting future situations. Naturally, her repeated advice of holding back was not very pleasant to the superiors. But the servant of God in her wisdom saved her Sisters many a crisis and disappointment.

With what great discretion she directed her congregation is also manifested in another point. Rapid expansion brings in its wake endless worries in the process of construction of new buildings and additions to existing buildings. When in need, the congregation was permitted to solicit in the example of St. Francis. Love of holy poverty caused this right to be anchored in the Constitution. Naturally enough Mother Maria Theresia saw the many dangers connected with this practice if the Sisters were constantly on the road. Therefore, in no uncertain terms she counseled:

> If you must build … then in the Name of God do it! But do not overburden yourselves with heavy debts that the Sisters must go soliciting funds. Such practice is likely to cause a loss of religious spirit, and a loss of respect by the people of the world for the religious habit if seen too much on the public streets. Our constitution attaches the blessing of obedience to begging; but be circumspect! The greatest misfortune can happen before one scarcely suspects it. O dear Sister Deogratias, what happenings I could tell you! May our dear and merciful Lord preserve us from sin and disgrace! (I 15)

Instructions of this nature are always valuable in studying the position Mother Maria Theresia had in regard to her Sisters. The objectives, activities, and organization of the congregation did not constitute her conception of greatness. She thought of the individual Sister. She was not prepared to endanger the physical nor the mental health of a Sister to reach an external goal, as for example in construction projects. Her foremost objective was and remained the formation of her Sisters as religious. If any task or activity threatened that goal, it had to be postponed or delayed.

Her mature wisdom and maternal solicitude were qualities manifested long before her advanced age of seventy-five. When she wrote these instructions, she was but in middle age and still was to lead the congregation for another twenty-five years. It is unfortunate that we have no direct personal letters of her earlier years, but only the official correspondence to the ecclesiastical and civic authorities in which the personal is veiled or held in reserve. From 1879 on, her letters are much more personal and clearer to us for they are repeatedly interwoven with confidential remarks. Thus from the following letters it is possible to glean how much Mother Maria Theresia suffered from illness and bodily infirmities. She never expressed this openly, but to her confidant, Sister Deogratias, such remarks flowed from her pen unnoticed, as follows:

> July 22, 1879: I do not recall whether in my last letter to you I mentioned the fever with which I suffer severely. Sometimes I am so weak and fatigued that I must go to bed. Our dear Lord, I am confident, will help again. (I 4)

> March 15, 1881: On Christmas Day last, I had a contest with death. All of us thought the time had come. I offered the Christ child the sacrifice of my life, but our dear Lord spared my life dedicated to him alone, in sorrow and penance, in love and suffering. The dear Sisters sustained me through their prayers. May it please the Lord to bless my continued work in the congregation and may it redound to his greater honor and glory. I realize my nothingness only too well, but if the Lord in his mercy will strengthen me, I shall serve him with joy. May my sinfulness not stand

> in his way. Pray much for me, dear Sister Deogratias, for my physical weakness is still great; I am still confined to my room and only now and then go to the chapel choir to greet the Lord in the tabernacle. I still may not go downstairs. This is very hard for me. Still Christ is rich in mercy; he comes to me and gives me strength and energy and fills his poor one with grace and patience. Writing saps all my strength. Will you please be so good and give my best wishes to Sister Josepha for her nameday. (I 11)
>
> November 18, 1881: It has been quite some time since I last wrote to you, my dear good child. First I was travelling; then I became ill and my head is still good for nothing . . . I was thinking that if my health permitted, I would accept it as God's will that I accompany the Sisters leaving here for America in the winter. Now, however, I think differently, for even before the winter has set in, I am confronted with all types of illness and infirmities. (I 15)
>
> October 13, 1882: As to the condition of my health; it is not good, but I trust there will soon be an improvement. (I 14)
>
> January 25, 1883: If one is well, he can work; but feeble and weak, what then? My little energy is not worth much and I drag myself along, awaiting spring. (I 27)
>
> March 8, 1883: Healthwise I have not been very well all winter; I was often confined to bed; but now I take part in all; but I am so fatigued. (I 29)

This comprises a little chronicle of suffering and illness but no complaints and self-pity. Because she was so afflicted with illness herself, she had such great kindness and sympathy for the sick Sisters. On December 12, 1882, she wrote:

> The weather here is really cold and I feel sorry for the Sisters who came from the missions to make the retreat. It invariably seems cold to them here. Good Sister Juliana is miserable; she suffers much from a bad cough and severe weakness. It is hard for me to see her so wretched. May the

> Blessed Mother soon make her well again. Sister Laurentia is bedfast and is really pitiable. We never lack sick and infirm Sisters.

The manner in which Mother Maria Theresia accepted her illnesses together with much of her greatness of soul are clearly manifested in her letters of this period in an occasional exchange of ideas with her Sisters. This correspondence reveals the treasured depths of her thinking. In a biography of such a person not only the achievement of external goals are important but much more the personal interior attitudes. Thus the previous manifestations of her spiritual posture have not been overlooked. As a follower of Christ, we see how she had to struggle to hold to the way she had begun:

> It is our obligation in religious life to strive continuously for perfection by using all opportunities within our power to overcome ourselves and to gain merits, which united with those of Christ will draw down blessings for us from above. Please pray for me, dear Sister Deogratias, for I need help so very much. Although within my heart I yearn for crosses, sufferings, and contempt, yet miserable human nature struggles against all those things. But it should be and must be so to follow our Savior step by step on his way to Calvary. (I 7)

Before her Sisters, she did not pretend to be a person who had reached perfection long ago. She admits that all her longing is for complete union with Christ, her cross-bearing Redeemer. But at the same time she humbly acknowledges how insistently her nature rebels against it and, therefore, pleads for prayers that God may give her his grace. For no matter how much good man may do, it is not sufficient that man may expect grace from God as a reward. Only in union with that which the Lord did for us do human deeds count before God; only through Christ does human activity become pleasing to God.

How often in those things against which her nature especially rebelled, she, recognizing the cross, renounced herself with firm determination. The following lines speak of it:

> ... in this vale of tears what else can we expect but crosses and adversities! ... may our dear Lord grant us patience to pass through all sorrows with gain. In spite of the Lord's graces, I am poor and troubled. Let us never cease to entrust all to God in prayer, hold everything earthly as passing and subject to change. Let us keep our eyes on what endures eternally. I feel deeply, dear Sister Deogratias, the words spoken against me. What Father Agnellus has said about me, gives me a greater incentive to pray more and more earnestly for him. God be praised for all! (I 10)

Not always is the difficulty so easily discerned as in these words. Many of her difficulties could not be explained clearly through correspondence. Toward the end of 1879, she could only write: "Pray much for me! The Lord has permitted a heavy cross to fall upon me concerning which I am not able to write. May the Lord turn all to good! His name be praised! (I 10). The nature of this heavy cross can no longer be ascertained at this time. Either it was a personal spiritual affliction, or one caused by some persons whose identity she wished to protect.

Mother Maria Theresia was compelled by God to be the superior. She never let her Sisters feel that she was the exalted all-wise leader. "In spite of all that I have experienced and gone through, I am still such a stupid, stupid creature. That the Lord should use such a wretched person as I am! May all tend to the greater honor and glory of God and may no harm come to the congregation through my stupidity" (I 16).

These words give an insight into the nature of Mother Maria Theresia. Before God and man she was truly poor in spirit and firmly convinced that it was not her personal qualities that recommended her as major superior. Because of her feelings of inadequacy, it was a constant mystery to her that God should wish to use her as his instrument for this service. As gathered from her life story, God had to let her know quite clearly that he wished her to be the Mother of the congregation. As soon, however, as she recognized his wish, she said "yes." Her deep spirit of poverty gave her that great confidence in God, and not in her personal qualities; also, that firm certitude and manifest goodness her Sisters always admired in their Mother.

As one thoroughly poor in spirit, she could thus praise the Lord:

> How unspeakably great is the goodness of God to each one of us! How unendingly the mercy of the sacred Heart of Jesus is manifested to me the most miserable one! Therefore I am convinced that he will also draw other souls to himself, souls more loyal to his call and to the workings of his grace than I am, whom the powers of his boundless love has overwhelmed. Eternally I am pledged to gratefulness! Forever I shall praise his mercy! (I 19)

Only the person who sees himself poor in spirit and finds himself so enriched by God, can thus praise him. For one poor in spirit knows more of God's goodness and sees the wonders of God in his own life.

This inner attitude gave her the strength to accept all difficulties as providential even when caused by the idiosyncrasies of men. On January 25, 1883, she wrote to Sister Deogratias regarding a special sorrow:

> Before Christmas I received a letter from Paderborn stating that the divine services in our chapel should be limited to the absolutely necessary, only one Holy Mass a day. Also no visiting priests may say Holy Mass in our chapel except with the permission of the Reverend Vicar Tigges. Your own Reverend brother was not permitted to say Mass in our chapel on his last visit here. The Reverend Vicar knows that priests love to come to our chapel; he wants them to go to the hospital more frequently. Our superior, Reverend Dechant, was bypassed in this matter. However, we must have patience until it please God to help us. It is hard to realize such sentiments in priests. But I sincerely trust that, through the powerful intercession of the Mother of God, a change will come soon. (I 27)

Although she was keen-sighted and reasonable enough to discern and regret an unusual disposition in a priest, yet characteristically she blamed herself for this predicament and accepted this trial as a punishment. "We should have complied better and cooperated more with the many graces that were ours through the Holy Masses."

To see one of her Sisters die was especially hard for Mother Maria Theresia. On February 12, 1883, a letter was sent to Sister Deogratias in North America, in which she reported the death of two Sisters. The manner of reporting it portrays her maternal love for them:

> Certainly you will become alarmed upon opening this letter and seeing the black-edged cards. Our dear Sister Laurentia died peacefully and tranquilly on January 8, after a long and very painful illness. The evening before she had again received the Sacrament of the Anointing of the Sick. She was well prepared and resigned to the Will of God. How we feel the loss of this young, energetic, and talented Sister, you can readily conceive; but, dear Sister Deogratias, our dear Lord did it. May his holy will be done and may he be adored and praised! Inform the Sisters that they may soon receive Holy Communion and perform prayers and indulgences for the repose of her soul that she may soon be admitted to the Beatific Vision.
>
> Dear Sister Deogratias, my writing was granted a rest for eight days. Now again I must report a death, that of our dear Sister Josephine. After receiving the Sacrament of the Anointing of the Sick on Wednesday, the 7th, she made her profession of final vows. In the evening she rejoiced so loudly over the many and great graces that were hers in the religious life that the jubilant tones were heard in the chapel. The following morning at 5:30 she died. Both sisters died in youth, but I trust, well. (I 28)

This letter not only speaks of the way this true Mother reports the death of the deceased so lovingly, but also adds a personal meditation which gives a picture of her inner life:

> The number of our deceased intercessors in the next world is already great. I have been at the deathbed of so many of our beloved Sisters. May God grant that these dear ones, joyous in the Lord, may come to meet me and escort my

> departing soul, after having prayerfully surrounded my deathbed. O my beloved Sister Deogratias, what ardent longing fills my heart that soon, really soon, that hour may come for me to bring me to my Jesus! Pray much for me and have all the Sisters there also pray. (I 28)

Scarcely would Sister Deogratias have prayed for that intention of Mother Maria Theresia. Even if at that time, 1883, the wish of the servant of God was that her last hour be near for complete union with Christ, God willed otherwise. The Lord wished her to remain many years more on earth to labor in his service. This she did faithfully. Just at this time she confessed: "All as our dear Lord wishes! He leads, I follow!" (I 32).

The words, "He leads, I follow!" can be taken for the life of this servant of God. In connection with the foundation in North America it can be seen clearly how well she fulfilled this saying. She recognized the guidance of God: her obligation to care for the future of the congregation and to provide for the physical and spiritual welfare of the Sisters. But God's guidance also had a design unknown to the servant of God. What energy and what depth of soul she had was revealed in the foundations in North America. She compelled herself to manage affairs in a regular exchange of correspondence. Her whole method was such that over and over again she permitted very personal expressions of leading ideas in her own spirituality to color the directives given to her Sisters. Thus unintentionally she betrayed what power her life possessed. Here she does not communicate as one committing herself to death and seeing her life terminated, although she often believed that hour was at hand. Through her personal abilities, she had already accomplished much at this period in her life and at a time when she still had many years ahead of her. This shows what great power this life bore in all its phases. A person readily recalls this in all the tasks she still had to accomplish. Why the Sisters always reelected her as major superior even again shortly before her death at the age of seventy-five is now easily understood. "He leads, I follow." This her expression also contains all that the major superior had to accomplish in the German homeland during the *Kulturkampf* and after it abated.

CHAPTER IX

NEW DEVELOPMENTS IN THE HOMELAND

During the days of the *Kulturkampf*, Mother Maria Theresia probably often wondered whether the congregation could possibly survive in Germany, or whether with all her Sisters she would need to go to North America. She wrote as follows to North America on November 4, 1880: "If you have to build, provide sufficient space for all of us; here there is no change nor end in sight" (II 2). On July 16, 1879, the confessor Bishop Martin, exiled to Mont St. Guibert in Belgium, died. This death affected Mother Maria Theresia deeply. The congregation owed him a great debt of gratitude. That he had to die in exile aggravated the sad situation in the fatherland particularly. The administration of the diocese fell to the capitular Vicar Dr. Franz Kaspar Drobe.

The longer the unfortunate *Kulturkampf* held sway, the more oppressive conditions for the congregation became. The established houses were maintained but at the price of straining all energies. Many Sisters had gone to America. Death also took its toll. In Germany all investitures of Sisters were forbidden and their activities were severely restricted. The niece of Mother Maria Theresia endeavored to open an orphanage under her maiden name. She planned to use the space left vacant by the closing of the former orphanage, but her attempt under existing conditions came to nothing.

Catholic Germany, with few exceptions had remained loyal to the Pope and the bishops. During the struggle, energies and wills waxed stronger. Catholic associations registered a significant rise. Above all the Central Party had grown considerably in the elections and could wield a strong political influence. The country at this time had a group of extraordinarily energetic and fearless men: Ludwig Windhorst (d. 1891), Herman von Mallinckrodt (d. 1874), brothers August and Peter Reichensperger (d. 1895 and 1892), and others. These men confronted all injustices in Berlin with courage and skill. Results, however, would have been delayed still longer had the opponents not become weary of the struggle. It seems apparent that discussions with the Catholic Church weakened the authority of the state considerably. In judicious circles the desire for peace in the state grew. Also Bismarck, for various reasons, saw the advantage of a change in politics. The skillful politics of Pope Leo XIII met him halfway. The laws of the *Kulturkampf*, however, remained literally on the books, but the state after 1880, did not enforce them in fact. The time also came when the religious orders through prudent and wise management brought about alleviations in their situation.

FIRST INVESTITURE AFTER A LONG TIME

Mother Maria Theresia utilized this change in the political climate immediately. Dean Steinbusch, Wissen, a member of Parliament with good insight into possibilities that bade defiance, did not forget the cares of the Olpe Franciscans. He counseled Mother Maria Theresia to seek permission of the state to invest new members in the congregation. In such a petition, permission had to be obtained also from the episcopal authority. The servant of God, therefore, traveled to Paderborn on February 10, 1882, to present her petition to the Capitular Vicar, Dr. Drobe. He promised her that her petition would be considered and that he would then advise her. Ecclesiastical authorities work slower than the petitioner desires. Consequently, on February 23, Mother Maria Theresia felt instigated to write to the Capitular Vicar as follows:

> Your Reverence, did I take too much liberty on the 10th of this month in presenting a proposal from Dean Steinbusch, a member of the Parliament from Wissen, relative to the acceptance of new candidates? Your Reverence had the kindness to promise me that you would consider the proposal the following day in assembled chapter. Dean Steinbusch inquired from Berlin concerning the progress of our cause. Therefore, Your Reverence, I allow myself this most submissive request of asking you most graciously to inform me soon concerning the proposal. (VI 3)

Thereupon the proposal was returned to her on February 25, with the remark that the Capitular Vicar's decision will be one of approval of the request provided a formulated request be sent to the Minister that he remove the hindrances which forbade the acceptance of new candidates (VI 3).

On February 27, Mother Maria Theresia sent the formal request (VII 8); it had to pass through official channels and the first attempt reached only to the government of Arnsberg. Then the whole procedure started all over again a second time. The request was not to be granted so readily. After considerable correspondence and the negotiations of deputy, Dean Steinbusch, the Minister of Religious Affairs, under date of July 22, 1882, wrote to the district Magistrate of Olpe. He handed the script over to Mother Maria Theresia on August 11, 1882. She finally was pleased to read:

> ... under most practical considerations, we hereby approve the formulated proposal of the superior of the Franciscans in Olpe, that the foundation (motherhouse) of said congregation may admit new candidates to the number of 17 within a year, and further the approval of the state for the transfer of members of the order in accordance with prescribed rules. We take for granted the following regulations will be observed, especially that only persons of German citizenship be admitted and that the congregation obtain the permission of parents or guardians in the acceptance of dependents.

Whether Mother Maria Theresia in all her future years read another correspondence with such joy as this one is to be wondered. Did it not present her a new beginning? She did not have to search long for candidates to comply with the directive. Seventeen could be admitted within one year. Nine postulants had been waiting, and after a brief final preparation they were admitted on September 26, 1882; in April of 1883, five additional ones; and in July, 1883, three more. That completed the number with the given time.

One can readily surmise what that meant for the congregation. In 1875, her congregation in Germany had numbered fifty-five Sisters; in 1882, only thirty-eight. The present addition brought courage. Mother Maria Theresia petitioned for a greater number of candidates; on February 23, 1884, approval for forty-two was given, also within one year. On May 1, 1884, eight were invested; on October 15, twelve; on January 13, 1885, eight; and on March 9, 1885, again twelve. Must this not have seemed as a dream to the Sisters? Within two years, fifty-seven young Sisters swelled their ranks of thirty-eight. The number of the newly invested within two years was greater than the original fifty-five which in 1875 had entered during the previous twelve years. If we had no previous knowledge in the foregoing chapter how Mother Maria Theresia prudently and repeatedly counseled her Sisters to be cautious in the investigation and acceptance of candidates, one could readily surmise in the face of this large number of candidates that she simply accepted all who came in order to fill the ranks. But here as always prudence directed her course. Although forty-two were permitted, she invested only forty rather than deviate from her principles.

The year 1882 was a year of great rejoicing and thanksgiving for Mother Maria Theresia. The Diocese of Paderborn was permitted a new bishop, and in July the Capitular-Vicar, Dr. Franz Kaspar Drobe, was consecrated bishop of Paderborn. Ecclesiastical affairs as a whole could be regulated again since the diocese now had an officiating bishop. Mother Maria Theresia turned to the bishop on July 12, 1882 for the reappointment of a Rector for the congregation. For this office she suggested Dean Pielsticker of Attendorn. She wrote as follow: "Since the death of superior Schroeder, he was so kind as to fulfill the functions of superior to the congregation without having been appointed officially to that position because of the chaotic ecclesiastical conditions." The General Vicar consulted Dean Pielsticker. The latter realized the difficulties entailed in the distance of Attendorn from Olpe. He consequently suggested that if a new pastor be appointed for Olpe, the office of superior be given to him. In the interim he commented that he was prepared to continue as he had done since the death of Superior Schroeder to direct and counsel the congregation in purely spiritual matters. He retained this office until 1885. A provisional arrangement had been necessary previously because of the *Kulturkampf*.

The year 1882 brought further joy for the whole Franciscan family, namely, the seventh centenary of the birth of St. Francis. This event, which gave a strong impetus to Franciscan thought throughout the world, was opened by a festive triduum beginning in the chapel of the motherhouse from October 4 to 6 and was attended by many of the faithful.

FURTHER FOUNDATIONS

The congregation was again supplied with young energy. The regulations of the *Kulturkampf* were no longer enforced in their complete dimension nor with their earlier rigor. Plans for the future could now be made by religious orders. Thus also Mother Maria Theresia made new strides. She sought state approval for establishing new foundations. Suitable proposals were offered them. The state granted the requests. On May 19, 1883, the bishop also gave his permission for three new foundations: Jülich, Bonn-Poppelsdorf, and Heimerzheim. Jülich was opened on July 24 with five Sisters; Heimerzheim, October 4 of the same year, with three Sisters; and Bonn-Poppelsdorf on May 5, 1884, with four Sisters. Contact for the Jülich foundation was made by two Sisters on a soliciting tour. The impression they made must have been significant. The alderman, Theodore Schmitz, a brother-in-law of the Archbishop of Cologne, and Cardinal Dr. Antonius Fischer, suggested that the Olpe congregation undertake the care of the aged, the poor, and the sick in Jülich. Mother Maria Theresia accepted the offer and complied with it as soon as circumstances permitted.

The foundation at Poppelsdorf owes its beginning to a woman's love of home, that of Mrs. Rolffs, a native of Olpe. She was Councilor of Commerce and a member of Poppelsdorf's Education Association. As Poppelsdorf at this time was considering the establishment of a kindergarten, she directed attention to the Franciscans of her home town, Olpe. The pastor agreed to the proposal. He added that the Sisters could begin home nursing in Jülich as well as open a boarding school for children and a sewing school.

On August 12, 1882, the servant of God was again reelected major superior of the congregation. The election always had the same outcome. The rule of the Church restricting the period of office for superiors of a congregation is one of wisdom in order that in the repeated elections a change might occur when plausible. That the Sisters always reelected the servant of God, shows they really wanted her as mother; it is not a sign that the congregation probably did not consider other qualified or capable Sisters. Who would want to lose a good mother? Or who would want to exchange her with another every three years, without necessity?

At this time, at least in Olpe, the servant of God endeavored to follow the lines of the former apostolate. Since 1882, she had adopted a plan to care for epileptic children. This activity was different from caring for orphans, but the time was not ripe to open the orphanage again. As far as the objectives of the congregation were concerned, the care of epileptics was more in keeping — to help the most needy children. Untold hardships confronted the Sisters at this stage. Mother Maria Theresia repeatedly went from one official court to another with petitions. Finally, through tenacious patience she overcame all difficulties.

On April 25, 1884, the Minister of Home Affairs granted that the epileptic children may be cared for in the former orphanage, where the children were obliged to attend the common school in Olpe. This was in full conformity with the *Kulturkampf*. In all these negotiations, the servant of God was ably assisted by the Baron von Herremann in Berlin.

PROHIBITION OF NURSING THE SICK IN OLPE

In the midst of this promising unfolding, a very severe shock came upon them. The old opponent, Auxiliary Bishop, Dr. Freusberg, superior of the Vincentians, started the old struggle anew. The Vincentians had reason to rejoice that they had a superior who fought so relentlessly for them. He manifestly hoped that under the new bishop, he would be able to accomplish his goal — to oust the Poor Franciscans from Olpe. He announced his intended visit to the motherhouse. His purpose was evidently clear to Mother Maria Theresia. She left for Hüsten, obviously for a conference with her superior, Dean Pielsticker, and thus avoided a confrontation with the auxiliary bishop. From there on September 22, 1883, she wrote to Sister Deogratias, who at that time was in Olpe:

> I am, as you can well imagine, with my thoughts almost always in Olpe; yesterday afternoon I was miserable; today I am somewhat better. But I am not satisfied with the little I hear from Olpe; I beg you share the happenings there with me. I rejoice, dear Sister Deogratias, that you and Sister Paula are in full agreement regarding all. I can only pray for you. That I must be at a distance is hard for me. Still it seems the best course to take under our present difficulty, and I am at peace. As always the good pastor here is encouraging, although he cannot understand that Mr. Altscheid in Olpe has not made adjustments to comply with the will of the Reverend Bishop and the Auxiliary Bishop. Who can foresee the final outcome of conditions! We must all continue in humble prayer for an account will have to be rendered to God. God in his divine mercy has permitted this conflict to come upon us; and he knows best how to help. I rejoice that your brother is acquainted with the situation.
>
> Please inform Sister Paula that when the bishop comes to her, she should have someone send a telegram to Sister Margaretha immediately. One word will be sufficient 'CAME.' Perhaps Rector H. or the Doctor will send it. Your brother is too far distant. Upon receiving it all of us together will pray fervently that the Sacred Heart and St. Anthony be in your midst. What are the Sisters saying? The reason for the trip was not revealed to them. The Dean would not have wanted that. Or, has it leaked out in Olpe? You can well imagine, dear Sister Deogratias, what anxious and tortuous thoughts fill my mind; this is a terrifying time through which we are passing; still we must be cheerful. Yes, "I can do all in him who strengthens me."... When I reflect on the fact that I did leave Olpe, I think that should

> satisfy the auxiliary bishop. God knows all that may still come. However, the thought that it could not have been otherwise and God directs his own in a wonderful way, encourages me. Yes, it is only in prayer that I find rest.... All as God wishes! He leads, I follow. He has preserved us from so many dangers. Now, too, he will save us in his own time. Praise and thanks be to him for joys and also for sorrows. Let us be united in holy love, then strength will be given us to speak and do for the things of God. (I 32)

It was good that Mother Maria Theresia went to Hüsten. But the auxiliary bishop did not give up so readily. He was appointed visitator of the Poor Franciscans. Was that appointment probably made at his request? Was it a wise decision to make him visitator of the Congregation of Sisters that he would like to oust from Olpe, or at least see their activities there definitely restricted? But Mother Maria Theresia had to face the ordeal for she now had to confront him. The visitation in Olpe commenced on October 1, 1883. The auxiliary bishop conferred with Mother Maria Theresia relative to the visitation on October 2. He informed her that the bishop of Paderborn was in agreement with the regulation that the Franciscans under no condition were to engage in the nursing care of the sick in Olpe any longer. He demanded a promise from the servant of God that this regulation would be scrupulously observed. Mother Maria Theresia was in a more difficult position. In the interest of her congregation, she considered herself unable to make the requested promise, before conferring with the diocesan bishop and presented the letter to the Auxiliary Bishop Dr. Freusberg for comments, before sending it. He wrote his comments in the margins. We shall give the entire correspondence of the servant of God and also add the remarks of the auxiliary bishop.

> *Your Grace and Most Reverend Bishop!*
>
> Respectful greetings to Your Grace. I beg pardon for interrupting your time by this letter.
>
> Yesterday morning, the Most Reverend Auxiliary Bishop Dr. Freusberg, while conducting the visitation here

incidentally remarked that the Sisters of this congregation refrain from the nursing care of the sick here in Olpe, and asked the submissive undersigned to give a promise that from now on the Sisters of this congregation would no longer engage in that apostolate except in a situation in which the Sisters at St. Martin Hospital would be unable to do so. In consideration of the interests of the Congregation of the Franciscan Sisters, where my responsibility lies, I felt that immediately and offhand, I could not give that promise. But that I would first submit the request to Your Grace before I would respectfully take an opposing stand.

To support my most submissive request, I permit myself to present the following with deepest respect: The Constitution of our congregation obligates us to works of charity, among which the nursing care of the sick takes first rank since the education of youth has been absorbed by the state.

* * *

Marginal notes by the auxiliary bishop: Decisions concerning places and phases of activity relative to the Constitution of a congregation belong to the jurisdiction of the Most Reverend Bishop.

* * *

Our Constitution was approved by the Most Reverend Bishop Konrad Martin of blessed memory. The establishment of the congregation was brought to the attention of the Papal chair and praised by it. Accordingly Bishop Martin granted us the right to engaged in nursing the sick in Olpe.

* * *

Marginal notes of the auxiliary bishop: If this is really a fact, it must have been in the earlier and not the later years of his pastoral activity. However the superior has not produced the written account of this permission

* * *

... and at the time of the *Kulturkampf*, only the fact that we were engaged in the care of the sick, saved our congregation from being suppressed by the government. Thus through the requested verbal promise, I would not only restrict the Constitutional activity of the congregation and obstruct its way, but also surrender a practical right of years and increase the danger of suppression by the government. Also, I must consider it an obligation since I am responsible to the congregation for the furthering of its charitable activity and preservation of the rights of the members and especially their maintenance. Also, it is not conducive in furthering the spiritual life especially that of the younger Sisters to send them into the country, where frequent changes can become very burdensome. This condition can be managed much better within the town. Our congregation is very poor. Because the country people are also very poor, the nursing care in that area yields little returns for our sustenance. On the contrary, we often give alms where we expect to get some. Thus the nursing the sick in the town gives us the needed support. If we must forego this, material disadvantage would result. A situation in which two different congregations exercise the care of the sick in the same town is often the case.

* * *

Marginal note of the auxiliary bishop: But certainly never in such a small and sparsely settled place as Olpe.

* * *

This ought not to cause discord between the two congregations since we do not intrude ourselves, but only do nursing where and when called upon. Many of the townspeople here would take it amiss if they were restricted in their choice of nursing care personnel.

* * *

> Marginal note of the auxiliary bishop: by far the greatest number of people here, Christians and Jews, desire the nursing care of the Vincentians, for they know that these are specially trained for this service.

* * *

> I therefore humbly and respectfully beg Your Excellency, to kindly consider the explained reasons and graciously consent to differ from the expressed request of the Most Reverend Auxiliary Bishop that the children of St. Francis sorely oppressed here may retain a better and securer existence under the paternal protection of their beloved and revered Bishop.

In interpreting the marginal notes of the auxiliary bishop, it cannot be determined exactly whether these intended to touch the nature of the case, or endeavored to end the activity of the Poor Franciscans. They treat facts that were not under discussion. But he did not let the matter rest with these marginal notes. In a very long correspondence of December 22, 1883, he gave his opinion of the Olpe situation to the bishop. However, he did not research thoroughly into the Olpe Foundation, for he remarked that the 1859 foundation was a branch of the Paderborn Vincentians. In this writing, he also disclosed the fact that he had undertaken the visitation of the Franciscans in Olpe with the approval of the bishop admitting however that it was on his own initiative.

The decision evidently was carefully weighed. It was issued on February 9, 1884, in answer to Mother Maria Theresia's letter to the bishop:

> Concerning your petition of October 3 of last year, I have intensely scrutinized the conditions you elaborated. As a result I find myself obligated to prescribe that the nursing of the sick in the town of Olpe, except in cases of emergency, be carried on by the Vincentians alone; that the nursing of the sick in the outlying districts and parishes be the care of the Franciscan Sisters. Only under such arrange-

> ment can peaceful relations be maintained. I am making the strict and exact observance of the prescription a duty for the Poor Franciscans.

How did the servant of God react to this hard blow? She revealed it in a letter written on February 28, 1884, to Sister Deogratias who had recently returned to America:

> On the Monday after your departure from here the superior came and suggested that we send a petition to the Most Reverend Bishop regarding our nursing care of the sick. I was really in low spirits as though I had a premonition. The petition was soon formulated and was to be delivered to the superior on the next day, when on Saturday the prohibition came to us. The care of the sick within the town would be taken care of by the Vincentians and in the country by the Franciscans. Finally I was strongly obliged to adhere to it. The agitation in Olpe is great and many petitions have been sent to Paderborn. The turn of events has made it very difficult for us. If previously His Excellency had the exact knowledge of circumstances that he has now, I believe it never would have happened. But also now our dear Lord can and will help. We must pray much. . . . You should be here now for excitement is high. The Most Reverend Bishop is bombarded on all sides. The Blessed Mother will surely help, for she has the Heart of Jesus and all hearts in him within her power. If it is for our good, conditions will change. Your brother, Anton, together with Maus, Schmidts, and the Doctor are active, and with Maus there is no cessation. Lord Vicar Feldmann has also joined the group. The superior has counseled us to stay clear from all demonstrations. At times it becomes very difficult, but I am glad that the people are interested in us. Next week confession will be difficult for me, but our dear Lord must help. This will also pass. (I 33)

The following reveals that Mother Maria Theresia had indeed often considered transferring the motherhouse to another locality. For she wrote:

> From Aachen word was received from Mother Vincentia through Sister Paula that Mayen was not a suitable location for a motherhouse. Later a Sister wrote and suggested Kirchen, but that place is too small. To accept the administration of the hospital at Kirchen would probably be good because it is near. But the question arises whether the bishop of Trier would accept another congregation within the diocese.

Evidently she had sought information from the Franciscan Sisters as to the feasibility of transferring the motherhouse to Mayen. But she closes this deliberation with the remark: "I think that under present conditions, we may not leave Olpe" (I 33).

In another letter of March 28, 1884, we find the statement:

> The board of directors here in Olpe hourly await an answer from the bishop to their letter regarding the prohibition; I am fearful none will come. Pray much for me, dear Sister Deogratias, for God must uphold me; storms from all sides rage about me; will an Easter also come for us after this Good Friday? God will grant it. (I 35)

The situation had still not reached its peak; the real Good Friday was close at hand. On April 9, 1884, Dr. Kaufmann, the brother-in-law of Mother Maria Theresia, died. He had been the community physician for the Franciscans and had always become deeply involved in all that concerned the congregation. As he became seriously ill, the relatives wrote the bishop begging him to please make an exception in this one special instance and permit the Franciscan Sisters to undertake the nursing care of Dr. Kaufmann. He answered that they should submit. Mother Maria Theresia wrote about this in a letter to Sister Deogratias, April 18, 1884, and added the following:

> I visited him; our Sisters shed tears in being unable to give nursing care to him who had done so very much for all of

us. Our dear Lord permitted all this; it hurts and is very hard to bear; but God knows what is best for us. (I 36)

MÜLHEIM ON THE MOHNE

It has been stated earlier that the servant of God had seriously considered transferring the motherhouse to another locality and had sought information regarding various possible places. The situation in Olpe had become very complicated, not only because of the prohibition relative to nursing care but also for various other reasons. Much as the growth in membership, namely, fifty-seven Sisters within two years, was to be admired, it had nevertheless created serious problems for the congregation in that the living quarters had become entirely too limited. Since permission to care for epileptic children in the former orphanage had been granted, those quarters could be used no longer as housing for the Sisters. In this dilemma the purchase of the castle at Mülheim offered a solution. In this castle of the Knights of the Teutonic Order, the Salesian Sisters had, until the *Kulturkampf*, conducted a boarding school for the higher education of girls. Mother Maria Theresia had been attracted, and was accepted by this order of Sisters in her early years, but was hindered by a sudden disease, mentioned earlier. In 1857, the Salesians went to Höxter. But as this city offered no practical possibilities for them, they went to Mülheim in 1860. Missionary Hillebrand gave the impetus for this transfer. He had also counseled Mother Maria Theresia in her earlier years as she struggled with her religious vocation. During the *Kulturkampf* the Salesians' boarding school for girls was suppressed. They, consequently, went to Tilbury, Holland. The many unfortunate happenings in Mülheim before it was suppressed, left the Sisters with no desire to return after the *Kulturkampf*.

The press publicized the castle for sale at various times. Finally the Domkapitular, Dr. Schulte, purchased it. Personally, he could not do much with it and had no special designs for its use. Most likely he bought it to prevent it from falling into wrong hands; he wished to preserve it for ecclesiastical purposes. Thus he readily sold it to the Franciscans in Olpe. Mother Maria Theresia had read the notice in the papers and negotiated for it. The business transactions ended successfully. Through a bill of sale, September 19, 1884, the castle at Mülheim passed into the possession of the congregation. Its roomy quarters and serene atmosphere and locality made it a more feasible area for a novitiate than the limited quarters of the motherhouse in Olpe. The first group of Sisters left on February 5, 1885, to prepare the place. These were Sister Deogratias, recently returned from America, as superior with three other Sisters. On Ash Wednesday, Mother Maria Theresia accompanied a second group there. From that date until 1895, the novitiate of the congregation was conducted at Mülheim. Later the novitiate was transferred back to the motherhouse in Olpe. During these ten years, six hundred novices received their schooling in the religious life within the walls of the old castle.

When the Sisters first arrived at Mülheim, the castle had been unoccupied for ten years. The grounds were overgrown with weeds and required much attention. Much energy had to be expended to make the devastated buildings take on an appearance of habitation. Its roomy areas were difficult to heat to any degree of comfort. In the early years, Mülheim often felt real need, for it was difficult to secure outside employment for a livelihood. A novitiate is not self-supporting.

Mother Maria Theresia always loved to linger in Mülheim. On one of her visits she experienced the real poverty that reigned there. During the noon meal the bowls were soon empty. She intimated to a Sister to get more food from the kitchen. The Sister concerned, knowing there was no more, hesitated for a moment. Another Sister thinking the one addressed was tired, picked up a bowl and went to the kitchen. She, however, soon returned and placed the empty container on the table. Mother Maria Theresia surprised asked if there were no more food in the kitchen. When she learned the situations, she said: "O Sisters, how happy I am that I can share your poverty!" She added; "You probably do not honor St. Joseph sufficiently here. Have you no St. Joseph here to whom we can bring our need and beg him for help?" A Sister mentioned that upstairs in a corner there was a dust-covered statue of St. Joseph. The Mother advised that it be brought down, cleaned thoroughly, and displayed honorably. Mother Maria Theresia then prayed with the Sisters before the little altar of St. Joseph and begged fervently for his mighty help. The short devotion ended with a hymn to St. Joseph, *Go All Ye to Joseph.* The trustful prayer was soon answered. That same afternoon a person from a neighboring estate announced himself and said that he thought the Sisters probably did not have enough to eat; and consequently he had brought a wagon load of eatables, and added a donation of one hundred marks.

Again St. Joseph proved himself the trusted helper of Mother Maria Theresia. Even in a more significant way than in the early days of Mülheim, St. Joseph demonstrated his help in Olpe during the great worries of Mother Maria Theresia's construction projects. Her brother-in-law, Dr. Kaufmann, who knew the exact financial status of the congregation, asked Mother Maria Theresia at that time with what moneys she was actually building. She answered St. Joseph will be our help. She then gave him a more detailed explanation that in the motherhouse there was a statue of St. Joseph that had a large opening on the rear side. Within that opening she placed all the unpaid bills when she did not know what else to do. Puzzled, he could not understand such a procedure: "Do not worry, Lorenz, all such accounts I place in the statue of St. Joseph; you just watch, someone will come with the money." This unshakeable confidence in her heavenly helper was again rewarded. Just then benefactors came and brought the urgently needed money.

In Olpe a large building sum was due and Mother Maria Theresia did not have the money to pay. The account was placed in the statue of her heavenly helper. On the same day a citizen of Olpe, Johann Schmidt, came to the convent in the evening and handed the Sister portress a sum of money. He explained: "I had the intention long ago of giving the Sisters this gift but always forgot. Today I was again reminded of my intention and I now bring it before I forget again." Strange to say he brought the exact sum designated in the account.

Now back to Mülheim. There were many traces of the activity of the Salesians. The cemetery had a Way of the Cross on the wall. Many Sisters found their final resting place in that cemetery. Mother Maria Theresia was influenced by the piety of those who live and served as religious in the castle before her Sisters: "The cemetery must be preserved. In the midst of life we are embraced by death. The thought of death should ever be near; then it will lose its fear for us, and we shall welcome it as readily as a known friend."

The foundation at Mülheim and the transfer of the novitiate there brought on more problems other than that of support. A large building and beautiful surroundings are not enough in themselves. Shortly after their arrival in Mülheim, the servant of God endeavored to establish Mülheim as a center. Thus on February 9, 1885, she wrote to the bishop of Paderborn. After first thanking him for his mediation in securing the required state approval of the transfer to Mülheim, she added:

> We should be very happy if Your Grace would use your influence to realize the prospect of the new hospital in Rüthen for our congregation. Much will depend upon our having hospitals in the vicinity of Mülheim.

The bishop contacted the mayor of Rüthen and asked him to give over the operation of the new hospital to the Franciscans. He wrote:

> I must note that it is in the interests of the congregation to operate hospitals in the vicinity of their motherhouse in Mülheim to give their Sisters opportunity for educational development in nursing care. Besides I can assure you that the Franciscans enjoy a good reputation in the nursing of the sick.

Although the bishop in this way endeavored to make reparation to the Sisters for forbidding them the nursing care in Olpe, his action produced no results.

Spiritual direction had to be provided for the Sisters. On her own initiative, Mother Maria Theresia put out feelers to Reverend Vicar Lappe in Drolshagen asking him if he were willing to assume the position as spiritual director. The request resulted in Vicar Lappe being appointed spiritual director of the Sisters at Mülheim. The stipulations of the General Vicariate were that the congregation offer him free board and room and annually give him three hundred marks as Mass stipends.

June 24, 1885, marked the date of the first profession in Mülheim. As representative of Superior Pielsticker, Dean Gochel, as appointee of the bishop, officiated at the ceremonies. The question arose whether Superior Pielsticker wanted to give up the office of superior? The obligations of superior were rather difficult to fulfill because of the distance of Attendorn from Mülheim. At the wish of the congregation, the bishop appointed Reverend Domkapitular Dr. Schulte as superior in June, 1885. The office of superior was again in very good hands, for Dr. Schulte had made the foundation in Mülheim possible and therefore had a great personal interest in the advancement of the congregation. He fulfilled the office faithfully until he was made General Vicar. Reverend Vicar Lappe was appointed superior in February 1889. General Vicar Wigger succeeded him after a three-year period.

FURTHER FOUNDATIONS

In 1885 the convent at Mülheim was opened. Kirchen on the Sieg was the tenth foundation in Germany. Five Sisters took charge of the hospital there on January 5, where they also engaged in home nursing. In the same year, Merten near Bonn was undertaken. An unmarried woman of the nobility called Josephine from Boeselager placed her possessions in Merten at the disposal of the Franciscan Sisters to enable them to engage in the care of the sick there. Because of the *Kulturkampf* she had been advised not to deed the property directly to the congregation. Thus the landed estate was deeded to the parish church in Merten with the stipulation that it be given to the Franciscans as soon as conditions were such that they could accept it in order to form a foundation. Since the time was now favorable, Mother Maria Theresia was able to bring her first Sisters to Merten in May 1885.

The beginning was made, but soon many cares and difficulties arose. The organization and plan had not been completely formulated. The nobility had pressured and the Sisters accepted prematurely. The donors specified the area of activity. It is scarcely possible for outsiders to plan feasibly the life and apostolate of religious women. There no advancement was made. Other arrangements had to be made. At all events, it is questionable whether these would have succeeded had the Archbishop of Cologne and Cardinal Phillipus Krementz not intervened. During a visit in Merten the archbishop advised the Sisters to arrange for a boarding school in that beautiful building. To defray the cost of renovation for that purpose, he gladly permitted a collection in his archdiocese, though personally he was much adverse to such a collections. Today it is customary for a parish to announce collections taken for various purposes and then manage them. At that time it was customary to solicit funds from house to house. We saw earlier that Mother Maria Theresia was against the house to house soliciting in the various towns and villages unless absolute necessity demanded it. Although begging is permitted in the statutes of the congregation, she clearly saw what harassment the Sisters suffered from it. She was unwilling to jeopardize the spiritual welfare of the Sisters to obtain money. Thus under a special condition, she wrote to Merten:

> … to send a Sister to Merten for the purpose of collecting would not be acceptable since such practice is forbidden in the Archdiocese, and even our asking for permission would be looked upon with disfavor. (I 44)

This letter had been written before the archbishop gave permission. The servant of God was therefore surprised at the archbishop's approval. But she recognized an outstanding sign of his good will toward the congregation.

But she was deeply concerned lest the Sisters in Merten venture into projects that were to be accomplished by others, and in the same letter she wrote:

> The necessary construction must be done … if the pastor and the good lady wish to build, I have nothing against it; but we cannot undertake a new construction project in Merten, but can only make the necessary renovations. The house has been deeded to the parish church; therefore, further construction work is the affair of the parish pastor, consequently, be discreet.

Again she admonished: "Also regarding the collecting, we must be very alert and also obedient" (I 44).

From this last statement we learn how very considerate Mother Maria Theresia was that the ecclesiastical regulations and orders be respected. Wise reflections played their part. For if a congregation, by whatever means, tries to carry its own will through, against the will of the presiding bishop, it will suffer shipwreck. The servant of God in this special situation expressly declared, "We shall be obedient," manifesting her deep knowledge of the situation. She once mentioned to her Sisters, "How confidently an obedient soul can appear before her Judge; to all questions put to her she can reply that she acted in obedience to his representative." This was not said as a warning to her Sisters. She regulated her own life according to the directives of God's representative. Herein she greatly resembled holy Father Francis, who confessed that the Lord made known his will to him through the mouth of the bishop of Assisi. But her willing obedience was not an unenlightened one. She distinguished clearly between diocesan bishops who within their domain could exact obedience from her and her congregation, and others who by force desired to force their own ideas to the detriment of the congregation. "Open your eyes to faith" was once said in connection with obedience, giving the intrinsic and basic roots of a genuine enlightened obedience. It seems that at this time their readiness opened the doors of the apostolate to the Sisters. Entirely contrary to his accustomed way, the archbishop of Cologne permitted not only a collection in the archdiocese for the reconstruction of the foundation in Merten, but even went a step farther. He obtained a teacher with the necessary qualifications required by the state for licensing a school. This teacher was Miss Fischer, from Cologne. At this time the congregation had no qualified teaching Sister for the *Kulturkampf* had interrupted the education of the Sisters. In Miss Fischer the Lord gave the Sisters an outstanding benefactor, for she devoted not only her name and energies to the school at Merten, but through her monetary donations made a chapel for the Sisters a possibility.

The development of education in Merten was a mark of distinction and very significant for the Poor Franciscans. Because of the restrictions of the *Kulturkampf*, their apostolate had been limited to the nursing of the sick. The times now afforded their earliest opportunities for the education of youth. In the early years of its foundation, the chief activity of the congregation was the care of orphans. This apostolate in Olpe earned them the designation of "orphan Sisters." After the suppression of the orphanage, Mother Maria Theresia, under great difficulties, obtained permission to care for epileptic children in the orphanage quarters. In this way she furthered to some degree the Sisters' formative work among youth. She now learned that many religious congregations had again obtained permission from the state to operate nursery schools and kindergartens. She endeavored to try such an undertaking in the motherhouse because of its close relationship with their first activity. On October 15, 1885, a corresponding visit by the government was arranged. Sister Paula, the assistant made the contact since Mother Maria Theresia had gone to America toward the end of September. On February 4, 1886, the approval of the state was received. It stipulated that orphan children not of school age may be cared and provided for at the orphanage. On August 19, 1887, the ministerial permission was granted for the acceptance of children of school age also. This permission had riders attached: when the orphanage is reopened, epileptic children will have to be removed; the education of the orphans may not take place in a private school conducted by the Sisters; orphans must attend the elementary school of the town. These conditions were satisfactory. The Sisters rejoiced greatly that their original apostolate again could be exercised in full.

The Constitution of the congregation determines definitely: "In the apostolate of the congregation, one of the chief objectives is the instruction, care, and formation of poor, orphaned, or neglected youth." There can be no indifference as to activity. Her fidelity dictated the resumption of the original objective as soon as possible.

Mother Maria Theresia Bonzel (1830–1905). *Photo taken in Lafayette, Indiana*

The home of the Bonzel family located next to St. Martin Church in Olpe, Germany. Mother Maria Theresia developed a strong devotion to the Eucharist from an early age, praying at her first holy Communion, "O Lord, I am Thy victim; accept me as Thy victim: do not reject me."

Adoration Chapel at the motherhouse which had once been Mother Maria Theresia's bedroom.

Mother Maria Theresia prayed many hours in adoration before the monstrance pictured here. She had a great love for Jesus and a powerful devotion to Eucharistic Adoration, beginning Perpetual Adoration in the community immediately after it was founded in 1863.

During her first visit to America, Mother Maria Theresia visited Columbus, Nebraska, where the Sisters later established a hospital. She was a true Mother to her Sisters and came to visit them three times in America.

A class of novices with Mother Maria Theresia after their investiture. When the *Kulturkampf* restrictions in Germany had been lifted, young women entered the community in great numbers. The decade following this period saw 600 novices pass through the novitiate in Germany.

Mother Maria Theresia near the Lourdes Grotto at the motherhouse in Germany.

Statue of St. Joseph where Mother Maria Theresia placed her special intentions. She brought both spiritual and practical needs before St. Joseph, dedicating each Sister to him with the title "of St. Joseph" added to her name.

Mother Maria Theresia on her deathbed. Her last words were: "Patience! My dear Savior, come soon!" She died on February 6, 1905, after a life of adoration and selfless service, leaving a work richly blessed by God and a well-established congregation. At the time of her death, nearly 1,500 Sisters served the Church in Germany and the United States.

The unveiling of the portrait of Blessed Maria Theresia Bonzel at the Beatification Mass in the Cathedral in Paderborn, Germany, on November 10, 2013. Bishop Kevin Rhoades of the Diocese of Fort Wayne–South Bend, Indiana, is to the right of Cardinal Angelo Amato.

The remains of Blessed Maria Theresia were transferred from the motherhouse in Germany to the Adoration Chapel in St. Martin Church, Olpe, Germany on November 11, 2013.

CHAPTER X

AGAIN ANEW TO AMERICA

The Congregation of the Poor Franciscans had now been in existence more than twenty years. Those were years filled with hopes and sorrows, severe trials, and renewed beginnings. They walked the way of the cross. But God also blessed their activities. Especially in North America the congregation experienced an almost phenomenal growth at the exact time when all was at a seeming standstill in Germany. In the homeland all wisdom and energies had to be expended to hold and justify existing positions, while in the New World conditions were in a genuine upward swing.

When Mother Maria Theresia drafted the first Constitution in 1865, Olpe was the only house of the congregation and the Sisters were few in number. Twenty years later the situation was entirely different. A change had also occurred in the inner structure of the congregation. After consultation with Sister Paula, her assistant, the servant of God undertook a redrafting of the Constitution. She submitted the revised copy to the Reverend Superior for examination, and in an accompanying note she gave the reasons for the suggested changes:

> As Your Reverence readily sees, the revision of our Constitution was a necessity. The original Constitution had been approved by Bishop Konrad of blessed memory in 1865, with the reservation that he endorse later necessary and useful modification. After the expansion of the congregation here and in America, some regulations had to be deleted and others added. In consultation with the Very Reverend Provincial of the Franciscans, Othmarus Maasmann, the changes were made. The provincial had one of his priests help us redraft the Constitution. Most changes were taken from the Constitution of the Franciscan Sisters of Heidhausen (Capellen), which in three instances had been approved by Rome. (V 15)

The reference above was made to the Franciscan Sisters of Penance and Christian Charity, who had their motherhouse in Haydithuizen, Holland. These Sisters had a foundation in Capellen, Germany, and were well known in the country and had a splendid reputation. Mother Maria Theresia never hesitated to acknowledge that she learned much from this congregation. By basing the organization of her congregation on the Constitution of other congregations approved by the Holy See, she avoided unnecessary experimentation. Upon reflecting the ways of the servant of God, the conclusion might easily be drawn that she had no method of her own. Nothing could be more untrue. What she learned from others she reworked in her own mind making the final result her own. She was the spiritual leader of her congregation in every way. Her letters to America prove this fact.

In 1885, the congregation in the United States of America, besides a motherhouse and novitiate in Lafayette, operated six hospitals and seven schools, more foundations than the congregation had in Germany. Since Mother Maria Theresia's return from America on June 5, 1879, during which time she had learned conditions there, she was keenly devoted and interested in developments across the sea. She showered all the love of her maternal heart upon her Sisters, took an intimate part in all their endeavors, and endeavored to lead all on the way they had begun in the name of God. Repeatedly her circular letters crossed the ocean to all the Sisters, to separate convents, to individual Sisters, and sometimes to superiors only. The Sisters in America sensed and realized deeply what they had in their Mother from Olpe. A large number of letters were carefully preserved and today disclose the deep concern of the mother for her daughters. Sooner than laud these letters in beautiful terms, let her words speak for themselves.

Let us now consider her letter of November 3, 1880:

> *Dear good Sisters!*
>
> I thank you most sincerely for the loving and gracefilled wishes you sent me on the occasion of my nameday, the feast of St. Theresia, especially for the Holy Communions and prayers you have offered for me. May it please our dear Lord to answer your petitions in my behalf and gra-

ciously grant me the graces I need. I have presented all of you, my dear Sisters, above all others, to my patron saint and have begged her to grant you a holy love of God and neighbor. May this great grace be ours; may we be grounded and strengthened in this love, according to the wish of our divine Savior! The group of our dear Sisters in America is growing ever more numerous. God be praised! Although an ocean separates us, we shall ever remain intimately united in the Sacred Heart and in all seek to advance the greater glory of God by walking according to our holy Rule. Our dear Lord has called us to this way of life as a means to save our souls and those of others. Let us guard against following the phantoms of evil! Walk in the way of obedience for it guides with certitude. Whoever seeks her own self in the convent, loses what is common, and whoever withdraws from obedience, withdraws from grace. A nun without obedience is a misfit in the convent. Walk in fidelity and guard the grace of vocation. God himself has called and selected us and we shall be held accountable for all he has entrusted to us, especially for the great grace of vocation.

Dear good Sisters, remain faithful! For the love of God I beg all of you, be faithful! Consider nothing mean and trivial, for the evil one prowls about seeking to bring us to destruction. The holy Rule and the regulations of our superiors are a staff giving us needed support. Let us walk in the footsteps of our holy Father Francis with simplicity and humility for we are the lesser ones. For this may God be praised a thousand fold. Let us not be satisfied by being lesser in name only, but with true humility of heart let us also rejoice when we are despised by others and considered unimportant, for that is fitting to us.

I am trusting that you are all in good health. Most likely your conversations often turn to your many experiences and happenings in the motherhouse; dear Sister Johanna and the other Sisters accompanying her will have much to tell you upon their arrival. Your membership will again increase as more candidates will be invested. May great graces and spiritual joys be yours on that day. May our holy Father Francis obtain his spirit for you that with the laying aside of worldly attire, the worldly heart may also be rent asunder and a truly crushed and humbled spirit be granted in its stead. Therefore, we shall pray for all of you here; dear good Sisters, be fervent in prayer. Since you have many contacts with the world, your remaining faithful to your prayers and spiritual exercises is all the more important. Adieu, my dear Sisters! In true love and devotion, I bless you every morning and evening.

Your least,
Sister Maria Theresia, Poor Franciscan
(II 1)

These words are simple and unpretentious. Still they are characteristic, not insignificant chatter, let alone empty repetitions of pietistic expressions. That was not Mother Maria Theresia's way, and just that made her words so directly relevant for conversation. Definitely many an exhortation and demand are embodied therein. But these are more the delicate pressures of a loving mother than the words of a writer who wishes to show his superiority to others, or of one in office who wishes to pose as superior. Whether the exhortations to humility refer to certain incidents is not clear. Possibly they could have been, for Mother Maria Theresia generally was not accustomed to give general admonitions, but only with reference to specific situations. She signed the letter as "Poor Franciscan." The entire letter is an acknowledgement of this expression, "For we are the lesser ones!" This humble poverty in spirit made her the genuine daughter of the Poor Man of Assisi. A scrutiny of this letter reveals why the letters of the Mother were so carefully preserved. In their straightforwardness they offered a reliable guide for the spiritual life of her Sisters.

How in difficult times she revealed the fullness of her loving maternal heart to her Sisters in North America and encouraged them, is manifested in the following letter:

> As I learned from your letters, my dear Sisters, you are overburdened with work for some of the Sisters are weak and sickly. My heart aches for you and I would love to write a word of comfort to each of you individually, but time will not permit. May the loving and ever comforting Heart of Jesus, in whom we can always seek refuge, give you a certain new courage and joyousness in his service. For the yoke of the Lord is sweet and his burden light! Undoubtedly, my dear Sisters, we all have repeatedly experienced, after returning from the confused entanglements and strivings in the world and spending a few moments with our Beloved Savior, what grace, what peace, and what quiet has stolen into our heart! Times will be better again, only keep up your courage. Let us rejoice if the Lord demands sacrifices of us, for it marks us as his own. The spirit of sacrifice is the criterion of God-loving souls. Therefore, my dear Sisters, rejoice for your reward will be exceedingly great.

After she had encouraged her overburdened Sisters, not with more consolation, but with substantial thoughts, she advised further how to manage their two fold obligation of work and prayer:

> How much you can accomplish. Do not let it disturb your recollection nor destroy your union with God! Although Martha's work rests upon you, let Mary's attitude of prayer abide, for the Lord's word is valid for us too: "Only one thing is necessary."

She reflected the regional superior, Sister Deogratias, would soon be visiting the Sisters; then there would also be days of rejoicing after all those of work and cares: "I would also love to visit you but must rest satisfied with the good will. It is always a great joy to hear from you and I beg you to write to me frequently" (II 3).

In another letter she wrote of the chief objective of our congregation, namely, the Perpetual Adoration. This should not only be a beautiful title of the congregation but should be basic in the formation of the Sisters and give meaning to their lives. She added a thought she herself conceived during a retreat:

> We had a retreat some time ago; how indelibly the retreat master impressed the idea of prayer on our hearts. To belong to a Congregation of Perpetual Adoration can never be cherished adequately. What innumerable graces flow down upon us during the quiet hours of adoration. Let us fulfill this obligation very faithfully; then we can look forward to our last hour with confidence, for in eternity we shall continue the loving labor of our grateful hearts begun in this life: the adoration of God.

Then she added:

> Here we are looking forward to the Holy Night with great joy; we shall have exposition of the Blessed Sacrament. I trust our dear Lord will grant me the grace of participation. Last year I was seriously ill and was able only to look down upon the crib from the choir loft. Our dear Lord knows what is best for all of us. May he be praised! (II 4)

How often similar hints appear in her letters! A long chain of illnesses and physical sufferings are thus revealed. It is astounding how this servant of God could fulfill the manifold duties of office so well. Yet she never mentions her sufferings in a tone of pride or in the sense of a victim soul. She also never complains about sickness. As Mother she simply relates it to her Sisters, thanks God for recovery, and expresses resignation to his will.

Because she knew suffering so well, her words connoted a characteristic depth and warmth when she comforted her Sisters undergoing crosses and afflictions. She recognized the hardships entering more or less into the founding of a new mission. In the opening of a new school in St. Mary's, Nebraska, the difficulties seemed almost insurmountable. On February 18, 1882, she wrote to her Sisters there:

> From Sister Magdalena's letter just received, I have learned that you are enduring many crosses and oppositions. I

> rejoiced and thanked God, but I also prayed for you, my dear, good Sisters, for patience and joy in suffering. Above all keep a joyous heart; all comes from the hands of God, our best of Fathers in heaven; he loves us tenderly, more than the kindest of mothers could love. In the knowledge of so much providential goodness, how could we be sad or discouraged? Let us grieve over our sins, failings, and shortcomings through which we daily offend the tender Heart of Jesus. That alone is unfortunate and deserves to be lamented. Accept all with courage in childlike prayer, dear Sisters, and seek the Lord and his honor in all that befalls you; the Lord is good to the soul that seeks him! In all our activities let us preserve a good intention and an upright heart; let us offer all to him, who besides his many graces, has given us the great grace of a religious vocation. Let us rejoice here on earth when the Lord considers us worthy to wear his livery, for it is his sign of predilection. As his exemplar let us bear the cross with courage. A very brief time and the crown will be ours and that for eternity! (II 5)

Evidently, because St. Mary's was a new foundation, Mother Maria Theresia, from thoughts experienced in faith, added several points. She was concerned that this foundation, from its very beginning, live in a truly religious spirit. Therefore, she desired to give her Sisters, to a certain degree, a special synopsis of the spiritual life. She wrote:

> Let us act in obedience, dear Sisters, then we cannot go wrong and will enjoy the blessing of God. Love holy poverty and practice it with joy of heart; it is the greatest treasure left us as legacy by St. Francis. Let us live as true Franciscans, my dear Sisters; poverty brings us many blessings and preserves us from much evil. Our Savior did not find this treasure in heaven but on earth; he learned it in the stable and preached it from the cross by his example. Gladly make the sacrifice! Bear with patience and love all and everything burdensome entailed in contact with the children, in the spirit of the Lord. Times will certainly

> come when you cannot attend the spiritual exercises. Be prepared also for that if there is no other way. But on the other hand in fidelity to your congregation try to rearrange conditions if possible. Let love reign among you, for love is the queen of all virtues of the soul. With her even the most difficult will become easy. If then you meet difficulties and oppositions from the outside, bearing them together in love can even make them sweet. Pray much, my dear Sisters, and seek to maintain an ardent and living spirit of devotion. You can even pray while engaged in external activities if you keep your heart at rest in God. This union with our Lord I wish for you with all my heart and beg that you also pray for me, as I do for you. (II 5)

How exactly she had sized up the situation at this newly founded mission passing through the throes of its initial hardships! There was much that had to become matter of custom. Her stressing love above all gave evidence of her clear insight into the situation. Under such conditions overwork is natural. The fact remains that an overstimulation of nerves from all this overwork can readily result. She was wise enough to realize that also in a convent, especially under strained conditions, great difficulties can arise from life in common. "See, it is the Lord who has thrown us thus together," she once humorously wrote to Sister Deogratias (I 25).

Also, in this letter a characteristic of Mother Maria Theresia becomes evident in a specific way. She does not wish a general religious life for her Sisters but one impregnated with Franciscanism. So many religious congregations came into being in the nineteenth century, and many chose their Rule by chance. Charitable activity called and congregations were founded to fill the need to serve God and man. With some it seemingly made no difference what religious rule was followed for all were good and sanctifying. Opinions concerning specific spiritualities came much later. With Mother Maria Theresia the situation was entirely different, for from the very beginning it was definitely clear to her from what spiritual store her Sisters were to be nourished.

She never ceased to point out to her Sisters the great legacy of St. Francis, as her letters to America repeatedly show.

Most probably during the *Kulturkampf* eyes often turned to North America especially upon hearing of the rapid expansion and the fruitful results of the Sisters' apostolate there, and melancholy readily stole upon the Sisters in the homeland. Comparisons were made with the situation in Germany which at that time seemed almost hopeless. Were conditions in the New World not much easier than those at home? At one time this idea also entered the mind of Mother Maria Theresia, but she thought it over with serene calmness. Thus she wrote to North America:

> One hears that in America everything is easier. But I think the way to heaven there is just as steep and just as strewn with crosses and thorns as here in Germany. (II 6)

She takes this opportunity to inform the Sisters there of the situation in the homeland, which was of particular interest to them. She does not relate incidents in a straightforward manner, but intersperses them with recognitions of divine Providence. She continues further:

> Here winter has set in with energy. You have most likely heard of the flooding in the Rhine Province and in Tyrol. It was a terrible misfortune and the devastation was formidable. Our dear Lord comes in various ways to bring men to their senses, but it almost seems as though nothing has any effect. Dear Sisters, let us pray much especially to the Blessed Mother that the dreadful punishments threatening us will be held back. The enemies of holy Church appear in the open and almost daily one hears insulting remarks about the Catholic religion. Missionaries will soon be more necessary in Germany than in India or China. The scarcity of priests is felt more and more, although the weapons of the *Kulturkampf* are at rest in some areas, they crop out anew in others. May fervent prayers and zealous works effect reparation to our Lord and save souls from the swelling tides of perdition. (II 6)

From these letters the Sisters in America must have sensed clearly what the servant of God once wrote to Sister Deogratias:

> Oh, how often I think of you, dear Sisters, in the morning, in the evening, many times during the day, and in the sleepless nights. (I 14)

When a widely spread congregation must be kept together, there certainly is justification for simply forbidding every separation and every attempt at autonomy. But such decisions carry weight only when the consciousness of community is alive. How the servant of God brought about this consciousness of community in truly maternal fashion is shown in her letters. She was not so much a dictating superior as a solicitous mother. She was the heart of the congregation.

What she did not communicate to the individual houses or certain Sisters in North America, was her great concern whether all was going well. She had her fears. In her letters to the regional superiors she wrote:

> I am very concerned about you and all the Sisters in America; I have always been concerned, but recently my fears have increased with each day. (I 9)

As learned from her letters, one fear was that disunity and discords might arise among the Sisters. This explains why her letters so often exhorted the Sisters to charity among themselves. A second fear was the attempts of the bishops to place themselves in a position of greater strength in the administration of the congregation. Evidently Mother Maria Theresia wished her congregation to adapt and adjust itself to the special regulations and proposals of the diocese. The bishops have the right and the obligation to direct the religious life in their dioceses and to issue orders for that purpose. Hers was a fear that bishops would go farther and set up definite statutes for religious women active in the respective dioceses. For two different constitutions in one and the same congregation would create havoc and lead ultimately to separation. Thus Mother Maria Theresia became alarmed rulewise when she was notified in 1884 that Bishop Dwenger had in mind to change the Constitution of the congregation. However, she soon learned that that was not his intention. The bishop wished only several changes in the investiture and profession ceremony. Regarding this the servant of God had no objection: "The change the Most Reverend Bishop wishes in the rite can readily be made; that no change is requested in the Constitution is good." (I 35)

The bishop had obviously urged that the questions regarding the novitiate be settled more effectively. The problem had the appearance that the great distance of the North American foundation had produced certain difficulties. Mother Maria Theresia consequently in a letter of March 28, 1884, expressed an opinion whether it might not be better to establish a second novitiate in Omaha, Nebraska (I 35). Two months later, May 26, 18814, she wrote with great concern:

> *Dear, good Sister Deogratias,*
>
> Now I am really greatly disturbed since the Most Reverend Bishop of Fort Wayne, with the approval of Rome, has effected a change in our seeking the establishment of a second novitiate in another diocese. (I 39)

The sentence is not clear nor complete. It seems as though the restless thoughts ran away from the pen. The impression is given that the regional superior in the North American foundation had written to the effect that, with the approval obtained from Bishop Dwenger, the novitiate could be conducted more effectively in another diocese. Great dangers were concealed herein for the sisters in North America. Therefore she continued her letter as follows:

> I believe in this we shall meet with great dissatisfaction toward our congregation and make bishops and priests ill disposed toward us. The bishop has advised that a well-conducted novitiate would be of interest to the congregation and of great importance to it. If this will not be accomplished, priests will be dissatisfied and will not direct postulants to our sisterhood. (I 39)

At that particular time it would have been hazardous to attempt to play one diocese against another for the sole purpose of securing better regulations in the conduct of a novitiate. Mother Maria Theresia had been informed that the bishops of North America would soon meet in general council at Baltimore. One point on the agenda of this national synod was the relationship of the bishops to the various religious congregations in the United States of America.

To prevent any unwise act, especially in this point, would serve the best interests of the servant of God. Consequently, on June 10, 1884, she admonished with great urgency:

> Under no conditions may you disregard the decisions of the Most Reverend Bishop of Fort Wayne. We will and must obey after the Holy Spirit has spoken. Because of the great distance a second novitiate might have to be established in the West at some time; but for the present, dear Sister Deogratias, let us not consider it. The decision of the Most Reverend Bishop Dwenger must be respected for our motherhouse is in his diocese. I beg you be deeply concerned about the formation of the young Sisters; they are souls God entrusted to you. The true religious spirit is easily lost if too soon they mingle with the world again. Also you can readily imagine the subjects under discussion by the assembled bishops. The Reverend Bishop of Cleveland, a good and outstanding prelate most certainly collected information from none other than Bishop Dwenger. The results could cause great unpleasantness for the entire congregation. I beg you be prudent, listen to advice, consult with the older Sisters! My fears and cares concerning conditions there are inexpressible. May our dear Lord in his goodness sustain you that all be for his greater honor. (I 40)

Sister Deogratias seemingly did not have sufficient maturity to handle the manifold situations crowding in upon her. In the same letter she had to face another reprimand:

> It grieved me greatly that you took over the hospital in Denver; really if one places himself in your position, he

> can easily see that it is not easy to refuse a bishop; still you knew our situation. It would have been better for you had you first consulted with Sister Johanna and the older Sisters in Lafayette; good Sister Johanna would have accompanied you on the toilsome journey and been faithfully at your side with assistance and advice. But now she must learn (the acceptance of the hospital) through public media. Dear Sister Deogratias, the Sisters are becoming dissatisfied; you know I mean it well, but for the sake of God, be careful. (I 40)

All this probably caused Sister Deogratias to recognize her limitations humbly and to beg to be relieved from the office of regional superior. This was granted her and in the same year (1884), she returned to Germany and was appointed superior in Mülheim. The office of regional superior was given to Sister Hyacinth. That this was not a happy choice soon became evident. She was a person who by her rigidity repulsed others. Also, she did not have the correct attitude toward North America and was adverse to American culture. When an American girl applied for admission, she was subjected to an overly critical test by Sister Hyacinth. This fact caused new unrest in an already overcharged atmosphere.

To understand the meager entry, all things must be placed in proper perspective. The Chronicle reads:

> As disturbing reports were received from across the ocean, Mother Maria Theresia decided to make a second trip to North America to be of assistance in word and deed to her Sisters in their difficulties. Toward the end of September accompanied by several of her Sisters she made the journey and disembarked in New York on October 3, 1885. There, after a tiresome voyage, she made the first stop with the Sisters of Mother Schervier, and then proceeded to Lafayette, which she used as a center for visitation to the various houses of the region. She probably had previously conceived plans of how she would solve the personnel problems, but first she wished to contact all the Sisters to hear their wishes and cares.

For many Sisters the visitation was another visit with the Mother; for others it was their first personal contact with her. What impression did the latter gain from this first meeting with her? It might be questioned whether these Sisters experienced the same reaction as many others. After the death of the Mother, they said they had. The attention of the Mother emanated from the loving serenity of her heart, and often at her first glance she comprehended what engaged the Sister before a word was spoken.

How the servant of God was treasured by outsiders in this segment of her life is shown by a letter from Mother Josepha Hersel, O.S.U., in 1885, to a girl who applied for admission to the Olpe congregation:

> In that convent you wish to enter, I perceive, as in the greatness of the call itself, a very special love and grace of God. The Venerable Mother Maria Theresia I honor and revere as a saint and also esteem Sister Paula highly.... You will be in a cloister where word and example will be your guidelines to a life of virtue and sanctity.

Bishop Dwenger of Fort Wayne must have esteemed Mother Maria Theresia highly also. An incident illustrates this fact, although it is not evident whether it occurred during her first or second visit to America. It had come to his attention that the Sisters had no photograph of their Mother. He influenced Mother Maria Theresia to have her picture taken. Although such was not in harmony with her unpretentiousness, she acceded to the wishes of the bishop. Thus the Sisters had at least one photograph of the Mother they could show to new entrants.

The twenty-fifth anniversary of Mother Maria Theresia's investiture fell within the visitation period. She had not intended to mention her silver jubilee. But the Sisters had been informed and instructed by the first assistant, Sister Paula from Olpe. The anniversary day, December 20, 1885, occurred when Mother was in Omaha. Naturally the Sisters planned a beautiful feast for the occasion. Numerous letters from Germany as well as from America signified the great love and gratitude of the Sisters. She, of course, had planned within her own mind to spend the day by herself in quiet reflection. But since things were different and our Lord in love had willed otherwise, she was grateful to the Sisters for their dedication and attachment. She expressed this in a letter, dated December 28, 1885, to her Sisters in Lafayette:

> *Dear, good Sisters,*
>
> My sincere thanks for your loving letters and felicitations on the twenty-fifth anniversary of my investiture and also for your joyous Christmas greetings, which Sister Hyacinth has already surely conveyed to you. They gave me great joy. Let us thank our dear Lord, for it is he, who daily overwhelms us with his benevolence and his benefits, who ordained the congregation for his glory and sustains us in his service. May the good pleasure of the Lord be ours in the future also. Let us endeavor through intimate union with his holy will and fidelity in his service to become favorites of God. Dear, good Sisters, I am greatly indebted to you for the prayers and Holy Communions that you have offered for me, though unworthy, to the all-good God; may your love and confidence be mine also in the future. I was sorry that our dear Sister Paula had informed you, for I had hoped to reflect before the Lord in all serenity, to review the past, in grateful love, and to praise the Lord for his mercy. But the Lord permitted otherwise. Too fatigued after the journey, I could not then proceed to Lafayette. But I hope soon to spend more time in your midst. What a joy it will be to see all of you again and realize your happiness in the service of the Lord. (II 7)

But this letter could not reveal her thoughts nor the thoughts of her own life experience. Before God she was and remained responsible for her Sisters and consequently added some thoughts for advancement in the spiritual life:

> Let us, my dear Sisters, make good use of this beautiful Christmas season and learn from the loving Christ child and his Blessed Mother. May humility be anchored firmly in our hearts and may we learn the practice of silence from

> the silence of the Mother of God that in the stillness of our inmost hearts we may hear the exhortations of grace and arrive at a deep inner union with God. At the approach of the New Year, I wish all of you really great graces, consolations, and blessings. May the Name of Jesus be our power and strength enabling us to renounce ourselves that on the ruins of self-love, we may grow in virtue and love of God. May the New Year bring much good to all of us. Graces most certainly will not fail us if we are grateful to God and in humility correspond to his graces.

The visitation, a time of great labor and exertion, had ended for the servant of God in America. She encountered many problems that required prudent consideration and careful solution. However, she did not forget her obligations toward her Sisters in the homeland. On April 12, 1886, she wrote a letter to Mülheim where the novitiate was at that time:

> The glorious day of Easter is fast approaching and I hasten to send my wishes for a gracefilled, peaceful, and joyous feast. May the risen Savior grant you special consolations and blessings that all may enjoy intimate union with God. You, my dear sisters, will most certainly be granted great graces in the solitude of the cloister. Make yourselves steadily more worthy through great love and fidelity, through courage in sacrifice and renunciation, childlike obedience, humility, and mutual charity. The world little knows the joys hidden in trusting intercourse with God. We have joyfully left the world and desire to live our lives in the love of our crucified Savior. May his holy love strengthen us and grant victory to our weak wills. The good Sisters who recently made their profession are most likely there no longer. Our Lord whom they have chosen as Spouse will draw them to his heart and preserve them from the wiles of a wicked world. I have prayed much for those good Sisters and also for you, and will continue to offer prayers for you in the future. I am sorry that you, my dear postulants, must wait so long for investiture; but it must be the will of God, otherwise, he, the Almighty,

> would have ordained differently. Use the intervening time conscientiously in preparation that with greater humility and more inflamed love you may approach the Lord: then richer graces will be your portion. Pray much for me, dear Sisters, that the beloved Mother of God will lead me again into your midst that together we may sing the praises of God. (I 41)

This letter shows her powers of empathy with all the Sisters and above all her identifying with the younger Sisters. With special sympathy for the postulants, she expresses her heartfelt regret regarding the delay of their investiture. In this matter there was a special condition. It is manifested in a letter of March 17, 1886, to Sister Deogratias, superior at Mülheim:

> ... it is a peculiar situation and difficult that the Reverend Superior is sick and cannot find a free day to officiate at the ceremony. Our Lord knows how to turn all to our good; now as heretofore let us trust in him. That the investiture is postponed so long is very disturbing to me. (I 41)

Mother Maria Theresia had no idea that the investiture was delayed because of her. The Sisters desired to wait until her return to Germany in order to give her an additional joy in the celebration of her silver jubilee. Had she known she probably would not have attributed low spirits to the postulants.

The letter to Sister Deogratias mentioned just previously permits deep insight into the thoughts of Mother Maria Theresia that disturbed her at that time. She was in Lafayette again, the chief convent of the area. The visitation of the houses was completed. It was necessary now to make the required decisions. From this situation, we have the following:

> ... it is a sweet consolation: the Lord looks down upon the lowly but gazes at the lofty only from a distance. If the glance of the Lord rests complacently upon us, what more can we desire! May this gracious glance preserve us, most of all, from ourselves, from the egoism and deceptive self-love; let us inundate our hearts in the furnace of the love of the Sacred Heart and from there draw forth a pure

> and holy love of God and a faithful and selfless love of neighbor. May it be given us in this holy season to become his sacrifice through a complete sacrifice of self. For the next celebration of the feast of St. Joseph, I hope to be in Germany again. The Most Reverend Bishop Dwenger is good and desires adequate preparation and formation of the novices; that we also wish. I, too, realize it were better if our main convent were in the West, but a transfer cannot be made at present. If we pray and are faithful, our Lord will help us when the right time arrives. Let us endeavor to be true children of St. Francis, die to self, and lead a crucified life. Then at Easter we shall rejoice in the Lord and celebrate a spiritual resurrection with Christ. Pray much for me that the Sorrowful Mother remains near for at times tears and sorrows come over me. (I 41)

From these words we can readily surmise there were great problems that had to be solved. As to dates, we know that on May 1, 1886, Mother Maria Theresia was present at the investiture and profession ceremonies in Lafayette and in the second week after Easter for profession ceremonies in Omaha. Before her return trip in May, she set about solving the questions that called for solution. Realizing how very much depended upon the person of the superior, she appointed Sister Alphonsa Neuhoff as superior provincial of the North American foundation. How she esteemed this Sister is shown in a letter to Sister Deogratias, when the latter was still regional superior in America. The following is her estimate:

> I respect Sister Alphonsa greatly. She has always been a loyal member of the order and a good support to every superior. You can entrust Sisters to her without concern. She is well-intentioned and strives for the glory of God and in that also for the welfare of the congregation and also for yours. (I 13)
>
> From Omaha the Sisters have informed me that Sister Alphonsa is in poor health; I am grieved and beg you sup-

> ply sufficient help that she may be spared. She is a blessed power in the congregation. (I 36)

Sister Alphonsa was among the first Sisters to come to America and consequently was acquainted with the developments from the very beginning. This incident sounds like a well-known passage taken from the Legends of Saints, but nevertheless is true in fact. When the news of her appointment was received she was in the laundry of St. Joseph Hospital, Omaha, engaged in washing clothes.

What a happy solution Mother Maria Theresia had found in this appointment is shown in the further activities of the first provincial in North America. She held that office until her death on May 18, 1900. Reverend Bonaventure Hammer characterized her in the following words:

> As provincial superior she chose Lafayette as the provincial motherhouse. The beautiful new hospital she had erected in 1896 gave ample evidence of her great aptitude and her glowing surrender to works of charity. Under her leadership the province prospered and its activities attracted attention. In her position as head of the province she came in contact with many people. All were influenced by her gentle nature, her genuine womanliness, and her noble and agreeable personality. She was a woman of superior intelligence and great culture. It was a pleasure to converse with her. She lived entirely for others and entered wholeheartedly into everything she undertook. Her greatest joy was to help the suffering; according to human reckoning, her life's work ended too soon.

On May 12, 1886, Mother Maria Theresia embarked at New York on her return trip. Sister Hyacinth and Sister Dominica accompanied her. The voyage occasioned much concern as a heavy fog lay over the Atlantic. The travelers will not soon forget the sound of the foghorn. But all turned out well. Soon after their arrival in the homeland the fourteen postulants were invested in Mülheim with Dean Gokkel of Warstein officiating and Mother Maria Theresia present. They had waited a long time and in the meanwhile must have heard all the reports of Mother Maria Theresia with great suspense.

Soon after the celebration, the servant of God returned to Olpe. There in the beginning of June the General Council met in session. At this time it was determined that the congregation be divided into two provinces. The German Province was entitled "The Province of the Sacred Heart of Jesus" and the American province "The Province of the Sacred Heart of Mary." The great expansion in North America necessitated the division.

CHAPTER XI

SUPERIOR GENERAL

The last election by the congregation as a whole had taken place on August 12, 1883. According to the old Constitution, the term of office had been three years. Since the congregation now had two provinces, the election of 1886 was highly significant. The Sister elected would be the first Superior General of the Congregation. Basically, the official tasks of this office were the same as those of the former major superior. But it was a great joy to the congregation that this distinction was now clearly defined, for this title marked its growth and expansion. According to the new Constitution, amended with the approval of the bishop, elections take place every six years. Because of the continuous expansion of the congregation, it was deemed advisable that the Superior General have a longer term of office than three years, for only then could she, to some extent, fulfill the duties of her office consistently.

The General Chapter was held at Mülheim. In this chapter, America was represented by Sister Alphonsa, Provincial Superior, and Sister Rosa. In Germany, in addition to the council members, four Sister delegates were elected. Thus the General Chapter had twelve electoral votes. Reverend Dean Gokkel presided as representative of the diocesan bishop. His assistants were the ordinary confessors, Vicar Platte and Vicar Lappe, and the latter served as director of protocol. There was no other expected outcome but that Mother Maria Theresia would be elected Superior General for the next six years. The Sisters gave her their unanimous vote. The council members elected were Sisters Dominica, Johanna, Juliana, Paula, and Scholastica. As first assistant, Mother Maria Theresia again appointed her loyal Sister Paula. At this time the position of Provincial Superior for Germany was not set up; those duties remained with the Superior General.

The general council met on August 14 and appointed or reappointed the superiors for the German province. Mother Maria

Theresia who had previously also been local superior in Olpe was relieved of that burden by the appointment of Sister Juliana for this position. Although she had ardently wished to be relieved as Superior General, Mother Maria Theresia held that position until her death. In her repeated reelections, she however saw the Will of God. But with every term the burden grew heavier. She tried many alternatives to prevent reelection but to no avail. This is the record of her conformity to the will of God and at the same time the confidence of her Sisters.

August 12, 1892, marked another election for Superior General. Representatives from America were Sister Alphonsa, Superior Provincial, and one delegate, Sister Josepha; from Germany there were the council members and nine elected delegates. The chapter comprised sixteen electoral votes. Superior Wigger, who resided in the Olpe Motherhouse for the first time, presided as representative of the bishop. He was assisted by the ordinary confessor of the Sisters, Vicar Budde. Of the sixteen electoral votes fifteen were cast for Mother Maria Theresia. Council Sisters elected were: Sisters Dominica, Hyacinth, Johanna, Paula, and Scholastica. From among these, Mother Maria Theresia again chose Sister Paula as her assistant.

Again, in 1898, the General Chapter assembled in Olpe for the election of a Superior General. Representatives from the United States of America were: Sister Alphonsa, Superior Provincial, and two delegates, Sister Rosa and Sister Raphaele; from Germany there were twenty-two delegates. The number shows the great growth of the congregation. With those of the council Sisters, there were thirty electoral votes. Superior Vicar Wigger again presided. Once more the Sisters unanimously elected Mother Maria Theresia as Superior General. To accept the office again was difficult for her and she voiced this in the assembled chapter. But she bowed to the will of God. No one, as well as she, knew the requirements of this office.

What this reelection did to her condition can readily be conjectured from the fact that the day after, at the advice of the doctor, she went to the Baths at Wildungen to seek relief from nephritis. The year before she had recuperated there with good results. At that time the congregation had no foundation there but one was opened in 1902. It must have been a real joy for the servant of God that she was not obliged to go to the Baths at Wildungen alone, but with Sister Alphonsa who frequented the baths for the same purpose. Both Sisters remained there for a month, and then returned to Olpe. Sister Alphonsa, greatly improved in health, returned to America toward the end of September 1898. But her days were numbered. She died from heart failure on May 18, 1900. Mother Maria Theresia appointed Sister Josepha as Superior Provincial in North America, who held the office until 1923.

August 12, 1904, marked another election for the office of Superior General. In a circular for the feast of Pentecost the servant of God wrote to the Sisters:

> Then, dear Sisters, please say the following prayers, in common if possible, and daily: "Come Holy Spirit, etc., three Hail Mary's with the ejaculation, O Holy Mary, Mother of Perpetual Help, pray for us; St. Francis, pray for us;" for God's blessings upon the general chapter to take place on August 12. (IV 159)

Concerning the atmosphere prevailing before the general election, the Sister chronicler of the congregation made the following observations:

> The venerable Mother caused us more than little concern when she declared herself incapable of reelection. The more urgently she pleaded that the infirmities of age, her almost constant illnesses, and the great responsibilities of that office incapacitated her for continuance in that position, the greater our concern became. The more determined Mother became to lay aside the burden of office together with its honors, the more vehemently we implored God to direct the minds of all for the best and placed our trust in his guidance.

Sister Josepha Dirkmann and Sister Augustine Dirkmann came from America. The chapter opened on August 12, 1904, after a solemn high Mass in honor of the Holy Spirit imploring his light. Superior Wigger presided. It was a singular situation. As on the preceding days so also in this holy Mass the Sisters and Mother Maria Theresia prayed in opposition to each other. Mother begged the Lord that for the welfare of the congregation, he should direct the hearts of the Sisters to elect another Sister as Superior General. The Sisters prayed that God guide the heart of Mother to accept another reelection. The chapter met at eight o'clock in the morning. Mother Maria Theresia made a final plea to prevent her reelection. Sister Paula was commanded to endorse the request of Mother Maria Theresia and beg the Sisters not to reelect Mother but to consider another Sister, for it would be impossible for her to function through another term. She felt herself incapacitated to give the congregation what a Superior General ought to give. Sister Paula was very reluctant to make the preliminary statements, but she had been commanded in obedience to do so.

The time for elections was at hand. The Sisters made known their will through the ballot. The Reverend Superior called aloud the names appearing on the ballots, one after another. Ever and again the name of Mother Maria Theresia was called. It was a cry of the Sisters for their Mother. Indeed, all knew how frail she was at present. Although she could not possibly be as active as she had been formerly, however, in the estimation of her Sisters, she possessed qualities more worthy for she was the heart of the congregation. The election dispensed with drama. What must have been the reaction of the servant of God? She had so hoped that another Sister would be elected and had done all in her power to bring it about. Ballot after ballot registered only her name. Acceptance of the result was very difficult for her. Could she not have considered this attachment to her as a cruel love? She had experienced many situations similar to this in her life. God had constrained her to walk in her destined way until the end. She consequently hesitated no longer to assume the task again with its burdens. She accepted the results of the election in obedience to the will of God.

The balloting for the council Sisters followed. The Sisters chosen were: Deogratias, Dominica, Hyacinth, Paula, and Scholastica. After the election all went to the chapel. There the Reverend Superior announced the results of the election to the assembled congregation, and ended with a prayer of thanksgiving. The Sisters sang the *Te Deum*. Was not the primary intention in this great song of praise a thanksgiving for the elected one? "Your mercy be upon us, O Lord, as we have hoped in you. I have trusted in you, O Lord, as we have hoped in you. I have trusted in you, O Lord, do not let me be put to shame."

The council met in the afternoon of the same day. Not only the Sisters were indisposed to have a change in the office of Mother, she likewise was indisposed to make the change if a Sister wielded the office in a trustworthy manner. Consequently, she again appointed Sister Paula as her assistant. Sister Verena was appointed as substitute should one or other of the council Sisters be unable to attend the council meeting. At that time no one could have surmised that Sister Paula and Sister Verena were later to follow Mother Maria Theresia in the office of Mother General. Mother Paula held the office from 1905 to 1914; Mother Verena was assistant from 1914 to 1916, and Mother General from 1916 to 1947 during the war years.

After the elections and appointments were completed on August 12, 1904, the Sisters prepared a feast for their Mother in the refectory. They celebrated with skits and songs and wishes for the blessings of God. She thanked them for all their good wishes and their expression of confidence, and then added: "You wanted me again; now you must accept me as I am and be satisfied with my weaknesses." With great kindness she then admonished the Sisters that if her office was to be administered efficiently, all must help to carry the burden by being faithful in their duties and zealous in the observance of the Holy Rule.

Mother Maria Theresia had to be satisfied to administer the high office of Superior General until the end of her life. What she felt interiorly was somewhat revealed during the elections, but voluntarily she said much more in a letter: "At times I become despondent in having no one who can help and with whom I can weigh matters. I cling to St. Joseph, who has always helped me" (I 111). In these words she did not wish to complain that she had no help from her assistant nor from the council members. She had reference at that time to the economic difficulties relative to which she was unable to get competent or expert help from the outside. In order not to disturb her Sisters regarding these business matters, the servant of God bore the difficulties alone. Although energetic and capable Sisters were at her side, she was obliged to suffer much in solitude regarding matters inherent in the office of a major superior. Probably the experience of her own life prompted her to write as follows to her Sisters:

> He (the Holy Spirit) will be near us, when the burdens of life press upon us and afflictions of all kinds crowd in upon us. His grace will not fail us if we beseech him humbly and reveal our own wretchedness to him with confidence. How often, my dear Sisters, we complain to others and plead for a word of comfort, but forget to go to him, who alone can give true comfort, light, and help. Let us now try to do better, and go to him with great confidence. He can truly and really help us, for he is the dispenser of grace, the Holy Spirit.

She then added:

> Pray earnestly for me, for the grace of piety and strength that I may fulfill the heavy duties of my office with fidelity, and that I may live and die in a way pleasing to God. (IV 154)

These words were written in 1901. But similar requests appear in her earlier letters: "Pray much for me, for I feel the heavy burden severely at this time; I often think it will oppress me and only a gaze at the crucifix gives me strength and courage." That this is not pietistic talk only, is sensed from a similar letter written in 1895:

> On Wednesday six Sisters will leave for a new foundation in Leichlingen . . . The celebration preceding their departure affected me severely; it is still not well with me, my heart condition is not good. Saturday I thought I should die. (I 50)

Sometimes the burden is merely touched upon as in the following sentence:

> Pray much for me, dear Sister, the burden often weighs down heavily; but all for the love of God. (I 67)

The above is really not a complaint nor an accusation against her Sisters, who repeatedly elected her to the position. She ever again pleaded for prayer, gained energy by gazing at the crucifix, and strengthened herself in the love of God.

Her burdens of office increased year by year together with her bodily infirmities. Although she rejoiced in the growth and expansion of the congregation, she suffered from another aspect: "Pray much for me for cares and obligations increase with the expansion of the congregation; I need the guidance of the Holy Spirit above all" (IV 140). Hers was not a playful sort of self-confidence in directing the Sisters. She was honest before them and before God. Her Sisters realized her honesty and the full meaning of her words: "Pray often for me, dear Sisters, that I may fulfill the obligations faithfully that rest upon my weak shoulders" (IV 107). She could speak plainly and openly to the Sisters regarding her weakness without losing a fraction of her authority.

She often acknowledged how much she depended on the loyal help of her assistant, Sister Paula. Thus, at the close of the year 1890, she wrote the following in a circular letter:

> I feel very exhausted and my limbs are very painful; arthritis is an illness in itself. Dear Sisters, now I must give up; I scarcely know where my head is. Sister Paula has not been here since Thursday and you can readily imagine how things are with me. (I 121)

This is not the only letter that speaks so sincerely and openly of her condition. With aging superiors it could in some way be the panic of age. They wish to document their full energy and irreplaceability in such a tragic way. But none of this was found in Mother Maria Theresia. She viewed her situation soberly as it really was, but not with bitterness nor despair; rather she viewed it with the normal attitude toward dissolution of life in advanced years. In her straightforward acceptance of her weakness and frailty, she found her great strength in God. Why God continually wanted her as his instrument was a mystery to her, one she could not understand. She only understood that he wished to use her as his instrument and she acquiesced. Perhaps this resolves the question why her Sisters, in spite of all, repeatedly elected her. They must have sensed how, in the weakness of their Mother and her simple endurance, God wished to make his power effective in blessing the congregation.

What was the relationship of the Mother General to the local superiors administering the various foundations? How she saw the cooperation of these local superiors is expressed beautifully in the following words:

> Heartfelt thanks for your letter, also for the good wishes for the further bearing of the heavy cross; our dear Lord must help and send me a Simon of Cyrene in each local superior who through good example and fidelity to obligation and Rule can alleviate the cross; also, now as before I count on the fervent prayers of the Sisters. (III 13)

To carry the cross together was her idea of the relationship of herself to the local superiors in the service of the congregation. In all probability could not such pious thoughts be readily employed to help a Sister overcome all difficulties in her obedience to her present superior? Mother Maria Theresia realized only too well that such qualities can be found also in religious superiors. And in her honesty she might have included herself when in 1872 she wrote instructions regarding the difficulties of perfect obedience:

> Burdened are the superiors who lead us. It is certain that at times we have superiors whose administration troubles us. One lacks prudence and wisdom, another ability to know her Sisters and to deal with each individually. At times there is lack of love, often of sympathy, often concern for others. One fails in mildness, another in friendliness, whereby she could win hearts and make obedience sweet. Another has need of a ready heart, impartial toward all.

For the other Sisters she added:

> A truly obedient heart rises above all these weaknesses. Our exemplar is Jesus Christ!

In these words she showed her Sisters the real purpose of religious obedience. She not only advised them and explained that in their superiors they were dealing with humans, but much more endeavored to show what qualities are necessary in a superior. She often mentioned that if no suitable superior was to be had, the congregation should forego the establishment of a new foundation.

Those who were installed as superiors received repeated instructions from her relative to the administration of their office. She also instructed the Sisters carefully on their correct relationship to their superiors:

> Dear Sisters, have patience with the weakness of the Sisters and show great love to the afflicted, for patience conquers all! Our dear Lord bears with all of us also, for love endures forever; let us also gladly bear each other's burden to win all for God. (III 499)

To a superior she wrote:

> May the Lord strengthen you and grant you patience and resignation to fulfill your duties with courage and great confidence in him. May he grant you the grace to carry the cross of your office for his honor and glory and the salvation of those entrusted to you. Dear Sister, you will soon come to see what is wrong with Sister B. It is good to be silent, pray, and endure, but not always. You have obligations to each and every one of the Sisters. You must be vigilant. Admonish, correct, and be able to punish if necessary; but as you know from experience, under four eyes (between you and the person concerned), lest it turn to public scandal. (III 65)

When she became convinced that a local superior had made an open error in judgment, the venerable Mother took the situation in hand immediately. Thus, during her last days, as reported by the Sisters, a superior had given orders that except for the set times of prayer, no Sister was to spend time in the chapel. Scarcely had Mother Maria Theresia heard of this when she appeared in the place to set things aright. For she had emphasized over and over that as religious the Sisters were to have definite time for private prayer.

In North America the Provincial Superior naturally installed the local superiors. When Mother Maria Theresia learned that a Sister had been installed as superior for the first time, she instructed and advised her relative to the duties of that office. Such letters give a synopsis of what Mother Maria Theresia expected of the superiors of the congregation. On March 18, 1901, she wrote to a newly appointed superior in the United States:

> From your little letter of the 3rd of the previous month, I learned that you are carrying a heavy burden. Try to see the will of God and endeavor to be a good example to the Sisters and to edify them through love, humility, and fidelity to the Rule. Offer yourself to our dear Lord each morning for your Sisters, in union with the sacrifice of our Lord, who offered himself completely for all of us. Be a guardian angel to your Sisters, watch and pray, that God's grace and blessing be ever with you. Love poverty, have concern for simplicity in all things. Let your communications with outsiders, whether clerics or laity, be restricted to necessities. Have deep concern for the spiritual and the bodily welfare of the Sisters. (II 25)

How her concern for good superiors increased can readily be seen in the many foundations she established. She once mentioned to Sister Deogratias that at her judgment the Lord would not ask her how many new foundations she made, but what she did for the sanctification of her Sisters. Although made for the honor and glory of God, she did not wish the foundations to be considered the primary end of the congregation; yet, they belonged to her life's work and were noteworthy. Since the founding of a definite province in North America, the establishment of new foundations practically belonged to the Provincial Superior there. It was understood, of course, that the Superior General be informed of all new foundations. Thus here we shall confine ourselves to the new foundations in Germany.

To establish the new foundations is not an easy task. Much planning and preparatory work had to precede each new establishment. Before Sisters could be sent to a new place, Mother Maria Theresia made all required arrangements to avoid a repetition of conditions at one new foundation in America. Here she arrived with five Sisters where she was to establish a new branch convent. A house was available. It was well furnished. A wealthy farmer had donated it. But the most necessary requisite for the life of the Sisters was missing — food provisions and money. At all events, the Sisters that evening had to retire without an evening meal. Only Mother Maria Theresia did not retire. Pleadingly, she prayed to St. Joseph, who always came to her aid. Although no provision had been made for food, a statue of St. Joseph was there. As the servant of God had done frequently, she did now again. She placed a beggar's purse about the neck of St. Joseph and in fervent prayer sent him out to procure bread and money for the Sisters. The next morning as the Sisters were chanting the divine office, a vehicle laden with all necessary provisions stopped at the convent door: flour, coffee, bread, eggs, butter, etc. Naturally, the Sisters were eager to know who their generous benefactor was. But the driver would only say that he was commanded by a prominent man to deliver the provisions to the Sisters. St. Joseph had again helped in a very wonderful way.

Such instances did not induce Mother Maria Theresia to be careless in her preparations for the establishment of new foundations. All dealings whether of a spiritual nature or business matter had to be settled carefully before she would send her Sisters to the place. Consequently, there were many and sometimes long delays before the actual foundation could be made. Many a plan was never realized because the necessary requirements could not be met.

FOUNDATIONS AFTER 1886

When Mother Maria Theresia was elected Superior General on August 12, 1886, the congregation in Germany had twelve foundations: Olpe, Blankenstein, Hüsten, Morsbach, Eckenhagen, Wissen, Heimerzheim, Jülich, Mülheim, Bonn-Poppelsdorf, Kirchen, and Merten. The following foundations were established by the servant of God after 1886:

13. Meckenheim near Bonn. Preparations for this foundation were started as early as 1884. New difficulties had to be overcome constantly. Finally, on September 28, 1886, Sister Johanna, a councilor, was able to accompany the first three Sisters to Meckenheim. Their apostolate was home nursing, a nursery, and a school for sewing. Some years later the parish determined to construct an addition to serve as convent for the Sisters. A section of the wing was arranged to accommodate patients. Later this developed into St. Joseph Hospital.

14. Bonn-Kessenich. This house was taken over in 1887. From the very beginning, the apostolate, namely, home nursing, nursery and school for sewing, was the same as in Meckenheim. The congregation soon acquired an adjoining tract of land on which it constructed a home for women and later St. Francis Hospital.

15. Torgau on the Elbe. For the time being, the Sisters' activity was not to be restricted to Catholic areas only, but extended to the Diaspora of Germany. They were to render help in areas in which the Catholics were few. Thus three Sisters left for Torgau on October 7, 1887, where on October 11, they undertook the management of St. Pius, an institution for communicants. These institutions were very worthwhile developments in these areas. Only in such institutions could the Catholic children receive proper instructions in preparation for their first Communion and also fundamental instruction in the Catholic religion. Later an orphanage was opened in Torgau.

This foundation in Torgau holds a very special position in the life of the servant of God and in the history of the congregation. In September 1888, one year after its establishment, Mother Maria Theresia visited the Sisters there. On this occasion she had the opportunity to experience in a very conspicuous manner the unhappy results of the Protestant Revolt. The day after her return she wrote to Mülheim of her experience:

> In Torgau one could scarcely do anything else but weep and pray over the shocking results of the revolt of Luther. Never would I have believed such a situation, nor even thought of it. It is a new paganism. How very deeply are we

> obligated to thank God for having been born and reared in the bosom of the Catholic Church. The clergymen are unbelievers and their religion is one of hate, a bitter hate of the Catholic Church and of the Holy Father. The few Catholics there are ashamed of their religion and will probably soon fall away. Dear Sisters, only the almighty and all-merciful God through the intercession of his holy Mother can help in this situation. Do pray with the Sisters. Our Sisters, otherwise, are well there; they must see their way through and I trust that later this will become a fruitful field of endeavor. (I 85)

This experience must have convinced her that she was right in her decision to send her Sisters into an area in which the Catholic Church was passing through hard times.

Torgau became a symbol of holiness to the Franciscans in Olpe. The following event reaches out beyond the lifetime of the servant of God. Still it should not be forgotten when thought is given to this foundation. During the night of April 20-21, 1906, fire broke out in the charitable institution, St. Pius. The Sisters' first thought was to rescue all the children from the flaming building. Both, Sister Connexa, twenty-nine years of age, and Sister Optata, twenty-four years of age, had been rescuing the children when they realized that two were still missing. Courageous in the face of death, the two Sisters dashed into the burning building again to save the two children. But they did not return. After the fire had subsided the bodies were found, each Sister held a child in her arms. They had given their young lives in an act of love. The Chronicles of the Congregation report the event in the obituary of the two Sisters as follows:

> You, our dear deceased Sisters, are worthy to be envied that you gave your lives in an act of love for the children in your charge; and so early scattered your bodies in the furrows of time as seed enduring in fruit glorified through eternity.

The remembrance of the heroic death of both these Sisters is commemorated to the present day with great honor in the motherhouse in Olpe.

16. Holzweiler, District Erkelenz. On May 14, 1888, Sister Johanna, a councilor, accompanied the first Sisters to this new foundation. Property had been donated to the parish Church with the stipulation that the gift should be utilized for a foundation of a religious congregation. The parish suggested the procurement of the Olpe Sisters to engage in home nursing, nursery care, and a school for sewing. Later this establishment developed into St. Mary Hospital.

Two other foundations were made in 1888. The pastor of Hochneukirch contacted Sister Deogratias, superior at Merten, about the possibility of making a foundation there. Although the contacts were not made with the motherhouse, Mother Maria Theresia occupied herself earnestly with the negotiations which progressed satisfactorily and were completed in 1888. In the same year Mother Maria Theresia several times mentioned her intention of making a foundation in Bardenberg near Aachen. On May 2, she wrote: "Soon Sisters should be going to Bardenberg, but since Reverend Hitt died recently, there will probably be a delay of a few weeks" (I 74). And on August 6: "This week Sister Paula will accompany the first Sisters to Bardenberg." At all events, the congregation never noted Bardenberg in the list of foundations. Probably the establishment of this place was dropped, or else was given up shortly after it was established.

17. Geistingen in Siegkreis. The initiation of this foundation came from the Reverend Ritsch in Geistingen. He wanted religious Sisters in his parish to take care of the poor, the sick, and the children. Since in Geistingen a rather large and roomy house with a spacious garden was for sale, he called this to the attention of Mother Maria Theresia. Did he probably have more confidence in the business ability of the Sisters than in his own? At all events, the Superior General acted immediately and transacted a business deal on May 8, 1889. Eleven days later the first three Sisters went to Geistingen. They began their apostolate with home nursing and instructions in manual work and also in needlework. Later, through new additions and further growth, the foundation developed into St. Joseph Hospital.

18. Altenhundem, District Olpe. The foundations in 1890 were established in rapid succession. Altenhundem started with three Sisters. From a small beginning it developed into St. Joseph Hospital.

19. Winterberg, District Brilon. The day after the foundation in Altenhundem, three Sisters went to Winterberg, May 18, 1890. From this foundation St. Francis Hospital evolved

20. Oschersleben on the Bode. A second request came from the area of the Diaspora. On May 31, 1890, the congregation sent three Sisters to undertake the administration of the existing Montana Orphanage. An institute for communicants was connected with the orphanage. The children were educated in the orphanage by two certified lay teachers. Because of existing circumstances the management of the institution was not easy for the Sisters. Only in 1896, were the Sisters permitted to do home nursing within the city and in its vicinity.

In the early part of 1890, it appeared that a foundation was to be made in Friesheim. But this plan came to naught.

21. Beuel on the Rhine. St. Joseph Hospital was initiated by four women who wished to do good and at the same time provide security for themselves in their declining years. They were daughters of the Winterscheid and Sains families who conducted a business in Mechernich. In Beuel they had a house erected surrounded by a garden. Their intention was to deed the house and garden to the Olpe Sisters as a gift, with the stipulation that each would have a room in the establishment, free of cost and care, throughout the winter of their lives. On August 12, 1891, the first Sisters took possession of the house. An addition was built in the year that Mother Maria Theresia died.

22. Jülich. From the establishment of St. Elizabeth Hospital in 1883, another foundation was made in Jülich, namely, St. Joseph School. This was conducted by two Sisters. They boarded and roomed in the hospital and taught in a private home close to the Church. Since the school prospered, the congregation purchased a tract of land on which a building was situated. Thereby a self-supporting foundation was made that developed into a large boarding school necessitating additional acquisition of land and further construction work.

23. Rödingen, District Jülich. A hospital had been donated to the parish. For its administration the members endeavored to secure the Olpe Sisters. On December 3, 1891, four Sisters undertook the apostolate and also started a nursery and home nursing. From the activity of the Sisters there, St. Joseph Hospital evolved.

24. Fredeburg, District Meschede. The Sisters took charge here on December 9, 1891. As in most of the other foundations, a hospital evolved from a small beginning. In 1909, this place was known as St. George Hospital.

25. Bonn-Venusberg. Perhaps no other foundation had to mount such great obstacles and overcome such strong opposition as St. Mary Hospital on Venusberg near Bonn. With the exception of Mülheim there is no foundation to which Mother Maria Theresia was so definitely attached as to that of Venusberg, which she loved to compare to Mount Alverna. Here later she sought personal help from prominent physicians. She ever had in mind and sought a large well-equipped hospital for the training of the young Sisters to qualify them as efficient nurses. The initiative for this foundation lay with a Protestant, Mr. Rudolf Jung. He had repeatedly observed the Sisters from his residence, as they left Poppelsdorf to do home nursing in Bonn. He offered the Sisters, as a gift, a tract of land on Venusberg where they could have a quiet and convenient home. This offer aroused serious and vigorous debate in the council meetings. The tract of land offered was in a solitary, ill-reputed region and was used as a rubble-refuse dump. All this caused great concern to Mother Maria Theresia's acceptance of the gift. Even Sister Paula was against the plan. Since the servant of God still held out for the plan, they sought the advice of Reverend Huerth of Poppelsdorf. He decided in the affirmative and his advice was decisive. In order to bring the landed tract into a consummate whole, parcels of land sandwiched in between had to be purchased; this naturally involved many business deals and great costs.

The preparations for building disturbed the management of the nearby imperial parks. This group did all in its power to hinder the building of a hospital. It even offered to assist the Sisters financially to build the hospital in the city if they would forego building one on Venusberg. Again, Mother Maria Theresia was urged to relinquish the plan and to have the hospital built in Bonn, for it would be more convenient and would also lessen the construction costs. Although she realized the difficulties, she adhered to her original opinion. Strongly influencing her decision was the idea that the hill represented Mount Alverna and that later she would change the name of "Venusberg," to "Alvernaberg," a name holy to the Franciscan family.

Thus in the spring of 1890, construction was begun on the project. The first financial offering six thousand marks, was given by Mr. Jung. Although the foundress had little capital at the beginning of this construction, she trusted in the mighty help of St. Joseph, who also at this time did not disappoint her in her need. It was a heroic time for the Poppelsdorf Sisters, who by their manual work reduced construction costs. Wherever they could make themselves useful as unskilled laborers, they did. During the night they were seen among those nursing the sick; during the day they were among the construction workers. The deep confidence of Mother Maria Theresia inspired her Sisters. In the spring of 1891, Rector Neu in a solemn celebration laid the cornerstone. If only the home for the Sisters had been erected at this time, the construction would have been completed, but the plans in the meantime had been changed considerably. A hundred-bed hospital was under construction simultaneously. This was the large hospital Mother Maria Theresia had envisioned for the education of her Sisters. By winter the project had advanced to the stage that enabled the Sisters to do the painting jobs.

The building, however, was not ready for occupancy when the first Sister was hospitalized, the critically ill Sister Antonia Stangier. Two rooms were readied for Sister and her nurse. She underwent surgery on January 12, 1892, at the hands of Professor Krukenberg. Since the operation was performed there it can easily be surmised that it was an emergency. But it was too late. Sister died on January 20. Thus the new building was consecrated by the death of one who had devoted all her energies to its construction. The very death of a Sister in this still unfinished building in some way instigated the determined pugnacious spirit with which the hospital was completed.

In March 1892, the Sisters from Poppelsdorf were able to occupy the building. Mother Maria Theresia again had the occasion to thank St. Joseph that with his help the seemingly insurmountable difficulties had been overcome. On his feast, March 19, 1892, the first Holy Mass was offered in the chapel. On March 25, the feast of the Annunciation, St. Mary Hospital was solemnly dedicated and opened for occupancy. "Mary of the Angels" was chosen patroness of the building and especially of the chapel. Through this gesture Mother Maria Theresia eternalized "Venusberg" as "Mount Alverna," as she envisioned before construction began.

Up to this time no direct action had been taken to secure an energetic doctor for the hospital. Mother Maria Theresia entrusted this question to our dear Lord and St. Joseph. Help soon came. Already during the illness of Sister Antonia the university professor, Dr. Witzel, looked about the new building. This esteemed and energetic surgeon announced himself voluntarily. After the hospital was completely furnished – the kitchen range was still missing – he began to send patients. The initial difficulties were soon overcome. The hospital won renown rapidly because of this doctor. Already in 1896, an addition to the structure had to be built. Since it attracted outstanding specialists, it became the leading hospital of the congregation. Many Sisters received help at the institution, even Mother Maria Theresia.

26. Herbede on the Ruhr, District Hattingen. St. Joseph Orphanage had evolved from a communicants institute, whose management was undertaken by the Sisters on February 20, 1892. The Reverend Missionary Waechter had observed the Sisters from neighboring Blankenstein, had learned to treasure them, and had asked for them.

27. Welschennest, District Olpe. The parish had received a donation of a house and sufficient capital to conduct a hospital and a home for the aged. The Olpe Sisters were asked to undertake the project. On April 30, 1892, St. Mary Hospital was begun by the Sisters.

28. Lübbecke, Precinct Minden. The St. Paul Corporation for Weaving had founded a Catholic convalescent home and looked for a religious order of women to undertake the housekeeping. Mother Maria Theresia was favorable. Thus on May 2, 1892, the first Sisters came to this foundation.

29. Neunkirchen, Precinct Cologne. St. Francis Hospital had its origin through a gift of a landowner, named Schmitz, to the civic community. The returns from the donated property were used to purchase a house that could serve as a hospital and a home for the poor. Mother Maria Theresia was approached to undertake the work. On December 9, 1892, the first Sisters opened this new foundation.

30. Richrath, District Solingen. The parish priest, Reverend Boddenberg, had purchased a roomy house with a garden and had given it together with eleven hundred marks to the Olpe Franciscans. The furnishing of the house for which he gave the money was left to the discretion of the Sisters. On June 4, 1893, four Sisters came to open this foundation. As there was a statue of St. Martin above the front entrance they named the building St. Martin Hospital. On March 1, 1894, the property was deeded to the congregation.

31. Eitorf on the Sieg. On December 11, 1893, the Superior General sent five Sisters to administer St. Francis Hospital. It was furnished and arranged by the citizenry.

32. Allendorf, District Arnsberg. In March 1894, some Sisters came to this area to do home nursing and to open a school for instruction in sewing. As so many other foundations of the congregation, this one also was placed under the mighty protection of St. Joseph.

33. Uckerath, District Sieg. The parish had furnished a small house accommodating twelve to fourteen patients and asked the Olpe Sisters for nursing service. On May 28, 1894, three Sisters undertook this service in St. Gertrude Home and also engaged in home nursing.

34. Gütersloh, District Wiedenbrück. Here the parish priest had his former large residence converted into an infirmary for incurables. He asked for Sisters and on September 21, 1894, they began their apostolate here. From this small beginning, St. Elizabeth Hospital developed.

In December 1894, a parish priest in Cologne-Kalk asked for a new foundation to be undertaken by the Sisters. He was informed that this could not be done in 1895, since six new foundations had already been promised for that year. He, however, was unwilling to wait indefinitely, and consequently that foundation was not realized.

35. Neuenkirchen, District Wiedenbrück. In 1894, the parish had commenced the construction of a larger hospital. Up to that time two tertiaries had taken care of the sick in a small, modest building. As their energies were insufficient for the larger hospital, the priest approached the Olpe Sisters. On March 4, 1895, the first two Olpe Sisters arrived and when St. Margaret Hospital was completed two more Sisters came. Besides giving nursing care, the Sisters also established a school for lessons in sewing.

36. Drolshagen, District Olpe. The parish requested the Olpe Sisters to undertake the administration of St. Gerhardus Hospital and besides the regular patients to care for the feeble-minded and the epileptics. Mother Maria Theresia was unable to refuse this help to a neighboring parish. On May 2, 1895, the hospital was taken over.

37. Longerich near Cologne. The Frederick-Catherine Institution goes back to its founding by Lady Frederick Contzen. She had donated a furnished house to the parish with the necessary money for its upkeep. She expressed a wish that the Franciscan Sisters of Olpe do the nursing. On May 21, 1895, three Sisters undertook the administration and the nursing in the institution. In 1897, this apostolate developed further into a nursery and a sewing school.

38. Leichlingen, District Solingen. The parish priest requested Sisters for St. Heribertus Institution to undertake the management and administration of the orphanage and communicants' institute. On December 4, 1895, the Sisters began this work.

39. Eslohe, District Meschede. St. Joseph Hospital thanks its origin to the initiative of the manufacturer Gabriel. He had erected a house and his wife and the Eslohe women furnished the interior. They did this by means of collected furnishings and through purchases made from the results of programs sponsored by benefactors. The project was presented to the Olpe congregation as a gift from Mr. Gabriel. On February 14, 1896, the institution was taken over by the Sisters. Besides nursing care, the Sisters engaged also in a school for sewing and a kindergarten.

40. Gelsenkirchen-Uckendorf. On July 14, 1886, the Sisters had opened St. Anthony Home. Home nursing and teaching sewing were the spheres of activity for the Sisters.

41. Mariadorf near Eschweiler, District Aachen. The Mining Society had arranged a house in Mariadorf for which they wanted Sisters to carry on an apostolate of home nursing, kindergarten schools, and instructions in sewing. Through the instrumentality of the parish priest this request went to Mother Maria Theresia. On January 15, 1897, St. Mary's was taken over by the Sisters of Olpe.

42. Haaren near Aachen. Home nursing, kindergarten, and a school for sewing were the activities prevailing in St. Joseph's. That the Sisters are engaged here is owing to Reverend Loper. This foundation has great significance relative to Mother Maria Theresia. The superior Sister Agatha, like sister Deogratias, preserved all the letters received from Mother Maria Theresia.

43. Eitorf on the Sieg. The activities of the Sisters in St. Francis Hospital had been observed in the community since December 11, 1893. They consequently requested Sisters from the same congregation for home nursing, kindergarten, and instructions in sewing. For various reasons, it was determined not to combine these activities with the hospital; consequently a separate house was acquired. On November 11, 1897, St. Anthony Convent was established as a second foundation in Eitorf.

44. Elspe, district Olpe. This foundation as so many others began with home nursing. At the request of Reverend Budde three Sisters began an apostolate here in January 1898. Later they opened a school for sewing and built St. Francis Hospital.

45. Weiden near Aachen. Reverend Westenberg arranged a convent and requested Sisters to undertake home nursing, a nursery for children, and a Sunday guidance program for girls working in the factories. Three Sisters came and were conducted with great festivity to their convent home, St. Mary Convent.

46. Korschenbroich, District Mönchengladbach. The district commission donated a tract of land and 7,500 marks to the congregation for the construction of a hospital. But Mother Maria Theresia delayed her decision for some time for she did not wish to overtax the energies of the congregation. At this time there were requests for Sisters from all sides. Only in 1898, was she able to give serious thought to the offer made to her in Korschenbroich. In the summer of 1898, the congregation commenced the construction of the hospital and at the same time a kindergarten. On November 18, 1898, the first Sisters arrived to begin home nursing. They lived in rented quarters until March 1899, when they took possession of the newly constructed St. Elizabeth Hospital.

47. Herdorf near Betzdorf. The pastor requested Sisters for home nursing, conducting of kindergartens, and a sewing school. On December 14, 1898, St. Barbara Convent was opened with the arrival of four Sisters.

48. Bonn, Bachstrasse. The Reverend Director Neu of Bonn cherished the activity of home nursing by the Sisters, but he realized the great inconveniences endured by the Sisters in commuting from Poppelsdorf to Bonn to do so. This situation had prevailed for some time. He suggested that a house in Bonn would be far more convenient. At his advice Mother Maria Theresia purchased a place on Bachstrasse. The Sisters occupied the house on May 27, 1899, called St. Elizabeth Home. It also had special quarters for lay women.

49. Troisdorf, District Sieg. St. Joseph Hospital erected later goes back to the initiation of Reverend Meyer, pastor. For a long time he had harbored the idea of securing Sisters for his parish. To give his desire greater weight and to have something to offer, he purchased a residence. On June 14, 1899, the Olpe Sisters took possession of the dwelling and occupied it until the hospital and quarters for a kindergarten were completed. The parish donated additional land adjoining the hospital to the Olpe congregation.

50. Betzdorf, District Sieg. The hospital dedicated to St. Joseph was administered by five Sisters. It was constructed from contributions collected by the pastor.

51. Lüdenscheid in Westfalen. As the Sisters administered the existing hospital, they also undertook the management of St. Joseph Orphanage on May 29, 1900. They also conducted a kindergarten and a school for domestic arts. Later, home nursing and the orphanage were discontinued.

52. Olpe, St. Martin Hospital. At the beginning of 1900, the Superior General of the Paderborn Vincentians approached Mother Maria Theresia with the suggestion that it would probably be best if the Franciscans were to take over the administration of St. Martin Hospital. One can recall readily the many sorrows the servant of God suffered relative to this hospital. She had just expressed her wish for the year 1900 to her Sisters: "May this be a year of great rejoicing for us" (IV 23). And now the great gift for jubilation came! In reality, under close scrutiny, the gift came back to her. A very peculiar association can be discovered here. The servant of God at one time spoke to one of her Sisters regarding the situation:

> Just think how really good God is! The ground on which the hospital stands was my possession, and now the whole comes back to me. As a hospital was to be built the town was unable to secure a building site. I then said to my mother: "give them this yard," and now the Superior General of the Vincentians of Paderborn contacted me to take over the hospital. I did that gladly for now I have a place to train our novices in nursing.

When the hospital was under construction the twenty-six year old Aline was battling with her religious vocation. This heartfelt generosity was probably a part of her great renunciation in total poverty. Now it came back to her one hundred fold. On Judy 13, 1900, the Sisters of the servant of God took possession of St. Martin Hospital. Mother Maria Theresia directed that the change in administration should take place quietly and without any public demonstration.

53. Laibach in Slovenia. Were there possibilities here that a new province was in the making? For a time it appeared that way. A province at that time could have expanded into Eastern lands. Such thoughts were prevalent then. The Countess Auersperg from Laibach became greatly interested in the Poor Franciscans of Perpetual Adoration and for a long time had endeavored to have these Sisters in Laibach. In this pursuit the prince-bishop supported her. In 1899, the Countess herself made a trip to Olpe and spent a rather long time there. She had a very special gift for the congregation: several postulants whom she in her enthusiasm for the Olpe Sisters had won for them. Here we can see an indication of the impulsive temperament that marks her later life. Nevertheless, the postulants she brought were to be a sign that a foundation in Laibach had excellent prospects for the expansion of the congregation in those areas. The Archduchess Valeria, daughter of Emperor Franz Joseph, helped in these negotiations. Countess Auersberg, who wished to enter the congregation, wanted to give her property to the foundation. She had the house in Laibach arranged and furnished.

On August 13, 1900, Sister Paula accompanied by six Sisters traveled from Olpe to Laibach. Sister Verena was appointed superior for the establishment. Mother Maria Theresia would have liked to make the trip herself, but her physical condition at that time forbade such a strenuous journey. Because of her heart condition she went to a health resort in Brückenau in Lower Franconia for the cure. She had advised Sister Paula to make the return trip through Italy to visit the Holy House of Loretto, the home of the Franciscan Family in Assisi, and the Eternal City Rome. It meant much to Mother Maria Theresia to have her Sisters visit the holy places to call down the blessings of God upon the congregation. Sister Paula and her companion had the good fortune in Rome to have an audience with the Holy Father, Leo XIII, and to receive his blessing for themselves and for all the Sisters of the congregation.

Soon after the foundation in Laibach, the Countess Gabriele Auersperg was admitted to the congregation. On May 15, 1901, she was invested by the prince-bishop and received the name of Sister Maria Francesca of St. Joseph. After a great improvement in health, Mother Maria Theresia herself in 1901, made the trip to Laibach. On August 8 of the same year, accompanied by Sister Josepha, the North American provincial, she arrived there, and remained with the Sisters for twelve days. Over all she obtained a favorable impression as to the possibilities of the foundation. Difficulties were there to be sure, but what new foundation is without its hardships? The servant of God returned to Olpe by way of Villach and Innsbruck.

But soon serious difficulties marked the development of the activities of the Sisters in Laibach. The prince-bishop was well-disposed toward the Franciscan Sisters. Even he was unable to change conditions. With the passage of time it clearly became evident that the problems were more than initial foundation difficulties and would have permanent effects. Continuous nationality frictions between the Slovenians and Germans hindered the fruitful development of activities. To prevent disastrous consequences, Mother Maria Theresia recalled her Sisters, the first of whom returned home in the beginning of October and the others on October 14, 1904. Countess Auersperg did not return with them; she left the congregation. Of the young Sisters whom she had brought to Olpe in 1899, only one returned to Laibach; all the others remained in the congregation.

54. Neunkirchen, Precinct Cologne. Since December 9, 1892, the Olpe Franciscans labored in St. Francis Hospital and among the poor. Now the household management of St. Anthony Hostel was also entrusted to them. This second foundation in Neunkirchen was made in September 1900.

55. Aldenhoven, District Jülich. On December 9, 1900, the Sisters occupied St. Elizabeth Convent. They engaged in home nursing and in conducting sewing schools.

56. Elspe, District Olpe. On January 10, 1901, three Sisters came to Elspe to form a second foundation where they conducted an agricultural school and a department of domestic science, a great need in this area. On January 15, 1901, the school was opened.

57. Duisdorf, District Bonn. St. Francis Institute was opened by the Sisters on July 18, 1901. As in so many smaller foundations the Sisters devoted their energies to home nursing, sewing, and kindergartens.

58. Bonn, Lenne Street. Since the summer of 1901, Mother Maria Theresia planned to take over the private clinic of Professor Krukenberg, located on Lenne Street. After his death, several doctors were in favor of continuing the clinic. They turned to the Mother General of the congregation with the request to undertake the nursing care and financial affairs of the clinic. The congregation consequently purchased the clinic and expanded the building with the construction of a new wing, providing a rather large hospital. The Sisters took possession of the buildings on December 6, 1901. It became known as Sacred Heart Hospital. In the lifetime of Mother Maria Theresia, she also built a convent for the Sisters with the requisite enclosure.

In 1901, a plan was suggested to Mother to make a new foundation in Wien. With a foundation there, the Sisters in Laibach would not be so isolated from the other foundations. On April 23, 1901, Mother Maria Theresia wrote concerning this plan:

> The undertaking of a foundation in Wien would give me great joy and I favor it greatly if we only had the required personnel. It would also please the Sisters in Laibach to know that some more of our Sisters were in the same country. But I cannot possibly do it this year. (III 41)

Since the foundation in Laibach was dissolved later, the one in Wien was never realized.

59. Cologne. St. Elizabeth Home on Victoria Street reverts to a Miss Frey, who gave the initial stimulus of having Franciscans undertake home nursing in Cologne. The pastor of St. Gereon suggested that the foundation be made in his parish. The congregation purchased a house with garden located on Victoria Street for fifty thousand marks from Mrs. Guillaume. She accommodated the Sisters still further by waiving the interest if the amount could not be paid at the stipulated time. On her deathbed, she gave her entire estate to the Sisters as a gift. On February 2, 1902, eight Sisters took over this foundation, which served also as a home for lay women. They began home nursing with the city immediately.

60. Berlin. On February 15, 1902, Mother Maria Theresia sent seventeen Sisters to Berlin. Their purpose was to undertake the nursing of the sick in Westsanatorium. The medical officer of the Board of Health, Dr. Ruegenberg of Bonn, and Dr. Kaute of Westsanatorium, had previously gone to Olpe in January to persuade the Superior General to accept the nursing in Westsanatorium. Before their trip to Olpe they had contacted Superior Wigger and Bishop Dr. Wilhelm Schneider and brought it about that the bishop positively recommended the acceptance. The position of the bishop proved decisive for Mother Maria Theresia although it was very difficult for her to accept. She knew it would be hard to collaborate with Dr. Kaute, the leading physician. Already on June 12, 1902, we read in the correspondence of the servant of God: "Our dear Sister Paula has been in Berlin eight days. Certain conditions prevail there that show beyond doubt that their way is not bedded with roses" (III 53). The unfortunate situation led to the withdrawal of the Sisters in mid-August, 1905, soon after the death of Mother Maria Theresia.

61. Wickede on the Ruhr. On June 3, 1902, the Sisters arrived in Wickede and lived in a house rented from the parish. They began their apostolate with home nursing and later added a sewing school. Conditions in the rented house were too unfavorable for the Mother to expect her Sisters to live there for an extended period of time. She consequently determined to build a hospital. The project was completed in 1903. This foundation was dedicated to St. Joseph.

62. Kurl, District Dortmund. On August 12, 1902, the Sisters were able to take over the newly constructed St. Elizabeth Hospital. Besides the nursing of the sick in the hospital, the Sisters also did home nursing. Later they conducted a kindergarten and a school for sewing.

63. Asseln, District Dortmund. Three Sisters went to Asseln on November 24, 1902, to administer the new St. Francis Hospital, and also engage in home nursing. In the spring of 1903, they opened schools for kindergarten and sewing.

64. Bad Oeynhausen, Precinct Minden. A Catholic priest had purchased a home for patients under treatment and endeavored to secure Sisters to conduct the home. On December 11, 1903, the first three Sisters from Olpe came to St. Bernard Home. With the increase of patients more Sisters arrived.

65. Oberpleis, Siegdistrict. The parish priest, Rev. Matthias Schmitz, on January 8, 1903, donated his practically new villa "Constantia" to the congregation. Mother Maria Theresia entered into an agreement with him that seemed plausible to her: the villa was to be used either as a hospital or an institution for other charitable purposes. Immediately after the donor moved out, the first Sisters occupied the villa on April 2, 1903. They began their apostolate with home nursing while the villa was remodeled and set in order for a hospital. To keep the memory of the donor alive, the villa was called "Constantia" Hospital.

66. Bad Wildungen, Waldeck. The much frequented "hot baths" had no Catholic convalescent home. The need was repeatedly lamented, and Mother Maria Theresia realized it only too well from her own experience. She herself had sought help here in August and September of 1898. The cathedral provost Wigger, superior of the congregation, was instrumental in that the Diocese of Paderborn acquired a tract of land there. He persuaded Mother Maria Theresia to build a convalescent home. The project was started in 1902, and was completed without interruption. On June 25, 1903, the Sisters were able to occupy St. Liborius convalescent home.

67. Ramsbeck, District Meschede. On November 14, 1903, the Sisters came to undertake home nursing. This foundation, likewise dedicated to St. Joseph, evolved into a hospital.

In 1903, Mother Maria Theresia was approached concerning a foundation to be made in Odendorf. We have this information from her letter to Sister Deogratias, superior at Merten, written on July 29, 1903:

> I beg you to drive to Odendorf — it is between Meckenheim and Rheinbach. There is a beautiful piece of property there which we have been asked to undertake for a new foundation. The Reverend pastor has requested our consent to enable him to obtain permission from the spiritual administrative authorities in Cologne. I wrote to him that you would make a visit there to investigate the situation and to confer with him concerning the terms. Please go there as soon as possible and write to me concerning it. (I 197)

The foundation, however, was not realized. Whether the undertaking of the Carmelite convent at Rolduk, Holland, mentioned in the same letter, was considered further is questionable for no other mention of it was made.

68. Wipperfürth. St. Anthony Hostel was occupied on April 30, 1904 by three Sisters. Reverend Schaaf founded this hostel for boys and gave the management over to the Olpe Sisters.

69. Miesenheim near Andernach. On June 14, 1904, Sister Verena installed three Sisters here. They engaged in home nursing and kindergarten. This foundation had but a brief existence.

70. Nievenheim, District Neuss. This foundation came into existence through the instigation of a married couple surnamed Schmitz. They had given over a residence with the surrounding areas to the archbishopric of Cologne with the stipulation that after their death the entire estate be given to the Olpe Sisters, to be used for the care of the sick and a nursery school. On October 12, 1904, three Sisters took possession of the house and began their specific activities.

71. Anröchte, District Lippstadt. This foundation was accepted by the Sisters on October 26, 1904, at the time when typhus raged among the people. It founded St. Elizabeth Hospital.

72. Gelsenkirchen-Hüllen. This was the last foundation made personally by Mother Maria Theresia. Sister Verena accompanied four sisters to St. Elizabeth Home. Home nursing, domestic arts instruction, and kindergarten comprised the activities of the sisters. "I am very grateful that we are released from Tiergarten; even as a gift, we could not accept it" (III 82). This was written in one of her letters, dated May 25, 1904. More definite information was not given.

It is certain that since the middle of 1903, Mother Maria Theresia had negotiated a foundation in Lengenfeld below Stein on the Eichsfeld. The foundation was delayed because the pastor feared difficulties with the government. The matter was resolved only after the death of the servant of God, and the foundation was opened on May 29, 1905.

The chronicle of the various foundations can be interpreted in different ways: as proud results of increasing activities, as an exhibition of unpretentious services for the honor of God and the welfare of mankind, as a visible sign of the blessing and help of God. All depends upon the point of view. Mother Maria Theresia did not experience the feeling of spiritual triumph over this her great development. "He leads, I follow," that was her guideline. She, as an instrument of the Lord, directed her congregation and often wondered why he had chosen her for this task. Whether plans for a new foundation materialized or whether they failed, much work was always expended on the undertaking. The Mother had to see that her Sisters had a real home and adequate facilities for work. Every time a new group of Sisters prepared to leave for a new foundation, she experienced the same feelings she had when the first Sisters left for Poppelsdorf. Assuredly with the growth of the congregation, office work also increased. That, however, did not lead the venerable Mother from the right road to govern her Sisters as a bureaucrat. To them she simply remained the Mother who had concern for all.

Although the Mother General entrusted her congregation completely to the providence of God, she nevertheless did all in her power to make the existence and the welfare of the congregation secure. For many years, she together with Superior Wigger, had studied the possibility of giving security to the finances of the congregation through the ministration of civil law. She had endeavored repeatedly but in vain to secure a community lawyer. With the issuing of the new civil code in 1900, she tried again, but without results. Therefore, it was determined to found a juridical corporation as many other congregations had done. Through the assistance of the court of law in Cologne, the situation progressed to the extent that on September 8, 1902, the corporation was established before the Notary Kleber in Cologne. It was titled as a private corporation with limited liability for the nursing of the sick and teaching kindergarten in Olpe.

CHAPTER XII

MOTHERHOUSE IN OLPE

Mother Maria Theresia established many foundations for her Sisters. But how did the motherhouse itself develop? Although Mother followed all the events in the various foundations with great watchfulness, she was a reticent partner. Therefore, the development in Olpe from the beginning of the Generalate of the servant of God until her death will be related. Those happenings that regard her personally: her illnesses, her joys and feasts, and her sufferings will be treated. This supplementary aspect can so easily be forgotten, when considering the activities surrounding the new foundations.

The novitiate had been in Mülheim since 1885. The nursing of the sick was prohibited in Olpe proper. The year 1887 showed signs of a more favorable development: the permission of the government was no longer required for investiture, the orphanage could again admit children of school age. How did events progress?

Mother Maria Theresia's letters showed that in 1887 children were again admitted to the orphanage in the town of Olpe. The women of the town did not consider the care of the orphans as the entire responsibility of the Sisters. They helped to prepare a real Christmas for the children. With gratitude to God, the venerable Mother remarked: "They assembled to sew clothes for the children, bought linens, and knitted stockings." (I 59)

In April, she herself acknowledged: "Lately I have not been very well. I would gladly have written to the Sisters again, but I must avoid the bending position required in writing" (I 42). In the beginning of June, she wrote:

> In a previous letter I was able to inform you that the situation relative to my health was good, and that condition still prevails. But the foregoing week edema set in and my legs were swollen well above the knees; it seems to be fluid and makes walking difficult for me. (I 47)

In August, the doctor diagnosed her case not as a defective valvular heart condition, but as a shortage of adipose tissue around the heart. She wrote this concerning her suffering: "Whatever it is makes little difference to me as long as I am able to fulfill my duties" (I 51). Although she was better at times, on October 5, she wrote, "since yesterday erysipelas is in my foot again holding me captive in my beloved solitude" (I 53). But at the close of the year, she wrote a more cheerful note: "If our dear Lord permits my health to remain as it is at present, I shall be able to take several hours of adoration for in this the feet are not engaged" (I 59). Each year followed this same pattern, one marked by sickness and suffering. However, there were never any signs of self-pity nor impatience. All this was written only in her letters to her confidant, Sister Deogratias, and not in her letters to all the Sisters.

The year 1888 saw workmen in the motherhouse. Mother Maria Theresia was determined to have water piped into the house. She wished to ease the heavy burden of the Sisters, especially on wash days. Whether it was due to the piping of water supply into the house, or not, she was short many thousand marks that had to be paid at the end of the year. Greater need of an ample food supply and other provisions for the orphans caused her many headaches. But the Sisters in various branch houses came to the rescue, especially Sister Deogratias, superior at Merten.

The Mother's health condition early in 1889, was not at its best as she reveals:

> It is well with me, but one extremity of my body is in constant pain. For some time now, I can scarcely hear; now my foot is filled with fluid again and is very painful. Thank God for all. (I 91)

With such a report, it may be wondered what her condition must have been, since she herself said that conditions were bad with her. And the year 1889 closes with the remark: "As always my stand is beneath the cross" (IV 4).

The greatest cares of this year concerned the chaplain in the motherhouse. At the beginning of the year, Vicar Droege, whom the Sisters cherished greatly, stated that he would have to relinquish his chaplaincy completely because of illness. He would be unable to carry out his duties and he felt that the Sisters consequently would miss too much. Since Vicar Droege was no longer able to celebrate Holy Mass after the beginning of April, the Sisters were obliged to attend Mass in the parish church. Not to have Holy Mass in the convent chapel was very difficult for Mother Maria Theresia. She consequently approached the Franciscan Provincial for a temporary Franciscan substitute. But soon, on April 17, a priest from Altengeseke, Pastor Herdes, was sent as the new chaplain. Vicar Droege died on April 26, 1889. Mother Maria Theresia honored him in the following statement:

> He suffered so very much and so patiently and always prayed; we trust that he will be our advocate in heaven. Let us offer all the prayers for the repose of his soul as we offer them for a deceased Sister. (I 98)

Rector Herdes remained but a very short time. Because of a public statement made from the pulpit, he was sentenced to imprisonment. Thus for another period, Holy Mass was not celebrated in the convent chapel in the motherhouse. At this time, an event, insignificant in itself, happened which Mother Maria Theresia used in her own original way to her advantage:

> To date we have no regular divine service in the motherhouse chapel and no spiritual director will be with us until October.... This morning St. Joseph provided a Holy Mass for us. There was an excursion in the town and Sisters were in the church to attend the student Mass, but no priest arrived. Suddenly the rector stormed into our chapel to celebrate Holy Mass; he and his entire party had overslept. We rejoiced greatly and wished for more pastors to oversleep in the same manner. (I 104)

On October 11, Vicar Plesser arrived to assume the office as chaplain in the motherhouse. Mother Maria Theresia thanked

> ... the dear Lord who has sent such a good priest, Rector Plesser. The priest is rather poor in health, but very pious and punctual. (I 106)

But there were other cares as well. The living quarters in the motherhouse were too limited, and the structure was damp and unhealthy. The number of orphans too had increased to the extent that they were overcrowded. Since the Superior General also had in mind to transfer the novitiate back from Mülheim to Olpe, she had to plan for new buildings. But before the actual planning could progress, she had to consider the purchase of more land and a house. Mother consequently began to negotiate but experienced such great difficulties that the negotiations dragged on and on and, in the end, she had to alter her original plans. However, she did not lose courage: "If our building project here is pleasing to God, he must help us" (I 97). Not until the following year was she able to begin her building program.

In July 1889, she experienced a very special joy. Bishop Wigger, a native of Olpe, and Bishop Joseph Rademacher visited the Olpe Motherhouse. Bishop Rademacher was the successor of Bishop Dwenger of Fort Wayne, Indiana, and, like his predecessor, had great respect for the Poor Franciscans in his diocese. During their stay in Olpe, both bishops nearly always celebrated their Holy Masses in the motherhouse chapel. On July 18, fifteen postulants were invested in Mülheim by Bishop Wigger.

"Building" was the great theme of Mother Maria Theresia's letters to the Sisters during the 1890s. One contains the following comments:

> In building one meets with difficulties that were not even surmised beforehand, but all turns out as the Great Builder wishes. (I 109)

Further plans were made for the orphanage. The old Koester home was razed and in its place a larger new building was erected. With this new project as many difficulties as possible were met — rocky soil had to be blasted, bad bricks — (the architect had considered an Olpe firm for the bricks, but was obliged to have them brought in by an outside firm), changes in the original plan and, to top it all, the finances were running low. To replenish her dwindling fund, Mother Maria Theresia came upon the idea of contacting the leading authorities for permission to take up a collection in the area of Arnsberg, since the majority of orphans came from that administrative area. This collection would do much toward the comfort of the orphans and alleviate the burdens of the motherhouse. Thus her letter:

> In reference to the financial status of the orphanage, there was no existing capital. For the individual children in the orphanage, their relatives or the parish pay 30 to 40 pennies a day, and in exceptional cases, 50 a day. With such a meager sum, the orphanage often finds itself in dire straits. Then the Sisters through the sale of needlework and with the generous donations of benefactors help supply the need. (VII 24)

Concerning the planned construction of the new building, the Mother wrote as follows:

> Because of the new construction, with the exception of a dining room for boys and one for girls, all the other quarters of the orphanage could be used by the convent. The addition to the old orphanage, as planned originally, met with opposition from the local authorities. Consequently a new building became a necessity, one that permitted a great number of orphans to be admitted. The planned new construction would place the community in a secure position for a long time. The three stories provide ample and healthful quarters for the orphans. It will house from 80 to 100 children. (VII 24)

In spite of all the difficulties, the rough brickwork was completed by winter.

Finally, the burdensome restriction forbidding the Sisters to nurse the sick in Olpe was lifted. The citizens of Olpe had not remained silent nor idle. Pleading petitions were being sent constantly to the general vicariate of the diocese. On May 24, 1890, he granted the Sisters the freedom of caring for the sick wherever their help was requested. On October 28, 1890, Mother Maria

Theresia sought the lifting of another restriction from the general vicariate. This had reference to the restriction of December 4, 1882, forbidding the celebration of more than one Holy Mass in the convent chapel daily without the express permission of the local parish priest. On October 29, the general vicariate withdrew this restriction also.

Mother reckoned that also in 1891 much sorrow and suffering would await her:

> In the varied needs and sorrows that the new year will bring, our dear Lord will again care for us in fatherly fashion as he did in the previous year and be a Father to us with his almighty help. Often as I look into the future, I am filled with anxiety, but in prayer I must again seek help and courage. (I 124)

Not only in Olpe was building going on, but also in Venusberg. Besides, it was the year for her to make her third visitation trip to North America. She was eager to meet the Sisters again, if her health permitted.

In Olpe the construction of the new orphanage was progressing. Until its completion, living quarters were very limited. Thus Mother Maria Theresia wrote to Sister Deogratias as follows on February 7, 1891:

> From your loving letter ... I see that you wish to send Sister Thecla and Sister Silveria to Olpe for health reasons. Dear Sister Deogratias, not to Olpe, for we have no quarters either for sick or well Sisters until the orphan children are able to move into the new orphanage. (I 126)

In the fall of that year, the children occupied the new building which was called St. Joseph Orphanage:

> It was some time before the new building was clear of debt: It was so necessary for us to build here, but we could not clear the debt until more funds were received from the branch convents. We are in debt deeply enough and the interest eats up all our savings, but our dear Lord will come to our aid again. (I 30)

These lines were written in the beginning of 1892 and give a resume of the burdens of the coming months. But at the same time, they again bring the great confidence of the servant of God to the surface. Her work was dedicated to God and he was her secure help at all times. From July until October divine services in the motherhouse again took a critical turn. Reverend Plesser was transferred to Herzebrook. Only in October of that year was a chaplain assigned to the motherhouse. He was a Carmelite, Reverend Hilarian Lucas.

In April 1893, Reverend A. Schroeder was appointed chaplain and spiritual director at the motherhouse. Until then he had been a co-worker with the Dean at Westönen. Reverend Schroeder remained with the Sisters in the motherhouse until his death, July 16, 1913 — a period of twenty years.

Another eventful happening of 1893 was the opening of a school in Olpe by the Sisters for the higher education of girls. In her early activities in the 1870s, Mother Maria Theresia had greatly desired this type of school; now it was being realized. We can readily remember her early zeal. In 1892, however, more families approached the Sisters to consider the opening of a school in Olpe. In the fall of 1892, two Sisters were giving private instructions. Mayor Roeper of Olpe became intensely interested in obtaining certification.

During the Easter season in 1893, the school was opened with three Sisters as instructors. St. Francis School, so famous today, developed rapidly from its very beginning. The accomplishment of great things through hard work characterized the activities of the religious orders during the nineteenth century. Except for a firm will to work, all else was temporary. Three Sisters instructed seventeen girls in two classes. The classrooms were in the new St. Joseph Orphanage. After the new additions to the motherhouse were completed, the classrooms occupied the lower floor of the west wing. The first instructors were deeply concerned for the development of higher education in the congregation. Besides their actual teaching duties, the Sisters coached some of their fellow religious in preparation for their certification examinations. How deeply Mother Maria Theresia appreciated the hard work of her Sisters can be learned from many incidents. She did all that she could to maintain their health. Even during her lifetime, the number of students in St. Francis School increased to eighty.

Because of the great demands on the motherhouse through the increase of orphans, students, and Sisters, it became an absolute necessity for her to engage in further building expansions. But there was one great difficulty to be overcome by the Superior General before she could commence. A small house owned by its occupants stood between the wings of the convent; this space was needed for expansion. It had to be purchased at an exorbitant price. In the winter of 1893, shortly before Christmas, Mother moved the orphans attending school into this house together with several women who occupied portions of the west wing. The rooms previously occupied by the women could now be used by the Sisters. Thus Mother Maria Theresia arranged that the construction of a new wing could begin in the following year.

Mother Maria Theresia began the new year of 1894 with great joy. She could not refrain from making mention of it in her next letter:

> Now something gratifying. Through Father Hilarian, the Holy Father gave me his picture as a gift and his apostolic blessing to all the Sisters of our congregation and to all their relatives to the third degree, including a plenary indulgence for the hour of death. Let us all endeavor to become worthy of so great a grace. (III 4)

For the servant of God, this was something extraordinary. The blessing of the Holy Father meant much to her. And she realized how much she needed this blessing at this time. The motherhouse was in the process of being enlarged.

Next the choir of the Sisters had to be razed, for in its place a new chapel was to be erected. Since construction would require time, the Sisters attended Holy Mass in the choir loft of the chapel in the orphanage. Community prayers were said in the chapel proper. In the spring of 1894, the razing of the old building began. In June, 1894, the cornerstone of the new chapel was laid with great solemnity and amidst profound rejoicing. In this, as in all previous expansions of the motherhouse, the living conditions throughout the period were uncomfortable. Mother Maria

Theresia also suffered much as her letter of October 22 reveals: "The work here is terrible; with the weather as it is, together with a building in progress, one cannot avoid dirt" (I 137). She had hoped that the building would proceed uninterruptedly. Beyond all, she was awaiting the completion of the chapel. But on November 15 she began to realize: "We shall not have the chapel under roof this year; I am sorry, but one must be satisfied with what God does" (I 138). An expression born of her deep interior faith! Whether everyone would come upon such an understanding even amidst the halting of a building program and consider it the will of God was a question.

She had many difficulties to overcome relative to health during the winter. For the most part she usually wrote that all was well with her, but a letter of October 22, 1894, reads rather differently:

> At this time my health is not very good; although the cardiac pains have subsided somewhat, a severe coughing has set in. Who knows what will follow. (I 137)

A month later she wrote the following in a rather humorous vein that "my cold held on a long time and coughing plagues me. Well, old age has its oddities" (I 138). "Who knows what more will come?" And in the middle of November: "Our dear Lord knows how to find each one" (I 138). The Lord found her in a very special way on Christmas night. According to conventual custom, the Mother personally wished to carry the figure of the Infant at midnight and place it in the Crib set up in the chapel. But in the process, she slipped and fell on the stony winding stairs and struck her head a heavy blow on the stone floor. She raised herself with all possible energy. Her first thought was to see whether the figure of the Infant had suffered any damage. She then carried the Infant into the chapel and placed it in the Crib and attended the midnight Mass. She mentions a severe headache, but stayed on for the two Masses that followed immediately and was present in the morning for the solemn closing of the adoration. Then, however, she was forced to seek the bed. The doctor diagnosed the injury as a severe concussion. She remained unconscious for several days in restless fantasy. The Sisters feared for her life.

However, she recovered slowly and felt the consequences of her fall for a long time.

Thus she began the year 1895 in a state of illness. In the words of her letter of January 19, she had reference to her own illness: "… there always remains something to wish for, and since the beloved cross may not be wanting in our following of Jesus, the way of the cross is always the best way" (III 6). In love of her crucified Lord, she often prayerfully made the Way of the Cross, which the parish had erected on the Mount of the Cross on the opposite bank of the Bigge River. She arose early and rejoiced greatly when one or another Sister accompanied her. She always returned in time for the opening of the conventual morning exercises and prayers in the chapel. Above all she loved to make this Way of the Cross barefoot and humbly. During intervals when her health was better, she must have walked very briskly for the distance from the convent to the first station required almost thirty minutes. When more or less overcome by ill health, her steps became slower. The Sisters who accompanied her jokingly remarked that they were glad the Mother was not so well, for they could then keep pace with her especially while making the Way of the Cross.

The experiences of her own sickness and suffering in 1895 dictated the words that fell from her pen at Easter:

> May Jesus, who was crucified for us and arose from the dead, dwell in each of us, and may we live, suffer, love, work, and die for him. We live such a happy life of grace in our religious vocation, and, if conditions at times become hard to bear, we have something to endure for him who has suffered so much for us, for each one of us, even to the death on a cross. There is no love without suffering. Therefore, my dear Sisters, let us love him, who first loved us and let us gladly suffer for love of him. If we are entirely united with Christ in love, then with and through him all our activities will be blessed and we shall be happy in life and also in death. (IV 98)

In these words she revealed how she considered her life of suffering and infirmities: "There is no love without suffering!"

How earnestly God accepted her preparedness to suffer, how unpretentiously she entered into it, can be sensed readily by her abrupt close of a letter of May 13: "Now I must stop; most likely you have surmised that I am not well! my heart pounds mightily."

In addition to all this, she was oppressed by the worries of building. The program was moving very slowly:

> Our building program, despite the good weather, is progressing slowly; workmen often fail to appear; it is very disagreeable. In August or September, the Reverend Superior will come for dedication, if the work is far enough along. (I 144)

But it was November before the Mother could occupy her cell close to the new chapel.

On the feast of St. Elizabeth, November 19, 1895, the building was completed sufficiently that the Reverend Wigger could dedicate the chapel. The Blessed Sacrament was carried in solemn procession from the existing chapel into the new house of God. Two days later twenty-six novices pronounced temporary vows for five years in the new chapel. It had been a long time since such a ceremony was solemnized in Olpe. In the following weeks, all the novices and postulants transferred from Mülheim to Olpe. The novitiate was again established and housed in the motherhouse.

Mother Maria Theresia suffered many and great hardships in 1895. In the beginning of the year, her heart condition was so bad that she could not write a letter without frequent moments of respite. How must she have reflected upon this year. Some inkling of it is given in a letter to Sister Deogratias:

> Friday will be the thirty-fifth anniversary of my receiving the religious habit. How much is hidden in these years! If I had only done all meritoriously for heaven. But the human always remains with us. Our dear Sister Caroline is approaching her end. I doubt whether she will be with us at Christmas. Hopefully, she is awaiting the last hour; I would love to die with that devoted soul. (I 151)

Mother Maria Theresia took her illness with her into 1896. Her infirmities did not seem to her as a dark, inescapable misfortune of which she must rid herself, but as a way of the cross she wished to walk in the strength of love. Healthwise she was not able to make the visitation in America this year. Sister Paula substituted for her. She still had much work at home; new foundations and further expansion at the motherhouse. Why was she not more sparing of her strength? Thoughts of death often occupied her mind: "I am on the home stretch" (I 154). Did she try to benumb thoughts through work; or did she not wish to admit how very weak she was? Once she wrote of all this:

> Although I am completely resigned to God's holy will, still the thought of death is and remains more specific; may we all learn to die well. The consideration of death engages me very frequently, for my heart condition has become more severe lately and the "keep-yourself-quiet" and "spare-yourself" seems unprofitable to me. Still I think: to those who love God, all things turn out for the best. Then do all slowly in God's name. Pray much for me, dear Sister. Our dear Lord tries me in various ways. Although often oppressive, the beloved cross is always most welcome. May our dear Lord continue to give us the necessary strength and courage to imitate and persevere with him on the way of the cross. (I 152)

It was destined for her from now on to proceed slowly in the name of Jesus. She utilized her remaining strength quietly and simply and in a tenacious manner continued to follow the way God destined for her.

After the dedication much remained to be done in the motherhouse. The former chapel was converted into two stories and fitted to the lower two stories of the building. A gymnasium was arranged for the school on ground level; the first story was converted into a conference hall. The choir apse of the old chapel remained intact until the erection of a new novitiate. Then the roof of the choir apse was removed and a balcony made for the sick Sisters, giving them the opportunity of being in the fresh air. This same balcony also plays an important role in the letters of the Mother. She writes that after an illness it is a pleasure to spend time recuperating there.

On May 12, 1896, investiture again took place in Olpe. The Reverend Superior presented the religious garb to thirty-nine postulants. Mother Maria Theresia was happy that she no longer needed to travel to Mülheim for the ceremony, as travel had become burdensome to her.

With especially deep feelings, Mother Maria Theresia must have spent Christmas this year. In her letter she writes:

> On the day before Christmas from six o'clock in the morning until six o'clock on Christmas morning, we had exposition of the Most Blessed Sacrament. From midnight Christmas until four o'clock in the morning we had five Holy Masses. Our chapel was decorated so beautifully and lighted so profusely that it seemed a foretaste of heaven. (III 7)

The great and outstanding event of 1897 happened on April 28. The superior handed Mother Maria Theresia the Papal Decree of Commendation of the Congregation. It was issued in Rome on April 13. Some changes in the Constitution were prescribed by Rome. Among these was the stipulation that temporary vows were no longer to be made for five years immediately after the novitiate, but in three periods of two years each, followed by final vows. For Mother the decree was a source of very special joy, for such decrees are commonly the forerunners of pontifical approbation of a congregation.

In mid-May, Mother agreed to her hospitalization in Venusberg near Bonn. Her condition is described briefly and to the point in the close of one of her letters: "My hand is painful and swollen, and consequently I must give up" (I 60). She remained in St. Mary Hospital, Venusberg, until the end of July. The doctor did all in his power to bring her back to health. To his endeavors in her behalf, she replied: "As God wills! I gladly work, pray, and suffer as long as the Lord wills" (I 162).

Such quiet resignation to the will of God was the source and secret of her strength. This also accounts for her cheerfulness and her serene composure of heart that was a part of her in difficult times. She herself marveled at that gift which God had granted her. But of this fact she spoke only to Sister Deogratias to whom she could confide the inmost secrets of her heart: "Such various things happen; often I marvel at myself that I can retain a joyous disposition; I am glad that misfortune does not bear me down. I can only say thanks to God for all" (I 164). In this same letter of February 17, 1898, she touchingly speaks of the spirit of sacrifice of the Sisters and, how on the Day of Atonement, they were so zealous in prayer and in acts of mortification. She herself wore the hair shirt every morning when her condition permitted. She never spoke of it. She had retained this act of penance for herself. It was customary in the congregation only in its early days. She did not require it of her Sisters, but she herself practiced it.

To have all her Sisters gain all the blessings of the Church, Mother at this time made a special request. She petitioned the Holy Father in Rome that the Sisters be given the privilege of gaining all the indulgences in the convent chapel, for which, according to regulations, they would be obligated to visit specified churches. Rev. Anselm Budde, O.F.M., presented this petition to the Holy Father on April 1, 1898. His Holiness, Pope Leo XIII, granted the request for a period of seven years. This quite well covered the time that Mother still lived on earth.

In the same year, Mother Maria Theresia witnessed the first advance in the further development of the school in Olpe. During the Easter season, a new division was incorporated which comprised three years of elementary education.

After Mother had again been reelected as Superior General on August 12, 1898, she for reasons of health was obliged to revisit the medicinal baths at Wildungen. Sister Alphonsa, the Provincial of the North American missions, accompanied her and remained at Wildungen until September. After her departure, Mother Maria Theresia felt very lonely and asked the Sisters to pray that her "exile" be shortened. The letter was written on September 11 and contains a short description of her situation:

> Very many patients are here; seemingly the favorable weather keeps them lingering. I, too, am getting along

> nicely. Twice a day I go to the well in a 20-minute walk from here to drink water and then climb the high hills. You have no idea how difficult it was for me at first to go that great distance; but practice makes perfect. It is much better now. Although my sore feet and kidney pains often growl, they must go with me. (III 13)

Mother did not reckon on a complete recovery for herself. Soon she wrote again: "Healthwise I am not very good; I feel that I cannot make it much longer and thank our dear Lord for all! Soon my life on earth will be a thing of the past." And this letter ends: "Now I must stop; with the least endeavor, perspiration rolls from me" (I 166).

This chronicle of her sufferings should be read with the chronicle of the new foundations as given in the previous chapter. It is difficult to realize that in both, the same person was the actor who administers all and who suffers all. Sister Paula, her assistant and greatly devoted to her, took over most of the external administration of the congregation, but the interior administration Mother reserved for herself, especially the guidance of the Sisters. This she exercised faithfully through her letters.

Thus she lived through the year 1899. On May 25, the novices pronounced their temporary vows for two years for the first time in accordance with the directives from Rome. The Bishop of Paderborn approved the new Constitution on July 2 and gave permission to have it printed. The apostolate of Mother Maria Theresia was exercised in obedience to the Church and her work developed internally and externally.

In the beginning of the year 1900, Mother was able to write humorously: "I also am better than during the previous year, but my antiqueness remains with me" (III 21). A singular honor came to Mother Maria Theresia on January 27, which she accepted calmly, for it was an acknowledgment of the work of her Sisters. Emperor William II granted her the medal of the Order of the Red Cross, Second Class, in recognition of the great work of the congregation. The District Magistrate, the Mayor, and the Pastor appeared at the motherhouse to bring the good news. The bestowal was made in a festive manner by the Reverend Rector

Schroeder. The address which he gave for the occasion was presented to Mother in written form. It tells of the great esteem in which Mother Maria Theresia was held even in her life time. It reads as follows:

> A very honorable task has been assigned to me to present the great distinction His Majesty, our Most Gracious Emperor and King, has been pleased to award our Venerable Mother. My pleasure is so much the greater since I have been associated with the congregation for many years in closest ties through my activeties, and most likely I will always remain with it. Thus I esteem it an eminent honor that during my time here, the Venerable Mother receives this outstanding distinction. To my knowledge His Majesty has not granted such a favor to any other congregation. Mother receives two decorations in one, for the bestowing of the higher decoration includes the lower. As I mentioned, no other congregation to my knowledge can rejoice in such an honor. The Venerable Mother has deserved it; the decoration will serve as an acknowledgement of work and endeavor. She founded the congregation under the greatest difficulties. The obstacles confronting her seemed insurmountable. Most certainly she was not bedded on roses. Apart from her severe physical pains, which she suffered almost uninterruptedly, manifold storms battered the young congregation just as it was beginning to develop and blossom. Only the Mother's great and firm confidence in God and her unbending energy preserved the congregation from ruin at this time. Seemingly the *Kulturkampf* wished to deal a death blow, since it forbade the development of the Sisters and the acceptance of further new members. But these very storms served its salvation. They led to the foundation in North America where a branch congregation developed, in which the selfless activities of the Sisters unfolded gloriously for the salvation of men.
>
> I need not quote all the particulars of the Venerable Mother's activities. God has recorded them in the Book of Life that will be revealed on the day of reckoning.

Now I would like to direct a word of exhortation to you, dear Sisters, because words spoken on such a worthy occasion make a profounder impression and persist longer. You must endeavor to maintain the congregation at the height of its present honor and esteem; and it will if you remain loyal to the duties and tasks of your calling; if you willingly and uprightly follow the commands of your superiors with confidence and esteem. The superiors must know what they can expect from their Sisters. Only then is it possible for a congregation spread so widely to develop through fruitful activity and to remain at its present height or even mount higher.

Novices and postulants, you can consider it an honor to belong to such a congregation. Endeavor to become good and worthy members! Not only is Mother held in high repute by ecclesiastical circles which have observed her quiet unselfish endeavors for a long time, but also by civil authorities which have recognized her worthy and knew how to honor her as this decoration given the Venerable Mother shows. Should you then not rejoice to belong to such a congregation and vow to remain true to her even in stormy and sorrowful days? Ever bear in mind that you are poor Franciscans! Harbor a sincere sympathy for the poor, the forsaken, and the sick. Preserve the genuine spirit of the congregation. The superior has the obligation to foster the spirit of the congregation and to provide for the formation of the Sisters to enable them to qualify for the great objectives of the congregation. Endeavor to sustain her in all and in every possible way.

Now I shall perform my assigned task to adorn the Venerable Mother with the decorative medal. I know that you in no way desire worldly distinction, otherwise you would not have entered the convent to travel the thorny way of religious life. In spite of all, the honors have come to you and with so much the greater joy I present this decoration which you have not sought. May you wear this distinction for many years in the joy of your Sisters, in the joy of your

> flourishing congregation! Others at your age have retired long since to enjoy their merited rest. But, you only two years hence have again shouldered the burden of Superior General in the trust and confidence that God will strengthen your weak condition. Even if at times you lament that you no longer possess your former energy to devote to the Sisters, still they have your love and confidence and realize that in you they have a heart of sympathy and love. Although you have not the strength to devote your energies to external affairs, the calm courageous bearing of your many sufferings is an example to all the Sisters how they must persevere. May you, therefore, Venerable Mother, wear this award in love and joy for many years more. Here I offer you also the congratulations of the Reverend Superior which I unite with mine in the certainty that as always I shall genuinely further your interests.

It was a fine gesture on the part of the civil authorities to assign the presentation of the award to a priest. A representative of the government would certainly have closed the festive occasion with the threefold "Hail" or even a "Hurrah" to the Emperor. It was a day of joy for the motherhouse that the State recognized the activities of Mother in such a remarkable way.

Naturally, it became known to the various branch houses that the Superior General received this distinctive decoration. Congratulations poured in from all sides, also from Sister Bonaventure of Jülich. Mother sent her a reply on March 12,1900:

> You also wrote your congratulations to me relative to the honor which I received. I thank you and rejoice at the recognition of the congregation; otherwise the medal rests peacefully in its coffer and does not disturb me. (III 24)

Could Sister Bonaventure, out of sheer joy, have promised to send Mother a cake? Nevertheless, she continued:

> In your last letter you mentioned that Sister Beata would bake a cake and consequently made the mouth of this aged child water. Did she probably give it to you! If you send it, please send some violets, also.

In addition, this same letter gave some idea of the condition of her health:

> Healthwise I am better than last winter, but not too much better. One or two, sometimes three days of every week are days of pain, making it necessary for me to be quiet. This is not a complaint, far from it. In the interim, I have work and plenty of it.... Now the feast of St. Joseph is fast approaching; how greatly I rejoice on that beautiful day, but he must not put me to bed; that would be hard, but even then I would be satisfied.

Otherwise, her health seemingly was better this year. She was able to make the visitation of several branch houses. However, she was old and felt the burden. Thus she wrote: "It is with me as with the aged in general, sometimes better, then again so worn out and weak that I could weep" (III 30). Was it not an inhuman attachment for the Sisters to elect and reelect her again and again as Superior General? On the other hand, did this not portray forcibly what the Sisters had in their Mother could not readily be given by another who might have been chosen to succeed her?

It was now forty years since she had been invested with the religious habit. How very much had happened since then! She reminisced and wrote: "When I look back over the very agitated years of life, bitter hours come to mind. Much I should have done better, but all is now past and the good Lord will turn all to the best" (I 76). But she could not recall the day of her investiture without bringing to notice: "Today, forty years ago our dear Savior came into our chapel" (I 178). This grace she could never forget! Since that day she was a Poor Franciscan of Perpetual Adoration.

In this thought, she began the year 1901. What at that time she wrote to one of the superiors, she herself experienced deeply:

> ... and it will be a great comfort for you to live under the same roof with our Lord. All will be well if oftener during the day, we spend some moments in prayer. In every situation and in all places hardships are present and the cross needs to be carried, but our Helper and Comforter is so

> near. He waits for us to hear our petitions and to help us. (III 34)

As a guideline for the Sisters, especially in this year, she wrote: "Be concerned not to neglect your prayers and see that silence and charity are practiced" (III 46). She saw prayer, love, and silence as worthy supports for the upright life of a Poor Franciscan. Her Sisters should seek strength in prayer to enable the love of their hearts to overflow on mankind. Their love should be silent, their ego recede before the Lord, who wishes to pour out his love through men upon mankind. Silent love was to her the mark of one who knows himself gifted by God to distribute his love to others.

As to her personal well-being in this year, she wrote in January: "It is better with me at present. I had the grippe and my feet were bad again, either from the infirmities of age or from laziness" (III 35). She accepted her illnesses with patience and could even joke about them. But during the same year, she suffered much from arthritis, and the burdens of her office weighed more heavily upon her. Although she rejoiced at the approaching investiture and profession, she mentioned, in her letter of May 6, that the days would be onerous:

> I look forward to the 29th and 30th of this month with fear and anxiety. The tasks are difficult: first, the spiritual exercises of retreat, then the renewal of vows, profession, and investiture. Our dear Lord must strengthen all of us in a special way, or we shall scarcely see the way through. (III 42)

The Sisters knew that the Mother was available to them at all times. She herself often had to exert all the strength she had to bear up when one Sister after another came to her for advice and comfort.

In July, Mother Maria Theresia had to frequent the Baths at Brückenau: "Pray much for me that our dear Lord shorten the days of my trial" (III 47). Even though one Sister spent the time with her, she longed to be with the Sisters at the motherhouse. From a letter, we get a rather clear idea of how matters stood in Brückenau:

> Often, in the solitude of the woods, my thoughts go to you. I long for your companionship but fear that the trip will be too hard and that has kept me from asking you to come. Up to now I had been quite well, but today nephritis set in requiring me to keep myself quiet, but I trust that it will be better tomorrow. The peace and serenity here are so wholesome that I often sit on the hills for hours, praying, reading, and doing some embroidery. I believe one could recuperate here without the water and baths. We must take twelve baths, and I have taken four thus far. The baths are filled to capacity with patients. To date we have had only one priest here who celebrates each morning, but on Sundays, Tuesdays, and Thursdays, a Franciscan Father from Volkersberg comes to celebrate Holy Mass and, also, to hear confessions. May our Lord grant that I may soon return home strengthened; it is not a small sacrifice to live entirely among strangers. (I 185)

Perhaps her greatest joy of the year was the celebration of Mass on Holy Thursday in the chapel at the motherhouse for the first time. Heretofore, the Sisters were obliged to go to the parish church on Holy Thursday and this was impossible for the infirm Sisters. Mother, full of joy, reported the event as follows:

> Today for the first time we celebrated Holy Thursday with Holy Mass in our convent chapel and thereafter our beloved Savior was carried to the tomb where today and tomorrow we shall have quiet adoration. Now this so-long-desired wish has been fulfilled. We rejoice greatly over this grace and thank our dear Savior for the privilege. (I 183)

Earlier a Reverend Superior had said that, relative to divine services, the Venerable Mother will not rest until she has obtained all. Concerning the liturgy of Holy Week and Easter, she obtained all in 1902. During a visit of the Diocesan Bishop, Dr. Wilhelm Schneider, on October 4, she asked him for permission to have the complete liturgical services from Holy Thursday to Easter in the convent chapel as celebrated in the parish church. Immediately the Bishop gave her this permission verbally.

Illnesses and infirmities were her constant companions. In the spring of 1902, she had a rendezvous with death. A serious heart condition was always with her. In the night of April 12 and 13 she had an onset of heart paralysis. The Sisters were awakened and assembled, praying and weeping, at her bedside – which appeared to be a deathbed. After a long and anxious half hour, regular heart action again returned.

Mother awakened from her unconscious condition. She saw the Sisters assembled around her bed and calmly said: "Go to bed; I shall not die." But it took her a long time to recuperate from this attack. Toward the close of the year, she was able again to hold visitation in some of the houses.

Perhaps it was the experience of this attack that occasioned her to write at the end of the year: "Would that I had passed through the last hour, but it cannot be far away and how ardently I long for it. Still I cannot exclude fear and anxiety" (II 33). Again at the end of the year, she reminisced relative to the day of her investiture, the first Holy Mass offered in the convent chapel on the following day, and the inauguration of the Perpetual Adoration:

> Today marks forty-two years that our Lord is living in our midst. Thus our hearts are full of good fortune. But also sorrow and shame oppress me, and I must woefully accuse myself of ingratitude in the face of such great graces. Yes, dear Sisters, thank the Lord that in his goodness he has granted us time to make satisfaction and through the divine Child offer amends for the past. (I 195)

January of 1903 set in with many difficulties for Mother — not only ill health, but sorrows because of individual Sisters. Otherwise, she most likely would not have written as follows:

> The month of January has brought me many and great sorrows. It seems as though the older one becomes, the more he has to endure. We are and remain poor creatures. If all would seek only God in their activities, and practice charity regularly, and observe conventual silence, many

> evils would be avoided and all would be happy in their holy calling. (II 34)

In these lines can be sensed the ideas that embody Mother's directives in her last years: love and be silent. The whole crystallized itself for her thusly: in the life of her Sisters, all must harmonize.

February 1903, brought anxious weeks to the congregation. For a second time a report that Mother was near death, went out to the Sisters. Sister Andrea Bussien, the chronicler of the congregation, had written the report. It almost seems that, up to this point, she had compiled the chronicle from hearsay, but now she became an eye witness. It is evident that the story was made at the time of happening for it breathes a directness not to be replaced by anything else. It seems most fitting to quote the entire account as written by Sister Andrea:

> On February 19, the Thursday before Shrove Tuesday, the Sisters, according to custom, observed Great Penance Day to make amends to our dear Lord for the many wrongs committed against him on those exuberant days of merriment. Oh, could we by our penances form a phalanx on which the strokes of wickedness could rebound before they strike the gracious paternal heart of God! Our beloved Mother was unable to take part in our atonement hour. Heaven had imposed a severer atoning sacrifice on her. She is seriously ill today, her chest is contracted, her coughing is tight. Until early afternoon, she remained up, praying and sacrificing, but later had to retire and was unable to arise Friday morning.
>
> Today, Sunday, January 22, Sister Helene was taken from her cell to the infirmary. She had felt wretched for several days but was definitely resolute in refusing to take to bed. She thought: "In bed, I must die." She was right. On Sunday morning she was found unconscious in her cell breathing heavily. She was taken to the infirmary again. The doctor pronounced her condition critical, a severe case of pneumonia had set in. She remained unconscious

and only on Tuesday were there some minutes of awareness. Anointing of the Sick was then administered.

The doctor also visited the Venerable Mother and said that her condition resembled that of Sister Helene. Her chest became contracted and her breathing wheezed and whistled, but there was no immediate danger. On Ash Wednesday, Sister Paula remained with Mother during the St. Joseph devotions. Her condition worsened suddenly. Sister Paula made all the preparations for the administration of the Anointing of the Sick. The Sacrament was administered immediately after the devotions, while the Sisters prayerfully remained in the chapel to storm heaven for the recovery of their beloved Mother.

Dr. Fuchius, a relative and personal advisor of the Mother, approached the local physician, Dr. Stuehlen, regarding the condition of the patient, and the doctor readily agreed that Professor Ungar of Bonn should be brought in for consultation. Thursday, about midnight, while the two doctors were still waiting, the professor arrived. The diagnosis of the professor coincided with that of the two doctors and he also said that their medications were good. However, he gave but little hope for Mother's recovery. Although she was suffering severely, she did not forget to order proper hospitality for the doctor from Bonn. She gave orders and was solicitous that they be taken care of. In the night of January 26 and 27, Sister Helene died at about three o'clock. May she rest in peace!

Professor Ungar returned to Bonn on Friday morning and promised to come back on Sunday. Mother remained critical through Friday and Saturday. During Friday night, she again received the Anointing of the Sick. All possible nursing care was given to her to alleviate her suffering. Sister Paula gave herself no rest either day or night in order to be available at every moment. The Venerable Mother was unconscious most of the time and consequently unaware of what was happening.

The often repeated injection of camphor revived her spirit. The doctors had given up all hope of recovery and several times gave her but a few more hours to live. The Sisters, however, have not given up hope. As a drowning man clasps a straw, so the Sisters cling to hope as long as there is a spark of life left. The greater the danger, the greater their confidence in God's almighty help. Who can count the petitions and the sighs coming from the hearts of the Sisters and uninterruptedly ascending to heaven? Who can count the sacrifices offered to turn the heart of God to grant their request? Sunday afternoon the doctors declared her condition worse and gave up every hope of recovery.

Sister Paula wished to give all the Sisters the opportunity of seeing the Mother once more. She gave notice for all the Sisters to assemble and informed them that the doctors had given up all hope. Since the Venerable Mother was lying in a coma, the Sisters were to file past her bed to see her beloved face once more. Her countenance was greatly swollen, her laboring breast was heaving and wheezing and a rattle was in her throat. She knew nothing of what was transpiring. It was a sad farewell, but even now the Sisters did not lose hope. Sister Paula placed a relic of St. Crescentia on Mother. All began a novena immediately. On Sunday, about five o'clock in the afternoon, Professor Ungar came once more. He also gave up hope and returned to Bonn the same evening. That same evening the sad news of the hopelessness of recovery was sent to all the houses. From hour to hour, the Sisters in the motherhouse feared for that precious life. The greater the anxiety, the more fervent their prayers that soared to heaven without interruption.

Toward midnight Mother asked to see the Sisters once more. Soon as many Sisters as the room could hold were gathered at her bedside. Although gasping for breath, the sick one spoke to her Sisters in a loud voice amidst frequent pauses: "Dear Sisters, now it will not be much longer before I must leave you. Be loyal, dear Sisters, obey the Rules and practice obedience, for disobedience leads to ruin. One thing, dear Sisters, lay the following to heart

— be one and practice charity. If you practice charity, all will go well. I have loved all of you with my whole heart. Do not forget me after I have passed into eternity. Dying is not easy; you can see that from me. Lead good lives that you may die well. Remain loyal."

Amidst tears, Sister Paula begged Mother in the name of all the Sisters for forgiveness. She answered: "I have forgiven all. There is no more to forgive. There were only small faults and imperfections. Let us mutually forgive one another. Do not forget me after I have passed into eternity."

Sister Paula then asked Mother not to exert herself any longer, stating that talking is above her strength. She then gave the blessing to the Sisters who were kneeling around her bed, in the words of her much used and loved benediction wish: "May the Virgin, pure and lowly, bless you with her Child most holy, in the name of the Father, and of the Son, and of the Holy Spirit." Then she added: "Dear Sisters, I have loved all of you, all without exception, and this love will endure."

Touched deeply, the Sisters left the sickroom and in intense prayer before Christ, they remained a long time pleading for the life of their dear Mother. The night finally passed and their Mother was still with them.

Monday morning Sister Helene was buried, and we asked ourselves anxiously and with fear whether we would not soon accompany our Venerable Mother on the same road. Several days more, in fact, an entire week, Mother remained critical; since the threat of death was there constantly, she received the Sacrament of the Anointing of the Sick several times more. She was joyously prepared and waited hour by hour to follow the call from above. Still what a loving alleviation for all to see her return to clear consciousness.

With what love and joy she noted the jubilee of His Holiness, Pope Leo XIII, celebrated solemnly by the entire Church on the second Sunday of Lent in early March. She thought of Olpe's celebration on March 15 to be observed with great illumination and a candlelight procession and asked that nothing be neglected in the convent that could enhance the festivities, for this was in honor of the ecclesiastical head of the Church. She was attached with childlike love to the Holy Father and regarded him with deep respect and holy awe. On Friday before the feast, she wished for once to hear the Leo Hymn which the Sisters had practiced for the occasion, for she did not expect to live through Sunday. The singers assembled in the opposite room; the door of the sickroom was partly ajar. Attentively and with great joy the seriously ill folded her hands while she listened to the subdued tones of the beautiful hymn. All the Sisters in the sickroom let the tears flow freely, for they could not be restrained.

Slowly, very slowly the condition of the Mother gave signs of slight improvement. One scarcely dared to believe, for as the sick one felt better for several hours, soon thereafter she succumbed to extreme languish. Also, the pains in her heart, from which she suffered so much, caused her many painful hours. As her condition showed some improvement, Professor Ungar visited the Venerable Mother once more. He found her condition definitely improved; still she had to be careful especially regarding much talking. She had to avoid all drafts. As soon as she had recovered sufficiently to travel, she was to leave the raw air of the Sauerland and be taken to the milder and warmer air of the Rhineland, that is, to Bonn. Since the Mother was unable to do without liquids during the night because of the mucous collecting in her throat, the Reverend Rector was so kind as to bring her Holy Communion at midnight so that during her long siege of illness she would not be deprived of this great spiritual help, the reception of her divine Bridegroom for whom she longed most lovingly. (At this time the Church required a Eucharistic fast from midnight for all who wished to receive; abstaining from water was included.)

At the beginning of April, her recuperations had advanced to the point that she could spend some time out of bed, and soon she could take a few steps. She permit-

> ted Sister Paula to help her to the choir so that she could adore her Savior in the tabernacle and to thank him for adding more days to her life. On Holy Thursday, April 11, she entered the convent for the first time after her illness. On Easter Sunday, she joined in the jubilant celebration. On this day she again attended Holy Mass. The Sisters, deeply moved, thanked God for having heard their fervent prayers.
>
> Her recuperation progressed slowly. The doctors urged that she be taken to a warmer climate as soon as possible to overcome the effects of her serious illness more readily. Thus toward the end of April, the Venerable Mother was taken to Venusberg. She traveled via coach to Bergneustadt and from there by coach to Siegburg; then again by coach to Venusberg. The trip was hard on her and she needed several days of complete rest before the effects wore off. Here the warmer weather was favorable and she improved rapidly.

This closes the Chronicle report.

Mother Maria Theresia remained in Venusberg from the beginning of May until the end of July. Henceforth, a very special individual disposition must have governed the relations between her and her Sisters. The Sisters had experienced the imminent death of Mother; once again she was given back to them. The love with which Mother clung to her Sisters, and their love for her were submerged in the evidence of death. And still nothing fundamentally changed, except the new delicacy of their relations to each other. For both, Mother and the Sisters, in the serious moments at the end of February, what they said and what they did in the face of death, gave the appearance of mending all strain. In reality, all manifested genuine love and attachment. Therefore, Mother could be herself now as she had been before, for there was actually no break in their former relationship. Whether in life or in death, her motto was always: "He leads, I follow."

She serenely relived in memory her danger of death during her stay in Venusberg with these words:

> I passed through a very severe illness and would so gladly have died, but our dear Lord most assuredly wishes me to suffer my Purgatory here; I shall be satisfied with his Will in all. But I have one request, that, if my life is prolonged, he will improve my health to the degree that I shall be able to accomplish more for him. (III 70)

At that time, she acquainted a superior with her own method and attitude toward some Sisters and how she guided them:

> The Sisters that are with you now will surely endeavor to be good supports to you and give you much joy. But God permits the adverse to happen; one must take the Sisters as they are, and not as they should be. (III 70)

Mother Maria Theresia had planned to be present at the investiture ceremonies and profession at the motherhouse in Olpe on May 27 and 28. But Sister Paula urged her to remain in Venusberg for it would be better for her. She mentioned that, if she were in Olpe, none of the younger Sisters would want to leave without seeing her personally to receive her instructions and advice. There were thirty-one postulants, forty-two novices for temporary vows, and thirty Sisters for final vows. Sister Paula knew only too well that Mother would not spare herself and would not refuse to see a single Sister. Such a large group would definitely overtax her strength and might cause a setback. Mother Maria Theresia acquiesced. For their great feast, she sent the Sisters her most heartfelt wishes and congratulations with her maternal blessing.

Since she had recovered sufficiently now, she visited the various houses in Bonn and in the vicinity. On July 24, she returned to Olpe. She was met by coach in Bergneustadt and arrived at the motherhouse about four-thirty in the afternoon. All the Sisters met her at the entrance. She seemed recovered, but it was clear that the infirmities of age would remain with her.

It was again a pleasure for her to send her Sisters heartfelt and grace-filled blessings for the feast of Christmas (IV 51). She reminisced over the year of 1903:

> Now this year will soon end; it will pass with its sufferings and joys; its cares and endeavors. Happy are we if we have utilized all well and increased our merits for heaven! What we have recognized as faulty in the past, let us endeavor to correct in the future and faithfully correspond to the grace of God that we may become ever dearer to the Divine Infant. As in the past so also in the future, we shall encounter many trials. Let us in no way refuse these nor become discouraged, definitely not! We know under what banner we march, and victory will be ours if we have confidence and beg our Lord for the grace to remain loyal. (IV 65)

She entered the last year of her life: 1904. At its very beginning we hear: "Again I have lived through some very hard days, heart spasms accompanied with severe pains" (III 77). Also, at this time a request was made to the superior of Haaren, near Aachen, to ask the Schervier Sisters to borrow their Book of Customs (III 78). Mother Maria Theresia was in the process of revising the Book of Customs and wished to compare hers with that of another congregation. The General Chapter was to take place in August; she wished the revision completed by that time. As long as the Lord granted her life, she wanted to work although she realized that her days were numbered.

As she wrote to the Sisters at Easter, she weighed her own life and confessed, not that which man accomplishes is great, but only that which God accomplished in man. Here her vision born of the wisdom of age becomes significant, and she traces the way of a Poor Franciscan to the very end as one in poverty and forgetfulness of self:

> Let us not consider that we have done something great, my dear Sisters, by entering religious life, definitely not! The Lord has done great things for us by giving us the call! Let us endeavor to remain true to our Lord and, in leaving the world, let us also leave ourselves, the ego. Each morning let us endeavor to give a blow to self-love, then we can joyfully sing Alleluia in the evening as we review the day. (IV 127)

Mother Maria Theresia was in Olpe for the investiture and profession ceremonies in May, but she was unable to participate in the solemnities. At the beginning of June, her condition had not improved. On June 1, she wrote:

> On Friday the spiritual exercises began for the Sisters who are to renew their vows. I wish the strenuous festivities were over. I am not well; my feet simply refuse to be active. I scarcely ever leave my room. I would love to go out into our beautiful garden, but up to now, it has been impossible. (III 83)

In the same letter, she again stressed her thoughts relative to religious life on which she concentrated more and more in later years:

> Endeavor earnestly to observe silence and practice true charity to each other. Do not omit your spiritual exercises nor your prayers. The religious spirit and joy in sacrifice in religious life must be sustained by prayer. (III 83)

To improve Mother Maria Theresia's condition healthwise was the concern of all in anticipation of the General Chapter. The plan was to send her to the Baths at Wildungen for a few weeks' stay. But Professor Ungar advised against this. Thus on June 15, she went to Venusberg near Bonn to recover her strength. However, she did not have much rest for the preparations for the coming General Chapter were in progress.

On July 26, she interrupted her stay in Venusberg to go to Geistingen. Sister Johanna, one of the first Sisters who with her had started anew in Olpe in 1863, was at the point of death. She still recognized Mother Maria Theresia upon her arrival. It seemed as if she had just waited for her coming. Then the end came rapidly. Mother closed Sister's eyes in death. Sister Johanna had been a loyal companion, one who had borne all the sorrows and hardships of beginning. Now she had gone home. This death was difficult for the Mother. She lamented:

> It is hard on me to see the old Sisters die before my very eyes, and I must continue as a pilgrim along the way. May

> it please our dear Lord to take me home soon, for all my longing and desires tend toward him, my only love. (II 39)

It is readily understandable how difficult it must have been for Mother on August 12, when the unshakeable and, at the same time, the inexorable confidence of her Sisters once more elected her as Superior General in the face of her opposition.

On November 26, she expressed humorously how she spent the last cold season: "My condition is similar to that of all elderly people; I must be careful and keep to my room more than ordinarily" (IV 134). Even at this time, she was not inactive. On December 5, she conferred with the Reverend Provincial Strassfeld relative to the conditions required for pontifical approval of the Constitution. Although she did not attain this personal objective in her lifetime, yet she initiated this important step for the congregation.

Her last Christmas on earth came. For her it was understood that she participate in the midnight services. As she returned to her room after the service, she rejoiced greatly over the small crib and Christmas tree that the Sisters, in the meanwhile, had set up in her room. She knelt before the Crib a long time, for in this Holy Night she had so very much to tell her Lord. Early in the morning, before five o'clock, she was in the choir of the chapel for Holy Mass. The Sisters received Holy Communion during this Mass. She also attended the Mass following and remained for the close of the Adoration. This exertion soon showed its effects. She was not at all well. As Sister Paula insisted that, "Next year you must spare yourself more and not go to the midnight services." Mother answered, "If I am still living next Christmas and God wills, I shall again attend the midnight services."

CHAPTER XIII

"SHE WAS MOTHER TO US"

Sister Hildegardis Schelle, in 1917, gave the above title to a chapter delineating the character of Mother Maria Theresia. There are no words that better characterize her effectiveness and summarize her life. The word "Mother" has rich connotations. It was customary for the Olpe Sisters, as well as Sisters of other congregations to call their highest superior "Mother." Seldom could anyone bear that title with greater right than Mother Maria Theresia Bonzel. From a really modest beginning, in 1863, until her death, a congregation developed that had one hundred ten foundations in America and Germany combined. Was not the Superior General compelled through such growth of the congregation to remove herself, as it were, more and more from the Sisters? Since she had to govern a large congregation, was she not unable to maintain close personal contacts with the individual Sisters? Was she not obliged to operate remotely? Did not her desk work come to the forefront so urgently that she had little time for anything else? This is the great mystery of her motherly love; she was there for every individual Sister and was concerned about each one. This attitude she preserved until death. It was characteristic of her that she seldom spoke about the congregation. She spoke about the "Sisters." Her last words to her successor were: "Sister Paula, take good care of the Sisters; I have told you all, dear Sister Paula, you know all."

As superior she most assuredly understood the desk work. Faithful care of a large congregation demands that the office carry on adequate correspondence. In this respect, Sister Paula assisted Mother with great efficiency; she cherished her assistant highly and was grateful to her. A letter of November 26, 1904, mentions that Sister Paula again conducted the visitation for Mother Maria Theresia. Mother, in her characteristic manner, prepared the way for her assistant when she wrote this message to a superior in one of the houses:

> In the near future, our good Sister Paula will visit you; she is at Wildungen now and from there has planned to go to Berlin, Torgau, and Oschersleben. How she will arrange her tour, I do not know, but I beg you most urgently to take good care of her for she takes cold readily and traveling in the cold of winter is not a small matter. (IV 134)

When toward the end of June 1904, Mother Maria Theresia had to stay at Venusberg, she longed to have her faithful assistant, Sister Paula, celebrate her own name day with her on June 29, for she wished to felicitate her devoted assistant personally on her feastday. Since the Sisters in the motherhouse did not wish to miss this celebration, they held the nameday festivities there on June 27. For the occasion Mother Maria Theresia had Sister Deogratias send some cherries from Merten to Olpe for the celebration.

With the work that she took upon herself, Sister Paula not only aided Mother Maria Theresia but also the other Sisters. Thus Mother had more time to devote to her correspondence apostolate with her Sisters. The catalogue of letters received from individual Sisters numbers five hundred seven. The first letter extant to one of the Sisters is dated May 22, 1879, and the last one was dated December 20, 1904. A great many letters were written to individual Sisters, which constitute only a fraction of the sum total of letters written by the Mother. Unfortunately, the letters that she wrote to Sister Hildegardis, her niece, have not been preserved. But the letters that have been preserved definitely show how she endeavored to guide her Sisters in a maternal way.

Then there were the circular letters written to the Sisters on feastdays. Here the reader comes upon an amazing fact. She wrote, and even toward the end of her life, not only one version of a circular for a feast. For Easter, 1904, she wrote four different letters; for Christmas of the same year, Mother wrote five. Why did she multiply her work in that way? Would not one letter have been sufficient? Others might be inclined to think so. But Mother Maria Theresia thought otherwise. She knew that the various houses of the congregation differed in their structure and problems, and, as much as possible, she wished to take this into consideration on these occasions. To understand this better, we will take a look at the four circulars written for Easter 1904. Two were written on March 30, and two on March 31.

The first circular contains the following thoughts:

> May the tremendous love our Savior has for us, comfort us at all times. May this love let us recognize that we live not for ourselves but for him. May this love awaken a corresponding love in us and arouse in us a loyalty and love of sacrifice. We are weak and wretched creatures. We must humbly acknowledge this and beg our Lord to help us lowly ones, that, through his assistance, we will be enabled to do great things for him.
>
> How much a fervent and zealous soul can accomplish through good example; the eyes of the world are upon us and will readily detect the least fault or imperfection. Therefore, dear Sisters, let us above all be circumspect and vigilant that our conduct be exemplary, that God's eye may rest upon us with complacency. (IV 126)

The second circular letter contains four admonitions. It deals with Lent:

> Who in this preparatory period has zealously meditated on the excessive love of God, must feel himself called to die repentantly to himself; to arise with Christ, which means to detach ourselves, with the grace of God, from all that is displeasing to him. After such considerations, it should not be difficult to renew joyfully our surrender and our vows to him. Let us not think that we have done something great in entering the religious life, dear Sisters, certainly not! The Lord has done something great in calling us! Let us endeavor to remain loyal to the Lord, to leave the world, our relatives, but most of all ourselves by surrendering the ego. Each morning let us endeavor to give a blow to self-love; then in looking over the day in the evening, we can sing a joyful Alleluia. Happy are we if in retrospect we find a rich self-sacrificing life. Here below life seems but a dream, but eternal will be the joyous Alleluias of heaven — a reunion for which we all long. (IV 127)

The third circular urged the Sisters to overcome sadness and sorrow in the light of what the Risen Christ bestowed upon mankind. Then in a special way she presented Christ as their exemplar and wrote:

> In his imitation let us sanctify ourselves and in holy love and patience bear the burdens of life. Also in religious life, unexpected things happen; still, dear Sisters, we are in the Lent of this life. Let us turn our gaze on our loving Savior and with him and for him carry our cross; let our evil inclinations die the death that we may rejoice in his and in our resurrection, and be glorified with him. Above all, dear Sisters, let us endeavor to practice charity toward our Sisters faithfully, that the bond of perfection may unite us ever more deeply and firmly, for love is the greatest of all virtues and draws God nearer to us. When in our daily relations, something weighty happens, let us endeavor to preserve our charitable sentiments and let us consider the meek Lamb of God in his sojourn with his disciples; yes, with his enemies. Let us imitate our divine Master, then all will be well. (IV 131)

The fourth circular begins:

> Although we may consider ourselves fortunate during Lent to rest in the Sacred Wounds of Jesus and in meditation to immerge ourselves into the bitter passion, still we yearn for the holy Easter Season where the jubilant Alleluias ring out so gloriously.

Then Mother Maria Theresia refers to Mary Magdalen and elucidates her joy on having found the Lord again. She reminds her Sisters of the good fortune and grace of Holy Communion, for there they come in contact with the Redeemer. Her thoughts lead over to the practical life, telling how it must be borne and lived prayerfully and continues:

> Still, my dear Sisters, we do not receive all these graces for ourselves alone. We are to cooperate faithfully and, through word and example, endeavor to win others for

> the Lord and to encourage them wherever we can. True love is never inactive; we must gladly and joyfully bear the burdens of others; although it be hard at times, love overcomes all and knows no hardship. In intimate prayer let us beg strength and courage to work faithfully in our holy calling; let us be forgetful of self and lead a life of sacrifice as God wills it for us. Definitely, crosses will not be wanting in religious life, and we might also become discouraged and impatient. But, dear Sisters, let us not permit ourselves to be robbed of merits, for we know only too well why we have left the world and what we have promised God at the altar. Still greater things have been promised us. Therefore, let us go forward with confidence in God. Only a little while and our goal is reached, and we may celebrate Easter in heaven. (IV 133)

These are the four circulars for one Easter feast! The reader senses definitely that each letter contains a specific message. That four such significant letters were written on this one occasion was not mere accident. Every letter carries an important message. Does this fact not show how earnestly the servant of God understood her duty as guide to the Sisters? Without effort, her thoughts seemed to flow from the maturity and richness of her life. It might be concluded that her letter of exhortation on bearing hardships had reference to the recent foundations. These foundations had many pioneering difficulties to overcome. Concerning the letter referring to the critical judgment of the world, either those of the Diaspora or those foundations employing many lay persons could be considered. Sisterly love is a general theme in all convents and a subject repeatedly called up for reflection. Still there could have been several houses of Sisters where such written admonitions were necessary. The Superior General, either from her own visitations or from the reports of her assistant, Sister Paula, knew her convents well and their existing conditions.

Apart from all these considerations, amazing is the fullness of thought that welled from her motherly heart, when the Mother wrote to her Sisters of the mysteries of faith and the essential characteristics of the congregation. Sister Paula, as Superior General of the Congregation from May 25, 1905, to December 10, 1914, the date of her death, accomplished great things for the congregation. But without a doubt, her greatest contribution to the Sisters was her unselfish assistance to the Mother while she was living, thus freeing her for the formation and guidance of the Sisters.

NORTH AMERICA

Of all her spiritual daughters, Mother Maria Theresia was especially devoted to her Sisters in North America. She had made two visitation trips there at the time when the foundations were not yet formed into a province and were still dependent on Germany for their decisions. On May 1, 1891, the Superior General made her third visitation to America from Bremen on the ship *Hohenzollern.* Sister Alphonsa, Provincial, accompanied by Sister M. Bernarda Weller, met Mother in New York. Sister Dominica was with Mother Maria Theresia. From New York they traveled to Lafayette, Indiana, where a joyous welcome was extended them. Shortly thereafter Mother began her tour of the American foundations.

Since her last visitation in 1885-86, the number of foundations had increased substantially: in 1887, St. Anthony Hospital, Denver, Colorado: St. Francis Hospital, Grand Island, Nebraska; St. Francis Hospital, Colorado Springs, Colorado: St. Joseph School, Kentland, Indiana; St. George School, Hermann, Missouri; in 1889, St. Joseph Hospital, Memphis, Tennessee; St. Elizabeth Hospital, Lincoln, Nebraska; in 1890, St. Stanislaus School, Duncan, Nebraska. In the year of visitation, 1891, St. Mary Academy, Memphis, Tennessee; Sacred Heart Academy, Fowler, Indiana; and St. Michael School, Tarnov, Nebraska, were founded.

Unfortunately, only a few details are known of this third trip to North America. The chronicle merely states that the Mother was received with the greatest joy and cordiality by all the Sisters in each of the houses. Unfortunately, also, the letters of Mother are missing from this period. Much might have been gleaned from her correspondence. Assuredly, she wrote letters to her Sisters in Germany during this time, but none are extant.

On October 20, 1891, Mother Maria Theresia and Sister Dominica left Lafayette on their return trip. They embarked in New York on the ship *Spree*. Although encountering severe storms on the fifth day of the journey, the ship arrived on schedule. They disembarked at Bremen, November 28; after a short rest, they returned to Olpe by train.

In 1896, Mother desired to make another visitation trip to North America. However, the Sisters were deeply concerned whether her condition healthwise would permit such a strenuous journey. The Reverend Superior also advised against it. Therefore, Sister Paula, as Mother's representative, undertook the visitation. Again, the congregation had expanded greatly in America. In 1893, the following foundations were added: St. Joseph Hospital, Logansport, Indiana; St. Mary School, Dunnington, Indiana; St. Joseph Orphanage, Lafayette, Indiana; and, in 1896, St. Lawrence School, Lafayette, Indiana.

Under the efficient administration of Sister Alphonsa, additional foundations were made as follows: in 1897, Immaculate Conception School, Omaha, Nebraska; in 1898, St. Margaret Hospital, Hammond, Indiana. The year 1899 saw no new foundations. Thus the year 1900 was all the more fruitful: St. Francis Hospital, Evanston, Illinois; St. Anthony Hospital, Louisville, Kentucky; St. Edward Hospital, New Albany, Indiana; St. Boniface School, Monterey, Nebraska; St. Casimir School, Hammond, Indiana. The foundations of 1900 were not all made under the leadership of Sister Alphonsa, but, since she initiated the plans for them, they may be considered her work.

The year 1900 also was a difficult one for the North American Province. The Provincial, Sister Alphonsa, had been ill for some time. Toward the end of March, she became seriously ill from a cardiac condition. Expert help was sought from the best doctors to bring her some alleviation and a cure. But it was only possible to prolong her life somewhat. Thus on May 9, 1900, a telegram reached Olpe concerning which, on the same day, Mother Maria Theresia wrote in a letter:

> This morning I received a cablegram from Lafayette stating that Sister Alphonsa, who had been ill since the middle of Lent, is critical from a heart and kidney disease without any hope of recovery. It is hard, but in all may the will of God be done. (I 171)

In every letter that Mother wrote to the Sisters at that time, she mentioned the serious illness of Sister Alphonsa and asked the Sisters to pray earnestly for her. But the life of the Superior Provincial ebbed away. Sister Alphonsa, serenely and resignedly, died on May 18. She was conscious to the last moment. On May 21, amidst a great throng of people and clergy, she was laid to rest. Bishop Rademacher of Fort Wayne was ill at the time, and consequently the administrator of the diocese, Reverend John H. Guendling, officiated at the Requiem and Reverend Pius Niehaus delivered the sermon.

How intimately this death touched Mother Maria Theresia and how her sentiments went out in empathy to her Sisters in America is revealed in her letter of May 22, 1900:

> Our dear Lord has called our Beloved Sister Alphonsa to himself; she now rests from all the troubles and difficulties that she bore for love of God and love of you, dear Sisters, and has now begun her eternal life. We lament our great loss with deep grief and sorrow. Each one of you knows what the dear one meant to you personally; how by word and example she walked before you to teach you the way to true happiness in religious life. Although our hearts are heavy, let us say with resignation: "Lord, may your holy will be done."
>
> The final hour will also come for each of us, dear Sisters, and blessed are we, if we be found as faithful as our dear departed Sister, as true to what we have promised God, and of one heart with our superiors. Then we may rejoice eternally in God. Although I have the confidence that our dear Sister Alphonsa is already enjoying the beatific vision, let us nevertheless say all the prayers for her as prescribed by our Constitution.

> As her successor in office, I have appointed Sister Josepha; she will certainly endeavor to perform her arduous duties with affability and kindness and try to replace Sister Alphonsa in your lives. From you, my dear Sisters, I expect and await love, respect, and trust in your newly appointed Superior. Bear in mind that the Superiors must give an account before God for you; assist them that they may do so with joy and not with sorrow. Do not make their office more burdensome through disobedience and self-will, dissatisfaction and other failings.
>
> Dear Sisters, I sincerely hope that not one of you will be guilty of such ingratitude. Pray much for your new Superior and, as true Franciscans, endeavor to give her much joy through love of holy poverty, simplicity, and true observance of the Rule. Through the graces of the Holy Spirit, may the bond of love unite us ever more closely together and unify us in God. (II 22)

The North American Province had a new Provincial in the appointment of Sister Josepha Dirkmann. Before she took over this office, she had been Superior at St. Francis Academy, Columbus, Nebraska. She led the province with great ability until her death in 1923. Mother Maria Theresia, in all ways possible, helped the new Provincial in the administration of the province. Seemingly, it was difficult for the Sisters to brave the death of Sister Alphonsa. Also, Mother Maria Theresia was ever mindful of her with great fidelity. Even on August 7, 1902, she wrote: "Often, yes very often, I think of our good deceased Sister Alphonsa." (III 31)

But she realized that it would be detrimental to the new administration if the Sisters did not relate to the new Provincial with the same confidence they had shown to the deceased. Seemingly it appeared especially difficult for Sister Bernarda, the Provincial Assistant, to relate completely to the new Provincial. Not that she withheld her confidence, but her thoughts continued to linger on the deceased Sister Alphonsa. Sister Bernarda was thus reminded by Mother Maria Theresia:

> Do not grieve so excessively that Sister Alphonsa is no longer with you, for she is probably nearer to you now

> through prayer and union than heretofore: most certainly, dear Sister Josepha is good, too. Time will heal all wounds. After you have been with her as long as you were with dear Sister Alphonsa, both of you will be intimately amalgamated in God. Characters, of course, are different, but in time adjustment will come. (II 24)

Thus through prudent leadership, Mother endeavored to help her Sisters adjust to new situations.

In the first year of Sister Josepha's provincialate, the twenty-fifth anniversary of the foundation of the congregation in North America occurred. The new bishop of Fort Wayne, Bishop Herman Joseph Alerding, opened the silver jubilee festivities with a pontifical High Mass. Numerous members of the laity and the clergy, together with the Sisters, were present to thank God. Mother Maria Theresia participated intimately in the celebration as her letter shows:

> All of us, the Sisters and I, participated most intimately and genuinely in the Twenty-fifth Anniversary of the foundation there. It was a feast of thanksgiving for all of us. That the feast was glorified by the presence of His Excellency, the Bishop, was fine. All day my thoughts lovingly reverted to Sister Clara and Sister Alphonsa, who bore many pioneering difficulties. As regards age, both could have been present, but our dear Lord has given them a better place and they are praying for us now. (II 24)

Mother Maria Theresia remembered the founding Sisters, who with courage and love, endured the beginnings, now twenty-five years in the past. As she at that time sent her first Sisters to America, it was in part with the purpose of having a place where all her Sisters could go if they should be banished from their own country. Did God perhaps permit difficulties in the mother country so that attention would be turned to North America? However, it had not become necessary to have chosen North America as a place of refuge for the entire congregation. The Lord granted a period of great progress in the homeland and blessed wonderfully the activities of the Sisters in North America.

"He Leads, I Follow"; with reference to North America, was not that the source that brought about the blessing?

Although the subsequent foundations in the United States of America were brought about through the initiative of the Provincial Superiors, essentially they belong to the work of the Mother Foundress. During the last years of her life, further foundations were made including: in 1901, St. Ann School, Clover Bottom, Missouri; in 1902, St. Anthony Hospital, Michigan City, Indiana; in 1903, St. Anthony Home for the Aged, Lafayette, Indiana; Sacred Heart School, Remington, Indiana; St. John School, St. John, Indiana; in 1904, Our Lady of Guadalupe School, Pena Blanca, New Mexico.

Mother Maria Theresia was grateful to God for this development. Unfortunately, it was not her privilege to see her Sisters in America personally once more. More and more vocations had been realized in North America. Still, Mother took pains to see to it that over and over again young Sisters and candidates from Germany would devote their energies to the North American Province. This can be taken as evidence of her maternal concern and her loyal attachment to the Sisters. Mother's last letter to the Sisters in North America was written on January 3, 1905, just one month before her death. This letter shows how thoroughly she was informed regarding all occurrences, and how, through advice, she wished to help the Superiors and thereby all the Sisters. She saw all in the light of God in a moderate way and made a special point of the danger for a religious to compromise too much with the world. Since this letter is the last witness of her concern for the Sisters, whether in America or in Germany, it is presented here:

> It is time to write a letter to you, my dear Sister. Assuredly you have enjoyed the beautiful festive days and have commenced the New Year with God. Dear Sister Josepha will certainly take a little winter rest, then you can discuss your experiences and other matters with her at leisure. I have no doubt that Sister Kunigunde was always loyal and well intentioned. When a Sister fulfills her duties conscientiously as she sees them, and observes the Rule and

> prays well, God will be with her, even if some of the Sisters would like to have things otherwise according to their own wills. Sister Kunigunde is probably very economical and that is what some do not like.
>
> Sister Jacobine wrote that she suffers from hernia and is weak; she must go back to Denver to undergo surgery. They will have room for her. Since she herself is sickly and weak, she will the more readily have sympathy with the sick and infirm Sisters.
>
> Relative to Cleveland, I have written to dear Sister Josepha expressing my views. It is necessary that Sister Leonarda have two faithful and energetic Sisters at her side. She is shouldering a heavy burden because of the building program, and especially since, during her long absence, many irregularities and liberties crept in. Force and strictness cannot help much in such a situation. Love, kindness, and great patience are required. Sister Leonarda means well, but she must have good and loyal help. Sisters who do not wish to be of service, may not go there for the time being. If at all possible, it would be well for Sister Josepha to go there and remain for three or four weeks. We will trust and pray that dear Sister Leonarda will not be too greatly discouraged. May our dear Lord change all for the best. (II 44)

This letter shows very clearly Mother's ability to guide. Without complaining, she draws on her experience with human nature in directing her Sisters. She will not govern her congregation by force nor rigidity. She knows that love, kindness, and much patience are appropriate to lead souls and to lead them to see the right.

In this manner, the Sisters had their contacts with the Mother; this was true above all in regard to the German Sisters who were constantly near her. Many Sisters acknowledged later that they envied the Sisters who lived in Olpe and were always near Mother. Even the postulants and novices experienced her kindness, for she was an example to all. Apparently, many young girls entered in Olpe because Mother Maria Theresia was still there. One Franciscan priest gave Sister Fortunata the following advice: "Go to Olpe. There the foundress is still living, whom I greatly revere, and a good spirit still reigns there."

CANDIDATES

The mothers of the Sisters also perceived that their daughters were in good hands with Mother Maria Theresia. One mother who brought her daughter to the convent observed the foundress with keen eyes, wondering within herself whether her daughter would have it good in the convent. Sister Gerhardis, reminiscing relative to her investiture, remarked that her mother had spoken with Mother Maria Theresia and upon leaving said: "Now I can go in peace. With such a holy woman, I can calmly leave you."

The servant of God had never been novice mistress. From the very beginning, this office had been entrusted to other Sisters in the Community. But the examination of the candidates for reception and profession was the concern of the Mother herself. In her first meeting with the candidates for religious life, Mother often portrayed a surprisingly deep penetration of soul relative to those asking for admission. One of the Sisters reported concerning this:

> She had a deep understanding of the individual Sister and her difficulties and saw through the Sister to the inmost depths of the soul. Thus she readily recognized the genuineness of the vocation. I myself had great inner struggles in the early years of my religious life and despaired of my vocation. I shared my difficulties with Mother. She thought, however, that my calling was genuine and I could remain in the convent with a peaceful conscience. As I was not convinced, she permitted me to return to the world. She said, "But you will come back." Mother was right, for I returned within the same year. Consequently, I had the impression that she saw through the happenings in my life to the very depths and could foretell events that were fulfilled exactly.

Another Sister, who as a candidate had harbored the thought of entering the religious life for three years but could not bring herself to take the decisive step, was visiting a relative at the motherhouse in Olpe where she met Mother Maria Theresia. Without ever having spoken of this, the foundress asked her directly how long she had harbored the idea of entering the convent. "Three years," she answered. Thereupon, the servant of God told her to make the feast of the Immaculate Conception the day of her definite decision. In fact, this feast was her entrance date. This must have occurred in 1885, for in giving this account in 1917, the Sister concerned had been in the convent thirty-two years.

Naturally, such first meetings could also result in opposite decisions. A young woman, who had already begun her studies in medicine, believed herself to have a religious vocation to spend her life in service to the poor and sick. Incidentally she met Mother Maria Theresia at Venusberg near Bonn. This first meeting made such an impression on her that she asked for an appointment with Mother and applied immediately for admission. Calmly but firmly the Mother answered her, "My dear child, you have no calling to the religious life." The refused candidate was disappointed and complained to a Sister in the hospital about the matter. Later, after living some time at home, she recognized how quickly the Mother had judged and how correct her judgment had been.

Religious have often been told that during the periods when large groups of candidates regularly applied for admission, decisions relative to admission were often made too quickly and many good candidates were turned away. From this fact, the conclusion may be drawn that the genuine decision of a religious vocation does not depend solely upon the will and character of the applicant but also upon her acceptance. This is an essential point! Mother Maria Theresia cannot be accused of considering admissions superficially, as can be seen in an incident that happened in 1900. There was no lack of vocations at that time, for in that very year sixty-one were invested. Mother Maria Theresia states in a letter:

> On Tuesday morning Miss Gabriele, with her aunt, came to see me at Venusberg. She was very disappointed because

> of your letter; however, she could not give up the hope of coming to us. She told me all. I could not understand her urgent pleading and told her that if besides a bun, she could eat several slices of buttered bread for breakfast, and in fact eat well at all times, then she should write to me. Slowly, she should also try to arise earlier in the morning; then she should consult a good Catholic doctor and inform him also of her earlier condition. Have him write a testimony of her condition healthwise and his opinion as to whether she is strong enough for religious life and forward it to me. Now let us recommend all to God. Since Miss Gabriele does not wish to marry, it would be well to have her become a Tertiary of St. Francis and practice good works in the world. There are so many societies in Bonn, in which renowned women who cannot enter religious life, share their activities. (III 29)

It is not known how this affair ended, but we can sense that when Mother was confronted with such a serious question as a vocation in life, she felt obligated before God to help the individual concerned to follow the way really best for her. Concerning admissions into her own congregation, she gave evidence of having a very definite procedure, as her letters show. The requirements of the Church for admission to a religious order, she took very seriously. Thus she wrote at one time to Sister Deogratias, who manifestly interceded for the admission of an elderly person:

> You have written regarding Miss R., but we may not make an exception. Forty-four years is too old; she is very contented in Merten and, as a Tertiary, she can sanctify herself. If I should, although the Sisters are not in favor, consult our Reverend Superior, he would oppose the move. (I 151)

How conscientious she was in not admitting a postulant because of illness, is evidenced in a letter to a superior:

> My purpose in writing to you is in regard to Miss Agnes. We cannot admit her to investiture for health reasons. On the occasion when a doctor removed a nail from her toe, he gave her a physical checkup and discovered that she

> had cardiac trouble. He informed me. I have since spoken with her and told her that she could not be invested at present. This summer we shall send her to Wildungen and, if she recovers, she can be invested at a later date. Do not become alarmed over this, dear Sister; we may not invest sick postulants. If she recovers, we may invest her in the fall. It surely is a sad situation for the dear child, for she may not return to her parental home. We shall do all for her that we possibly can; she could be employed in one of our houses. (III 80)

These lines show that Mother Maria Theresia was not superficial in her decisions regarding the admission of postulants to investiture. Besides her concern for the individual postulants, it must be observed that, in the same year, fifty-two were invested in Olpe and thirty-four of them went to America. Mother's attention to the individual postulant was not the result of their small number, but was the outflow of the kindness of her maternal heart.

In the matter of admissions, she was always clear and decisive, especially in regard to those candidates who portrayed character faults. "If Miss Agatha is not happy and satisfied, let her go," she wrote to a superior (I 52). When an application was accepted and the day of entrance set, she expected punctuality and a sign of willing obedience:

> How is Sister A's sister? She should have entered on February 2, but did not come, nor did she write if she may come later. Such arbitrary action is not permitted. (I 164)

Many Sisters later commented that Mother Maria Theresia surprisingly asked them in their interviews as applicants to sing a song. It may be that in this manner some information of character might be revealed. But this way of gaining information was not characteristic of Mother Maria Theresia. The "singing test" was not original with her. Contemplatives formerly tested their applicants to ascertain if they had a suitable voice for choir. It can scarcely be imagined that Mother would refuse a candidate for lack of a singing voice, although she treasured good singing.

On the other hand, an applicant might reveal much in song. Surprised but self-assured, she can lead forth in a good voice, or in a simple and unpretentious way, or with humble courage no matter how unmusical.

POSTULANTS AND NOVICES

"Good, loyal, and conscientious Sisters are very necessary in a congregation and of greater value than foundations" (I 39). That was her guiding principle for the acceptance and formation of Sisters. Normally, the novices and postulants would not seek out the much-engaged Superior General. Understanding mistresses gladly arranged for meetings with the venerable Mother. The latter utilized opportunities to show her loving concern for the young Sisters. She did not adhere to the point of view that the postulants had their own mistress who must regulate all. When Mother met a postulant, she always had a kind and encouraging word for her. Upon meeting the Sisters, she loved to quote the phrase "climb upward" in the Low German of the Sauerland in order to stimulate their zeal. Upon meeting a postulant who was alone, she showed her personal interest and inquired of her whether she were adjusting well and if she felt attracted to the religious life. What Sister Hildegardis Schelle reported is really surprising:

> Not seldom it happened that Mother had a novice come to her to ask for prayers, or in free conversation ask her opinion in a certain instance, or what she would do in a grave or given situation.

Perhaps this is also the basic reason for the attachment of the Sisters to her. Mother took them seriously! Hence, the young Sisters approached her with great confidence. They found the love of a mother in her. Maternal love often sees deeper than discreet reasoning.

Since approach to Mother was so easy, the postulants and novices could bring their personal cares and questions to her without hesitation. Thus, Sister Nuntia, before her investiture, approached the Mother to ask whether as a religious she would be in a position to nurse her foster parents should they become ill. The answer was, "That you should do; you should take good care of your foster parents. But let us first pray that our dear Lord will preserve them long in good health." Sister Nuntia added that she had not expected such an answer and was greatly gratified.

Although Mother Maria Theresia demanded of her Sisters the basic principles of religious life and renunciation of family ties, she nevertheless urged them to hold the obligations of children to their parents as sacred, even to foster parents. In her opinion the Fourth Commandment was not obliterated by entrance into religious life. She cherished highly the gratitude of children to their parents as is manifested in many of her letters. Thus, without further reflection, she sent her Sisters to the bedside of seriously ill parents. She did this at a time when, in most congregations, it was not a practice. Perhaps rooted in this policy is the comment of the Sisters: "She was Mother to us."

Also relative to the younger Sisters, the servant of God never flaunted her rank. Otherwise, the experience as related by one postulant could never have been possible. One day at work scrubbing the floor, the postulant's oversleeve slipped down. Mother Maria Theresia incidentally passed by. As a matter of course, the postulant asked the Mother to readjust her sleeve. Mother in the same matter of course way adjusted the sleeve, without showing the least surprise at the request. It was clear to both: she simply was Mother.

However, the young Sisters were cognizant of the respect owing Mother and the honor due her. They tried to find ways and means of rendering her every service possible. But this was not easy. Sister Victoria relates a significant incident in her early convent years apropos to this situation: "Mother Maria Theresia did not readily permit a personal service. The then used kerosene lamps were all assembled in one definite place for cleaning and refilling. As the Mother wished to take a lamp from there, I made an attempt to carry it for her. Mother cordially refused with the words, 'I thank you. A sheep that does not carry its own wool is not a genuine sheep.'"

On the other hand, the Mother sometimes asked a direct service from the Sisters. One day during conversation, she asked a Sister at random if she had ever knitted a pair of hose in her life. The Sister answered in the negative and added that she doubted whether she could ever even finish one hose. On the following day, the novice mistress gave the Sister the surprising task of knitting a pair of hose for Mother Maria Theresia for Christmas. She considered it a joke and did nothing about it. Somewhat later she was questioned how she had progressed with the knitting, and then realized that it was not a joke. The Sister gave herself to the task with all earnestness and was able to deliver the pair of hose in due time. The Mother expressed her joy to the Sister that she could really knit. But thereupon followed an exhortation of how meritorious before God is simple obedience and how important it is for a religious to master as many kinds of work as possible.

A Sister recalled how she as Superior General committed an injustice to a novice. One day the novice was accused of a serious fault and was consequently called before Mother. As she constantly maintained her innocence, she was sent to the chapel with the directive to reflect over the matter before the Lord. On the same day, she had to return to Mother who met her at the entrance and said, "I have done you an injustice. I have just learned this fact from the Sister concerned and I now know that you are innocent."

In a glance, the Mother saw each one precisely and readily recognized any change. A postulant remarked concerning the Mother's reaction: "Are you ill? For some days I have noticed that you do not look well." The postulant had wished to mortify herself, or, not to appear oversensitive, had eaten some food that had not agreed with her. Mother told her never to do that again and gave her some practical advice on how to act sensibly without injuring her health and still be mortified.

These details should not lead to the conclusion that Mother Maria Theresia permitted everything to pass, excused all, and that only kind words were spoken to the younger Sisters. Naturally, the younger Sisters often experienced that the older members of the congregation found fault with them when they were too boisterous and hilarious during recreation. Yet Mother had a real understanding of the younger Sisters in this regard, and she endeavored, in her calm way, to teach them proper religious behavior. Stairways have always been a temptation for young people and the cloister is no exception. In this connection, when Mother noticed a Sister had taken the steps by storm, she ordered, "So now, go up those stairs and come down again." A postulant at one time marched along a corridor holding a mop high with the tuft up like a standard. Mother met her, sent her back and said, "Go back again past the picture of the Mother of God."

With all her understanding of the temperament of youth, she directed the young Sisters to work at improving themselves and overcoming their imperfections. In a few words she could persistently show them the correct way to follow. One postulant, for whom rising in the morning, as for many young people, was very difficult experienced Mother's remedy. The said postulant usually came late for prayer. Whoever came late, knelt near the superior, and excused herself. Mother Maria Theresia had noticed the late comer several mornings. One morning the Mother let the tardy sleeper kneel a long time before giving her the signal to take her place with the other postulants. That method of cure worked.

At one time, a novice who was guilty of a fault committed against the Mother herself, caused either by over anxiety or over haste, received a very singular penance. Overcome by sorrow, the novice could not control her tears during Mass. She afterward went to the novice mistress, Sister Paula, and admitted her guilt and expressed her sorrow. Sister Paula related the incident to the Mother who had the novice come to her. She did not reproach her in any way, but set a piece of cake before the novice and had her eat it then and there. The sorrow that she had endured had been sufficient penance.

Thus the wisdom of her method of formation was not a standardized rigid plan into which all was compressed. She considered each Sister individually and directed as was best for each person. She had never studied pedagogy, nor had taken a course in psychology. Nevertheless, she came upon the right procedures. She was a mother, and a good mother knows without study what is best for her children.

SHE KNEW EACH OF HER SISTERS

Mother Maria Theresia ruled especially well when she knew one of her Sisters needed help. There was a very young postulant in the motherhouse, an orphan, who entered at the age of seventeen. Christmas came and on Christmas Eve all the Sisters received their packages from home. The young postulant had none. The loss of her parents and the joy of all the other Sisters at Christmas as they enjoyed their gifts was especially hard for her to bear. She went to the chapel to pray there alone. But she did not remain long, for she was called by the Mother. "The Christ Child is also giving you a special joy," the Mother said to her as she entered the room. Then she gave her a beautiful Christmas picture on which were written personal wishes in the Mother's own handwriting. The postulant was asked to be seated, a sign that the venerable Mother would spend some time with her. Then she was asked whether she had a desire for something special. The postulant was still confused and squirming in surprise. After some reassurance, answered that she would like to have a book that would give her helpful instructions for her professional training. Mother then inquired about her deceased parents and her relatives, for she did not want the postulant to miss her parents too much especially at Christmas time. Shortly after, she received the book that she requested. As long as she was in the motherhouse, each Christmas she relived her first Christmas there and the special maternal love of the Superior General.

Although the number of members grew steadily, Mother Maria Theresia knew each Sister by name and kept it faithfully in mind. Sisters often wondered how she was able to greet each by name, although she had not met some for many years. One Sister once asked the Mother about this amazing fact. The answer revealed much: "Why should I not remember? she replied. "Are not all of you entrusted to me by God? Not only in my memory, but also in my heart each of you has a claim to a place."

Her intimate union with her spiritual daughters was manifested in an incident that Sister Hildegardis faithfully reported. One morning Mother Maria Theresia told Sister Paula that she had had a remarkable visit during the night. A certain Sister from

America — unfortunately, the name of the Sister was withheld — knelt at her bedside and begged her in a childlike and imploring manner: "Dear Mother, bless me once more and pray for me." Thereupon, she awoke and knew definitely that she had raised herself in bed and blessed the Sister. "The Sister's petition may not be in vain," Mother said to Sister Paula. All the Sisters in the motherhouse were asked to pray for a special intention. The intention was not made known to them immediately. After a few weeks, notice came from America that the Sister had died; it was on the same night and at the same hour that she in a dream-vision took leave of the Mother.

As this incident became known to the members of the congregation through the communication of Sister Hildegardis, an elderly Sister said that she knew of a similar incident. Sister Hildegardis then wrote this second incident in the margin of the report. On a certain day, the notice of the death of a Sister in America arrived. All during the day, Mother Maria Theresia's time was much occupied. Therefore, she did not have the Office of the Dead prayed for the deceased Sister immediately as was her practice. During the following night, it seemed to her that the deceased knelt at her bedside begging. "Dear Mother, why have you not prayed for me? I, too, called you Mother." This was relative to a Sister with whom the Mother had visited during her last trip to America. At that time, the Sister was already ill. However, these two incidents may be interpreted, one thing is certain, they demonstrate, in an impressive manner, the maternal love that the foundress had for her Sisters.

In almost all the letters that Mother Maria Theresia wrote to the superiors is found the solicitous inquiry, "How are the Sisters?" Not only on the individual Sisters, but also on the superiors, she wished to bestow her love. Thus on one occasion she wrote:

> Do not become discouraged if the Sisters at times deviate somewhat from the beaten path; pray much and remain faithful to duty and approach each with great love and confidence. Love evokes mutual love and likewise confidence. The Sisters must be convinced that you bear and

> share their burdens and joys. Also, endeavor to study the character of each individual Sister and adjust to it, as St. Paul said that he tried to become all to all to win all for Christ. (III 81)

She often advised superiors: "When you must reprimand, never dismiss a Sister without having spoken some kind words to her."

The Sisters were always her first concern. Therefore she endeavored to control every possible situation in the various houses that could be a detriment to the Sisters. At one time she stated:

> It sometimes happens that good people contribute toward your activities or to the house, whereby they certainly had the honor of God and the welfare of the neighbor in mind. In return, they wish to be highly respected and to be consulted in all matters, and the Sisters in consequence must then play a subordinate role. Such a condition may not develop; the Sisters must always hold first place. The laity, no matter how good, may not interfere in the Sisters' affairs.

Whether the foregoing is the result of a particular problem is not known. Nevertheless, the advice bears the impress of mature judgment and experience.

CONCERN FOR THE HEALTH OF THE SISTERS

As a true mother, she was concerned about her Sisters in every respect. "Are you still in good health?" (III 72). This or a similar question peals forth in many of Mother's letters. She could urge vigorously when she believed that a Sister had not taken sufficient care of her health and had driven her energies to exhaustion:

> From your loving letter, I see that you were sick again. I am very sorry. You probably did not take enough care.... Now I beg you ... do take better care of yourself. It is your sacred duty! A person has constant anxiety and uneasiness concerning you. (I 67)

At another time the Mother wrote:

> You must gain in strength, dear Sister! Conditions are different now from the days of your youth. Then lost energies were quickly regained. Eat meat and eggs, drink milk and wine, or you will soon be sick again. (I 75)

Mother Maria Theresia repeatedly urged her Sisters to eat well to preserve their strength. Did she probably suspect that now and then a Sister fasted to maintain a slim figure? It appears so, for in one of her letters is found this amusing passage:

> Have a good pair of glasses. They are necessary for your weak eyes. And also you must eat well! The thought has come to me that you fear becoming stout and, perhaps through fasting, have incurred your illness. That would not be right. But you must forgive me that such thoughts have come to me. (I 72)

Then follows the significant sentence: "Being stout and also healthy is good for humility" (I 72). Just such expressions as these give witness to her resolute and humorous ways of giving advice.

She observed closely that her Sisters committed no indiscretion in respect to health. To one who needed tactful treatment, she wrote briefly that she must eat five times a day. In the motherhouse during meals, Mother sometimes arose from her place and went along the entire length of the table. Some Sisters received a calm admonition to take more food. Oftener she went to the kitchen to encourage the Sisters working there with heartening words. The statement, "Just think, you are cooking for the brides of Christ each day," was often repeated to them. To a young Sister about to take charge of a kitchen she said:

> Take good care of all things! The Community table must be good. The food must be tastily and nourishingly prepared so that the sick can eat and the weak regain their strength and the working Sisters be able to fulfill their duties without wearing themselves out before time.

In a letter of January 11, 1890, the following passage is found:

> We again drink corn coffee here, and all relish the taste of it; coffee beans are considered harmful for they impoverish the blood in humans. (I 108)

In other respects, also, Mother Maria Theresia was concerned regarding the health of her Sisters. Thus she wrote to one superior: "You have certainly had yourselves dispensed from fasting. I do not think that a single one of you should fast" (II 36). To a house where the Sisters were heavily burdened, she wrote:

> Since you are engaged constantly in strenuous work in the school as well as in the hospital, you are not obliged to fast. But we shall try to use the short time profitably to prepare ourselves for the glorious feast of Easter by practicing interior mortification zealously. (IV 91)

Mother was often greatly alarmed because of the arduous work of her Sisters. Concerning this she wrote:

> Often I do not know how the work can be done here. The laundry of the week is always of so great an amount that the good Sisters often need to wash on Thursday also. (I 101)

When it became evident that one of the Sisters had suffered ill health, Mother Maria Theresia admonished the superiors in her letters to be very careful lest the same happen to some other Sisters:

> Impress it on the Sisters to be very prudent in lifting and carrying. Our Sister Antonia was in great danger and still is because of a physical injury incurred during her postulancy and, at that time, she did not realize what it was. (I 48)

Relative to the Sisters, the Mother thought of everything. One winter she wrote to the Sisters in Winterberg as follows:

> Trustingly you are all in good health! Today the ground here is covered with snow and in the higher altitude of Winterberg it surely must be white and cold. Protect yourselves as much as possible to prevent taking colds. (II 21)

As a native of the Sauerland, she realized the hardships of the cold winters. Thus at this time of the year, she thought with concern of the American Sisters who had just occupied a new house. She wrote to them as follows:

> Here the severe winter has already set in some time ago, and there most likely is much worse to come. Protect yourselves with warm clothing, lest the Sisters be the first sick ones in the new house. In a new building, at all events, it is most likely to be cold. (I 9)

Mother Maria Theresia always grieved when a Sister, for whatever reason, had to live apart from the congregation for an extended period of time. On one such occasion a Sister was called to a home nursing case the day before the feast of St. Theresa, and Mother realized that she would be gone for several days. As the Sister before departing came to say good-bye, Mother gave her a small package with instructions not to open it until the next day. It was customary for the celebration of the feast of St. Theresa for many benefactors of the Sisters to send pastry to the motherhouse. Mother Maria Theresia had cut sample pieces from various cakes and had packed them in a box and handed it to the Sister so that she might at least have something from the festive celebration. At another time, a Sister, because of illness, was obliged to remain at a health resort for some time. She received this sympathetic note from Mother:

> I hope that you are feeling somewhat better now. When first starting treatments, when one leaves the usual activities behind, one feels very weak, but improvement comes later. Have courage and confidence in God and follow faithfully the orders of the doctor. You are with such good Sisters, who willingly give a helping hand. Although the Eucharistic presence is not in the house, you can say your prayers well. The church certainly is not far distant.

> Dear Sister, I remember you lovingly and pray much for you. I know from experience how a person feels in such a place. But you are there in obedience, and God will be your strength and support if you should feel forsaken and lonely. Time passes quickly; soon you will be improved and healthy and will return to your sphere of activity to work for God. (III 73)

ILLNESS, DEATH, AND NEED OF RELATIVES

Mother Maria Theresia was in complete sympathy with the Sisters when death or severe illness occurred in their immediate families or among their relatives. There are many letters extant which she, in her maternal goodness, wrote to them. Thus on October 18, 1879, she sent the following message:

> With sincere sorrow, I have received the sad news of the premature death of your good father. Dear Sister Liboria, our dear Lord has done it and it certainly must be for the best. We shall in silence adore the will of God at all times. In all probability, this was the best hour for your dear father to appear before our dear Lord. What a consolation for you that he had the happiness to receive the Sacrament of the Anointing of the Sick and had time to arrange his business matters. With you, my dear Sister, we shall pray for his eternal rest. It will please me if you say the same prayers for him that we pray for our deceased Sisters. (III 90)

Mother also suffered with her Sisters when the family became involved in depressing hardships. In such instances, she, with wise considerations as to persons and situations, knew how to make exceptions to established rules. Definite hours were set for visits to the Mother. But one evening after night prayers, a young Sister came to the Mother. She only said, "Let me go home." Without further information, this request could not be granted. Gradually, Mother drew out from the Sister the cause of her sorrow. The Sister was the eldest of eight children, and she had, since the early death of the mother, taken care of them. She had postponed her entrance into the convent for many years until her second sister was old enough to take over the management of the house. Now she learned that the father was contemplating a second marriage and that with a woman of ill repute. The Sister believed that, if she could speak with her father personally, she could influence him to give up the planned marriage which could not but have ill effects on the entire family.

Although many have been mistaken in regard to the power of their influence in similar cases, Mother Maria Theresia must have had confidence that this young Sister would be successful in this bold venture. She said to her, "If you, my dear Sister, think that you can do something to remedy this situation, you may go to your father." The next morning the Sister left on the first train, and, after three days, she returned happy to announce successful results. Naturally, the Mother would not permit her Sisters to go home for trivial reasons, but in cases of emergency, she was able to judge what was really urgent and necessary.

THOSE OPPRESSED BY NEED AND UNCERTAINTY

Perhaps no letter written speaks more forcibly of her goodness than that written to a Sister oppressed by need:

> For a long time an inner voice has urged me to write to you and this morning your signal of need reached me. How I would love to have you, my dear child, with me to give you words of encouragement. Since this cannot be, I pray for you all the more that the loving Mother of God grant you great confidence in God, that you remain zealous in the good you have begun and persevere to the end.

Unfortunately, this letter has not come to posterity in the original, but Sister Hildegardis Schelle recorded it in the Chronicles. Was this letter possibly addressed to her personally and then later destroyed with her correspondence?

To many a Sister in spiritual need, the clear and surmising glance of Mother was a source of allaying her fears. A Sister related a remarkable incident:

> It happened once that I was spiritually disturbed at the beginning of retreat. I wished to make a general confession. As I appeared before the foundress, she suddenly said to me, "Do not be disturbed; your past is entirely in good order." I was amazed, for I had told her nothing of my concern.

Mother Maria Theresia's letters also give an insight into her way of alleviating burdened minds. In 1887 she wrote:

> In your last letter you wrote that you were so disheartened. You must not be so, nor need you be. Who does not have her faults? Thank God, dear Sister, if your faults are perceived, for then they can be corrected. What you have written concerning the Reverend Pastor, that he encourages and reassures you, is good. Whether making a general confession of your life to him be good for you, I do not know. Daily living brings abundant opportunities for practicing humility, for in spite of the great and constant graces, one sees herself so full of sins and faults of the past and present which cause a stinging sorrow in the heart. Besides you have already confessed all. Shall I give you some good advice? With great devotion, pray the following petitions of the Our Father: Your will be done, and forgive us our trespasses as we forgive those who trespass against us! Perhaps you smile when you read this, but, dear Sister, you know that I mean it well with you and share my own experience with you ... Also, I do not wish to prevent your making a general confession to the pastor. (I 50)

Later Mother wrote to the same Sister:

> If you have made the annual confession, strain yourself no further. Our dear Lord looks into the heart and blesses our good will. (I 88)

Mother Maria Theresia repeatedly declared that if a Sister, before final vows, has not lived herself completely into religious life, or if she is the cause of difficulties, she should be dismissed. Otherwise others are burdened with a cross. But naturally, even precautions at the time of investiture and during the probation period, cannot prevent some instances in which Sisters later manifest character traits that cause grief to superiors and others. These Sisters, also, the Mother did not exclude from her concern. Here she did all that was possible to find a way of leading the Sister in the right direction. She wrote to a superior thusly:

> My personal thinking regarding Sister N.N. is, do not take any further notice of her. She must keep the holy Rule as far as possible. She does not have the energy for unusual exertion, but she should endeavor to give a good example. Whether she is sick or not, I do not know. I am fearful of committing an injustice. Try to see what is best to be done. One accomplishes most through love, patience, and kindness. (I 12)

In the letters of Mother Maria Theresia are often found directives for superiors, advising them how to deal with difficult characters. Although the bad behavior of her Sisters caused her pain, she condemned only the fault and not the failing one. She sought to win her into right ways, sometimes through sternness, but more frequently through patience and kindness.

On February 7, 1903, a letter was written by Mother Maria Theresia which manifests clearly with what kindness, but also with what earnestness, she could reprimand an erring Sister:

> My heart is very sorrowful at the thought that a soul, our dear Lord has called to be his bride and overwhelmed with so many graces, wishes to shake off his sweet yoke and prefer the pleasures of the world. Dear Sister, do not trust the cunning allurements of the wicked enemy. He uses our weaknesses. Certainly you must have neglected your prayers and spiritual exercises, and thereby weakened your powers for combat. These have become paralyzed. Get a hold on yourself and start to pray; then you will receive new courage. I have prayed very much for you and shall continue to do so. This you have not done heretofore. Start earnestly to serve the Lord in faithful love; then you may confidently expect graces. However,

> if you neglect our dear Lord, then you are not in a position to fulfill other duties. How near all of us are to the last hour, and what a passing it is for a soul that was unfaithful.

Unfortunately, this letter is not extant in the original but was taken from a copy.

In a special way, the Mother expected exemplary conduct from her superiors. But also with them, at times she had to solve problems which sometimes required the removal of a Sister. With great humility, one superior stated the following:

> The dear Mother certainly omitted no reprimand when it was necessary. When I was superior at one time I was asked to give up a certain Sister. I was in the motherhouse at that time on a visit and requested Mother to permit that Sister to remain and to transfer Sister N. giving my reasons for the request. At first, Mother was not in favor but later on acquiesced. As I bade her farewell, I asked for forgiveness and said that I would accommodate myself to her wishes, for I felt that I had not acted in the right manner. "Sister," she said to me, "you have hurt me very much, for you considered yourself and not the congregation." Then I recognized that a religious must forget self to become all to all. In similar situations, I often recalled the reprimand given me by the saintly Mother.

After a Sister left the congregation, or was dismissed, Mother still kept her in her love. "From the former Sister K., one hears many things. Let us pray for her that the Lord preserve her from all harm" (III 46). That was her reaction in such instances.

Love must adjust itself to the situation of the one to whom love is to be shown. Above all love must be guided by the virtue of wisdom that justice may prevail. Mother Maria Theresia at one time humorously remarked that our dear Lord himself had thrown the Sisters together. Each has her own manner, her own problems and experiences. For a mother it is not difficult, in true love, to direct her daughters on the right way. Her Sisters were accustomed to having their Mother direct lives in wisdom, not overburdening them with severities, always exhorting them to freely self-chosen mortifications. In such situations, the venerable Mother had to be vigilant lest some of the Sisters, through unwise penances, injure themselves in body or mind, for they were very zealous in performing penances. Thus she wrote to a superior concerning a Sister who had asked for permission to perform austere penances:

> I may not grant Sister E. permission for her requests. It is far better to offer up the small daily sufferings that come upon us with resignation and gain merit in that way. Through them we make satisfaction for many things and advance. I do not wish to quench her zeal entirely; therefore, if once a week she wishes to sleep on a board, she has my permission. (I 153)

DIFFICULT OFFICES AND DUTIES

Mother Maria Theresia realized how honestly the daily vicissitudes could be penance and mortification. She wanted her Sisters to become completely aware of this fact. Resignation to the will of God was much more essential to her than penances freely chosen. Thus she formed her Sisters lovingly in correct attitudes when they were transferred or appointed to burdensome offices. At such time, many feel incapable, believing themselves incompetent and unable to accomplish the task. In one such situation, the Mother made the sign of the cross on the forehead of the Sister and said to her, "Now go with God, dear Sister. If it becomes difficult, talk with full confidence to God: 'You sent me here; help me to do my assigned work.'" This Sister later declared, "This advice that the saintly Mother gave me as novice, I have taken into life with me. Often I have called it to mind and it has helped me in many trying circumstances." Does not this prayer of the servant of God, "You sent me here; help me to do my assigned work," reveal her own prayer? She may have said it when the congregation was young and also later when she was repeatedly reelected.

But the venerable Mother did not send her Sisters in simple obedience to a responsible position without first giving them a suitable preparation. This was especially true in regard to Sisters who had to qualify for teaching in schools. In the very beginning, the Olpe Sisters were sent to institutions of higher learning to prepare themselves for teaching. Incidentally, we read in a letter of the year 1904: "On Wednesday, three Sisters again left to pursue their studies at an institution of higher education in Münster. May our dear Lord protect them and lead them to the desired goal." Then in a genuinely maternal way, she added, "It pains me for all the poor Sisters must learn and read; may the Lord preserve them" (I 203). It is remarkable to note how early she saw to it that physical education (gymnastics) should be provided for the school teachers as well as instructors for the same. This training took place during the postulancy. There is a passage in a letter concerning this training and expressed in kindly humor; "We have two postulants in Poppelsdorf to take the physical education examinations. Postulant Helene is to return to Olpe tomorrow because her cardiac condition cannot take the jumps. The other postulant has lost courage. Thus we are in need again" (I 191).

After the *Kulturkampf*, the congregation could again resume its teaching apostolate in the schools. The teachers were severely overburdened at first. Teachers were few in number, for the *Kulturkampf* had forbidden further development. Mother Maria Theresia realized that the teachers were being overtaxed. She instructed all who had studied until eleven o'clock on any previous evening to report to her in the morning. When they came to her, she had them take a tonic right there in her presence. A Sister once said, "Dear Mother, I really do not need it, for I am very healthy." Then Mother answered, "I am deeply concerned that I have thus far been unable to make up for your loss of sleep."

Mother was deeply troubled regarding the health of the Sisters in the teaching profession. Therefore, she would tactfully advise the Sister students to preserve proper values in life. Thus to a Sister, about to commence study, she said:

> Child, study is not the chief essential! First, you must be a good religious, not to become a teacher. You entered to become a good religious, then a teacher. The latter is secondary, that is your activity. Do not lose sight of the essential.

Her motherly concern for her Sisters was not a characteristic of her advancing years only, but it was a trait of maturity that she always possessed. In the Chronicles of the Congregation of the Olpe Franciscans, there is an account that reaches back into the early years. This account, according to the Sisters, was typical of Mother. After her death, this incident was repeated frequently and handed down from word of mouth. As the Sisters in the early years lived in great poverty, a certain Sister was wearing a pair of shoes so torn into shreds that they were actually unwearable. But there was no money to buy a new pair. Mother Maria Theresia seized upon a clever stratagem. She put the torn shoes on her own feet and went to visit her relatives. The consternation of her wealthy family can readily be imagined when the members saw her, a relative and a superior, go about in such fashion. The Mother soon had a new pair of shoes for her Sister.

What she, in so many words and in so many deeds, did for her Sisters, is merely the living evidence of what she wrote in 1865 regarding sisterly love as embodied in the Constitution:

> Love is the soul of the religious life, but it may not have its source in human natural motives but in the holy will of God. The Sisters are to avoid an all too natural attachment to each other as also to all aversion and uncharitableness. Signs of friendship prevalent among people of the world are not permitted among the Sisters. They shall strive to be obliging and helpful to each other; one gladly bearing the burden of the other and thus fulfilling the command of the Lord. If one Sister has offended another, she should as soon as possible beg pardon of the other. It is not against love, but rather a mark of love, to acquaint the superior regarding a serious fault one notices, so that the respective Sister may be admonished. But this must be done with the purest intention. Although all Sisters owe equal love to each other, still the younger and subordinate members should endeavor to show special love and reverence for the elderly and those in authority.

THE SICK

In the same Constitution and in exact detail, Mother remembered another sphere of love — the care of the sick:

> The Sister infirmarian who has charge of the sick is to serve them with all charity and patience realizing that, in the person of the sick, she is serving the Savior himself. She is to keep the infirmary orderly and clean. The sick may not want for anything and are to be supplied with all that can bring them alleviation. The Sister infirmarian is to fulfill all directives of the doctor punctually. As far as the condition of the patient permits, the infirmarian is to assist her in saying her prayers and should provide suitable reading material. The superior is to visit the seriously ill daily and see to it that the infirmarian fulfills her duties faithfully. In a spirit of penance, the sick and infirm Sisters shall preserve patience and unite their sufferings with the bitter pains of the dying Savior. The Sisters may visit the sick, with the permission of the superior, for the purpose of edifying and comforting them. Let them avoid distracting their minds with idle talk. Convalescent and infirm Sisters, whose condition necessitates exemption from conventual routine, are to be vigilant lest they succumb to a desire for comfort and ease, readily acquired in their condition. Let them be satisfied with what the physician prescribes and the loving care that the superior and infirmarian provide. Let them look forward to the day when, exempt from all exceptions, they shall again be able, with renewed vigor, to observe the Rule in its entirety.

In the motherhouse in Olpe, the sick were accustomed to receive an early morning visit from Mother, even before breakfast, when she faced a full day. Concerned lest, in the many activities of the day, she would not have the opportunity to see them later, she would greet them and inquire about their condition. When she had to travel, she would always visit the sick before she left to bid them good-bye.

Of course, all her relations with the sick were reported by others. But her own words confirm the reports in all respects. In her Christmas letter to the various houses in the year 1890, Mother added the following:

> From Olpe I learned that our dear Sister Caroline is so very ill. Gladly would I have gone there, but the Reverend Superior will not permit me to travel. May our dear Lord prolong her life. I long to see her again and to speak to her. But all as it pleases our Lord. (IV 5)

In her last years, as the works of the congregation had multiplied greatly, Mother Maria Theresia's thoughts frequently reverted to her sick Sisters. Thus on July 11, 1904, she wrote:

> Sister Regis has improved somewhat and is now permitted to sit in an armchair near the grotto. I am trusting that her recovery will soon be complete. I have given permission to Sister Seraphia and Sister Cleta, consanguineous Sisters to the ill Sister Regis to come here next week. As to Sister Boniface, her pains have somewhat subsided; God grant that her hand will soon be better. Also, Sister Nathalia will soon be up again and exercise her infected knee. It is hard to have so many Sisters sick, still we must be satisfied. What our dear Lord does is always best for us. (I 207)

This is not the only letter which gives such an exact account of the condition of sick Sisters. Since Mother Maria Theresia was so devoted to them, she considered an account of them essential when writing to the Sisters. If at one time or another, she did not write about them, it seemed to her as though she had forgotten something important. If all of the letters of the Mother were extant, a summary of all the serious illnesses of the Sisters could be traced consistently from her letters. The accounts extend from the surgery of a finger (III 19, 20) to surgery involving life and death (II 38; III 17). And when the Mother learned that a Sister did not inform her regarding her illness, that Sister received a reprimand: "It grieves me that you did not inform me, for you were with me several times" (III 30).

When the Mother learned that a Sister was ill in one of the branch houses, she was not satisfied to learn of the sickness in a general way, but wanted to know particulars. She wrote the following to the superior:

> The illness of good Sister Capistrana disquiets me greatly. I beg you please to write the particulars, as to how she is getting along, the doctor's diagnosis, and what he says about the case. I am sure that the sick one is resigned to the will of God and patient in her suffering. I am also confident that you and the other dear Sisters are giving her devoted care. I am satisfied with all that God ordains, but I must know in detail how she is. Please be so good as to write me all the particulars! Kindly greet dear Sister Capistrana for me and tell her that I am praying for her that her illness may redound to the salvation of soul and body. (III 14)

When she learned that a Sister had recovered from an illness or received alleviation from a certain medicine or treatment, the Mother immediately made inquiries. Others might also be helped. However, she was different from many others who liked to force a "wonder drug" on the sick. Although she suggested methods of treatment, or certain medications, now and then, she always followed the decisions of the doctors and also advised the sick to follow their directives. In all her many illnesses, the Mother always reckoned with the doctor's orders, regarded them as the will of God, and obeyed them.

Medicine at that time was in a state of revolution. New ways were constantly discovered for curing diseases and for making the taking of medicine easier. But it nevertheless happened that remedies were often prescribed that required heroic self-control for medicines taken in oral dosages. A certain Sister had suffered a severe hemorrhage. The doctor ordered her to drink a cup of oxblood with salt added. "Dear Mother, please excuse me from this, for I cannot do it," the poor Sister pleaded. Mother Maria Theresia could have pointed to more self-control or commanded in holy obedience. But it was not the nature of the servant of God to order adherence in severe terms for it would have overwhelmed the afflicted soul. The Mother acted differently. She asked the Sister nurse to bring her a cup of it, too. When she had the cup filled with the peculiar drink, she said to the sick one, "Let us try it together, dear Sister, then it will be easier." This example of self-control was more effective than words and enabled the Sister to swallow the strange medicine.

Sister Hildegardis Schelle recorded this incident in 1917. "The Sister recovered completely and has since added eighteen years to her life as an efficient nurse." It took a great love to help a sick person in this manner!

Mother Maria Theresia often wrote to the superiors of branch convents to send certain tonics to the motherhouse for the sick Sisters. We read the following in a letter to a superior at Haaren near Aachen who could easily supply the renowned Aachen *printen:*

> Dear Sister Agatha, I should like to have you come to the motherhouse as soon as possible, and I beg you to bring some good *printen*. Our dear sick Sisters and also the sick Lina desire them. (III 17)

That was in 1898 when the congregation had forty-seven foundations in Germany alone. But in spite of her many and great cares, the Mother did not forget the little things that seemed so important to her sick Sisters.

"Let us be brides of the Crucified, and, as such, unite ourselves with our dear Lord on the cross," she exhorted her Sisters at one time (IV 99). The Mother was always filled with deep sympathy and great joy when her sisters bore their sufferings in this wise and with patience. She often said, "The sick Sisters here are good and edifying examples" (I 91). "Our good Sister Juliana is wasting away; she is an ideal and a model of patience" (I 53). "Let us all take an example from these good sick Sisters" (I 113).

Is it not more significant for a sick Sister, or person, to be resigned calmly to the will of God, than to recover her health? That the Sisters learn this was the loving intention of the Mother's heart, when she wrote:

> I am very sorry that your headaches continue unabated, and I often pray that you regain health if it is according to God's will and for your good. If it is for the best, the Lord

> will answer this prayer. There is great profit in suffering and through it you can gain much merit. Let us pray in the spirit of Mary. "Behold the handmaid of the Lord" and God will also be near us with his grace. (I 92)

THE DECEASED

"She was Mother to us." All the Sisters could make this statement. But those Sisters experienced it most emphatically whom the Lord called from this life. Mother Maria Theresia took many a trip in order to assist at the bedside of a dying Sister. "It is very hard for me to see the elderly Sisters die before my eyes, and I must journey on" (II 39). And thus she complained: "How grievously has the death of this Sister affected me; I had to take to bed for several days (III 17). She acknowledged at one time that it tugged at her heart when young Sisters were called in death. Even then the will of God was uppermost in her saddened heart, comforting her when a Sister ended her life well on earth. She wrote in August 1903:

> Thus far this year we have lost four young Sisters in death and several more cannot live much longer. This is hard to bear, but may the will of God be done in all things (III 35).

As a true mother, she remembered the deceased Sisters in her prayers and exhorted the Sisters to pray for them also:

> Tomorrow is the twenty-sixth anniversary of the death of our dear Sister Francesca. (I 138)

Thus she wrote on November 15, 1894. The Mother forgot none of her Sisters and her love was loyal and reached beyond the grave. It was significant that her last official act was a negotiation with the town of Olpe to secure a plot in the new cemetery for the burial of the Sisters.

THE ORPHANS

"She was Mother to us." Her Sisters were not the only ones able to say this. She meant the same to the orphans and to the poor. From the very beginning of the congregation, the care of orphans was undertaken as an apostolate. That is why the Olpians called the Franciscans the "orphan Sisters." Upon studying the history of the development of the old motherhouse, it can readily be recognized that, in the expansion programs, the orphanage always had precedence.

The venerable Mother provided for the efficient management of the orphanage. A charge was asked for the care of orphan children, but it was so meager that the institution could not have existed on it alone. This charge was canceled in case of need as is stated even in the oldest statutes. Mother Maria Theresia engineered this on a generous scale. A child should not lose its place in the orphanage because, for some reason or other, payments could not be made. One day a widow came to the administrator of the orphanage and lamented how difficult it was for her to support her six children since the death of her husband. The Sister consulted Mother, asking if she could accept one of the children without charge. The good Mother went a step farther: "Offer to take two of her children to care for them here."

At another time, the same administrator was accosted by Mother: "You appear so troubled; what is the matter?!" The Sister replied: "I am so sorry that they are taking little Karl away. His father is in the hospital and said he could no longer meet the payments. He has just sent an aunt to bring Karl home." Deciding quickly, Mother replied, "Just tell the aunt that we shall take care of Karl here."

One of the former orphans later told that, after his mother died, his father was at a loss as how to care suitably for the five children. At that time, he earned only ninety marks a month, and the charge for a child at the orphanage was fifty pfennigs a day, a very paltry sum, but under the circumstances, a prohibitive amount. As the father discussed his plan of possible payments with the Mother, she said, "Arrangements for payments can always be made later. Just bring the children, even if payments must be postponed for twenty years. Just forget about the interest."

Mother Maria Theresia would have considered it an injustice if material gain had been connected in any way with the administration of the orphanage. The showing of love to the orphans was not only the task of the orphanage Sisters. Mother also loved to be with them and have them crowd about her.

Her nameday was always a day of great festivities for the orphans. They celebrated with songs, speeches, and skits. The Mother made it a point to talk with each child individually. She followed the educational development of the children with great interest and was vigilant in discovering religious vocations among them either to the priesthood or the sisterhood. The fostering of religious vocations was dear to her heart. She was solicitous that the children regularly participated in divine services and said their prayers. Even after they left the institution, she assisted them in need. She saw that they secured good positions, and rejoiced greatly, when they came to see her later. Numberless orphans have witnessed to the fact that she was all love and kindness to them and was a real mother.

THE POOR

Mother Maria Theresia's love extended far beyond the confines of those cared for in the houses of the congregation. This is learned in manifold ways through her correspondence, in her mindfulness of the poor in crop failures, and during unusually cold weather. She wrote: "It certainly must be very cold there. Last night it was bitterly cold here, and seemingly it is getting colder. It is hard on the poor people since unemployment prevails. We feed many here daily" (III 49). This last statement endorses a powerful chapter in the liberality of the Olpe Franciscans. The venerable Mother had given instructions that no poor person nor beggar was to be turned away from the convent door without an alms kindly given. She called these poor her "brothers." Even the children at the orphanage realized this, for they experienced it one evening when they had no warm meal but only bread and butter. "The brothers of Mother Maria Theresia have eaten all the food," the children said.

There were times when the doorkeeper saw with fear and anxiety how the number of poor and beggars increased. Thus, together with the Sisters in the kitchen, she went to the venerable Mother to call her attention to the fact. She explained that wisdom demanded her setting a limit on her all too liberal hospitality at the convent door. But Mother Maria Theresia would not hear of it and said, "Did our holy Father Francis ever turn a poor one from the door? Are we not serving our Lord himself in serving the poor?" The Mother required that generosity at the door should continue undiminished. The doorkeeper obeyed. But she added to her assigned duties the self-imposed task of counting the number fed throughout one month. The number was seven hundred.

In addition, it must be emphasized that the Mother placed a great value on home nursing in the vicinity of the foundations of the congregation. In this phase of nursing the sick, the Sisters went among the really poor and were able to assist many who were too ashamed to ask for alms. Thus personally and through her Sisters, Mother sought whatever ways and means possible to carry her maternal kindness into the world.

CHAPTER XIV

LOYAL DAUGHTER OF SAINT FRANCIS AND HOLY CHURCH

In writing the original Constitution of the congregation, Mother Maria Theresia, in the very first words, set objectives and standards for her Sisters: "After the example of holy Father Francis, the Sisters shall endeavor to combine the contemplative with the active life."

The life of St. Francis served as guideline for Mother. With great persistency, the servant of God followed his way of life. It cost her many an argument and many a bitter hour. Posterity needs but remind itself of all the incidents connected herewith in 1863 and the written copy of the first Constitution. That the spirit of St. Francis be alive in her congregation was always a desire close to her heart. Not only in her letters did she repeatedly allude to St. Francis, but during retreats she urged the Sisters to pray that "all may thoroughly comprehend the spirit of St. Francis and earnestly endeavor to follow him" (III 65). When Mother instructed the young Sisters preparing for investiture and profession, she stressed this desire emphatically in her introductory prayer:

> In the names of Jesus, Mary, and Joseph, we shall begin under the guidance and protection of our holy Father Francis. May he implore his spirit for me that I may say the right things to you and lead all of you to sanctity and perfection. For this very reason we have left the world. Let us form ourselves according to the image presented us on the Mount of the Holy Cross. Our holy Father Francis fully grasped the truth of the Cross. He also wishes to lead us into the love and the wisdom of the Cross and desires to pierce our souls with his spirit. By subduing the world and the flesh through renunciation of self, we shall overcome the three-fold concupiscence of the world and put on our Lord Jesus Christ.

Mother Maria Theresia made many a glorious statement regarding St. Francis and wrote much in praise of the Franciscan way. But that is not the reason for her being called a genuine daughter of St. Francis. In the present generation, there might be many who have entered more deeply into the specifics of St. Francis, who can quote more from his writings than could Mother Maria Theresia. More is known today about the life of St. Francis than was known in her time. But it is questionable whether the essentials regarding St. Francis are better comprehended today than they were in the last century when, as with the servant of God, they were followed uncompromisingly. True Franciscanism does not depend upon the ability to quote the writings and words of the Poor Man of Assisi, or upon having his expressions at one's disposal in every situation, but upon the fact that one is impregnated with his spirit.

Mother did not come upon the Franciscan way through special study. That she, in the beginning, studied the various saints and their characteristics and then chose the Franciscan way, is not true. True it is that she considered St. Francis from various aspects. It is also true that the Franciscan way of religious life was not entirely new to her. She did not, however, have definite concepts and definite decisions in regard to St. Francis that influenced her ideas and decisions in favor of the Franciscan way. Much more to the point is the fact that she found in the saint of Assisi the exact example of the longing of her own heart. Her evaluation of the saint, his way of life, suited her own way of life. In this great saint, whose manner of life was recognized by Holy Church, she saw glorious possibilities to satisfy the yearnings of her life. His life was the holy inspiration of her own. Thus with joy she considered herself his daughter. As she thus began to impregnate her congregation with his life and spirit, her guidelines from there on became clear.

It was not apparent at their inception that the Poor Franciscans of Perpetual Adoration were obligated by ecclesiastical law to accept the regulations of an established congregation. Many foundations did this and followed an order already established and simply began in like manner. Only later was it discovered that, in following established orders, the new one accidentally seized upon a rich traditional treasure of religious life in the church and, consequently, a definite spiritual life. Mother Maria Theresia, on the contrary, through an entirely clear knowledge and endeavor became and remained consistently Franciscan.

There are many instances in her life that portray this. Wishing to designate them, a person would need to present her conformity to Francis in all circumstances of life. This could be done. But would it not seem that apparently she had no individuality, but lived the life of another, even if the other were a saint? Imitating a saint does not mean following his life literally, but rather to be permeated with his spirit. In Mother Maria Theresia, this was revealed with great certitude. Only a few instances are expounded here.

Francis left as a legacy to his followers: To walk in the footsteps of Christ. And in the rule of the order, he designated the main directive: To observe the Gospel of our Lord Jesus Christ. "Follow me" was decisive with Francis. What the Gospel reported of the life of Jesus Christ was a criterion for him personally. To act and to live the way Christ lived and acted was fundamental in his own life. This was very evident in Mother Maria Theresia also. In her circular letters written on the great feasts of our redemption is clearly portrayed how she always refers to Christ as the example that religious are to follow. In her admonitions to the Sisters in a circular letter of 1872, she sets up the life of Christ as the central point from which all thoughts should radiate. As a religious she was often mindful of the espousal with Christ, not in the sense of tranquil serenity but as his true follower. Later in life she conceived the espousal of a faithful follower in even more concrete terms: "Let us be brides of the Crucified and as such unite ourselves with our dear Lord on the cross" (IV 99). Is not the same development perceived in Francis? The expression, "Follow in the footsteps of Christ," he refashioned in his later years to, "Follow in the footsteps of our crucified Lord."

"Poor Franciscan," thus Mother Maria Theresia signed all her letters. She never abbreviated the words but wrote them out in full. In this can be recognized an acknowledgment on her part. How well she understood the poverty of St. Francis can be detected in the Constitution in which is manifested how the entire congregation, and not only the individual Sisters, were to live without property rights. The political regime, however, did not consider poverty without property feasible nor preservable according to the law of the land. By the administrative authorities of the state, the See of Paderborn was considered the possessor of the property that the Sisters needed for their life and apostolate. But it was clear to Mother Maria Theresia that such exterior manifestations of poverty were not the essentials. The essentials depended much more upon an unpretentious inner attitude. What this meant to her is clarified by a letter in which she wrote:

> Let us walk in simplicity and humility in the footsteps of our glorious father, St. Francis. We are the lesser ones! God be praised a thousand times for this! But let us not be satisfied, dear Sisters, by just being called the lesser ones! Let us strive for true humility of heart and let us in truth consider ourselves what we are – nothingness and sin. Let us rejoice also when others despise and disdain us, for that is our due. (II 1)

In this interior unpretentiousness of true poverty in spirit, lies particularly the basis for the essential character of the servant of God. She embodied this spirit of poverty in relinquishing all property rights, when it pertained to her own honor. If she was attacked, there was no counter attack. She left all to Divine Providence. "He leads, I follow," characterized her conduct. This is clearly demonstrated in a situation in which everything went contrary to her plans. She did not immediately resort to God with pleas and expectations that he carry through all that she had planned. Such pretentiousness was not in accord with her nature. Relative to poverty, she could readily resign herself to the will of God manifested to her through people and events of life. This is apparent in her numerous illnesses. Certainly she would have preferred to be well and to perform her task unhindered. But she preferred the will of God to personal preferences. In spite of her physical infirmities, she accomplished great things in her life. What was her attitude toward her work? As the chronicler, Sister Andrea Bussien began to write the chronicles of the congregation and approached the venerable Mother for information of the early years. She could obtain scarcely anything. Mother Maria Theresia did not wish to have the history of the congregation center about her. She did not wish to occupy the center of the stage for her success was solely the work of God. Thus her desire for unaffected poverty of spirit thwarted every attempt that was made to write a complete account of her life. She wished to retire before the Lord, wished to be only his instrument that he could use as long and in whatever manner he wished.

In her all-embracing poverty, she desired and was a loyal daughter of St. Francis, as well as in the perpetual adoration of the Blessed Sacrament, in conformity with the title of the Community. It is probably that this Eucharistic thought did not come directly from St. Francis, but in all probability from her boarding-school days with the Ursulines in Cologne where she experienced the perpetual adoration of the Holy Sacrament. Still this strong leaning toward perpetual adoration conforms exactly with the wishes of St. Francis. His great esteem for the Eucharist and the furthering of adoration was one of his chief objectives.

Previous statements in regard to Mother's great devotion to the Blessed Sacrament will not be repeated. However, one instance will be added to further confirm this particular attitude on her part. In her cell she had a small aperture through which she could see the tabernacle at all times and adore her Lord. This at least was true regarding the chapel erected in 1869. Her cell adjoined the chapel constructed in 1895. Nearness to the chapel was very important for her because of ill health, for then she would not have so far to go to the choir loft to pay homage to her Eucharistic Lord. Often during periods of illness, she went down to the chapel proper under great difficulties to receive Holy Communion. It was her custom, if at all possible, to go down to the chapel to venerate the Lord.

The foregoing stamps Mother Maria Theresia as a genuine Franciscan. She is further portrayed as a true daughter of St. Francis whom she resembled so closely in her absolute fidelity to the Catholic Church. Francis wished to live in poverty and humility. That was his ideal in life. But he wished also to live his poor and humble life only in the Catholic Church. He understood that he was called by God to live a new kind of life. For this also he wished the sanction of the church. His order, according to his desire, should always be "subject and subservient to Holy Church firm in the Catholic faith."

A clear idea of Mother Maria Theresia's ecclesiastical convictions can be gleaned from her official correspondence with bishops and pastors, which most certainly is characterized by humble submission to the representatives of the Church. How many, in certain circumstances, would not have been courteous and yielding in order to achieve some personal objectives. That such courteous loyalties were not mere forms or calculations relative to the Mother can be inferred from her many manifestations of conduct as a whole.

"How great is our good fortune to have been born children of the Catholic Church," she wrote to her Sisters (IV 122). She points out that only through the Church do we participate in the great mysteries of our redemption as commemorated in her ecclesial feasts:

> How fortunate are we to be children of the Catholic Church. In such beautiful succession, we celebrate feast after feast. We have the commemoration of the suffering and passion of our dear Lord, on which we meditate during Lent, culminating in the glorious solemnity of the Resurrection. (IV 114)

Since she clung so very closely to her Catholic Faith, it grieved her that the Church suffered so many persecutions. She wrote to the Sisters in North America in the year 1882 as follows:

> O dear Sisters, let us pray and implore the Blessed Virgin that the terrible judgments threatening us be averted. Almost daily we hear abusive language directed against the Catholic religion. Missionaries will soon be needed more in Germany than in India and China. The shortage of priests is being felt more and more; the weapons of the *Kulturkampf* have been at rest for some time now, but occasionally are taken up again in some isolated places. May we, through our fervent prayers and labors in his honor,

> render atonement to our dear Lord and save souls from the onrushing tide of perdition. (II 6)

Mother returned shocked from Torgau where she witnessed the terrible effects of the Reformation of Luther:

> In Torgau one can only weep and pray at the terrible defections caused by Luther. Never would I have believed such a situation. It seemed to me like a new paganism. How deep our gratitude to our dear Lord should be that we have been born and reared in the Catholic Faith. Many ministers themselves are skeptical and their religion is one of hate, bitter hate toward the Catholic Church and the Holy Father. The few Catholics there will be carried away easily and grow ashamed of their Faith. There only the long-suffering and merciful Lord, through the intercession of the Blessed Virgin, can help. But you and the dear Sisters help pray. (I 85)

As in Torgau, so also in other localities where Christians were few in number, Mother Maria Theresia established centers for the instruction of communicants. Thus, through her Sisters, she aided in confirming the Faith where Catholics were subjected to grave dangers against their Faith.

She was deeply disturbed in 1885 when one of her nephews married a Protestant woman. Upon receiving the news, she suffered a heart attack. Although saddened, she was not inactive in the matter. She wrote in clear terms, not only to her nephew in Berlin, but also to the bride:

> Dear A., I am very sorry that you concluded from my letter to Joseph, that I criticized you severely and unkindly; that, however, was far from me. I am lovingly inclined toward you as toward all. But I have Joseph's eternal salvation at heart. From a Catholic standpoint, I cannot consent to a mixed marriage. Differences in religion disturb the peace and happiness of the family, as each of us realizes from experience. You will find the following difficult to accept, also, but I am bound in sacred duty to write it. A Protestant is not obligated to rear the children in his religion.

> Contrariwise, the Catholic partner may not enter a mixed marriage unless beforehand he has the promise on oath that the children will be reared in the Catholic religion. In case of refusal, Joseph would be committing a grave sin. You, dear A., have promised me in your letter that it is your highest and holiest duty to make Joseph happy and contented. Then I can most certainly trust that Joseph's religion will become yours; otherwise it will be impossible. Dear A., an affirmative answer from you would give me great consolation and happiness! You and Joseph would be spared much grief and the blessings of God would rest upon your union.

Three years later she wrote to Sister Deogratias concerning her grief:

> Several weeks ago my nephew was here. He seemed well. But pray, pray, dear Sister Deogratias! I cannot dismiss the thought of his Protestant wife from my mind. I also wish that he would move from Berlin and come to reside in a Catholic town. Although the situation is bad, to God all things are possible. (I 84)

In June 1894, her prayers were finally heard. She could write to the wife of her nephew as follows:

> This morning I received Joseph's letter with the joyous news that you, dearest A., are now prepared to make our profession of faith and return to Holy Mother Church. With heartfelt joy, I communicated this blessed happening to the Sisters. All expressed sentiments of sincerest gratitude to the Lord for having heard our petitions and given you this great grace.

Did she hope at that time that another nephew of hers would also find his way back into the Church? It grieved Mother greatly when this second nephew married a Protestant divorcee in 1893. She bore this heavy sorrow all her life and tried all within her power to persuade him to recognize his wrongdoing; but in this instance she met with no success.

Mother Maria Theresia's concern was caused not from the mere fact that these instances stemmed from her own family. She always impressed emphatically upon her Sisters the importance of giving meaning to their religious life by making atonement in adoration for the sins of mankind and to plead for the return of the erring to his love:

> By faithful cooperation with his grace, we may accomplish much in the service of the Lord and be instrumental in drawing many sinful hearts back to God. Through prayer and good example, we are able to achieve much. (IV 3)

Mother's intentions for perpetual adoration are set forth in the Constitution:

> Through the perpetual adoration, the Sisters will make atonement to our dear Savior for the many insults heaped upon him, for the offences of Christians, heretics, and unbelievers. They will also pray for the intentions of Holy Church, for worthy vocations to the priesthood, and for grace and strength to fulfill the duties of their calling.

At one time, Mother Maria Theresia pleaded earnestly with her Sisters to:

> Please pray for Mr. B. He is critically ill and will not give any thought to confession. Pray, Sisters, and have others pray, and also perform good deeds. May our dear Sorrowful Mother assist us by her intercession. (I 193)

Likewise, she expressed great joy when someone on his deathbed returned to God through the Sacrament of Penance (I 179). Her letters registered sorrow when someone died without making peace with the church. Thus she wrote on March 8, 1883:

> Last week a very sad death occurred here. It is public information that Attorney X has not practiced his religion for many years. About eleven o'clock at night, when his sister came to visit him, she found him dead lying at the foot of the stairs. Naturally, a church burial had to be refused. Since the attorney otherwise was a very good man, the

> people were sorry. Let us trust that our dear Lord judged him mercifully. (I 29)

It is quite natural that Mother Maria Theresia participated in all the religious happenings of her home town. She rejoiced over the virility of Catholic life and the traditional customs that found expression in the town and vicinity. At one time she wrote about the celebration of Easter:

> It was beautiful here on Easter. In the evening, the Easter fire burned on all the heights encircling the town together with other fireworks. The singing of Easter songs resounded through the air. Celebrations are so beautiful in a Catholic land. (II 14)

Mother prayed much for her home town. When missions were conducted in the parish she doubled her prayers. In 1885, she wrote:

> During Holy Week, we shall most likely have a mission here in the parish. I beg all of you to pray that this great grace will redound to the salvation of souls. It is good that missions may again be conducted here, although they are carried on under new titles, "People's Retreats." Although the missionaries appear in diocesan attire, they are really religious priests. May our dear Lord grant that the Catholic Church will enjoy full freedom in its development and expansion here in Germany as in other countries. Please pray for that intention! (IV 89)

The Olpe parish mission of 1894 found an echo in one of Mother's letters: "Yesterday the mission closed, but some of the priests will remain until Wednesday.... May our dear Lord grant that conditions in Olpe will soon improve" (I 139).

Mother Maria Theresia considered it important that all branch convents have a chapel with the Blessed Sacrament, if at all possible. In this way she furthered the Catholic Faith in all the houses. She pleaded urgently with the Sister nurses to be very concerned that the dying receive the Sacraments. Convinced that in one of the houses a lay instructor was employed who no longer practiced her Faith, the Mother admonished the superior earnestly:

> I learned from Sister Paula that C. L. is with you. You probably have not considered that she no longer practices her Catholic Faith and thus might inadvertently drop a word here and there that might do great harm to the children. You may not keep her in your employ. Although you are confident that her being with the Sisters will bring her back to the Faith, and we should be happy if that were the case, still the probable harm that may come to one hundred children is too great. Please, dear Sisters, dismiss her, even if you must pay a higher salary to another lay instructor. The Lord will bless you in another way for it. These are matters of conscience; the parents wish their children to be educated in the Faith and preserved from harm. I consider it my duty to write this to you, and I beg you to take this counsel in the right spirit. (I 171)

The loyalty with which Mother Maria Theresia accommodated herself to the regulations of the Church was manifested in a very special way at the close of the *Kulturkampf* when investiture again became a possibility. For this permission had to be secured from the civil authorities. Mother wished to ascertain what stand the church authorities would take in this regard. She obtained an appointment in Paderborn and went there in person. Here, as in all the dioceses, the opinion was that to seek permission from the state was to be avoided, for this would give the state equal rights with the Church in exclusively Church affairs, a right that the state did not possess. Therefore, she presented a request to the state authorities that they set aside the obstacles relative to opposing the acceptance of new candidates into the congregation. The state, through its opposition, had not acquired the right to interfere in purely Church matters and this fact should be emphasized. Thus, in the petition formulated by Mother Maria Theresia, the wording is precise: "Will Your Honor kindly deign to remove the obstacles relative to the acceptance of candidates into our congregation?" (VII 13,14). The royal administration refused the request. Perhaps it was not proper to send the petition to the minister, but, undaunted Mother Maria Theresia sent it directly to the minister with success.

The future of the congregation depended upon the right of having investitures. Mother, however, did not wish to obtain the goal without full conformity to the wishes of the Church. Under no circumstances, would she go contrary to the regulations of the Church.

She exhibited another example of obedience to the Church after the Decree of December 17, 1890, relative to the guidance of souls, was issued. Until that time most superiors of the congregation required a manifestation of conscience from their Sisters in affairs that belonged to priests. This practice certainly did not stem from lust of power, but from a sincere endeavor to help the Sisters in matters of conscience from the experience drawn from their own lives and office. The rich experience of an exemplary religious superior who knows her Sisters well and is greatly interested in advancing them in their spiritual life may not be overlooked. But in all this the Church saw the danger of abuse that could enter if there was a complete confidence. Consequently, the Mother forbade the superiors to demand a manifestation of conscience or to question the Sisters pointedly regarding matters of conscience.

Shortly after the Decree had been issued, a Sister had a discussion with Mother. Somewhat later the Sister related:

> During a conversation, the venerable Mother asked a question, but, upon realizing immediately that the question was against the regulations of the Decree, she became quite disturbed and said, "I do not want an answer." I mentioned that I had intended beforehand to tell her. But she was adamant, "No, no, you may not tell me today." I had to acquiesce.

According to the Decree, the Sisters were free to interrogate their superiors in conscience matters, if they wished to do so. Mother Maria Theresia, however, wished to avoid all semblances of going counter to the Decree. Therefore, she simply would not consent to having Sisters lay conscience matters before her.

God has entrusted his Church to men. The Catholic Christian, on his way, repeatedly contacts men commissioned by

God. Thus he meets the human element in all its attractiveness, but also in its unfavorableness of the all too human. In such encounters, there is question of confirming faith in God through the activities of his representatives. Mother Maria Theresia also had contacts with the human element in the church, both relative to bishops and to priests. But she knew how to differentiate the office from the office holder, the personal and often really human conception from the actual ecclesiastical fullness of power. In her encounters with the Auxiliary Bishop Freusberg (+1889), this assurance shows up clearly. She honored him as bishop, although she could not acquiesce to his wishes with reference to her congregation. The Bishop of Paderborn was her superior, and, as such, she owed him obedience, but, when he was acting in an advisory capacity, she could justly refrain from action.

During the span of her religious life, four bishops administered the See of Paderborn. Bishop Konrad Martin is the one who gave the Sisters of Olpe autonomy. Through him, God pressured his servant to go her own way and become Mother to her Sisters. Up to this time, she had not seized the initiative, but had permitted the Bishop and his appointed superior to administer the Community, and the Mother accommodated herself to their decisions. Hers was a childlike submissiveness to the bishop as father. It was a great joy for her when he officiated at the laying of the cornerstone of the new chapel and also at the investiture ceremonies in 1869.

During the difficult period of the *Kulturkampf* which was especially severe for the Bishop, she wrote him a letter of sincere sympathy (VI 2). She felt bound to write a word of condolence. The death of the Bishop in exile, July 16, 1879, shocked her deeply as her letter to Sister Deogratias, July 22, 1879, portrays:

> Yesterday we received the sad news of the death, on July 16, of our Most Beloved and Highly Esteemed Bishop Konrad Martin. Your brother was just taking breakfast after Mass when Sister Francesca brought in the newspaper edged in black and handed it to me. Oh, how hard, how painful, this is for us poor children. (I 4)

Whether Bishop Franz Kaspar Drobe ever visited the motherhouse in Olpe during the term of his office is not known. If he had, the Chronicles of the Motherhouse would certainly have made mention of it. Of the servant of God, he demanded an obedience in all its severity and rigor when he forbade the Olpe Franciscans to nurse the sick in Olpe. During the same period, Reverend Tigges also ordered that only one daily Mass could be celebrated in the convent chapel. But the servant of God never complained. In her regard, the Bishop was the representative of God, and she adapted herself to his orders as is shown in her letters. Was he not in reality commissioned by God to direct her in obedience to the Church?

Bishop Hubertus Simar visited the motherhouse in Olpe twice. The Chronicle records his first visit on September 27, 1892. At this time, the Bishop conducted Chapter with the Sisters and also addressed them. At his second visit in August 1897, he commented favorably in his speech on the new wing at the motherhouse and the stately new chapel. In a fatherly manner, he exhorted the Sisters, that, as the new structures had successfully enhanced the exterior of the motherhouse, so each Sister should now endeavor to build her own interior as perfectly and as stately as the exterior. He then visited the orphanage where the children greeted him in song and speech.

Later the Chronicle recorded:

> The Most Reverend Bishop Simar was appointed Archbishop of Cologne. The Sisters rejoiced greatly when they learned that a new bishop had been appointed for Paderborn, namely, the Most Reverend Dr. Wilhelm Schneider from neighboring Gerlingen.

In the Bishop's display of a warm relationship to Mother Maria Theresia and her Sisters, it must be remembered that there was a close association, as he was formerly a resident of the same locality as Mother. When he visited his home on vacation, Mother sent Sister Paula and Sister Scholastica to greet him in the name of the congregation. She herself was unable to go on account of illness. But Mother took great pains to receive him honorably when he visited the motherhouse. This is sensed immediately in her letter of September 20, 1900, to Sister Deogratias, her helper in all needs:

> Next week we are expecting a visit from the Most Reverend Bishop. May our dear Lord quicken my feet. Today I am unable to walk because of arthritic pains. It would indeed be most hard for me not to greet our worthy guest. Dear Sister Deogratias, will you please be so kind as to supply me with a set of fine fruit knives as you have once before. If the Bishop is here for the noon meal, I would like to have the service nice and appropriate. You have granted me so many favors, and I know that you will grant me this one, too. We received the violet ribbon this morning and Sister Raphaela is already at work; the good Sisters will take care of the other things. (I 176)

Thus at the motherhouse, the esteemed guest received a well-planned and festive reception.

When Bishop Wilhelm Schneider administered the Sacrament of Confirmation in Olpe on September 25, 1902, he also visited the motherhouse. On this occasion, he gave the venerable Mother and the Sisters cause for real joy. The Bishop promised them that he would celebrate the feast of St. Francis, October 4, with them in Olpe and would offer a pontifical Mass in the chapel of the motherhouse. He arrived in the early morning by coach from Gerlingen, celebrated a pontifical Mass, and delivered an inspiring and festive sermon. All the clergy of Olpe gathered about the Bishop at the delicious noon meal. Later in the day, he discussed the cares and conditions of the congregation with Mother. At this visit, the Bishop verbally gave his permission to solemnize the entire Holy Week services in the chapel of the motherhouse, the same as was conducted in the parish churches. Before his visit, the Mother was rather disturbed as to whether she was making the proper preparations. In a rather humorous vein, she wrote concerning this in a letter:

> I have taken a severe cold and cannot rid myself of cough and hoarseness, and I fear I cannot say my little speech to the Most Reverend Bishop. (I 193)

He visited the servant of God again in September 1903. It had become a custom for him to visit Mother Maria Theresia every time he sought some relaxation in his own home in Gerlingen. His visits became informal; he could appear suddenly and unannounced. He knew the motherhouse and its entrances well. At one time, he entered the chapel way and appeared unexpectedly in the Sisters' refectory where some of the Sisters were taking coffee. One can readily imagine their surprise and embarrassment to have a bishop appear suddenly in their midst. The perplexed Sisters offered to call Mother Maria Theresia. The Bishop smilingly answered, "I shall find her myself," and he proceeded to Mother's office.

During the lifetime of the servant of God, her congregation was under diocesan jurisdiction. The Bishops of Paderborn appointed superiors for the congregation, who as their representatives cared for the interests of the congregation. Mother Maria Theresia showed these superiors the utmost respect and rendered them obedience. She willingly acquiesced to their guidance and considered them, not only as representatives of the Church, but also her personal superiors. What she wrote to the Sisters in America in a letter in 1882 is very characteristic of her:

> Up to the very last I had hoped to make a trip to America to see all of you during the summer months, but it must not be God's will. Last week our Reverend Superior, Dean Pielsticker, was here and in holy obedience my great desire had to be relinquished for the present. (IV 85)

A trip to America was always a big undertaking. But, also, in minor matters, the Mother was always obedient to the Superior. One time when she was in Mülheim, she wrote:

> From Olpe I learned that our dear Sister Caroline is very ill; gladly would I have returned, but the Reverend Superior was unwilling to have me travel. May God prolong her life; I desire to see her again and to speak with her. But all as God wills. (IV 5)

On her journey through life, Mother Maria Theresia encountered not only bishops and superiors, but in Olpe she had constant contacts with the parish priest. Under Reverend Bernard Hengstebeck, 1842-1873, she began her religious life. Owing to his initiative, the Way of the Cross on Finkenhagen was dedicated on December 4, 1850, as the Mount of the Cross, Olpe. How often the Mother of the Olpe Sisters made this Way. It is remarkable that the parish mission of 1851, arranged by the Reverend Hengstebeck, exerted no detectable influence on her. Could it be due to the fact that she had made the parish mission in Drolshagen the previous year? The mission in Olpe was likewise preached by Missionary Hillebrand who was assisted by two Franciscans. Could it have been that Aline Bonzel at that time was accepted in the Third Order of St. Francis Tertiaries? At this mission, the Sodality of Young Women for the Preservation of Christian Culture was founded. It can scarcely be imagined that Aline was not among them. In all probability, this Sodality was that of the Blessed Virgin, which during the youth of Aline was highly developed.

Reverend Hengstebeck wielded a decisive influence on the life of the servant of God. He mediated with Mrs. Bonzel in her opposition as Aline was aspiring to the religious life and prepared the way for her. He endeavored by word and deed to further the activities of the Franciscans in the parish, even though he protected the rights of the Vincentians in St. Martin Hospital.

After Reverend Hengstebeck's death, Reverend Heinrich Schroeder was installed as pastor of the parish in Olpe. His term was brief and regulated. Because of the *Kulturkampf*, he acted as administrator of the parish from 1873 to 1875. In 1876, he was named pastor and continued in this capacity until his death in the same year. Since he also held the office of Superior to the Franciscan Sisters, his benevolent leaning and attitude to Mother Maria Theresia was a matter of course.

His successor, Reverend Kaspar Tigges, was second assistant until 1886; however, he was responsible for the administration of the parish. During the *Kulturkampf*, he could not be appointed pastor, but his appointment to this position occurred in 1886. He accomplished much for the parish in Olpe. At times he appeared to be very demanding and convinced of his rights. His relationship with Mother Maria Theresia left much to be desired. Perhaps disagreements relative to the care of the sick arose. During this time, he was the confessor for the Franciscan Sisters. He caused many a cross for the foundress, but she carried them bravely and always met him courteously and objectively without raising any complaints against him. Was he unaware of the great gift God wished to give the parish in Mother Maria Theresia? He did much that must have pained her grievously. Yet, toward this priest she portrayed some of the behavior set forth by St. Francis in his Testament; even though a priest would persecute him, he would still have recourse to him because to him is entrusted the administration of the Blessed Sacrament. Reverend Tigges was reluctant to have any of his parishioners enter the Franciscan Community. When he became aware that someone wished to enter, he tried to prevent it. This situation was very painful and unpleasant for the servant of God, for on many occasions she had to rely on him in his official capacity.

He acknowledged his attitude toward the congregation openly. Mother, just as openly, told him that she realized his definite antagonism toward her Community. Nevertheless, she obliged her Sisters to pray for him daily. The question might be asked, whether or not he was influential in lifting the prohibition of the Franciscans relative to engaging in the care of the sick in 1890, and in the same year negating the requirement of celebrating only one Holy Mass in the convent chapel daily. In 1900, St. Martin Hospital passed into the hands of the Franciscan Sisters. With the Vicar General, who had the greatest influence, Reverend Tigges had no contact. Thus it appears that the animosity he felt toward Mother Maria Theresia had spent itself.

Mother Maria Theresia's letters clearly indicate that she thought these circumstances were providential for her. She suffered these situations, not only in the motherhouse in Olpe, but also from similar ones with pastors in the branch houses. When these occurred, the Mother was empathic with her Sisters, and she rejoiced with them when devout and zealous pastors were assigned to their houses.

What joy this loyal daughter of the church must have experienced as the Decree, giving ecclesiastical commendation of her congregation, was issued by the Roman Secretariat of Bishops and Religious on April 13, 1897. As this must have been one of the most joy-filled days of her life, the Decree is quoted here in its entirety:

> On December 20, 1860, the Congregation of the Poor Sisters of St. Francis of Perpetual Adoration was founded in the Diocese of Paderborn, through the pious endeavors of a devout woman, Maria Theresia Bonzel, with the approval of the Bishop of the named Diocese, Konrad Martin of blessed memory. The chief objective of the congregation, besides the sanctification of its own members through meditation and the adoration of the Most Blessed Sacrament, and besides the sanctification of the neighbor, as far as possible, is the active care of the sick in private homes and in hospitals, in the proper education of girls, and in the zealous performance of works of mercy toward poor, orphaned, and neglected children.
>
> Only a few years after its foundation, the congregation was persecuted through odious political laws. But in spite of all, Mother managed through the mercy of God an expansion that numbered seven hundred members and the possession of many branch convents and other houses suitable to its high objectives not only in Germany but also in many dioceses in North America. Although the Sisters are engaged in various areas far removed from each other, they operate under the administration of one Superior General, elected every six years in General chapter. After the novitiate, the Sisters make profession of the simple vows of obedience, poverty, and chastity.
>
> Since it is now well known that the said congregation has brought forth rich fruits for the glory of God and the salvation of souls, and that it exists in the firm confidence that in future it will bring forth even richer fruits, the Bishop of Paderborn, and also several other Bishops and Archbishops, among them His Eminence Cardinal Krementz of Cologne, have confirmed and attested that the said Sisters in their dioceses have given excellent ser-

> vice in the cause of religion and of the state. Therefore, they respectfully recommend them to the Holy See.
>
> All this was submitted to the Holy Father, Pope Leo XIII, by the undersigned Cardinal, the Prefects of this Sacred Congregation of Bishops and Religious, in an audience of April 5, 1897. His Holiness, listening attentively and weighing all, especially the letters of recommendation from said Bishops, vouchsafed in most honorable terms of praise to commend the said congregation because His Holiness wished to show the named Sisters a special mark of affection to encourage them to even greater zeal to attain their proposed objectives. Through this Decree this Congregation is praised and commended in an outstanding way. Nevertheless, the Ordinaries are to exercise their power in examining the congregation and its Constitution in accordance with the Sacred Canons and the Apostolic Constitution. Given at Rome in the Secretariat of the Congregation of Bishops and Religious on April 13, 1897.

The official approval of the congregation and also its Constitution was postponed until a later date. Relative to the Constitution, His Holiness ordered some changes to be made.

It was on April 28, 1897, that the Reverend Superior handed the Mother this Decree. This must have been a day of special joy for her. Unfortunately and regrettably no letters are extant regarding this incident. The next letter is dated May 17. It can be concluded that Mother Maria Theresia most certainly shared this great event of joy with all her sisters. In this incident the loyalty of the Mother to the Church again is proved. That she must have shared this honor with her Sisters can be concluded with certainty, judging from the manner in which she later reacted when the Minister General of the Franciscan order affiliated her congregation with the First Order whereby the Mother was given the highest recognition and estimation by the great Franciscan family.

From the very beginning Mother Maria Theresia had sought a close alliance with other Franciscan orders. She had the good fortune in 1863 to have Father Schmidt as Reverend Superior. He was a Tertiary of St. Francis and did all within his power to insure that the Sisters not only have the name but also the true spirit of real Franciscanism. The Reverend Bonaventure Wessendorf conducted the first retreat. In her first Constitution, Mother Maria Theresia stated expressly that she wished Franciscans to be chosen for all retreats. How persistently she followed the Franciscan way and close association with the sons of St. Francis, is shown in the letter that she wrote to the Reverend Superior on October 18, 1869: "Please obtain permission for us to use the Franciscan Ordo in our chapel. This is done in other Franciscan congregations" (V 6).

Olpe and practically all the foundations of the Olpe Sisters lay with the Franciscan Province of the Holy Cross. This province was very favorable to the servant of God. This is readily recognized by the fact that in 1869 the superiors of the order sent their highly competent architect, Brother Paschalis Gratze, to Olpe for the construction of a new wing and a new chapel. In 1879, the Reverend Provincial Othmar Maasmann planned to conduct the retreat for the Olpe Sisters in person, thus showing how the development in Olpe was dear to his heart and how he esteemed the Sisters. However, at the last moment, he was hindered from doing so. But as a substitute, he sent the Reverend Kaspar Heimer, one of the greatest spiritual forces in the province (I 10).

Mother Maria Theresia's connection with the Franciscans became especially evident as the Sisters went to America. The Franciscan, Reverend Accursius Beine of Lafayette, Indiana, worried much over the difficulties the Sisters suffered in the beginning of their work in that city. It appears that the second foundation made in America, in Columbus, Nebraska, was opened at the invitation of the Reverend Ambrosius Jansen who invited the venerable Mother to Nebraska. Sister Deogratias, the superior in America, was urged repeatedly by Mother Maria Theresia to seek counsel and advice in different situations from the Franciscans of the Sacred Heart Province. At this time, the Reverend Vincent Halbfas was Provincial. He was born in Olpe, Germany, on September 15, 1832, son of Mayor Joseph Adam Halbfas of Olpe. His brother was the mayor of Olpe during the period of the *Kulturkampf*. Thus Mother Maria Theresia knew the Provincial well as a native of the same town; she realized that her Sisters would be well advised and assisted. Just as in Olpe, where Brother Paschalis Gratze provided his architectural services to the Sisters, so likewise in North America, Brother Adrian Wewer, also a Franciscan, rendered his services to the Sisters as architect in the American province.

In 1885, as changes in the Constitution were necessary, the servant of God sought counsel from the Provincial of the Franciscans, Reverend Othmar Maasmann. The latter gave the task of making the required revisions to one of the priests of his province. Unfortunately, the name of this Franciscan is not known.

The year 1898 carries special significance relative to the alliance of the servant of God with the Franciscans. At that time a Franciscan cloister was founded in Attendorn, close to Olpe. Mother Maria Theresia rejoiced greatly, for it gave her hope that now her contacts with the sons of St. Francis would be ever more frequent. However, no mention is found of the foundation in Attendorn in any of her letters written in 1898, in spite of the fact that thirty seven of the letters are extant. Could it be that Sister Deogratias, who alone received thirty of these letters with the year, did not save all of them?

The first trace of the Franciscan cloister in Attendorn is found in a letter of April 25, 1902, to Sister Deogratias. In this letter Mother Maria Theresia writes concerning the chapter of the Franciscans of the Saxony Province, as follows:

> The chapter of the Franciscans at Düsseldorf was a shake-up! In Attendorn, Father Fridolin was chosen president, and I think Father Winifred is vicar in Düsseldorf. Reverend Vinzenz is canon at the Cathedral in Paderborn.... There is somewhat of confusion. (I 187)

In its own way, is not this brief reference a notable sign of how vitally the Mother was interested in all that pertained to the great Franciscan family? Although as evidenced above, the many changes that took place caused her much surprise and misgivings. How vital this association must have been is also recognized in her letter to Sister Deogratias on the day following the Franciscan chapter which included the comment: "May God's blessing be with them" (I 199).

At that time, Mother did not realize that the changes made in that chapter would be to her greatest advantage and the source of many blessings to her congregation. The Reverend Wenceslaus Straussfeld was elected Provincial. He prepared the way for the affiliation of the Olpe Franciscans. On July 14, 1904, Mother Maria Theresia, filled with joy, wrote from Venusberg to Sister Paula:

> Yesterday I visited Father Richard, the Definitor, who is ill. He will be instrumental in bringing about the affiliation or incorporation of our congregation and thereby we shall receive the same indulgences and privileges as granted the First and Second Orders of St. Francis. How long I have prayed for this and now our dear Lord has heard my prayer! Then we shall also receive permission that priests saying Mass in our chapel may use the Franciscan Ordo. The reverend Provincial and the guardian are in Rome at present and can arrange all with the Father General. (III 84)

As Reverend Anaklet Brogsitter was in Olpe on October 2, 1904, to begin the investiture retreat, Mother had an exhaustive talk with him in which she explained all that she had done on her part to bring about an affiliation. Immediately after the retreat, Father Anaklet discussed the matter with the Provincial and gave the Mother a decisive answer. She sent her petition to the Provincial who forwarded it to the Minister General in Rome.

On November 14 of the same year, Mother Maria Theresia received the following answer:

> Father Dionysius Schuler, Minister General of the entire Franciscan Order of Friars Minor, wishes the venerable Congregation of the Poor Franciscans of Perpetual Adoration of Olpe, Diocese of Paderborn, happiness and the Seraphic blessing. Since we recognize your zeal and attitude toward the Seraphic Order of which you, as presented in the document you issued, have the religious habit and also the way of life, we shall grant your petition in as far as is possible for us to comply. Furthermore, we are encouraged by the hope that your devotedness and love, through this

> new mark of favor, may increase steadily in the grace and strength of the seraphic spirit and through you bear ever richer fruit. We shall accept all your Sisters and all who shall enter in the future into our religious Union, from which you derived name and religious habit. We declare this Decree in virtue of the Sacred Congregation of Indulgences and Relics. From August 28, 1903, you can participate in all the indulgences granted directly to the First and Second Orders by the Roman Pontiffs. Your church will possess the same indulgences as the churches of the said orders enjoy.
>
> *Farewell and remember us*
> *and our Seraphic Order in your prayers!*
> *Given at Rome in our Monastery of St. Anthony*
> *on November 3, 1904.*
> *Fr. Dionysius Schuler*

We find the joyous message relative to this happy event in seven of her letters. Thus, Mother wrote in one of them on November 24, 1904:

> Now I can share with you that our congregation is incorporated into the First Order giving us the privileges of the First and Second Orders. May the Lord be praised! It is our obligation to show gratitude for so many and such great graces and to strive as true Franciscans to renounce ourselves and the world and bear with joy our daily troubles and hardships. Yes, dear Sisters, what should be difficult for us? Our dear Lord cares for us with an eternal love. (III 89)

That her congregation was recognized in such a manner and accepted as a follower of St. Francis was to her a great blessing from the Lord. Her endeavor from the very beginning was to be considered a poor Franciscan. The recording in the Chronicles relative to this event crowned her joy:

> Today, December 5, 1904, the reverend President of Attendorn and Father Provincial visited with Mother Maria Theresia. Besides the various situations and intentions of

> the congregation, they discussed the desired approval and ratification of the Constitution of the congregation by the Holy See. The Reverend Father promised to take all possible steps on his part to reach this goal. At the request and wish of the venerable Mother, he gave the Sisters a spiritual talk.

After the introduction, he remarked that, when such a loving, good, and aged Mother makes a request, it is impossible to refuse; he would speak no matter how poor the ending might be. He commenced with the idea that each individual Sister must endeavor to maintain the congregation at its height and to further its interests. This she will do, he added, if she meditates on the three following questions:

> Do I still cherish my religious life? Conforming to this call, I must be an adoring angel, a loving angel whose watchword is "My God and my all," a meditating angel, and a reconciling angel. Do I still bear in mind the reasons that led me into the convent? Was it perhaps the flight of time and the awaited reward in heaven, or the grateful love of my God who loved me to the extent of giving his life for me? Do I begin anew each day? Do I renew my vows each day and form special resolutions? The religious must also be prepared for the cross; yes, ready to accept it with joy. These will be the angel wings that will carry you to heaven. Such a religious gladly hears the words of promise from St. Francis: "We have promised great things, but greater things have been promised us. Let us keep the former and sigh after the latter and ours will be the crown of everlasting life."

CHAPTER XV

BLESSED PASSING

Toward the end of the year 1904, Mother Maria Theresia wrote to a Sister, "My condition is that of all elderly people; I am tired, but I am at peace and happy" (II 42). Mother had a right to be tired for hers was a long way. In fact it was the Way of the Cross. God had blessed visibly what she had begun under such great hardships. She was grateful to the Lord for all his goodness. Under his protection, she now rested. He guided her; she had walked his way.

The year 1905 dawned. In his New Year greetings, the Reverend Superior expressed the hope that, since the venerable Mother had successfully withstood the first half of winter without serious illness, she would also hopefully withstand the second. Although many visitors taxed her energies, she welcomed all who came to her with warm friendliness. In her cheerful way she endeavored to be the first to express the blessings for the New Year.

Increasing numbers in the congregation made it necessary to enlarge the motherhouse. It must have been at the turn of the year that Mother said to a Sister: "Our motherhouse will soon be too small for the congregation; we need a novitiate and a wing for the elderly Sisters. The latter are the pillars of the order and the best of care must be provided for them." First an addition was planned for a novitiate.

On January 13, the architect Huerth, from Aachen, was consulted regarding the addition. As an expert, he saw immediately that the motherhouse at the present location would be too hemmed in at a future time. He advised strongly that due consideration be given to building an entirely new complex for the motherhouse and novitiate in a more favorable locality. This eventuality could not be avoided indefinitely. At a meeting of the Council on January 17, the members determined to refer this matter to the Reverend Superiors of the Congregation to ascertain their viewpoints. Sister Paula went to Paderborn on January 18. The Reverend Superior of the Congregation advised against the undertaking of an entirely new construction project for the financial status of the congregation could not withstand the cost. He conceded that an addition could be built at the present site. Architect Huerth was commissioned to draw up plans for a novitiate. Another story was added to the present building where formerly the choir apse of the old chapel had been. The construction was begun on April 10, after Mother Maria Theresia had passed into eternity. She had planned and decided this structure. It was her last official business negotiation of far-reaching significance.

During the time that deliberations were taking place as to whether the present motherhouse be enlarged or an entirely new complex be built on another location, Sister Hildegardis recorded the following:

> At this time, I had a talk with our dear Mother. She shared her longings with me of how ardently she desired to build an entirely new motherhouse on Kimmicker Heights near the eastern outskirts of the town, where she possessed some land.

Would Divine Providence at some time fulfill that ardent longing of Mother Maria Theresia? Our day has seen its realization. At the Centenary Jubilee celebration of the congregation on July 20, 1963, on Kimmicker Heights bordering Olpe, the cornerstone of a new motherhouse was solemnly laid.

Relative to the days following the deliberations in regard to the new construction, we have from the hand of Sister Andrea Bussien, the chronicler, precise recordings written in the total love of a person who greatly revered Mother Maria Theresia. Nothing is more appropriate than to quote the entire account. It is the account of the blessed end of the Mother. Sister Andrea wrote:

> On January 18, we began our Wednesday novena in honor of St. Joseph. Although the feet of our venerable Mother were so painfully edematous with arthritis that she could scarcely step on them, she dragged herself downstairs in

the morning in order to receive Holy Communion with the Sisters. How burdensome were even these few short steps for Mother! When she arrived at the top of the stairs, she halted until the coughing brought on by the exertion subsided. She then proceeded to the choir loft to attend Holy Mass. Only utter impossibility kept her from making that distressing way again. She had always thought that she lacked reverence to the Blessed Sacrament if she did not exert herself physically and, instead, had Holy Communion brought to her.

On the following day, the condition of her feet had worsened; she could scarcely make a few steps. Since in the following week, her feet had improved somewhat, the venerable Mother, whose tenderness went out to the sick Sisters, had herself wheeled to Sister Edelberta, who was suffering from tuberculosis and nearing her end. Mother remained with the sick Sister a long time, and, when the Sister nurse wheeled her back to her room, she begged Mother to spare herself and to be careful lest the Sisters have the same worry concerning her that they had two years ago. Mother replied, "I shall gladly die, dear Sister, but as God wills. Take good care of the sick Sisters for me and serve them with ardent love. The sick and suffering Sisters are a blessing to the congregation and are God's favorites."

The exertion had been too much for Mother; she had to give up her intention of visiting all the sick Sisters at the same time. In the afternoon, she was wheeled to the other Sisters. Sister Verena was suffering from a severe case of influenza. As Mother visited her, the Sister with deep concern said, "You should stay away, dear Mother, for you might contract influenza." Smilingly, she answered, "It is not so bad; by the way, I have it already."

Before evening of the same day, tracheal catarrh had set in and by morning the Mother's coughing was excessive and her chest congested. She did not wish to miss Holy Mass, for it was Wednesday, the day dedicated to St.

> Joseph. Holy Communion was brought to her in the sick room. The venerable Mother felt very wretched.
>
> At eleven o 'clock in the morning, the motherhouse received word from Geistingen that Sister Angelica had passed away. The Mother postponed going to bed until after she had said the Office of the Dead for the deceased Sister. In the afternoon, she acceded to the pressures of the Sisters and went to bed.
>
> Sister Dominica, the devoted and loyal nurse of Mother Maria Theresia in better days, as well as, in sickness, became ill herself with influenza and also had to go to bed. In the first days of her illness, the Mother missed her nurse very much. On Thursday, she said to Sister Scholastica, "You cannot imagine how I miss that child. Tell her that if my last hour should be at hand, I would urgently beg her to come." However, Mother was not critical at that time, and the opinion was that several days of rest would eliminate her cold. On Saturday, Sister Dominica, although not feeling well, came to Mother's room. Later Mother Maria Theresia manifested to Sister Scholastica, "You cannot realize how happy I am that the child is here again. Often I was tempted to press the button to summon her."

As Sister Edelberta was growing weaker progressively, Mother urged that a petition be presented to the ecclesiastical directorate for securing a plot in the new cemetery for the burial of the Sisters of the congregation. On her sick bed, Saturday, January 28, Mother signed the petition, and no one at that time surmised that it would be her last official signature here below for the congregation. Her condition had not worsened. On the contrary, Sister Paula considered her on the road to recovery, giving the Sisters reasons for rejoicing. In the eternal designs, however, it was decreed differently.

On the evening of January 28, the venerable Mother's condition was not good. As she awoke during the night, after a brief slumber, her cough had become tight and her chest constrained. The Sister who was keeping vigil with the Mother called Sister

Paula. Within a few minutes, she was at the bedside. She found the Mother in a state of spasmodic insensibility, giving no response to repeated calls. The doctor was summoned and Sister Dominica, Sister Verena, and the Reverend Rector were awakened. Sister Paula, in the interim, attempted to revive the Mother by the application of remedies formerly used for spasms. Upon arriving, the doctor prescribed medicines to loosen the cough and relieve the chest. The sick patient, now somewhat revived, wished to know whether her condition was critical and whether she should receive the Sacrament of the Dying. Sister Paula inquired of the doctor. Although there was no immediate danger, he advised that she be anointed in the morning. After taking medicine, coughing again set in, thus relieving the chest. In this way the night passed.

When Sister Scholastica approached the sickbed on the morning of January 29, the Mother asked her, "Did you hear anything during the night?" "No, dear Mother, if I had heard, I would certainly have been here." "That is what I thought. But this time the end will come, dear Sister Scholastica." "Dear Mother, you may not leave us! What will become of us?" "I have instructed Sister Paula thoroughly and told her all. She knows how things should be. Only remain loyal and all will go well."

What fear and perplexity filled the Sisters as Sister Paula, after Mass on Sunday morning, begged them to remain faithfully assembled in prayer as Mother Maria Theresia would now receive the Sacrament of the Anointing of the Sick. Mother, who had so often been at the point of death, was ready to meet it with joy. But the Sisters, who had so often obtained her recovery, were again storming heaven with fervent prayers for their dearly beloved Mother. Since Mother Maria Theresia was very weak, Sister Paula had asked the Reverend Rector to hear her confession before Holy Mass and to administer the Sacrament for the Dying after the Mass. As a small altar had been placed in her room opposite the bed, the Mother remained in silent devotion awaiting the coming of her Divine Guest. Immediately after Mass, Sister Paula recited the preparatory prayers for Holy Communion with her. In spite of her weakness, Mother prayed audibly with her. As Sister Paula, overcome by emotion and tears, ceased to pray aloud, the Mother continued the prayers with great fervor: "Come, my dear Savior! Come for the last time in my life! Come!" Some of the Sisters, who were in the room with the Mother, prayerfully attended the administration of the Sacrament. Sister Dominica, still recuperating from the effects of her illness, undertook most of the nursing.

The news regarding the serious illness of Mother was sent immediately to all the branch convents of the congregation and cabled to America, such that the great number praying might effect the prolongation of the earthly life of Mother. It seemed as though the Lord would grant their prayers, for her condition had not worsened on Sunday and Monday, but even seemed to ameliorate on Tuesday so that the Sisters' hopes began to rise.

Hourly Sister Edelberta was awaiting the advent of her heavenly Bridegroom. When visiting her on Tuesday morning, January 31, Sister Verena bade her as first petition upon arriving above to beg our Savior to prolong the life of dear Mother Maria Theresia several years for the benefit of the congregation. In heaven her petition would be more effective, Sister Verena said. Smilingly the sick, scarcely able to speak any longer, nodded in approval and whispered, "Yes." As Sister Verena went to the venerable Mother, she said, "You shall not die, dear Mother. I have recommended your recovery to Sister Edelberta and she promised to intercede for you." The Mother smilingly replied, "You want me to stay here forever."

On Tuesday, about twelve o'clock noon, Sister Edelberta died. In the afternoon, as the death was reported to the pastor, he informed them that the Ecclesiastical Board of Directors had granted the Sisters a special area in the new cemetery. How Mother rejoiced that she had signed the petition. Wednesday morning, February 1, she was feeling better; it was believed that she had withstood the crisis. But in the afternoon, severe kidney pains set in accompanied by fever that continued to rise until evening. This rapidly absorbed her strength and, even that very night, the worst was feared. To revive her energies, Sister Paula prepared and administered a camphor injection. At about 11:30 p.m., the pastor brought Mother Holy Viaticum. The doctor also came and administered medicines to relieve the pain. Thus the night passed. To leave nothing untried, Professor Ungar, who had often before treated Mother Maria Theresia in her illnesses, was called by telephone and requested to come. He arrived on the next train. Contraction of the chest appeared on Thursday, February 2, the feast of the Purification of the Blessed Virgin Mary. Although in a somewhat slighter degree, the fever continued. Mother's weakness was so intense that, for most of the time, she lay in an unresponsive state. Professor Ungar had arrived at about five o'clock in the afternoon. In his diagnosis, he stated that her condition was similar to that of two years ago, only the fever was higher; unless that would subside, the worst was to be feared. The doctor ordered specific treatments that seemed to help. Upon receiving the sad news, several Sisters from branch convents came to see Mother. But her weakness was so great that she lay motionless most of the time. Sister Scholastica asked the seemingly unconscious one, "Dear Mother, do you know me?" Mother opened her eyes and answered, "Should not Mother know you?"

Sister Paula had contracted influenza and had to remain in bed on Saturday morning, February 4. Also, Sister Dominica, who had overtaxed her ailing physical condition in concern for Mother, had to take to bed the same morning.

As Sister Scholastica told the venerable Mother that Sister Paula was in bed, she said, "Both of you, Sister Scholastica and Sister Natalia, must stay with me; then the others can rest." When she learned that all the Sisters had retired, she said, "I am glad that they are resting; you stay with me." On Saturday, the fever had somewhat subsided. In the afternoon, she received the Sacrament of Penance. Also, in the evening, Mother's temperature was not as high as usual. Sister Paula was up again in the evening for her concern for the Mother gave her no rest.

Saturday night was tolerable for the Mother, but early on Sunday morning, she begged Sister Verena, who was keeping vigil with her at that time, "You must get me ready, for the Savior will come soon. Sister Paula will say the Communion prayers for me." Sister Verena said, "The Reverend Rector thinks you should forego a morning since it fatigues you so very much." Mother was satisfied and answered, "As God wills. Then I shall sleep a little longer." She knew how to keep herself in peace, contented with what God sent her, although it went against her most intimate desires. Although her temperature was not too high, she suffered very intensely. Mother did not speak, but the intent look in her eyes, seemed to express more maternal tenderness than usual. By her loving gaze, she rewarded each sign of love shown her. As though the imminent separation stirred her emotions, her expression seemed to say, "I must depart from all of you whom I have loved so dearly." At one time, she begged Sister Scholastica to pray very fervently to the Mother of God.

In the afternoon, she suddenly called aloud, "Sister Paula, take good care of the Sisters! I have told you all, dear Sister Paula; you really know all." Sister Paula replied, "Yes, dear Mother, I know all." Then she became calm again. It seemed as though she, once again, wished to recommend the Sisters to the tried and loyal love of good Sister Paula.

On Sunday evening, February 5, at about seven o'clock, a notable change for the worse took place in Mother Maria Theresia's condition. About nine o'clock she wished to be placed in an easy chair. While the Sisters were complying with her request, she became unconscious, and, only under great difficulty, could they return her to bed. Sister Paula immediately prepared a camphor treatment which revived her somewhat, accelerating her pulse and heart again. A short time later Sister Paula retired since the condition of the Mother had improved. But only a few minutes later, Sister Paula was again called to the bedside of the sick one. Deterioration of energy had once more set in. The Reverend Rector was called and at 10:30 Mother Maria Theresia received Holy Viaticum to strengthen her for the final combat. After the reposition of the Blessed Sacrament in the Tabernacle, the Rector returned to the sick room. The nearness of death was unmistakable. The dying Mother whispered, "Patience! Patience! My dear Savior, come soon." These were her last words.

The Rector commenced the prayers for the dying, joined by the Sisters, who in the meantime had been awakened and had assembled at the bedside of their departing Mother. The doctor arrived at midnight. He thought that she might live until morning. Soon after one o'clock, the rattle in her throat stopped and she became perfectly quiet. Then within moments, her head sank deeply upon her breast and, in one last gasp, she breathed forth her soul. It was early Monday morning, about 1:30, February 6, 1905.

For some moments, the Rector stood gazing upon the mortal frame of the Mother resting peacefully as in sleep. Then he turned to the Sisters:

> Dear Sisters, your good Mother is dead; she is now with God. The Foundress of the Congregation has departed. She now stands before the eternal Judge, and we may trust that she has found a merciful Judge. We have every reason to hope for this, when, in review, we look back upon the life of the good departed Mother. She always fulfilled the will of God conscientiously and to the best of her knowledge. She bore her great sufferings with enduring patience to the end of her life, not only physical pains but sufferings of all kinds. I scarcely need to remind you to succor the dear Mother through loving gratitude and fervent prayer.

Thereafter the Rector left the room. The Sisters, in deep sorrow, remained near Mother for some time. Sister Paula reviewed the last hours of the Mother for the Sisters. Together they prayed for the deceased and then repaired to the chapel to make the Way of the Cross for the departed one. Sadness had entered the motherhouse. Mother had gone home to God.

CONCLUDING REMARKS

In the same night, the deceased was clothed in her religious habit. On her head was placed the crown of thorns that she had received on her final profession day. Thus she lay in state. The Sisters immediately began the wake. As long as the Mother lay in state, two of her Sisters in regular rotation prayed at her side. Nearby branch houses were notified of the death of Mother Maria Theresia by letter or by telephone; others were sent telegrams. When the Sisters in America received the notification of the death of the Mother, they were astounded by a peculiar concurrence of incidents reported by Sister Josepha in her letter received in Olpe on February 15:

> Our dear Mother did not wish to arrive above alone. In her quick manner, she took a companion with her. During the same night, without previous illness and suddenly, our dear Sister Constantia, superior of St. Clare Convent, St. Bernard, Nebraska, died from a hemorrhage. She had always been attached to the Mother with a special intimate and tender love.

At break of day, the news of Mother's death spread throughout Olpe and the vicinity. Evidences of heartfelt sympathy were many. In ever larger throngs, the inhabitants came to view the remains of the deceased once more. Their desires were met. The death chamber became a small sanctuary into which not only the Sisters but also numerous people of all walks of life came for quiet prayer and a last farewell. From hour to hour tokens of sympathy from far and near multiplied in word and correspondence, giving testimony of the high esteem and grateful love in which the deceased was held. In their deep grief, it must have been a special consolation for the Sisters to learn that the first letter from a distance to arrive was from the Bishop of Paderborn. Also, the head of the German Government wrote words of the highest commendation in recognition of the activities of Mother Maria Theresia. He had not been notified directly, but received the news second-hand. That he wrote in spite of the oversight, showed his esteem for the venerable deceased.

The Reverend Superior, in a very special way, dignified the passing of the Mother in his letter of February 7, directed to Sister Paula:

> *Very Venerable Sister Paula:*
>
> With profound sorrow I have received the notification of the death of our good Mother. To all the Sisters, I express my feelings of deepest sympathy. We all know what a loss it is for the entire congregation and for each individual Sister. For long, long years, the good deceased has managed the affairs of the congregation with the greatest conscientiousness and joyous self-sacrifice, with discretion and wisdom. She spared neither hardship nor pains to fur-

ther the welfare of the congregation and of each Sister. She did all this amidst generally poor health and often severe physical pain, coupled with the infirmities of age.

How visibly God has blessed the works of his loyal servant. From small beginnings and under great difficulties, the congregation developed rapidly and energetically, and now it stands in full stature. The Sisters assemble as orphans at the bier of their loyal Mother. Their grief is natural and justified. I know that the Sisters grieve as self-sacrificing children of St. Francis, but with a pious turning to God: "The Lord has given; the Lord has taken away. May the name of the Lord be blessed." Yes, evidently our dear Lord gave the Sisters this good Mother as his loyal representative, and, contrary to all expectations, gave her a long life, certainly in answer to the fervent prayers of the Sisters. Finally, Divine Providence deemed the time opportune to adorn this good soul, faithful to the end, with the crown of eternal glory. We may not complain, but, in all humility, say: "Lord, may your will be done; may your name be blessed."

You dear Sisters, are not orphans as might be judged by the world. Your good Mother has been removed from the care of the world and has wandered to her Father's house, her eternal home in God. There, at the source of divine love and grace, she undoubtedly has met a great multitude of her glorified Sisters with whom she will plead for blessings and salvation for her Sisters still on earth that they may persevere faithfully to the end and render themselves worthy of eternal blessedness. Yes, dear Sisters, at the bier of your good Mother, resolve to follow her exemplary life as genuine Sisters of St. Francis, that a good religious spirit may persist in the congregation and may be established ever more firmly and developed further. I need not urge you to pray for the dear deceased. God's judgments are severe. I had decided to come to share my sorrow with that of the Sisters, but I must relinquish the plan because I am not well.

With sincerest sympathy, your resigned Superior greets you.

Wigger
Cathedral Provost

The remains of Mother Maria Theresia lay in state on a bier until the evening of February 8. About ten o'clock that night, the Sisters placed their deceased Mother in a coffin and bore it to the chapel. On February 9, as on the previous day, a Requiem High Mass was sung in the convent chapel for the repose of her soul. The Levitical Requiem funeral Mass was read in the St. Martin parish church, February 10, at 7:45 a.m., for the motherhouse chapel was entirely too small to accommodate the crowds wishing to attend. After the Mass, the clergy, eighteen in number (only two had been invited directly), proceeded to the motherhouse to join the cortege removing the deceased from the convent chapel. Pastor Tigges said the prayers of blessing; then came the departure. The deceased was borne from the sacred edifice that she had erected to the honor of God, and, in which through the years, she had prayed and obtained the needed strength for her labors of love among the Sisters.

The funeral procession to the cemetery followed. Never before had Olpe witnessed a similar cortege, one in which the participants manifested such esteem and gratitude. Many honors to the deceased were made. A military honor guard headed the procession, bearing a standard, unfurled and shrouded in black crepe, and a wreath in honor of Mother. Then came a veteran carrying a cushion displaying the decorative medals and other marks of distinction that the deceased had merited. The orphan children, instructors in the lyceum, students with white lilies and palms followed. Next followed the various organizations of the town with their respective banners. These groups were followed by the clergy. Immediately preceding the hearse were three little girls dressed in white, carrying candles entwined with myrtle and a white satin cushion bearing a vow formula and a copy of the Constitution. The coffin was borne along amidst a veritable sea of wreaths and flowers. The Sisters followed the hearse; their number totaled two hundred twenty. Then came the relatives, magistrates, leading officials of the town of Olpe, and a vast number of people of all walks of life. After the prayers and blessings at the grave, the choir sang, *Ueber den Sternen, da Wird Es Einst Tagen*. This solemn funeral terminated with three salvos by the military detail. She who had once said, "We are the lesser ones," was at her funeral the center of a genuine triumph of reverence and respect.

Relative to her Sisters, Mother Maria Theresia was a living memory. Many Sisters remarked later that they prayed to her for they were convinced that their Mother was in heaven. They entrusted their affairs to her with the conviction that her maternal love was an everlasting one, extending beyond the grave. They visited the cemetery frequently to pray at the grave of their beloved Mother. The longer the time of her absence from them, the more ardently they desired her presence among them.

On September 16, 1930, the Mother's grave was opened in the presence of the clergy, Mother Verena Schulte, several other Sisters, and some officials from the town. The remains were placed in a new oak and tin coffin. However, no official examination of the corpse was made at that time. Only a small hole was made at the head of the coffin. The sisters who peeped through the opening were of the impression that the countenance of the Foundress had darkened, but her features appeared the same as in death. At midnight, the coffin was quietly transferred to the chapel in the motherhouse where all the Sisters were awaiting their Foundress.

Here the Mother lay in state amidst flowers. Prayerfully, the Sisters held vigil with their Mother in rotation for the remainder of the night. In the morning of September 17, the one hundredth anniversary of her birth, the Archbishop of Paderborn, Dr. Kaspar Klein, celebrated a pontifical Mass in the chapel at 8:30 a.m. He gave a touching eulogy in which he lauded the activities and the personhood of Mother Maria Theresia. Then in solemn procession, the coffin was carried to the newly constructed Memorial Chapel in the garden of the motherhouse grounds. The Archbishop officiated at the burial services.

Mother had now returned home to her Sisters. It became a tradition that the young Sisters before their temporary profession attended Holy Mass in the Memorial Chapel of their Mother. To her were brought intentions relative to religious life during the days of the postulancy and novitiate. The professed entrusted to her their cares of years heavily laden, but also their joys of God's blessings upon them. The number of visits to the Mother's resting place have increased greatly since His Excellency, the Most Reverend Lorenz Jaeger, the Archbishop of Paderborn, entered the process of her canonization in 1961. Now the pages of the book are filled with the names of those who, together with the Sisters, beg God that he may soon raise his loyal servant to the honors of the altar.

In the first years after her death, her memory remained alive because of the personal contact that the Sisters had had with Mother. But soon there was an urgent request to have a biography of her life. Sister Hildegardis, a relative of Mother Maria Theresia, was commissioned to collect materials for it. She began the task in 1917. Apparently Reverend Antonius Hupperz was to write the life. He died on August 10, 1924; he had worked on the biography for several years and left a manuscript, not as yet ready for the printer. Then Reverend Salesius Elsner, O.F.M., undertook the work. Besides relating the life of the Foundress, he also developed the expansion of the congregation. His work appeared in 1926 under the title of *Mother Maria Theresia Bonzel and Her Foundation (Mutter Maria Theresia Bonzel und Ihre Stiftung).* The book was translated into English and published in 1955 under the title *From the Wounds of St. Francis: The Life of Mother Maria Theresia Bonzel.*

Reverend Salesius Elsner promised to write a short biography of Mother Maria Theresia Bonzel, and in 1933, in answer to an oft repeated request, he wrote *Mutter Maria Theresia Bonzel, Franziskanerin: Eine Grosse Frau Der Neuzeit.* H. Niebecker, in 1938, wrote *Mutter Maria Theresia Bonzel, Leherin Der Christlichen Volkommenheit,* containing the instructions which Mother gave the young Sisters before investiture and profession and adding his own interpretation. Since 1963, there has appeared *Mutter Maria Theresia's Ruf.* These are informative pamphlets concerning the servant of God, her veneration, and the progress of the process of canonization. They also give information about the life of the servant of God and expressions of gratitude for answers to petitions are herein made public.

May the veneration of this great religious woman increase! May rich blessings be the part of those who entrust their intentions to her! May Holy Mother Church soon grant the wish and prayers of her devotees by admitting her to the honors of the altar!

AFTERWORD

With joyful anticipation and excitement, an overflowing congregation of the faithful gathered in the 700-year-old Paderborn Cathedral on Sunday, November 10, 2013, for the beatification of Mother Maria Theresia Bonzel, the foundress of the Sisters of Saint Francis of Perpetual Adoration. I was privileged to concelebrate the beatification Mass.

The Rite of Beatification took place after the Penitential Rite when the Archbishop of Paderborn, Hans-Josef Becker, officially petitioned Cardinal Angelo Amato, the Prefect of the Congregation for the Causes of Saints and the celebrant of the Mass, that Mother Maria Theresia Bonzel be declared "Blessed." Sister M. Mediatrix Nies, the former Superior General, then gave an overview of the life of Mother Maria Theresia, after which Cardinal Amato read aloud the Decree of Beatification from Pope Francis.

The whole congregation responded in song with the solemn "Amen" and thunderous applause as the portrait of the new "Blessed" was unveiled in the sanctuary. It was an emotional moment as the beloved Servant of God, now "Blessed Maria Theresia," now officially recognized by the Church for her heroic virtues, is able to be venerated with public devotion by the faithful. The Beatification Mass was a celebration of the wonderful things the Lord had done in the life of Mother Maria Theresia, a celebration of her holiness that can inspire the faith and piety of all the faithful.

The beatification of Mother Maria Theresia occurred during the 150th anniversary of her founding of the Sisters of Saint Francis of Perpetual Adoration. For many years, the Sisters had prayed that the Church would officially recognize her heroic virtue and declare her "Blessed."

I traveled as a pilgrim to Germany for the beatification, along with forty-seven of the Sisters of Saint Francis of Perpetual Adoration who are members of the Immaculate Heart of Mary Province, one of the four provinces of the Sisters founded by Blessed Mother Maria Theresia. The motherhouse of this province is in my diocese, in Mishawaka, Indiana. Previously located in Lafayette, Indiana, it was moved to Mishawaka in 1943. Even when it was located in Lafayette, it was part of the Diocese of Fort Wayne, since the Diocese of Lafayette was not established until 1944.

I attended the beatification because of my deep affection and gratitude for the Sisters of Saint Francis of Perpetual Adoration and their important contribution to the Church's mission in my diocese since 1875. It was one of my predecessors, Bishop Joseph Dwenger, the second Bishop of Fort Wayne, who visited Mother Maria Theresia in Olpe and invited her to send sisters to the diocese. Mother Maria Theresia quickly accepted Bishop Dwenger's invitation since the anti-Catholic *Kulturkampf* in Germany at that time was restricting the work of the sisters and Mother Maria Theresia's acceptance of new candidates for her new congregation.

The first Sisters sent by Mother Maria Theresia, six in number, arrived in Lafayette on December 16, 1875. Within a month, they rented a store and began a hospital as requested by Bishop Dwenger. The modest Saint Elizabeth Hospital was the beginning of the Sisters' extensive health care ministry in the Midwestern United States. In the founding years of the sisters' apostolic work in the United States, the sisters opened hospitals in Indiana, Nebraska, and Kansas. Their work also extended to the staffing of schools and the diocesan orphanage. Their teacher training classes for the Sisters at the Lafayette motherhouse would eventually lead to the establishment of Saint Francis College in Lafayette, relocated later to Fort Wayne in 1944, the only Catholic college in Fort Wayne, now the vibrant University of Saint Francis.

The presence and apostolic work of the Sisters of Saint Francis of Perpetual Adoration looms large in the history of the Diocese of Fort Wayne (whose name was changed in 1960 to Diocese of Fort Wayne–South Bend), therefore, the diocese also rejoiced in thanksgiving when Mother Maria Theresia Bonzel was beatified. It is my fervent hope that, with her beatification, her life and works, including her spiritual teachings, will become better known. Already, so many of the faithful know Blessed Mother Theresia through the lives and works of her spiritual daughters, the Sisters of Saint Francis of Perpetual Adoration, who continue Mother's legacy, not only in health care, teaching, and other works of the apostolate, but also in their lives of prayer, especially adoration of the holy Eucharist. I am so grateful that the Sisters continue their holy foundress' practice of prayer before the Blessed Sacrament as the center of their lives and ministries. How many of the faithful of the South Bend side of this diocese visit the perpetual adoration chapel in Saint Francis Chapel in the Mishawaka motherhouse! Only the Lord knows the fruits of the prayers of the Sisters there and of the many other faithful who visit to pray in the chapel!

The Diocese of Fort Wayne was blessed with three extended visits by Mother Maria Theresia Bonzel, as recounted in this biography. Her community in America was growing rapidly, attracting many young women to their consecrated life. Mother Maria Theresia visited the newly established convents, hospitals, and schools. Most importantly, as a loving mother she came to offer her maternal care to her growing number of spiritual daughters. Her visits were received with joy. I think they were important visits since so many learned from her holy example and her insistence on the Sisters' lives of prayer as the essential center of all their activities, particularly their prayer of adoration before Jesus in the Blessed Sacrament.

On the day after the Beatification Mass in Paderborn, I participated in the festivities in Olpe where Blessed Mother Maria Theresia's body was transferred in procession from the motherhouse to the parish church of Saint Martin. On that day, November 11, the feast of Saint Martin of Tours, Mass was celebrated in the parish church and Mother Maria Theresia's body was laid to rest permanently in a newly constructed Eucharistic chapel in the church. This was the church where she was baptized and received her first holy Communion, her home parish as a child, where she also received the habit of her new congregation. Saint Martin's Church is located next door to Mother Maria Theresia's childhood home. It must have been difficult for the German Sisters who were used to praying at her tomb at the Olpe motherhouse, but they knew that their beloved foundress also belonged to the wider community of the Church. Now "Blessed," approved for public veneration, many more of the faithful will be able to pray before the Blessed Sacrament at her tomb in Saint Martin's Church.

Upon returning to the United States, our Sisters in Mishawaka brought with them a first-class relic of Blessed Maria Theresia, which is now displayed for veneration below her portrait in Saint Francis Chapel in the motherhouse. It is my hope and prayer that visitors to the chapel will be drawn to a greater knowledge and devotion to Blessed Maria Theresia, including young women whom the Lord may be calling to the consecrated life as Sisters of Saint Francis of Perpetual Adoration. I thank God that the Sisters continue to receive new vocations from the Diocese of Fort Wayne–South Bend and beyond.

Our Holy Father, Pope Francis, who decreed that the holy woman of God Mother Maria Theresia Bonzel be given the title "Blessed," has called the Church in our time to be a Church which goes forth "from our comfort zone in order to reach all the 'peripheries' in need of the light of the Gospel." This is what Blessed Mother Maria Theresia did 150 years ago. She is a model for the Sisters of Saint Francis of Perpetual Adoration and for all of us of "missionary discipleship." Her motto, "He leads; I follow," should be our model. The community of Sisters she founded is truly a community of missionary disciples whose apostolic work continues to bear much good fruit for the Church in my diocese and beyond. Their activities bear such good fruit because they are rooted not in themselves or purely human goals, but are rooted in the person of Jesus Christ and His grace, seeking the glory of the Father who loves us. They teach all of us that it is closeness to the heart of Jesus is primary. They learn from Blessed Maria Theresia also to look to the Blessed Virgin Mary, to Saint Joseph, and to Saint Francis of Assisi as their examples of prayer and service. As we implore the intercession of these great saints, we can now also publicly implore the intercession of Blessed Mother Maria Theresia to help us to answer the Lord's call to be His missionary disciples in the world today.

I conclude here with the newly composed prayer which is the Collect (Opening Prayer) on the feast day of Blessed Mother Maria Theresia. As you pray this new liturgical prayer, I also suggest adding a little prayer for the eventual canonization of Blessed Mother Maria Theresia:

> Almighty and merciful God, who strengthened the virgin, Blessed Maria Theresia, burning with a pure faith in the sacramental presence of Christ, to support her brethren in every need regardless of the cost, grant that we, in the spirit of her charity, may never tire of ministering to you in our neighbor. Through our Lord Jesus Christ, your Son, who lives and reigns with you in the unity of the Holy Spirit, one God, for ever and ever.

✠ Most Reverend Kevin C. Rhoades
Bishop of Fort Wayne–South Bend

INDEX

M

N

O

Z